Massage Test Prep - Complete Study Guide for MBLEx, Third Edition

Authored by
David Merlino, LMT, NCTM

**This book is dedicated to my dear wife Amanda and beloved son Owen.
You guys are pretty cool.**

Good Evening

My name is David Merlino. I am a Licensed Massage Therapist, Nationally Certified in Therapeutic Massage, and a Massage Therapy instructor. Needless to say, I'm pretty awesome. See?

You bought this book to help you prepare for the MBLEx, right? Great! I'm here to help! At one point, a long time ago, I was just like you. A student, preparing to take my licensing or certification exam. I was nervous, and rightfully so. It was a big test, and my entire career depended on me passing it. Can you guess what happened?

I passed! Of course! You think I'd write a book preparing you to pass the MBLEx if I couldn't even pass my licensing test? Over the past four years, I've been teaching students to pass the MBLEx and formerly the National Certification Exam. Students that follow my techniques and learn the information I provide have had an amazing amount of success on their exams. You are now my student. My goal is to not only teach you information, but to make you a well-prepared, test-taking machine. I want you to do even better than I did on any of my exams!

Just remember, you will get out of this book what you put in. Put this book to work for you. Study the information. Watch my video lectures. Take as many practice tests as you can. Adhere to the test-taking techniques I provide. The more effort you put in, the better your results will be. If you are confused about anything, please, I beg of you, email me and ask me questions.

Thank you for putting your trust in me, and in this study guide. I am here to help at every step of the way, because I care about you, the student, and I care about the future of the Massage Therapy profession. You can do it! Make me proud!

Sincerely,

David Merlino, LMT, NCTM

How To Use This Study Guide

This study guide was designed to be used by students preparing for the MBLEx, or for students who want to brush up on content while still in, or even after, school. This study guide encourages active participation of the student, allowing the student to learn as if they were in a school setting. This study guide was designed to give students the most important information, the information most likely to be seen on the exams, without the filler information. This gives the student the most effective and efficient way to study.

To utilize this study guide and gain the most benefit from it, the student will:

- Take notes using this study guide while following along with the video lecture provided via Vimeo, at Vimeo.com/MassageTestPrep.
- Complete all assignments given, including matching, crossword puzzles, etc.
- Take unlimited practice exams provided at MassageTestPrep.com/practice-test.html.
- While taking practice exams, student should focus on utilizing test-taking techniques discussed in the study guide and video lecture.
- While taking practice exams from the book, student should answer questions on a separate piece of paper, which will give the student multiple attempts at taking the test without the answers being written in the book.

If adhered to, the previous steps will fully prepare the student to pass the licensing/certification examination.

About the MBLEx

The MBLEx is utilized by many states and state massage therapy boards to show that the student is competent in every aspect of Massage Therapy. It was developed by the Federation of State Massage Therapy Boards, and in 2015 became the only licensing exam offered.

The test contains 100 multiple-choice questions, ranging from information on massage therapy to anatomy to pathology to muscles. Really anything you've studied in school could be on the exam. The majority of questions are questions only, but you will also have a limited amount of questions featuring pictures, in which you examine the picture and figure out the answer that way.

The official subjects and the percentage of questions on each subject are:
Anatomy and Physiology – 12%
Kinesiology – 11%
Pathology and Contraindications – 13%
Physiological Effects of Massage – 14%
Client Assessment and Planning – 17%
Massage Modalities and History – 5%
Ethics, Boundaries, and Laws – 15%
Guidelines for Professional Practice – 13%

The test is timed. You will have two hours to finish the exam.

Unfortunately, you are not able to skip questions and go back to questions you've previously seen, so you really need to know the information. Read all of the study and test-taking techniques provided below, and you should be well-suited to pass the test!

Source: https://www.fsmtb.org/userfiles/PDFs/as_of_July_2014_Content_Outline.pdf

Table of Contents

Study Skills/Test-Taking Strategies..1
Massage Therapy..6
    History..6
    Technique...7
    Modalities...10
    Business..12
Anatomy and Physiology..14
    Regional Anatomy...15
    Tissue...16
    Body Systems...18
Medical Terminology...26
Pathology..30
Kinesiology...48
    Attachment Sites..49
    Muscles..58
Assignments..94
Study Guide With Answers...103
David's Easy Ways to Remember Things............................194
Massage Therapy and Business Practice Exam....................200
    Massage Therapy and Business Answer Key.................224
Anatomy and Physiology Practice Exam..............................226
    Anatomy and Physiology Answer Key............................274
Pathology Practice Exam...278
    Pathology Answer Key...344
Kinesiology Practice Exam...350
    Kinesiology Answer Key..386
Flashcards..390
About the Author..439
    References...440

Inspirational Quotes

"Today I will do what others won't, so tomorrow I can accomplish what others can't."
– Jerry Rice

"Tell me and I'll forget, show me and I may remember, involve me and I'll understand."
– Chinese Proverb

"The art of being wise is the art of knowing what to overlook."
– William James

"What you do today can improve all your tomorrows."
– Ralph Marston

"Do as little as needed, not as much as possible."
- Henk Kraaijenhof

Study Skills

- Do not do all of your studying the night before or day of the test. Study consistently, up to several times per week. Cramming is good for short-term learning, but does not help with long-term learning. The more you study, the more likely you are to retain the information.
- Use all of your class and home work as study materials. The information in these assignments is information that might be on your exam.
- Take many short breaks as you study. Memory retention is higher at the beginning and end of study sessions than it is in the middle. This is called the Serial Position Effect. Study for no longer than ten minutes, then take a short break.
- Focus on one subject at a time while studying. You don't want to confuse yourself by mixing information.
- Study the subject you have the most difficulty with more than subjects you are comfortable with. Studying what you aren't weak in doesn't help. If you need work on a specific subject, focus the majority of your time learning that information, even if it means taking away study time from other areas. You're better off being 80% proficient in every subject than 100% in four subjects and only 50% in the last. Not studying this information could prevent you from passing the exam.
- While studying, take notes on important information, especially if it's information you don't recognize or remember. Use this information to study with.
- Assign yourself tests, reports, assignments and projects to complete. You are more likely to remember information if you write a report on it than if you just read the information.
- Teach information you are studying to another person. If you are responsible for someone learning something, you have to know and understand the material, and be able to put that information into the simplest terms possible, so someone else can understand it. This will only help you. Trust me, from personal experience, this really works.

- Understand the material you are studying. Do not just try to memorize certain answers you think may be on the test. Certain "key words" might not be on the test. Learn everything about a subject, and you'll never get any question on that subject wrong.

Serial Position Effect: http://www.simplypsychology.org/primacy-recency.html

Test-Taking Tips

- Go to the restroom before taking the exam. Using the restroom beforehand ensures that you are 100% focused on the exam, and not on your bladder.
- Read the entire question slowly and carefully. Never make assumptions about what a question is asking. Assuming you know what a question is asking may lead to you missing key words in the question that tell you exactly what the question is asking. Read every single word in every single question, multiple times if necessary. Understand what the question is asking before you try answering it.
- Identify key words in each question. Key words are words that tell you exactly what the question is asking. Identify these words easily by reading questions aloud to yourself. The words you find yourself emphasizing while reading aloud are likely the key words.
- Do not change your answers, unless you misread the question. Changing your answers puts doubt into your mind, and leads to more changing of answers. The answer you put first is usually correct. Do not change your answers!
- Match key words in the answers with key words in the questions. Sometimes it's as simple as matching terms, if you've exhausted all other avenues.
- Eliminate answers you know aren't correct and justify the reason they aren't correct. If you can eliminate one answer from each question, that brings your odds of getting that question right up to 33%. If you can eliminate two answers that can't be right, that brings it up to 50%. Then it's just a coin flip!
- Read the entire question before looking at the answers. Again, never make assumptions about what the question is asking.
- Come up with the answer in your head before looking at the answers. If the same answer you come up with is in the list of answers, that's most likely the right answer.
- Read every answer given to make sure you are picking the most correct

answer. Some questions have multiple right answers, and you need to make sure you're picking the most correct answer.
- Make sure you are properly hydrated before the test. Studies have been done on the effects of proper hydration on those taking tests. People who are properly hydrated tend to score higher than those who are not.
- Exercise for twenty minutes before the exam. Exercise has also been shown to increase test scores.

Exercise and Test-Taking: http://lifehacker.com/20-minutes-of-exercise-before-an-exam-may-boost-your-pe-1541773646

Reducing Test Anxiety

- Study consistently. If you understand the material, you won't be as stressed out about the test. There are ways you can study without this book or your class notes as well. An example, whenever you take a bite of food, think about every structure the food passes through in the alimentary canal and what each of the organs do. Another example, whenever you are massaging someone, tell yourself everything about every muscle you work on, like origin, insertion, and action.
- Keep a positive attitude while preparing for the test and during the test. If you think you're going to fail, you will not be as motivated to study, you won't adhere to your test-taking techniques, you'll become stressed out during the exam much more easily, and you'll be more likely to fail.
- Try to stay relaxed. Utilize deep breathing techniques to calm down if you start feeling nervous or stressed. You will have two hours to finish the exam. You can afford one or two minutes to calm yourself down if you need to.
- Exercise consistently up until the day of the test to reduce anxiety. Exercise has been shown to significantly reduce stress, and also helps with memory retention. Try utilizing flash cards while riding an exercise bike.
- Take your time on the test. If you find yourself rushing, slow down. Again, you have two hours to finish the exam. Do not rush through it. You may miss important information in the exam and answer questions incorrectly because of this.

Massage Therapy

History of Massage

China: Massage has been practiced in China as early as _____. Chinese massage technique known as _____ used rubbing and pressing movements.
Japan: _____ entered Japan around _____. The manipulation areas remained the same, but were known as _____. _____ points are pressed to increase circulation of fluid and _____. This technique is known as _____.
India: Massage has been practiced in India since before _____. The _____, or "Art of Life", was written around _____, and detailed massage treatments as part of personal hygiene.
Greece: Massage and exercise was a normal part of Greek life as early as _____.
America: Massage became popularized in America around _____ after the development of the _____.

People of Importance: p104
Aesculapius: _____ priest-physician who combined _____ and _____, which is known as _____, and founded the first gymnasium.
Celsus: _____ physician who wrote _____, which detailed the use of _____, _____, and _____ as prevention of disease.
Per Henrik Ling: _____ physiologist who developed a system of _____ and _____ to improve physical conditions, known as _____. This system of movements evolved into _____ and _____.
Charles Taylor: Introduced Medical Gymnastics to the _____, where it became known as the _____.
Johann Mezger: Established modern _____ for the _____, based in _____.
Douglas Graham: Helped to _____ the term "_____" in _____.
Emil Vodder: Developed _____ _____.

Massage Technique

There are _____ main massage strokes in Western massage therapy:

Effleurage: Long, _____ strokes directed _____. Used to increase circulation, apply massage lubricant, and transition between strokes. Primarily used at the beginning of a massage.

Petrissage: _____ strokes used to increase circulation, loosen adhesions and release metabolic waste from tissues.

Friction: Strokes that move _____ tissue. Used to increase circulation, break up scar tissue and adhesions, and stretch muscle. Examples include circular friction, cross-fiber friction, and compression.

Tapotement: _____ strokes used to increase muscle spindle activity, which stimulates the body, and loosen phlegm from the respiratory tract. Examples include hacking, cupping, and tapping.

Vibration: _____ or _____ movements. Fast vibration is used to stimulate an area. Slow vibration is used to sedate an area.

Nerve Stroke: _____ form of effleurage, used at the end of a massage to separate the therapist from the client.

Joint Movements:
Active: _____ performs an action _____ from the massage therapist.
Active Assistive: The _____ performs an action _____ from the massage therapist.
Passive: _____ performs a joint mobilization with the _____ _____.
Resistive: The _____ _____ a movement being performed by the massage therapist.

Assessment: _____ of the client before, during, and after a massage treatment. Used to determine contraindications, tailor massage treatments, and refer clients to other health-care professionals.

Methods: Intake forms, gait analysis, posture analysis, ergonomics, contraindications, listening, palpation.

Stretching: _____ a muscle.
Unassisted: _____ _____ into resistance _____ from the massage therapist.
Assisted: _____ _____ into resistance _____ from the massage therapist.
Proprioceptive Neuromuscular Facilitation: Unassisted stretch in which the muscle is _____ _____ _____, followed by an _____ _____ of the muscle by the client. The client relaxes the contraction, which allows the stretch to move further.
Reciprocal Inhibition: Used to _____ _____ a muscle by _____ the _____ muscle, especially useful in treating acute _____.

End Feel: _____ of a range-of-motion.
Soft End Feel: Stoppage of range-of-motion due to tight _____ pulling the joint in the opposite way, has a springy end of motion.
Hard End Feel: Stoppage of range-of-motion due to _____ preventing any further motion, has an abrupt end of motion.
Empty End Feel: Stoppage of range-of-motion due to _____ to an affected muscle or joint, limiting motion to prevent further injury.

Draping: Using _____ to cover a client during a massage session.
Top Cover: The linen placed _____, used to keep the client covered during a massage treatment.
Full Sheet: Using the entire sheet to enclose a client in a _____, primarily used in body wrap treatments.

Bolsters: Used to place a client into a comfortable position while receiving a massage.
Supine: Bolsters should be placed _____ and _____.
Prone: Bolsters should be placed _____.
Side-lying: Bolsters should be placed _____, and _____.
Semi-reclined: Bolsters should be placed _____ and _____. Use for pregnant women to reduce pressure on the _____ _____.

Body Mechanics
: Used to _____ to the massage therapist, _____ for the client, and to _____. The _____ should be _____, the _____ should be _____, _____ should be _____, and the massage _____ should be kept at the _____.
Archer/Bow Stance: Feet are placed _____ to the massage table, and allow the massage therapist to perform long _____ strokes like those found in effleurage.
Horse/Warrior Stance: Feet are placed _____ to the massage table, and allow _____, powerful strokes to be performed, such as petrissage, friction, compression, and tapotement.

Precautions:
Endangerment Site: An area of the body the massage therapist should take _____ on or near while performing a massage.
Local Contraindication: An area of the body that must be _____ while performing a massage.
Absolute Contraindication: A condition that _____ the use of _____ treatment.

Massage Modalities

Aromatherapy: Using _____ during a massage session for healing. Essential oils may have specific effects on the body, ranging from physical to emotional, depending on the type of essential oil used.

Craniosacral Therapy: Developed by John Upledger, very light massage technique that releases _____ in the flow of _____ _____ from the _____ to the _____ by working on the axial skeleton.

Deep Tissue: Deep pressure massage focused on treating _____ _____ and _____ _____.

Feldenkrais: Developed by Moshe Feldenkrais, massage technique designed to _____ the _____, allowing the body to move more fluidly and efficiently, which reduces pain.

Hot Stone: Treatment utilizing _____, which may be _____ or _____ on the body. Used to increase circulation throughout the body and relax muscles.

Hydrotherapy: Treatments utilizing _____ in any form.
Turkish Bath: A sauna inside a _____ _____ _____.
Swiss Shower: A _____ shower with _____ _____ _____.
Vichy Shower: A shower utilizing _____ _____ _____ with a client placed on a _____.

Lomi Lomi: _____ massage, similar to Swedish, using rhythmic strokes performed on the entire body with minimal draping.

Lymphatic Drainage: Developed by Emil Vodder, light massage strokes moving in the direction of the heart, used to increase _____ _____ and reduce swelling.

Myofascial Release: Massage aimed at releasing _____ in _____ and _____ utilizing light strokes moving in the direction of the restriction.

10

Polarity Therapy: Massage theory which states every ____ has a _____ and _____ _____, utilizes light strokes to balance the body.

Reflexology: Treating _____ _____ on the ____, ____, and ____, which may affect corresponding _____ throughout the body.

Reiki: Manipulation of _____ into and throughout the client, performed _____ _____ the client.

Rolfing: Developed by Ida Rolf, _____ _____ massage technique, which helps the client's body regain _____ _____. Takes place over ten sessions, with a focus on a different part of the body in each session.

Sports Massage: Massage for _____, performed before, during, and after athletic events. May be either fast-paced or slow and methodical, depending on the work that needs to be done.

Swedish Massage: Most common form of massage in the West, focuses primarily on _____.

Strain-Counter Strain: Also known as _____ _____, moving the body into a painful position and allowing the body to relax into a non-painful position, helping to release restrictions.

Thai Massage: Clothed massage performed _____, primarily utilizing _____ techniques.

Trager Method: Developed by Milton Trager, utilizing exercises called _____, performed with movement, gentle massage strokes, and rocking to produce positive sensory reception in the Central Nervous System.

Business

Certification: Credential obtained by completing a certification course, usually in a _____ setting, and may involve passing of a _____ _____.

License: Jurisdictional requirement to _____ the practice of massage therapy, allows a massage therapist to perform massage for monetary compensation.

Reciprocity: Massage license in one jurisdiction being _____ as valid in another jurisdiction.

Liability Insurance: Obtained through massage insurance providers, protects the massage therapist in cases such as _____ and _____.

Client Files: Any client file should be retained by the massage therapist for a minimum of _____, per the _____.

SOAP Notes: Used to _____ everything regarding a previous massage treatment.
S: _____, anything the client details about _____.
O: _____, _____ or techniques being performed, and any _____ the massage therapist _____ can physically see.
A: _____, any _____ in the client resulting from the treatment.
P: ____, any _____ for future treatment or exercises suggested to the client _____.

Communication:
Confidentiality: Keeping client information _____ and _____ in all ways.
Open-Ended Question: Used when asking for detailed _____ from clients.
Close-Ended Question: Used when asking for a _____ response only.

Transference: A client viewing a massage therapist similarly to a person in their _____.
Counter-Transference: A massage therapist bringing their _____ _____ into the therapeutic relationship.

Ethics: Guiding _____ _____ used to direct a massage therapist to proper course of action in ethical dilemmas.
Scope of Practice: Performing treatments and techniques only _____ _____.
Mission Statement: A short statement detailing the _____ _____ of the business.
Boundaries: Setting personal and professional _____ by the client or therapist.
HIPAA: Health Insurance Portability and Accountability Act of 1996. Enacted August 21, 1996. Created by US Department of Heath and Human Services.
Privacy Rule: Protects all individually _____ health information. Assures health information of individuals is _____ while allowing health information to be _____ between healthcare providers to provide high-quality health care.

Types of Employment:
Independent Contractor: A massage therapist who _____ to work for a person or company and receives _____.
Sole Proprietor: A business that has only _____.
Partnership: A business that has _____.

Tax Forms:
1099: Filed by _____ who make more than $600 in a year.
Schedule C: Filed by _____, details profit and loss for the previous year.
Schedule K-1: Filed by _____, details income and taxes for each partnership member from the previous year.
1040: Tax form detailing _____ and _____.
W-2: Filed by _____, details _____ and _____ from the previous year.

Anatomy and Physiology

Anatomy: The study of the _____ of the human body.
Systemic Anatomy: The study of the body's _____.
Regional Anatomy: The study of the different _____ of the body.
Physiology: The study of the _____ of the body.

Cells: Cells are the functional units of all tissues, and they perform all essential life functions.
Cellular Mitosis: A cell _____ from one mother cell into two daughter cells in order to replace cell loss.
Organelles are found _____ cells to make the cells function.
Nucleus: Contains _____, controls activity inside cells.
Nucleolus: Forms _____ and _____ _____ in ribosomes.
Mitochondria: Produce _____.
Golgi Apparatus: Allows _____ of _____ in cells.
Smooth Endoplasmic Reticulum: Synthesizes _____ and _____.
Lysosome: _____ _____ inside cells.
Ribosome: Contain _____ and _____, assemble cell proteins.
Cytoplasm: _____ inside cell.

Homeostasis: Homeostasis is the existence and maintenance of a _____ _____. Several factors contribute to the homeostatic process, including hormones, nerve impulses, and sweating.
Homeostatic Mechanisms: Homeostatic mechanisms are _____ things that happen in the body that alter the internal environment in response to a specific change. _____ reduces body temperature, and _____ increases body temperature.

REGIONAL ANATOMY

There are three main regions of the body:

Central
Upper Limb
Lower Limb

Central Body Region: The Central body region contains everything in the center of the body, such as the _____, _____, and _____. The trunk can be further divided into three other regions:
Thorax: The thorax contains our major internal organs, such as the _____ and _____. Also inside the thorax is the _____, a form of connective tissue that surrounds organs inside the chest(except the lungs), protecting them from too much jostling.
Abdomen: The abdomen contains the majority of our digestive organs, including the stomach, liver, gallbladder, pancreas, small intestine, large intestine, kidneys, and spleen.
Pelvis: The pelvis contains our _____, the _____ and _____, and the _____.

Body Cavities: Body cavities _____. There are two main body cavities:
Dorsal Body Cavity: Made by the _____ and _____, contains the _____ and _____.
Ventral Body Cavity: Made by the three trunk cavities(_____, _____, _____).

Directional Terms: Used to describe structures in the body in relation to other structures or body parts.
Superior: _____
Inferior: _____
Anterior: _____
Posterior: _____
Proximal: _____

Distal: _____
Medial: _____
Lateral: _____
Deep: _____
Superficial: _____

Body Planes: There are _____ planes used to divide the body.
Sagittal: Splits the body into _____ and _____.
Midsagittal: Splits the body into _____, runs down the _____ of the body.
Transverse/Horizontal: Splits the body into _____ and _____.
Frontal/Coronal: Splits the body into _____ and _____.

TISSUE

There are _____ types of tissue in the human body: _____, _____, _____, and _____.

Epithelial: Forms most _____, the _____, and the _____. Epithelial tissue is responsible for _____ the body, _____ nutrients, and _____ substances. Epithelial tissue is _____ and contains no blood vessels.

Nervous: Forms the _____, _____ _____, and _____ that emerge from both. Nervous tissue allows for _____, _____ _____, and _____ of skeletal muscle.
A _____ is a _____ _____. It contains a _____, the site of cell function. It also contains _____, branch-like projections that come off the cell body to receive nervous impulses, bringing them into the cell body.

Muscular: There are three types of muscle: _____, _____, _____.
Skeletal: Connects to the _____ and allows _____ _____.
Cardiac: Muscle of the _____, responsible for _____ _____ throughout the body.
Smooth: Found in locations such as the _____ (arrector pili) and _____ _____. Responsible for actions such as _____.

Connective: Connective tissue is formed by the "_____ ___", materials you don't find in cells. They can contain _____, _____ _____, and _____. Connective tissue is responsible for actions such as _____ structures, _____ structures, _____ of nutrients, _____ and _____ the body, and _____ the body.
Blast Cells: Immature cells that _____ the matrix.
Clast Cells: _____ _____ the matrix.
There are several types of connective tissue, including ____, _____, _____, _____, _____, _____, _____ _____, and _____. The most abundant form of connective tissue in the body is _____.

Blood: Consists of _____, _____, _____, and _____.
Erythrocytes: Also called ____ _____ ___, responsible for _____ oxygen and carbon dioxide throughout the body via _____, which is found in the cytoplasm of the cells.
Leukocytes: Also called _____ _____ ____, they are _____ that help fight off infectious agents and break down dead cells and debris inside the body.
Thrombocytes: Also called _____, they are responsible for _____ the blood.
Plasma: The _____ portion of blood, allows _____ of blood cells throughout the body.

Serous Membranes: Forms of connective tissues that _____ organs inside body cavities, preventing the organs from creating friction. There are _____ serous membranes inside the _____: the _____, which surrounds the _____, and the _____, which surrounds the _____. There is _____ serous membrane that is found inside the _____ and _____ that separates the organs from the muscle on top of them: the _____.
Inner wall of a serous membrane: _____ serous membrane
Outer wall of a serous membrane: _____ serous membrane

BODY SYSTEMS

Cardiovascular System: Responsible for _____ _____ throughout the body, bringing oxygen, hormones, and nutrients to tissues, and eliminating carbon dioxide and waste products from the body. Consists of the _____, _____ _____, and _____.

Heart: Pumps blood throughout the body. Consists of the superior vena cava, inferior vena cava, right atrium, tricuspid valve, right ventricle, pulmonary valve, pulmonary arteries, pulmonary veins, left atrium, bicuspid valve, left ventricle, aortic valve, and aorta.

Blood Vessels: Create _____ for blood to travel throughout the body.

Arteries: Largest and most internal blood vessels, move blood _____ _____ _____ _____, and almost always carry oxygenated blood.

Veins: Move blood _____ _____ _____, and almost always carry deoxygenated blood.

Capillaries: Microscopic blood vessels used to transport oxygen-rich blood _____ _____.

Digestive System: Responsible for bringing food _____ _____ _____, _____, _____ of nutrients, and _____ of waste.
Oral Cavity: Also called the _____, contains the _____, _____ _____, and _____. Performs _____ and _____.
Pharynx: Also called the _____, allows _____ of food from the oral cavity to the esophagus.
Esophagus: Tubular organ that allows _____ of food from the pharynx to the stomach.
Stomach: _____ and _____ _____ food into usable, absorbable nutrients.
Liver: _____ harmful chemicals from the blood, produces _____.
Gallbladder: _____ _____ and _____ _____ into the duodenum.
Pancreas: Produces _____ and _____ and secretes these substances into the duodenum.
Small Intestine: _____ nutrients into the body for use. Consists of the _____, _____, and _____.
Large Intestine: _____ _____, converts chyme to _____, assists in _____ of waste.
Between organs in the Digestive System, we have _____. Sphincters are _____ bands of _____ that allow food to pass through into other organs, and to _____ food from going _____ in the digestive tract. There are four main sphincters in the digestive tract:
Esophageal Sphincter: Located between the _____ and _____.
Cardiac Sphincter: Located between the _____ and _____.
Pyloric Sphincter: Located between the _____ and _____.
Ileocecal Sphincter: Located between the _____ _____ and _____ _____.

Endocrine System: Responsible for _____ the specific activities of cells and tissues via _____ release. Endocrine glands secrete hormones directly into the _____ _____.
Pituitary Gland: Secretes _____ _____, _____, and _____ _____ hormones. Responsible for _____ in bones, production of _____, and production of _____ cells in women and _____ cells in men.
Adrenals: Secrete _____ and _____, which elevate _____ _____, increase _____ _____, and increase _____ _____.

19

Pancreatic Islets: Secrete _____ and _____. Insulin _____ glucose concentration in the blood, while glucagon _____ glucose concentration in the blood.
Ovaries: Secrete _____ and _____.
Testes: Secrete _____.

Integumentary System: Contains the _____, _____, _____, _____ _____, _____ _____, and _____ _____. Responsible for _____, _____ of substances, _____ of substances, and detecting _____.
Skin: Made of epithelial tissue, skin is avascular and is used for _____.
Sudoriferous Glands: Secrete _____, which is a homeostatic mechanism. Sudoriferous glands are forms of exocrine glands.
Sebaceous Glands: Secrete _____. Sebaceous glands are forms of exocrine glands.
Sensory Receptors: Detect _____ in the skin.
Pacinian Corpuscles: Detect _____ pressure.
Meissner's Corpuscles: Detect _____ pressure.
Nociceptors: Detect _____.

Lymphatic System: Consists of _____ _____, _____ _____, _____, and _____ _____.
Lymph Vessels: They are a _____ system, meaning lymph in the vessels only flows one direction. The vessels _____ foreign bodies and nutrients from tissue.
Lymph Nodes: A lymph node is a ____ of lymph tissue, responsible for _____ and _____ foreign objects, helps to _____ _____.
Lymph: Made of mostly water, protein, leukocytes, urea, salts, and glucose.
Spleen: Removes old _____ _____ _____ from the blood stream.
Thymus: Produces _____.

Muscular System: Contains _____. Muscles are responsible for _____ and _____ _____.
In order for a muscle to contract, _____ must be present. The contractile unit of a muscle is called a _____. _____ are formed by _____ filaments(____) and _____ filaments(_____).

20

Muscle Contractions: A contraction is when _____ in a muscle _____.

Isometric Contraction: The _____ of a muscle _____ ____ _____, but _____ in the muscle _____.
Isotonic Contraction: The _____ in a muscle _____ ____ _____, but the _____ of the muscle _____.
Concentric Contraction: The _____ in a muscle _____, and muscle ____ _____.
Eccentric Contraction: The _____ in the muscle ____ _____ _____, and muscle _____ _____.
Prime Mover/Agonist: The muscle of a synergist group _____ for _____.
Synergist: A muscle that _____ the prime mover in performing the action.
Antagonist: A muscle that _____ the prime mover, performing the _____ action.
Fixator: A muscle that _____ an area so an action can be performed.

Nervous System
There are two branches of the Nervous System, the _____ **Nervous System** and _____ **Nervous System**. It also contains the _____ **Nervous System.**

Central Nervous System: Consists of the _____ and _____ _____.
Brain: Consists of the _____, _____, and _____ _____.
Cerebrum: The _____ part of the brain, split into left and right _____, responsible for _____ actions and _____ reception. Each hemisphere contains ____, named after bones overlaying them.
Frontal Lobe: Responsible for _____ motor function, _____, _____, _____.

Parietal Lobe: Responsible for processing most _____ information.
Temporal Lobe: Responsible for _____ and _____ processing, and _____.
Occipital Lobe: Responsible for _____ input.

Cerebellum: Responsible for _____ _____, _____, and _____.
Brain Stem: Contains three parts: _____ _____, _____, and _____.

Medulla Oblongata: Regulates the body's _____ _____.

Pons: Creates a pathway for _____ between the _____ and _____.

Midbrain: _____ reflexes.

Peripheral Nervous System: Contains _____. There are ___ **pairs** of _____ **nerves** that emerge from the spinal cord, and ___ **pairs** of _____ **nerves** that emerge from the brain.

Cranial Nerves: Emerge from the brain, numbered via Roman numerals. Olfactory(I), Optic(II), Oculomotor(III), Trochlear(IV), Trigeminal(V), Abducens(VI), Facial(VII), Vestibulocochlear(VIII), Glossopharyngeal(IX), Vagus(X), Spinal Accessory(XI), Hypoglossal(XII)

Autonomic Nervous System: Responsible for maintenance of _____ within the body. There are two autonomic nervous responses in the body.

Sympathetic Response: Also called "_____", when activated, increases _____ in the body, _____ heart rate. It also _____ digestive organs and pulls blood from them for use in the muscles.

Parasympathetic Response: Also called "_____", when activated, _____ heart rate, brings blood into the digestive organs to stimulate _____. Controlled by Cranial Nerve X, the _____ **Nerve**.

Respiratory System:
Exchanges _____ and _____ in blood, and aids in _____ from the body.

Nose: _____ and _____ coming in and exiting the body. _____ air via _____.

Larynx: Tube at front of pharynx, strengthened by muscles. Contains the _____, which prevents food from entering the larynx during swallowing. Allows _____.

Trachea: _____ inferior to the larynx, allows _____ of ____ into lungs.

Bronchi: Split into right and left, divides into smaller branches as they move through the lungs. Smallest branches are called _____. They secrete _____ to trap dirt and debris, which is then expelled from the lungs by _____.

Alveoli: _____ _____ at the end of bronchial tubes, connect to blood vessels. Responsible for _____ of oxygen and carbon dioxide.

Diaphragm: _____ attached to base of rib cage and vertebrae, creates a vacuum to _____ and _____. When the diaphragm _____, air _____ the lungs. When the diaphragm _____, air _____ the lungs.

Skeletal System: Contains _____. Responsible for _____ the body, creating _____, providing _____, and giving muscles a location to _____ to which permits _____.

Axial Skeleton: Consists of the _____, _____, and _____.
Skull: _____ the brain. Contains the following bones: Frontal, occipital, parietal, temporal, mandible, maxilla, sphenoid, vomer, nasal, ethmoid, lacrimal, and zygomatic.
There are four main sutures of the cranium, holding the bones of the skull together. They are:
Sagittal Suture: Connects the two _____ bones.
Coronal Suture: Connects the _____ bone to the _____ bones.
Squamous Suture: Connects the _____ bone and _____ bone.
Lambdoid Suture: Connects the _____ bone and the _____ bones.

Vertebral Column: _____ the spinal cord. Contains ___ individual bones. _____ **cervical** vertebrae, _____ **thoracic** vertebrae, ____ **lumbar** vertebrae, ___ **sacral** vertebrae, _____ **coccygeal** vertebrae.
Thoracic Cage: Also called the _____, _____ the organs inside the thorax. There are _____ **pairs** of ribs. The _____ **seven** pairs are called _____ **ribs**. The _____ **five** pairs are called _____ **ribs**. **Ribs 11 and 12** are called _____ **ribs**, and they do not attach to the sternum.

Appendicular Skeleton: Consists of the bones of the upper and lower _____, and the pectoral and pelvic _____.
Upper Limb: Contains the humerus, radius, ulna, carpals, metacarpals, and phalanges.
Carpals: Scaphoid, Lunate, Triquetrum, Pisiform, Trapezium, Trapezoid, Capitate, Hamate.
Lower Limb: Contains the femur, tibia, fibula, tarsals, metatarsals, and phalanges.

Tarsals: Calcaneus, Cuboid, Cuneiform I, Cuneiform II, Cuneiform III, Talus, Navicular.
Pectoral Girdle: Contains the clavicles and scapulae.
Pelvic Girdle: Contains the ilium, ischium, pubis, and sacrum.

Joint Classifications: _____(non-movable), _____(somewhat movable), _____(Freely movable)
There are _____ types of _____ joints.
Ball and Socket: _____ on the end of one bone fits into the _____ on another.
Hinge: Allows only _____ and _____.
Pivot: Allows only _____.
Plane/Gliding: Joints created by _____ bone surfaces.
Saddle: Created by two _____ articulating bone surfaces.
Ellipsoid/Condyloid: _____ of one bone fits into _____ cavity of another.

Movements:
Flexion: _____ the _____ of a joint.
Extension: _____ the _____ of a joint.
Adduction: Moving a structure _____ the _____.
Abduction: Moving a structure _____ from the _____.
Protraction: Moving a structure _____.
Retraction: Moving a structure _____.
Inversion: Turning the sole of the foot in _____ the _____.
Eversion: Turning the sole of the foot out _____ from the _____.
Elevation: Moving a structure _____.
Depression: Moving a structure _____.
Supination: Rotating palm so it is facing _____.
Pronation: Rotating palm so it is facing _____.
Rotation: Turning a structure _____ its _____ _____.
Circumduction: Turning a structure around the _____ of a joint.
Opposition: Moving structures in _____ directions.
Lateral Deviation: Moving a structure from _____.

Urinary System: Consists of the _____, _____, _____ _____, and _____. Responsible for _____ of waste from the body, _____ of nutrients, and _____ regulation.

Kidneys: _____ and _____ substances back into the body. Regulates the amount of _____ in the body. Inside each kidney, there are _____ _____ _____, which are responsible for reabsorbing vitamins, electrolytes, and water back into the blood stream.

Ureters: _____ urine from the kidneys to the bladder.

Urinary Bladder: _____ urine.

Urethra: _____ urine from the urinary bladder out of the body.

Medical Terminology

Medical terminology is widely used throughout the medical field, and is the primary way of communicating with other health-care professionals. Medical terminology has origins in Latin and Greek. A medical term consists of three parts: The word root, which is what the term is mainly talking about; the prefix, which comes at the beginning of the medical term; the suffix, which comes at the end of the word. Both the prefix and suffix help to further describe what may be happening in a certain medical condition.

Word Roots

Abdomin/o: _____
Acr/o: _____
Aden/o: _____
Adip/o: _____
Angi/o: _____
Ankyl/o: _____
Arteri/o: _____
Arthr/o: _____
Ather/o: _____
Audi/o: _____
Aur/o: _____
Bi/o: _____
Brachi/o: _____

Bucc/o: _____
Carcin/o: _____
Cardi/o: _____
Cephal/o: _____
Chlor/o: _____
Chol/e: _____
Cholecyst/o: _____
Chondr/o: _____
Cirrh/o: _____
Col/o: _____
Corp/o: _____
Cost/o: _____
Cry/o: _____

Cutane/o: _____
Cyan/o: _____
Cyst/o: _____
Dent/o: _____
Derm/o: _____
Dist/o: _____
Dors/o: _____
Embol/o: _____
Emphys/o: _____
Encephal/o: _____
Enter/o: _____
Erythr/o: _____
Esophag/o: _____
Gastr/o: _____
Gingiv/o: _____
Gloss/o: _____
Gluc/o: _____
Hem/o: _____
Hepat/o: _____
Hist/o: _____
Home/o: _____
Hydr/o: _____
Hyster/o: _____
Inguin/o: _____
Jaund/o: _____
Kerat/o: _____
Kinesi/o: _____
Kyph/o: _____
Lact/o: _____
Later/o: _____
Leuk/o: _____
Lip/o: _____

Lord/o: _____
Mamm/o: _____
Mast/o: _____
Melan/o: _____
My/o: _____
Myel/o: _____
Nas/o: _____
Necr/o: _____
Nephr/o: _____
Neur/o: _____
Ocul/o: _____
Onc/o: _____
Oophor/o: _____
Oste/o: _____
Path/o: _____
Ped/o: _____
Phleb/o: _____
Phren/o: _____
Pneum/o: _____
Proxim/o: _____
Pulm/o: _____
Pyr/o: _____
Ren/o: _____
Rhin/o: _____
Salping/o: _____
Scler/o: _____
Scoli/o: _____
Somat/o: _____
Spondyl/o: _____
Stomat/o: _____
Thorac/o: _____
Ventr/o: _____

Prefixes

a-: _____
ab-: _____
ad-: _____
af-: _____
an-: _____
ana-: _____
ante-: _____
anti-: _____
auto-: _____
bi-: _____
brady-: _____
circum-: _____
contra-: _____
di-: _____
dia-: _____
dys-: _____, _____
ef-: _____
endo-: _____
epi-: _____
exo-: _____
homeo-: _____
hyper-: _____
hypo-: _____
infra-: _____

inter-: _____
intra-: _____
iso-: _____
macro-: _____
mal-: _____
meta-: _____
micro-: _____
mono-: _____
multi-: _____
neo-: _____
pan-: _____
para-: _____
peri-: _____
poly-: _____
post-: _____
pre-: _____
pseudo-: _____
quadri-: _____
retro-: _____
supra-: _____
syn-: _____
tachy-: _____
tri-: _____
uni-: _____

Suffixes

-ac: _____
-al: _____
-algia: _____
-ar: _____
-blast: _____
-cision: _____
-clast: _____
-crine: _____
-cyte: _____
-derma: _____
-ectomy: _____
-edema: _____
-emia: _____
-esis: _____
-ferent: _____
-gen: _____
-globin: _____
-ic: _____
-ician: _____
-icle: _____

-ist: _____
-itis: _____
-lysis: _____
-oid: _____
-osis: _____
-pathy: _____
-phagia: _____
-phasia: _____
-physis: _____
-plasia: _____
-plegia: _____
-pnea: _____
-poiesis: _____
-rrhage: _____
-rrhea: _____
-stasis: _____
-tomy: _____
-trophy: _____
-uria: _____

Pathology

Cardiovascular

Anemia: Decrease in _____ of the blood, most commonly due to a lack of _____, _____, or both. Causes fatigue due to hypoxia.

   Massage is: _____.

Aneurysm: _____ of a wall of an artery outward, caused by a weakened arterial wall. Most likely the result of _____ putting strain on the arterial wall. May break open, resulting in severe _____ internally, which may be fatal.

   Massage is: _____.

Arteriosclerosis: _____ of the walls of arteries, caused by a lack of _____ in the arteries. Reduces circulation, which may lead to _____.

   Massage is: _____.

Atherosclerosis: Buildup of _____, or lipids, on the walls of the arteries, reducing blood flow. May result in _____ and the formation of blood clots.

   Massage is: _____.

Embolism: A _____ or bubble of gas freely moving throughout the circulatory system. May become lodged in the heart, lungs, or brain, resulting in lack of blood flow to those structures, causing _____.

Massage is: _____.

Heart Murmur: Flow of blood _____ in the heart due to malfunctioning _____, typically the _____ or _____. Formation of blood clots may occur, along with fatigue.

Massage is: _____.

Hypertension: _____, 140/90 mm Hg. Results in inelasticity of the arterial walls, reducing circulation.

Massage is: _____.

Migraine: _____ headache. Caused by _____ of extracranial blood vessels, which puts substantial pressure upon the _____, producing intense pain. May be caused by stress or smoke, among other things.

Massage is: _____.

Myocardial Infarction: _____ of heart tissue, usually caused by a blockage in the _____ arteries, which are responsible for supplying the myocardium with _____.

Massage is: _____.

Phlebitis: Inflammation of a _____, caused by trauma, pregnancy, prolonged periods of sitting or standing, and may present with _____.

Massage is: _____.

Raynaud's Syndrome: _____ of blood vessels in the hands and feet, which reduces _____. Caused by cigarette smoking, cold exposure, or stress.

    Massage is: _____.

Transient Ischemic Attack: Temporary cerebral dysfunction resulting from _____ in part of the brain. Also known as a "mini-stroke", it can be a precursor to a more serious stroke in the future.

    Massage is: _____.

Varicose Veins: Swollen veins, caused by dysfunction in the _____ inside the veins, resulting in blood pooling down the legs and forcing the veins towards the surface of the body.

    Massage is: _____.

Digestive

Cholecystitis: Inflammation of the _____, usually due to a blockage of the cystic duct, stopping the flow of _____ into the duodenum. Blockages most commonly caused by _____.

    Massage is: _____.

Cirrhosis: Destruction of _____ cells, resulting in the formation of adhesions and fibrous material in the _____, causing the _____ to become a yellowish-orange color. _____ function is gradually impaired.

    Massage is: _____.

Crohn's Disease: Autoimmune disorder which affects the _____ tract, resulting in _____ and _____ of the mucous membranes, in which scar tissue can develop.

    Massage is: _____.

Diverticulosis: Development of small _____ that protrude from the walls of the _____ _____, caused by weakening of the walls due to a lack of substances for the walls to press against.

    Massage is: _____.

Diverticulitis: Inflammation of diverticular pouches, which may become _____ and develop _____.

    Massage is: _____.

Gastroenteritis: Inflammation of the lining of the _____ and _____, most commonly caused by food poisoning or emotional stress.

    Massage is: _____.

Hepatitis: Inflammation of the _____ most commonly associated with a _____ infection, which may be acute or chronic. Results in pain, nausea, fatigue, diarrhea, and jaundice in the acute stage of infection.

    Massage is: _____.

Hernia: _____ of an organ through the surrounding connective tissue membrane. May result in pain and impaired body function, depending on the location and structures involved.

    Massage is: _____.

Endocrine

Addison's Disease: Autoimmune disorder which results in the degeneration of the _____, causing a decrease in _____ function.

    Massage is: _____.

Cushing's Disease: Overproduction of _____, resulting in increased _____ and muscle _____.

    Massage is: _____.

Diabetes Mellitus: Increased levels of _____ in the blood stream. Diabetes Type I is caused by a decrease in _____ levels in the body, which restricts the breaking down of _____, while Diabetes Type II is caused by the body being desensitized to _____, which is then unable to break down _____.

    Massage is: _____.

Goiter: Enlargement of the _____ gland, commonly seen with _____, _____, inflammation, or a lack of _____ in the diet.

    Massage is: _____.

Grave's Disease: Autoimmune disease resulting in _____, anxiety, trembling, and fatigue. May also result in protrusion of the _____.

    Massage is: _____.

Hyperthyroidism: Increased _____ function, results in a _____, hypersensitivity to _____, increased appetite, and increased respiration.

    Massage is: _____.

Hypothyroidism: Lack of _____ hormone in the body, results in _____, weight _____, edema, and sensitivity to _____.

    Massage is: _____.

Integumentary

Acne: Bacterial infection of the _____, due to numerous factors, including _____ production, stress, and hormonal imbalance.

    Massage is: _____.

Athlete's Foot: Also called _____ _____, it is a highly contagious _____ infection found on the _____, primarily between the _____, which may result in breaking of the skin and lead to bacterial infection.

    Massage is: _____.

Basal Cell Carcinoma: _____ serious, _____ growing, _____ common form of skin cancer, usually due to overexposure to sunlight.

    Massage is: _____.

Burns: First degree burn – Most common, least serious. Most common form is a _____, affecting the epidermis, resulting in inflammation and irritation of the skin.
    Second degree burn – Burn moves through the epidermis into the _____, which leads to the development of _____ and swelling.
    Third degree burn – Burn moves through the epidermis and the dermis, into the _____ layer. Results in _____ and _____ of the skin, and may lead to infection if not treated properly.

    Massage is: First degree – _____.
Second degree – _____. Third degree – _____.

Cellulitis: Acute infection caused by _____ or _____ bacteria, which often enters the body through exposure to _____, affecting nearby tissues. Presents with well-defined borders of inflammation.

    Massage is: _____.

Decubitus Ulcer: Also known as a _____ ulcer or _____ sore, results in ulcerations caused by prolonged _____ placed on a part of the body, causing _____ and ultimately _____ of the affected tissue.

    Massage is: _____.

Eczema: Idiopathic disorder causing dry, red, itchy _____ of skin. Maybe be either acute or chronic.

    Massage is: _____.

Herpes Simplex: Highly contagious chronic _____ infection, resulting in _____ sores around the mucous membranes.

    Massage is: _____.

Hives: Also known as _____, it is an inflammatory reaction in response to exposure to an _____ or _____. May be either acute or chronic, depending on the cause.

    Massage is: _____.

Impetigo: Acute _____ infection caused by _____ or _____, results in sores that form around the mouth, nose, and hands. Mostly seen in _____, it is highly contagious.

    Massage is: _____.

Lice: Highly contagious _____ infection, found in hair. Produce egg sacs called "_____".

Massage is: _____.

Malignant Melanoma: Overproduction of _____, resulting in formation of tumors that may _____ to other regions of the body. A = _____, B = _____, C = _____, D = _____, E = _____.

Massage is: _____.

Mole: Benign skin _____, resulting from an increased amount of _____ in an area.

Massage is: _____.

Psoriasis: _____ disorder in which the body's immune system attacks _____ tissue. _____ cells quickly regenerate at a rate quicker than normal, which results in thick, dry, silvery patches of skin.

Massage is: _____.

Ringworm: Also known as "_____ _____", it is a _____ infection resulting in circular raised patches on the skin.

Massage is: _____.

Scleroderma: An autoimmune disorder, resulting in excessive _____ production in the skin, causing the skin to become _____. Can be a sign of organ failure.

Massage is: _____.

Sebaceous Cyst: Blockage of a _____ gland, resulting in the body forming a thick membrane of connective tissue around the gland, limiting tissue damage as a result of infection.

    Massage is: _____.

Squamous Cell Carcinoma: Form of _____ cancer which develops into an area of _____, caused by overexposure to sunlight, or may be found in the mouth of a person who chews _____ or smokes _____.

    Massage is: _____.

Wart: Epidermal protrusion resulting from infection by the _____ _____ _____. Results in increased _____ production on the area of infection.

    Massage is: _____.

Lymphatic

Acquired Immunodeficiency Syndrome: _____ infection, caused by HIV, which destroys the body's _____, effectively disabling the _____ system.

    Massage is: _____.

Allergies: _____ of the body to agents which are normally harmless in most people.

    Massage is: _____.

Chronic Fatigue Syndrome: _____ disease which results in symptoms such as _____, low-grade fever, and irritability.

    Massage is: _____.

Lymphedema: Increased amounts of _____ fluid in a limb, resulting in _____. Caused by inflammation, trauma, or blocked lymph channels.

    Massage is: _____.

Lupus: _____ disorder affecting the _____ tissues of the body, resulting in a rash across the _____, scales on the skin, fatigue, fever, photo-sensitivity, and weight loss.

    Massage is: _____.

Mononucleosis: _____ infection, resulting in a high _____, fatigue, sore throat, and swollen _____ _____.

    Massage is: _____.

Pitting Edema: Swollen area, leaves _____ in the skin after applying _____. May be a sign of organ failure.

    Massage is: _____.

Muscular

Adhesive Capsulitis: Formation of _____ that stick the _____ capsule to the head of the _____, severely restricting the range of motion at the _____ joint. May also be caused by hypertonicity of the _____.

    Massage is: _____.

Atrophy: Loss of muscle _____ due to lack of ___ or malnourishment.

    Massage is: _____.

Fibromyalgia: Inflammatory disease affecting _____ and _____, resulting in pain, numbness, tingling sensations in the limbs, and fatigue.

    Massage is: _____.

Golfer's Elbow: A form of _____, results in inflammation and pain located at the _____ epicondyle of the _____. The _____ of the wrist are affected, as they originate on the _____ epicondyle of the _____.

    Massage is: _____.

Muscular Dystrophy: Autoimmune disorder, resulting in _____ of muscles. Muscle _____ leads to _____ and lack of use, eventually resulting in _____ and _____.

    Massage is: _____.

Strain: An injury to a _____ or _____, may be caused by overexertion or overstretching.

    Massage is: _____.

Tendonitis: Inflammation of a _____, results from injury to either the _____ or _____ junction.

    Massage is: _____.

Tennis Elbow: A common form of _____, results in inflammation and pain located at the _____ epicondyle of the _____. The _____ of the wrist are affected, as they originate at the _____ epicondyle of the _____.

    Massage is: _____.

Torticollis: Spasm of the _____ unilaterally, forcing the head to lean to _____. _____ may result.

    Massage is: _____.

Whiplash: Straining or spraining of tendons, muscles, and ligaments in the _____ due to violent forward motion of the _____ and _____. As a result, tendons, muscles and ligaments may be injured and weakened, with an increase in headaches, pain, and dizziness. Most commonly seen in _____.

    Massage is: _____.

Nervous

Alzheimer's Disease: Progressive _____ of brain tissue, resulting in loss of _____, _____, confusion and disorientation.

    Massage is: _____.

Bell's Palsy: _____ of one side of the _____ as a result of inflammation or compression of the _____ nerve. May be permanent, or may subside.

    Massage is: _____.

Carpal Tunnel Syndrome: Compression of the _____ nerve by the _____ _____ _____, resulting in loss of function and sensation in the _____.

    Massage is: _____.

Encephalitis: Inflammation of the _____, most commonly caused by a _____ infection. The _____ usually enters the body after contact with _____. Inflammation may result in necrotic brain tissue and death.

    Massage is: _____.

Hemiplegia: Paralysis of one side of the _____, usually as the result of a _____, which may impair function to specific regions of the body.

    Massage is: _____.

Meningitis: Inflammation of the _____. _____ meningitis is the most severe form, which may result in death. Symptoms include nausea, vomiting, dizziness, and headache. Highly contagious.

    Massage is: _____.

Multiple Sclerosis: Autoimmune disorder in which the immune system attacks the _____ _____ surrounding axons in the _____ nervous system, causing degeneration of the _____. Degeneration also results in scarring on the axons, which results in severe pain in acute stages.

    Massage is: _____.

Paraplegia: Paralysis of the _____ _____ due to an injury to the spinal cord anywhere below the ___ segment. Loss of function results in muscle atrophy.

    Massage is: _____.

Parkinson's Disease: _____ or _____ due to reduced levels of the neurotransmitter _____ in the body. Affects _____ motor movements at first, then affects _____ movements as the disease advances.

    Massage is: _____.

Quadriplegia: Paralysis of the _____ and _____, resulting from an injury to the spinal cord between _____ and _____.

    Massage is: _____.

Sciatica: Compression of the _____ nerve by hypertonic muscles, most commonly the _____. Results in pain radiating down the _____, and may even reach the bottoms of the _____.

    Massage is: _____.

Trigeminal Neuralgia: Compression of the _____ nerve, resulting in severe pain around the _____, _____, and _____.

    Massage is: _____.

Respiratory

Apnea: Cessation of _____, temporarily. Most commonly occurs during sleep, commonly caused by compression of airways by the tongue or pharynx.

    Massage is: _____.

Asthma: Spasm of _____ muscle in the bronchial tubes, which is a reaction to stimuli such as _____ or _____. _____ production is also increased, further reducing air intake, creating wheezing sounds upon inhalation.

    Massage is: _____.

Bronchitis: Inflammation of _____ tubes, with additional _____ production. Acute bronchitis is the side effect of a primary infection such as _____, while chronic bronchitis is the result of irritants entering the lungs over a long period of time, such as _____.

    Massage is: Acute bronchitis – _____.
Chronic bronchitis – _____.

Emphysema: Destruction of lung _____ due to exposure to irritants such as cigarette smoke, reducing oxygen intake and carbon dioxide output.

    Massage is: _____.

Influenza: Acute _____ infection, resulting in an inflamed pharynx and nasal cavity, increased mucous production, and fever.

    Massage is: _____.

Pneumonia: _____ infection in the lungs, which fills the lung _____ with fluid and waste products, reducing air intake.

    Massage is: _____.

Skeletal

Ankylosing Spondylitis: Progressive autoimmune disorder resulting in _____ of intervertebral discs. Disc _____ leads to loss of _____ of the spine, _____ of vertebrae together, and loss of motion at the site of bone fusion.

    Massage is: _____.

Baker's Cyst: Formation of a _____ behind the knee as a result of _____ fluid leaking from the joint cavity.

    Massage is: _____.

Bursitis: Inflammation of a _____, usually due to trauma to a _____. Often presents with _____ buildup, restricting range of motion at the site if around a joint.

    Massage is: _____.

Dislocation: _____ of a bone from its normal location, damaging tissues around the area. Severely weakens the joint following the dislocation, allowing for further dislocation to occur.

    Massage is: _____.

Fracture: A _____ in a bone. A _____ fracture remains inside the skin, while a _____ fracture breaks through the skin.

    Massage is: _____.

Gout: Excessive _____ _____ buildup in the body, resulting in a severely inflamed _____, and may also be seen in the arms and hands as well. Caused by an inability of the body to eliminate _____ _____ normally.

    Massage is: _____.

Herniated Disc: _____ of the gelatinous center of an intervertebral disc, known as the _____ _____, through the tough cartilaginous portion of an intervertebral disc, known as the _____ _____. Results in compression of spinal nerves, producing pain.

    Massage is: _____.

Kyphosis: Hyper-curvature of the _____ vertebrae, producing a hump-back appearance. Also known as _____ _____. Can be caused by a tight _____ _____, weakened back muscles, or other conditions such as osteoporosis or ankylosing spondylitis.

    Massage is: _____.

Lordosis: Hyper-curvature of the _____ vertebrae, forcing the vertebrae anteriorly. Also known as _____. Can be caused by hypertonicity of the _____ _____, or weakness in the _____ _____. May also result in overstretching of the hamstrings.

    Massage is: _____.

Osteoarthritis: Erosion of the _____ cartilage between articulating bones. Results in increased _____ between the bones, causing pain and inflammation. Also known as "_____" arthritis.

    Massage is: _____.

Osteoporosis: _____ of bone tissue, due to a lack of _____ entering into the bones. Usually seen in _____ women, due to a lack of _____ production. Bones become thin and brittle, making them prone to injuries such as fracture.

    Massage is: _____.

Rheumatoid Arthritis: _____ disorder in which the body's immune system attacks _____ membranes surrounding joints. Upon degeneration, the membrane is replaced by _____ tissue, which restricts range of motion in the joints. Usually takes place at the _____ joints of the hands. The fingers are turned to a _____ position, making function difficult.

    Massage is: _____.

Scoliosis: _____ curvature of the vertebrae, most commonly in the _____ vertebrae. Can be caused by severely hypertonic muscles, congenital deformities of the vertebral column, and poor posture.

    Massage is: _____.

Sprain: Injury to a _____, caused by overstretching or tearing of a _____.

    Grade 1: Stretching of a _____ without tearing.
    Grade 2: Partial tearing of a _____ that presents with bruising and inflammation.
    Grade 3: Complete rupture of a _____ which requires surgery to repair.

    Massage is: _____.

Urinary

Cystitis: _____ infection of the urinary bladder, resulting in bloody urine, pain, and increased urination frequency.

    Massage is: _____.

Pyelonephritis: _____ infection of the _____, usually results after obtaining _____.

    Massage is: _____.

Uremia: Excessive amounts of _____ in the _____ _____, usually a sign of _____ failure, caused by inability of the kidneys to filter properly.

    Massage is: _____.

Urinary Tract Infection: _____ infection typically affecting both the _____ and _____ _____.

    Massage is: _____.

Kinesiology

Bony Landmarks

Scapula: Acromion Process, Coracoid Process, Spine of Scapula, Supraspinous Fossa, Infraspinous Fossa, Superior Angle, Inferior Angle, Medial Border, Lateral Border, Glenoid Fossa, Supraglenoid Tubercle, Infraglenoid Tubercle, Subscapular Fossa.

Humerus: Head, Greater Tubercle, Lesser Tubercle, Intertubercular/Bicipital Groove, Deltoid Tuberosity, Radial Fossa, Coronoid Fossa, Medial Epicondyle, Lateral Epicondyle, Capitulum, Trochlea.

Radius: Head, Radial Tuberosity, Styloid Process.

Ulna: Olecranon Process, Coronoid Process, Ulnar Tuberosity, Head, Styloid Process.

Pelvis: Iliac Crest, Iliac Fossa, Anterior Superior Iliac Spine, Anterior Inferior Iliac Spine, Acetabulum, Obturator Foramen, Body of Pubis, Pubic Symphysis, Pubic Crest, Superior Ramus of Pubis, Inferior Ramus of Pubis, Ischial Tuberosity.

Femur: Head, Greater Trochanter, Lesser Trochanter, Gluteal Tuberosity, Linea Aspera, Adductor Tubercle, Medial Epicondyle, Lateral Epicondyle, Medial Condyle, Lateral Condyle.

Tibia: Tibial Plateau, Medial Condyle, Lateral Condyle, Tibial Tuberosity, Pes Anserinus, Medial Malleolus, Soleal Line.

Fibula: Styloid Process, Head, Lateral Malleolus.

Scapula (Anterior)

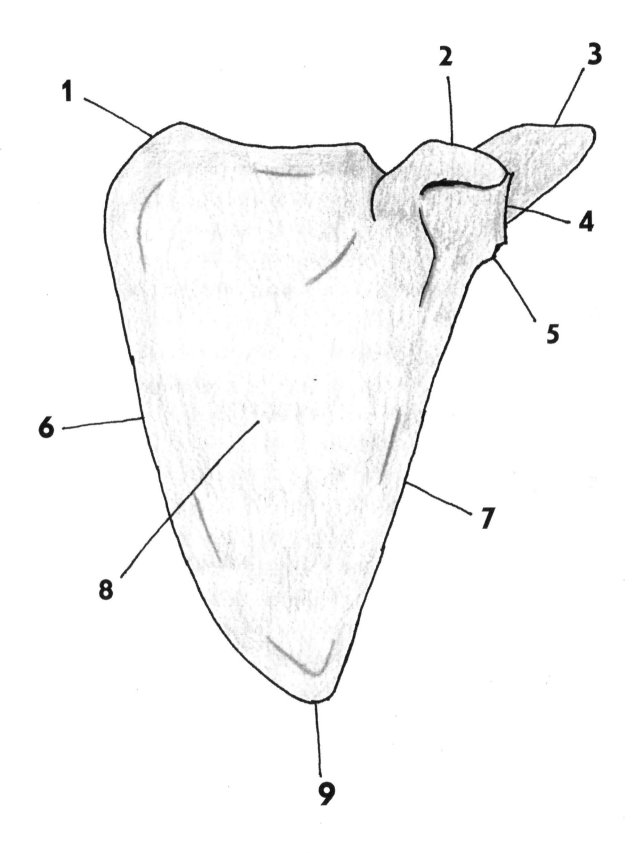

49

Scapula(Posterior)

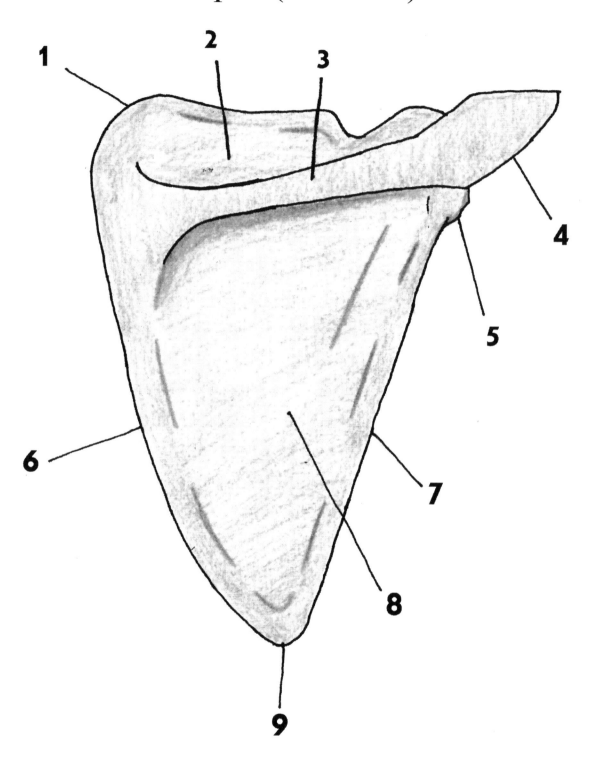

Humerus

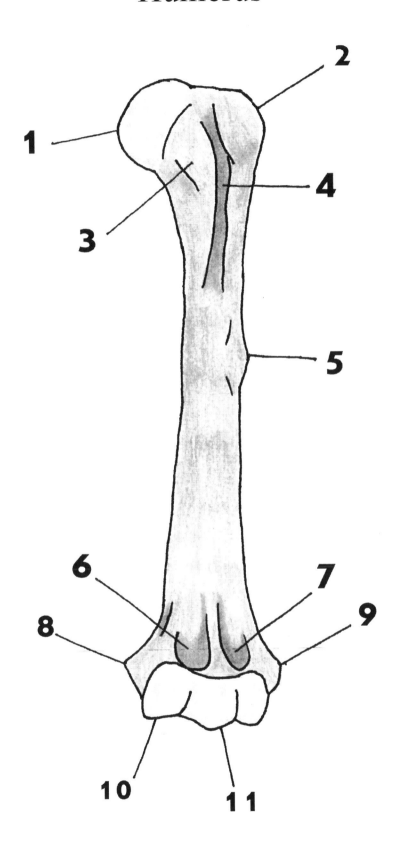

Radius

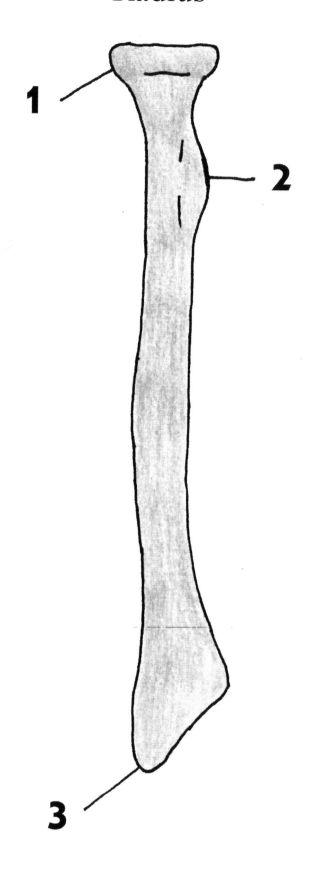

52

Ulna

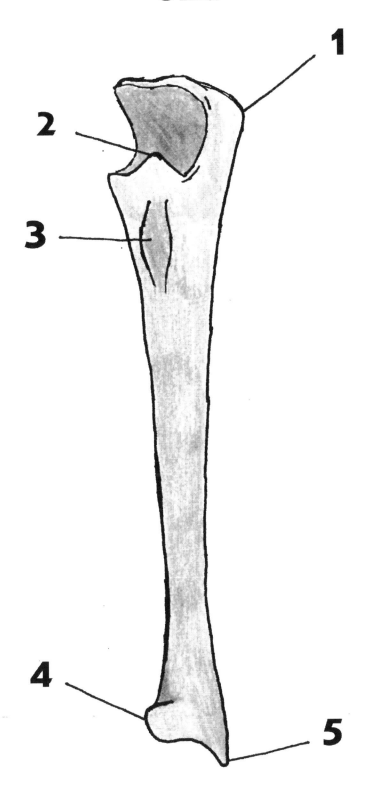

Pelvis

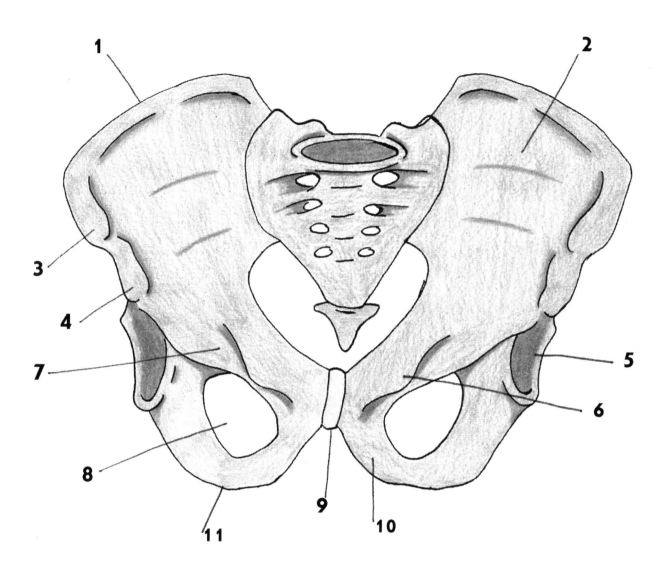

Femur

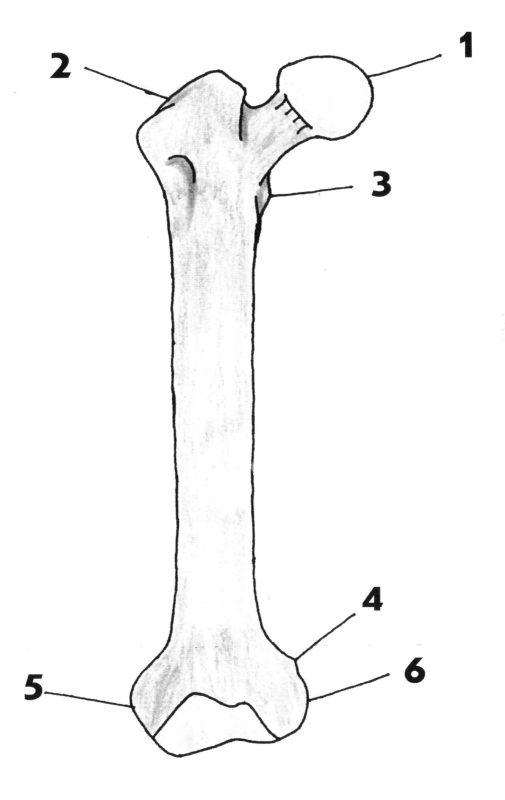

Tibia

Fibula

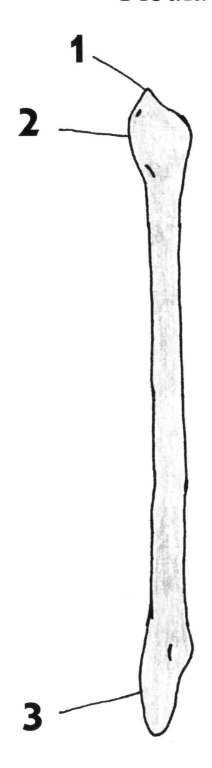

Muscles:

Fill out the information about all of the muscles listed, which includes all of the following:

Origin: Proximal attachment point, the least-movable part of a muscle.

Insertion: Distal attachment point, the most-movable part of a muscle.

Action: Joint movement performed when a muscle contracts.

Innervation: Nerve that stimulates a muscle.

Synergist: A muscle that assists a prime mover in performing an action.

Antagonist: A muscle that performs the opposite action of an agonist.

In the space below this information, draw the muscle and attachment sites.

Levator Scapulae

Origin:

Insertion:

Action(s):

Innervation:

Synergist(s):

Antagonist(s):

Draw the muscle and attachment sites:

Trapezius

Origin:

Insertion:

Action(s):

Innervation:

Synergist(s):

Antagonist(s):

Draw the muscle and attachment sites:

Anterior, Middle, and Posterior Deltoid

Origin:

Insertion:

Action(s):

Innervation:

Synergist(s):

Antagonist(s):

Draw the muscle and attachment sites:

Rhomboid Major and Rhomboid Minor

Origin:

Insertion:

Action(s):

Innervation:

Synergist(s):

Antagonist(s):

Draw the muscle and attachment sites:

Supraspinatus

Origin:

Insertion:

Action(s):

Innervation:

Synergist(s):

Antagonist(s):

Draw the muscle and attachment sites:

Infraspinatus

Origin:

Insertion:

Action(s):

Innervation:

Synergist(s):

Antagonist(s):

Draw the muscle and attachment sites:

Teres Minor

Origin:

Insertion:

Action(s):

Innervation:

Synergist(s):

Antagonist(s):

Draw the muscle and attachment sites:

Subscapularis

Origin:

Insertion:

Action(s):

Innervation:

Synergist(s):

Antagonist(s):

Draw the muscle and attachment sites:

Latissimus Dorsi

Origin:

Insertion:

Action(s):

Innervation:

Synergist(s):

Antagonist(s):

Draw the muscle and attachment sites:

Teres Major

Origin:

Insertion:

Action(s):

Innervation:

Synergist(s):

Antagonist(s):

Draw the muscle and attachment sites:

Pectoralis Major

Origin:

Insertion:

Action(s):

Innervation:

Synergist(s):

Antagonist(s):

Draw the muscle and attachment sites:

Pectoralis Minor

Origin:

Insertion:

Action(s):

Innervation:

Synergist(s):

Antagonist(s):

Draw the muscle and attachment sites:

Serratus Anterior

Origin:

Insertion:

Action(s):

Innervation:

Synergist(s):

Antagonist(s):

Draw the muscle and attachment sites:

Biceps Brachii

Origin:

Insertion:

Action(s):

Innervation:

Synergist(s):

Antagonist(s):

Draw the muscle and attachment sites:

Coracobrachialis

Origin:

Insertion:

Action(s):

Innervation:

Synergist(s):

Antagonist(s):

Draw the muscle and attachment sites:

Brachialis

Origin:

Insertion:

Action(s):

Innervation:

Synergist(s):

Antagonist(s):

Draw the muscle and attachment sites:

Brachioradialis

Origin:

Insertion:

Action(s):

Innervation:

Synergist(s):

Antagonist(s):

Draw the muscle and attachment sites:

Triceps Brachii

Origin:

Insertion:

Action(s):

Innervation:

Synergist(s):

Antagonist(s):

Draw the muscle and attachment sites:

Pronator Teres

Origin:

Insertion:

Action(s):

Innervation:

Synergist(s):

Antagonist(s):

Draw the muscle and attachment sites:

Psoas Major

Origin:

Insertion:

Action(s):

Innervation:

Synergist(s):

Antagonist(s):

Draw the muscle and attachment sites:

Iliacus

Origin:

Insertion:

Action(s):

Innervation:

Synergist(s):

Antagonist(s):

Draw the muscle and attachment sites:

Piriformis

Origin:

Insertion:

Action(s):

Innervation:

Synergist(s):

Antagonist(s):

Draw the muscle and attachment sites:

Gluteus Maximus

Origin:

Insertion:

Action(s):

Innervation:

Synergist(s):

Antagonist(s):

Draw the muscle and attachment sites:

Rectus Femoris

Origin:

Insertion:

Action(s):

Innervation:

Synergist(s):

Antagonist(s):

Draw the muscle and attachment sites:

Gracilis

Origin:

Insertion:

Action(s):

Innervation:

Synergist(s):

Antagonist(s):

Draw the muscle and attachment sites:

Pectineus

Origin:

Insertion:

Action(s):

Innervation:

Synergist(s):

Antagonist(s):

Draw the muscle and attachment sites:

Adductor Longus

Origin:

Insertion:

Action(s):

Innervation:

Synergist(s):

Antagonist(s):

Draw the muscle and attachment sites:

Adductor Magnus

Origin:

Insertion:

Action(s):

Innervation:

Synergist(s):

Antagonist(s):

Draw the muscle and attachment sites:

Sartorius

Origin:

Insertion:

Action(s):

Innervation:

Synergist(s):

Antagonist(s):

Draw the muscle and attachment sites:

Semimembranosus

Origin:

Insertion:

Action(s):

Innervation:

Synergist(s):

Antagonist(s):

Draw the muscle and attachment sites:

Semitendinosus

Origin:

Insertion:

Action(s):

Innervation:

Synergist(s):

Antagonist(s):

Draw the muscle and attachment sites:

Biceps Femoris

Origin:

Insertion:

Action(s):

Innervation:

Synergist(s):

Antagonist(s):

Draw the muscle and attachment sites:

Gastrocnemius and Soleus

Origin:

Insertion:

Action(s):

Innervation:

Synergist(s):

Antagonist(s):

Draw the muscle and attachment sites:

Peroneus Longus

Origin:

Insertion:

Action(s):

Innervation:

Synergist(s):

Antagonist(s):

Draw the muscle and attachment sites:

Tibialis Anterior

Origin:

Insertion:

Action(s):

Innervation:

Synergist(s):

Antagonist(s):

Draw the muscle and attachment sites:

Assignments

Body Systems
Complete the crossword below

Across
2. Produces hormones, consists of glands
4. Sensory reception and evaluation, consists of brain and spinal cord
5. Breaks down food and absorbs nutrients, consists of the alimentary canal
7. Allows for reproduction, consists of genitalia
8. Pumps blood, consists of heart and blood vessels
9. Protects the body and provides support, consists of bones
10. Aids in defense against pathogens, consists of lymph nodes and lymph
11. Creates heat and movement, consists of muscles

Down
1. Circulates air in and out of the lungs, consists of the lungs and airways
3. Filters, reabsorbs, and eliminates substances, consists of the kidneys and bladder
6. Protects the body, consists of skin, hair, nails, and sweat glands

Word Roots

Write the letter of the correct match next to each problem.

1. _____ Necr/o   a. Muscle
2. _____ Leuk/o   b. Liver
3. _____ Melan/o   c. Fat
4. _____ Cost/o   d. Kidney
5. _____ Spondyl/o   e. Arm
6. _____ Gastr/o   f. Blood
7. _____ Derm/o   g. Black
8. _____ Chondr/o   h. Tongue
9. _____ Adip/o   i. Brain
10. _____ Hepat/o   j. Rib
11. _____ Gloss/o   k. Spine
12. _____ My/o   l. Stomach
13. _____ Nephr/o   m. White
14. _____ Brachi/o   n. Vein
15. _____ Cardi/o   o. Lung
16. _____ Erythr/o   p. Skin
17. _____ Encephal/o   q. Cartilage
18. _____ Hem/o   r. Death
19. _____ Pneum/o   s. Red
20. _____ Phleb/o   t. Heart

Prefixes

Write the letter of the correct match next to each problem.

1. _____ auto-   a. Together
2. _____ a-   b. Change
3. _____ hyper-   c. Without
4. _____ meta-   d. Two
5. _____ mal-   e. Against
6. _____ syn-   f. Above
7. _____ homeo-   g. Through
8. _____ hypo-   h. Equal
9. _____ inter-   i. Slow
10. _____ dia-   j. Same
11. _____ bi-   k. Large
12. _____ macro- l. Towards
13. _____ brady- m. Small
14. _____ micro- n. Around
15. _____ anti-   o. Bad
16. _____ iso-   p. Excessive
17. _____ circum- q. Inside
18. _____ endo-   r. Below
19. _____ af-   s. Self
20. _____ epi-   t. Between

Suffixes

Write the letter of the correct match next to each problem.

1. _____ -ectomy   a. Nourishment
2. _____ -blast   b. Blood
3. _____ -pnea   c. Production
4. _____ -crine   d. Swelling
5. _____ -cision   e. Resembling
6. _____ -trophy   f. Condition
7. _____ -algia   g. Skin
8. _____ -stasis   h. Standing still
9. _____ -emia   i. Paralysis
10. _____ -derma   j. Break
11. _____ -plegia   k. Protein
12. _____ -gen   l. Germ cell
13. _____ -phagia   m. Removal
14. _____ -globin   n. Dissolve
15. _____ -clast   o. Cutting
16. _____ -edema   p. Pain
17. _____ -osis   q. Eating
18. _____ -cyte   r. Breathing
19. _____ -oid   s. Secrete
20. _____ -lysis   t. Cell

Muscles by Origin

Complete the crossword below

Across
1. Anterior Superior Iliac Spine
4. Posterior medial and lateral epicondyles of the femur
6. Ischial tuberosity
9. Anterior lateral shaft and lateral condyle of tibia
10. Coracoid process and supraglenoid tubercle
11. Iliac fossa
12. Inferior ramus of the pubis

Down
2. Anterior Inferior Iliac Spine
3. Transverse processes of C1-C4
5. Lateral supracondylar ridge of humerus
7. Subscapular fossa
8. Lateral border of scapula

Muscles by Insertion

Complete the crossword below

Across
4. Coronoid process and ulnar tuberosity
9. Olecranon process
10. Mastoid process of temporal bone
12. Head of the fibula

Down
1. Greater tubercle of humerus
2. Tibial tuberosity
3. Radial tuberosity
5. Adductor tubercle, medial lip of linea aspera
6. Base of first metatarsal
7. Medial border of scapula
8. Coracoid process
11. Deltoid tuberosity

Muscles by Action

Complete the crossword below

Across
3. Flexes, extends, and adducts the hip
9. Abduction, medial rotation, extension of the shoulder
11. Flexes the shoulder, flexes the elbow, supinates the forearm
12. Retract the scapula

Down
1. Flexes the knee and plantarflexes the ankle
2. Extend the shoulder and extend the elbow
4. Dorsiflexion and inversion of the ankle
5. Abduct the shoulder
6. Lateral rotation and extension of the hip
7. Flexes the hip and extends the knee
8. Flexes the elbow
10. Lateral rotation and extension of the shoulder

Muscles by Innervation
Complete the crossword below

Across
2. Tibial
4. Axillary
5. Superficial Peroneal
7. Obturator
8. Deep Peroneal
10. Median
11. Radial

Down
1. Musculocutaneous
3. Phrenic
6. Sciatic
9. Femoral

Full Study Guide With Answers

Massage Therapy 104
    History 104
    Technique 105
    Modalities 108
    Business 110
Anatomy and Physiology 112
    Regional Anatomy 113
    Tissue 114
    Body Systems 116
Medical Terminology 124
Pathology 128
Kinesiology 146
    Attachment Sites 146
    Muscles 156
David's Easy Ways to Remember Things 194
Massage Therapy and Business Practice Exam 200
    Massage Therapy and Business Answer Key 224
Anatomy and Physiology Practice Exam 226
    Anatomy and Physiology Answer Key 274
Pathology Practice Exam 278
    Pathology Answer Key 344
Kinesiology Practice Exam 350
    Kinesiology Answer Key 386
Flashcards 390
About the Author 439
References 440

Massage Therapy

History of Massage

China: Massage has been practiced in China as early as **3000 BC**. Chinese massage technique known as **Amma** used rubbing and pressing movements.
Japan: Amma entered Japan around **500 AD**. The manipulation areas remained the same, but were known as **Tsubo**. Tsubo points are pressed to increase circulation of fluid and **Ki**. This technique is known as **Shiatsu**.
India: Massage has been practiced in India since before **1000 BC**. **The Ayur-Veda**, or "Art of Life", was written around **1800 BC**, and detailed massage treatments as part of personal hygiene.
Greece: Massage and exercise was a normal part of Greek life as early as **300 BC**.
America: Massage became popularized in America around **1850** after the development of the **Swedish Movement Cure**.

People of Importance:

Aesculapius: **Greek** priest-physician who combined **exercise** and **massage**, which is known as **gymnastics**, and founded the first gymnasium.
Celsus: **Roman** physician who wrote **De Medicina**, which detailed the use of **massage**, **bathing**, and **exercise** as prevention of disease.
Per Henrik Ling: **Swedish** physiologist who developed a system of **active** and **passive movements** to improve physical conditions, known as **Medical Gymnastics**. This system of movements evolved into **physical therapy** and **massage therapy**.
Charles Taylor: Introduced Medical Gymnastics to the **United States**, where it became known as the **Swedish Movement Cure**.
Johann Mezger: Established modern **terminology** for the **massage strokes**, based in **French**.
Douglas Graham: Helped to **popularize** the term "massage" in **America**.
Emil Vodder: Developed **lymphatic drainage**.

Massage Technique

There are **six** main massage strokes in Western massage therapy:

Effleurage: Long, **gliding** strokes directed **towards the heart**. Used to increase circulation, apply massage lubricant, and transition between strokes. Primarily used at the beginning of a massage.

Petrissage: Kneading strokes used to increase circulation, loosen adhesions and release metabolic waste from tissues.

Friction: Strokes that move **across** tissue. Used to increase circulation, break up scar tissue and adhesions, and stretch muscle. Examples include circular friction, cross-fiber friction, and compression.

Tapotement: **Percussion** strokes used to increase muscle spindle activity, which stimulates the body, and loosen phlegm from the respiratory tract. Examples include hacking, cupping, and tapping.

Vibration: **Trembling** or **shaking** movements. Fast vibration is used to stimulate an area. Slow vibration is used to sedate an area.

Nerve Stroke: **Extremely light** form of effleurage, used at the end of a massage to separate the therapist from the client.

Joint Movements:
Active: Client performs an action **without assistance** from the massage therapist.
Active Assistive: The **client** performs an action **with assistance** from the massage therapist.
Passive: Massage therapist performs a joint mobilization with the **client completely relaxed**.
Resistive: The **client resists** a movement being performed by the massage therapist.

Assessment: **Preliminary evaluation** of the client before, during, and after a massage treatment. Used to determine contraindications, tailor massage treatments, and refer clients to other health-care professionals.

Methods: Intake forms, gait analysis, posture analysis, ergonomics, contraindications, listening, palpation.

Stretching: **Elongating** a muscle.
Unassisted: **Client stretching** into resistance **without assistance** from the massage therapist.
Assisted: **Client stretching** into resistance **with help** from the massage therapist.
Proprioceptive Neuromuscular Facilitation: Unassisted stretch in which the muscle is **stretched into resistance**, followed by an **isometric contraction** of the muscle by the client. The client relaxes the contraction, which allows the stretch to move further.
Reciprocal Inhibition: Used to **forcibly relax** a muscle by **contracting the antagonist** muscle, especially useful in treating acute **muscle cramps**.

End Feel: **Stoppage** of a range-of-motion.
Soft End Feel: Stoppage of range-of-motion due to tight **soft tissues** pulling the joint in the opposite way, has a springy end of motion.
Hard End Feel: Stoppage of range-of-motion due to **hard tissue** preventing any further motion, has an abrupt end of motion.
Empty End Feel: Stoppage of range-of-motion due to **trauma** to an affected muscle or joint, limiting motion to prevent further injury.

Draping: Using **linens** to cover a client during a massage session.
Top Cover: The linen placed **atop the client**, used to keep the client covered during a massage treatment.
Full Sheet: Using the entire sheet to enclose a client in a **cocoon-like wrap**, primarily used in body wrap treatments.

Bolsters: Used to place a client into a comfortable position while receiving a massage.
Supine: Bolsters should be placed **under the knees** and **under the neck**.
Prone: Bolsters should be placed **under the ankles**.
Side-lying: Bolsters should be placed **between the legs and arms,** and **under the head**.
Semi-reclined: Bolsters should be placed **under the knees** and **under the head**. Use for pregnant women to reduce pressure on the **abdominal aorta**.

Body Mechanics: Used to **prevent injuries** to the massage therapist, **provide a better massage** for the client, and to **increase the length of the massage therapist's career**. The **back** should be **straight**, the **knees** should be **slightly bent**, **joints** should be **stacked**, and the massage **table** should be kept at the **proper height**.
Archer/Bow Stance: Feet are placed **parallel** to the massage table, and allow the massage therapist to perform long **gliding** strokes like those found in effleurage.
Horse/Warrior Stance: Feet are placed **perpendicular** to the massage table, and allow **short,** powerful strokes to be performed, such as petrissage, friction, compression, and tapotement.

Precautions:
Endangerment Site: An area of the body the massage therapist should take **precautions** on or near while performing a massage.
Local Contraindication: An area of the body that must be **avoided** while performing a massage.
Absolute Contraindication: A condition that **prohibits** the use of **any massage** treatment.

Massage Modalities

Aromatherapy: Using **essential oils** during a massage session for healing. Essential oils may have specific effects on the body, ranging from physical to emotional, depending on the type of essential oil used.

Craniosacral Therapy: Developed by John Upledger, very light massage technique that releases **blockages** in the flow of **cerebrospinal fluid** from the **cranium** to the **sacrum** by working on the axial skeleton.

Deep Tissue: Deep pressure massage focused on treating **deeper muscular** and **fascial tissue**.

Feldenkrais: Developed by Moshe Feldenkrais, massage technique designed to **re-educate** the **body movements**, allowing the body to move more fluidly and efficiently, which reduces pain.

Hot Stone: Treatment utilizing **heated stones**, which may be **placed** or **rubbed** on the body. Used to increase circulation throughout the body and relax muscles.

Hydrotherapy: Treatments utilizing **water** in any form.
Turkish Bath: A sauna inside a **large stone building**.
Swiss Shower: A **standing** shower with **sixteen shower heads.**
Vichy Shower: A shower utilizing **seven shower heads** with a client placed on a **water-proof table**.

Lomi Lomi: Hawaiian massage, similar to Swedish, using rhythmic strokes performed on the entire body with minimal draping.

Lymphatic Drainage: Developed by Emil Vodder, light massage strokes moving in the direction of the heart, used to increase **lymph circulation** and reduce swelling.

Myofascial Release: Massage aimed at releasing **restrictions** in **muscles** and **fascia** utilizing light strokes moving in the direction of the restriction.

Polarity Therapy: Massage theory which states every **cell** has a **positive** and **negative pole**, utilizes light strokes to balance the body.

Reflexology: Treating **reflex points** on the **hands**, **feet**, and **ears**, which may affect corresponding **organs** throughout the body.

Reiki: Manipulation of **energy** into and throughout the client, performed **without touching** the client.

Rolfing: Developed by Ida Rolf, **structural realignment** massage technique, which helps the client's body regain **vertical alignment**. Takes place over ten sessions, with a focus on a different part of the body in each session.

Sports Massage: Massage for **athletes**, performed before, during, and after athletic events. May be either fast-paced or slow and methodical, depending on the work that needs to be done.

Swedish Massage: Most common form of massage in the West, focuses primarily on **relaxation**.

Strain-Counter Strain: Also known as **Positional Release**, moving the body into a painful position and allowing the body to relax into a non-painful position, helping to release restrictions.

Thai Massage: Clothed massage performed **on the floor**, primarily utilizing **stretching** techniques.

Trager Method: Developed by Milton Trager, utilizing exercises called **Mentastics**, performed with movement, gentle massage strokes, and rocking to produce positive sensory reception in the Central Nervous System.

Business

Certification: Credential obtained by completing a certification course, usually in a **school** setting, and may involve passing of a **certification exam**.

License: Jurisdictional requirement to **regulate** the practice of massage therapy, allows a massage therapist to perform massage for monetary compensation.

Reciprocity: Massage license in one jurisdiction being **recognized** as valid in another jurisdiction.

Liability Insurance: Obtained through massage insurance providers, protects the massage therapist in cases such as **accidents** and **malpractice**.

Client Files: Any client file should be retained by the massage therapist for a minimum of **six years**, per the **Internal Revenue Service**.

SOAP Notes: Used to **document** everything regarding a previous massage treatment.
S: **Subjective**, anything the client details about **themselves**.
O: **Objective/Observation**, **type of massage** or techniques being performed, and any **measurable data** the massage therapist can physically see.
A: **Assessment**, any **changes** in the client resulting from the treatment.
P: **Plan**, any **recommendations** for future treatment or exercises suggested to the client **between sessions**.

Communication:
Confidentiality: Keeping client information **private** and **protected** in all ways.
Open-Ended Question: Used when asking for detailed **feedback** from clients.
Close-Ended Question: Used when asking for a **yes or no** response only.

Transference: A client viewing a massage therapist similarly to a person in their **early life**.
Counter-Transference: A massage therapist bringing their **unresolved issues** into the therapeutic relationship.

Ethics: Guiding **moral principles** used to direct a massage therapist to proper course of action in ethical dilemmas.
Scope of Practice: Performing treatments and techniques only **qualified to perform**.
Mission Statement: A short statement detailing the **general purpose** of the business.
Boundaries: Setting personal and professional **limitations** by the client or therapist.
HIPAA: Health Insurance Portability and Accountability Act of 1996. Enacted August 21, 1996. Created by US Department of Heath and Human Services.
Privacy Rule: Protects all individually **identifiable** health information. Assures health information of individuals is **protected** while allowing health information to be **transferred** between healthcare providers to provide high-quality health care.

Types of Employment:
Independent Contractor: A massage therapist who **contracts** to work for a person or company and receives **no benefits**.
Sole Proprietor: A business that has only **one owner**.
Partnership: A business that has **two or more owners**.

Tax Forms:
1099: Filed by **independent contractors** who make more than $600 in a year.
Schedule C: Filed by **sole proprietors**, details profit and loss for the previous year.
Schedule K-1: Filed by **partnership members**, details income and taxes for each partnership member from the previous year.
1040: Tax form detailing **deductions** and **dependents**.
W-2: Filed by **employees**, details **income** and **taxes** from the previous year.

Anatomy and Physiology

Anatomy: The study of the **structure** of the human body.
Systemic Anatomy: The study of the body's **organ systems.**
Regional Anatomy: The study of the different **regions** of the body.
Physiology: The study of the **function** of the body.

Cells: Cells are the functional units of all tissues, and they perform all essential life functions.
Cellular Mitosis: A cell **dividing** from one mother cell into two daughter cells in order to replace cell loss.
Organelles are found **inside** cells to make the cells function.
Nucleus: Contains **DNA**, controls activity inside cells.
Nucleolus: Forms **ribosomes** and **synthesizes RNA** in ribosomes.
Mitochondria: Produce **ATP**. "Power Plant" Generates energy
Golgi Apparatus: Allows **transportation of protein** in cells.
Smooth Endoplasmic Reticulum: Synthesizes **carbohydrates** and **lipids.**
Lysosome: Break down **protein** inside cells.
Ribosome: Contain **RNA and protein**, assemble cell proteins.
Cytoplasm: **Gel-like substance** inside cell.

Homeostasis: Homeostasis is the existence and maintenance of a **constant internal environment.** Several factors contribute to the homeostatic process, including hormones, nerve impulses, and sweating.
Homeostatic Mechanisms: Homeostatic mechanisms are **physical** things that happen in the body that alter the internal environment in response to a specific change. **Sweating** reduces body temperature, and **shivering** increases body temperature.

REGIONAL ANATOMY

There are three main regions of the body:

Central
Upper Limb
Lower Limb

Central Body Region:
The Central body region contains everything in the center of the body, such as the **head, neck, and trunk.** The trunk can be further divided into three other regions:

Thorax: The thorax contains our major internal organs, such as the **heart and lungs.** Also inside the thorax is the **mediastinum**, a form of connective tissue that surrounds organs inside the chest(except the lungs), protecting them from too much jostling.

Abdomen: The abdomen contains the majority of our digestive organs, including the stomach, liver, gallbladder, pancreas, small intestine, large intestine, kidneys, and spleen.

Pelvis: The pelvis contains our **internal reproductive organs**, the **descending and sigmoid colons**, and the **urinary bladder.**

Body Cavities:
Body cavities **hold things inside them.** There are two main body cavities:

Dorsal Body Cavity: Made by the **skull and vertebral column**, contains the **brain and spinal cord.**

Ventral Body Cavity: Made by the three trunk cavities(**thorax, abdomen, pelvis**).

Directional Terms:
Used to describe structures in the body in relation to other structures or body parts.

Superior: Above
Inferior: Below
Anterior: Front
Posterior: Back
Proximal: Closer to the midline

Distal: Further from the midline
Medial: Middle
Lateral: Side
Deep: More internal
Superficial: Towards the surface

Body Planes: There are **four planes** used to divide the body.
Sagittal: Splits the body into **left and right.**
Midsagittal: Splits the body into **equal left and right sides**, runs down the **midline** of the body.
Transverse/Horizontal: Splits the body into **superior and inferior.**
Frontal/Coronal: Splits the body into **anterior and posterior.**

TISSUE

There are **four** types of tissue in the human body:
Epithelial, Nervous, Muscular, and Connective.

Epithelial: Forms most **glands**, the **digestive tract**, and the **epidermis**.
Epithelial tissue is responsible for **protecting** the body, **absorbing** nutrients, and **secreting** substances. Epithelial tissue is **avascular** and contains no blood vessels.

Nervous: Forms the **brain, spinal cord,** and **nerves**.
Nervous tissue allows for **sensation, mental activity,** and **movement** of skeletal muscle. A **neuron** is a **nerve cell**. It contains a **nucleus**, the site of cell function. It also contains **dendrites**, branch-like projections that come off the cell body to receive nervous impulses, bringing them into the cell body.

Muscular: There are three types of muscle: **Skeletal, cardiac, smooth.**
Skeletal: Connects to the **skeleton** and allows **voluntary movements**.
Cardiac: Muscle of the **heart**, responsible for **pumping blood** throughout the body.
Smooth: Found in locations such as the **skin**(arrector pili) and **digestive tract**. Responsible for actions such as **peristalsis**.

Connective: Connective tissue is formed by the "**extracellular matrix**", materials you don't find in cells. They can contain **protein**, **non-fibrous protein**, and **fluid**. Connective tissue is responsible for actions such as **separating** structures, **connecting** structures, **transportation** of nutrients, **cushioning** and **insulating** the body, and **protecting** the body.
Blast Cells: Immature cells that **build** the matrix.
Clast Cells: **Break down** the matrix.
There are several types of connective tissue, including **bone**, **cartilage**, **tendons**, **ligaments**, **adipose**, **fascia**, **serous membranes**, and **blood**. The most abundant form of connective tissue in the body is **blood**.

Blood: Consists of **erythrocytes**, **leukocytes**, **thrombocytes**, and **plasma**.
Erythrocytes: Also called **red blood cells**, responsible for **transporting** oxygen and carbon dioxide throughout the body via **hemoglobin**, which is found in the cytoplasm of the cells.
Leukocytes: Also called **white blood cells**, they are **phagocytes** that help fight off infectious agents and break down dead cells and debris inside the body.
Thrombocytes: Also called **platelets**, they are responsible for **clotting** the blood.
Plasma: The **liquid** portion of blood, allows **transportation** of blood cells throughout the body.

Serous Membranes: Forms of connective tissues that **surround** organs inside body cavities, preventing the organs from creating friction. There are **two** serous membranes inside the **thorax**: the **pericardium**, which surrounds the **heart**, and the **pleura**, which surrounds the **lungs**. There is **one** serous membrane that is found inside the **abdomen** and **pelvis** that separates the organs from the muscle on top of them: the **peritoneum**.
Inner wall of a serous membrane: **Visceral** serous membrane
Outer wall of a serous membrane: **Parietal** serous membrane

BODY SYSTEMS

Cardiovascular System: Responsible for **transporting blood** throughout the body, bringing oxygen, hormones, and nutrients to tissues, and eliminating carbon dioxide and waste products from the body. Consists of the **heart**, **blood vessels**, and **blood**.

Heart: Pumps blood throughout the body. Consists of the superior vena cava, inferior vena cava, right atrium, tricuspid valve, right ventricle, pulmonary valve, pulmonary arteries, pulmonary veins, left atrium, bicuspid valve, left ventricle, aortic valve, and aorta.

Blood Vessels: Create **passageways** for blood to travel throughout the body.

Arteries: Largest and most internal blood vessels, move blood **away from the heart**, and almost always carry oxygenated blood.

Veins: Move blood **towards the heart,** and almost always carry deoxygenated blood.

Capillaries: Microscopic blood vessels used to transport oxygen-rich blood **into tissues**.

Pulmonary Circulation (rt side)

Systemic Circulation (left side)

To body (12)
Aorta
(1) Superior Vena Cava
To lungs
(6) Pulmonary Arteries
→ To lungs (to be oxygenated)
Pulmonary Veins
(7)
(2) Right Atrium
(8) Left Atrium
(3) Tricuspid Valve
Bicuspid/ (9) Mitral Valve
Inferior Vena Cava
(4) Right Ventricle
(10) Left Ventricle
(5) Pulmonary Valve
(11) Aortic Valve

Digestive System: Responsible for bringing food **into the body**, **digestion**, **absorption** of nutrients, and **elimination** of waste.
Oral Cavity: Also called the **mouth**, contains the **teeth, salivary glands**, and **tongue**. Performs **mastication** and **swallowing**.
Pharynx: Also called the **throat**, allows **transport** of food from the oral cavity to the esophagus.
Esophagus: Tubular organ that allows **transport** of food from the pharynx to the stomach.
Stomach: Digests and **breaks down** food into usable, absorbable nutrients.
Liver: Filters harmful chemicals from the blood, produces **bile**.
Gallbladder: Stores bile and **empties bile** into the duodenum.
Pancreas: Produces **insulin** and **glucagon** and secretes these substances into the duodenum.
Small Intestine: Absorbs nutrients into the body for use. Consists of the **duodenum, jejunum**, and **ileum**.
Large Intestine: Absorbs water, converts chyme to **feces**, assists in **elimination** of waste.
Between organs in the Digestive System, we have **sphincters**. Sphincters are **ring-like** bands of **muscle** that allow food to pass through into other organs, and to **prevent** food from going **backwards** in the digestive tract. There are four main sphincters in the digestive tract:
Esophageal Sphincter: Located between the **pharynx** and **esophagus**.
Cardiac Sphincter: Located between the **esophagus** and **stomach**.
Pyloric Sphincter: Located between the **stomach** and **small intestine**.
Ileocecal Sphincter: Located between the **small intestine** and **large intestine**.

Endocrine System: Responsible for **coordinating** the specific activities of cells and tissues via **hormone** release. Endocrine glands secrete hormones directly into the **blood stream**.
Pituitary Gland: Secretes **growth hormone, prolactin**, and **follicle-stimulating** hormones. Responsible for **growth** in bones, production of **milk**, and production of **egg** cells in women and **sperm** cells in men.
Adrenals: Secrete **epinephrine** and **norepinephrine**, which elevate **blood pressure**, increase **heart rate**, and increase **blood sugar**.

Pancreatic Islets: Secrete **insulin** and **glucagon**. Insulin **lowers** glucose concentration in the blood, while glucagon **increases** glucose concentration in the blood.
Ovaries: Secrete **estrogen** and **progesterone**.
Testes: Secrete **testosterone**.

Integumentary System
Contains the **skin, hair, nails, sweat glands, oil glands**, and **sensory receptors**. Responsible for **protection**, **secretion** of substances, **absorption** of substances, and detecting **sensation**.
Skin: Made of epithelial tissue, skin is avascular and is used for **protection**.
Sudoriferous Glands: Secrete **sweat**, which is a homeostatic mechanism. Sudoriferous glands are forms of exocrine glands.
Sebaceous Glands: Secrete **oil**. Sebaceous glands are forms of exocrine glands.
Sensory Receptors: Detect **sensation** in the skin.
Pacinian Corpuscles: Detect **deep** pressure.
Meissner's Corpuscles: Detect **light** pressure.
Nociceptors: Detect **pain.**

Lymphatic System
Consists of **lymph nodes, lymph vessels, lymph**, and **lymph organs**.
Lymph Vessels: They are a **one-way** system, meaning lymph in the vessels only flows one direction. The vessels **absorb** foreign bodies and nutrients from tissue.
Lymph Nodes: A lymph node is a **mass** of lymph tissue, responsible for **filtering** and **destroying** foreign objects, helps to **produce antibodies**.
Lymph: Made of mostly water, protein, leukocytes, urea, salts, and glucose.
Spleen: Removes old **red blood cells** from the blood stream.
Thymus: Produces **T-lymphocytes**(T-cells).

Muscular System
Contains **muscles**. Muscles are responsible for **movement** and **creating heat.**
In order for a muscle to contract, **calcium** must be present. The contractile unit of a muscle is called a **sarcomere**. Sarcomeres are formed by **thin** filaments(**actin**) and **thick** filaments(**myosin**).

Muscle Contractions: A contraction is when **tension** in a muscle **increases**.
Isometric Contraction: The **length** of a muscle **stays the same**, but **tension** in the muscle **increases**.
Isotonic Contraction: The **tension** in a muscle **stays the same**, but the **length** of the muscle **changes**.
Concentric Contraction: The **tension** in a muscle **increases**, and muscle **length decreases.**
Eccentric Contraction: The **tension** in the muscle **stays the same**, and muscle **length increases**.
Prime Mover/Agonist: The muscle of a synergist group **responsible for movement**.
Synergist: A muscle that **assists** the prime mover in performing the action.
Antagonist: A muscle that **opposes** the prime mover, performing the **opposite** action.
Fixator: A muscle that **stabilizes** an area so an action can be performed.

Nervous System:
There are two branches of the Nervous System, the **Central Nervous System** and **Peripheral Nervous System**. It also contains the **Autonomic Nervous System.**
Central Nervous System: Consists of the **brain** and **spinal cord**.
Brain: Consists of the **cerebrum, cerebellum,** and **brain stem.**
Cerebrum: The **largest** part of the brain, split into left and right **hemispheres**, responsible for **voluntary** actions and **sensory** reception. Each hemisphere contains **lobes**, named after bones overlaying them.
Frontal Lobe: Responsible for **voluntary** motor function, **motivation, aggression, mood.**
Parietal Lobe: Responsible for processing most **sensory** information.
Temporal Lobe: Responsible for **auditory** and **olfactory** processing, and **memory**.
Occipital Lobe: Responsible for **visual** input.

Cerebellum: Responsible for **muscle tone, coordination,** and **balance.**
Brain Stem: Contains three parts: **Medulla Oblongata, Pons,** and **Midbrain.**
Medulla Oblongata: Regulates the body's **vital functions.**

Pons: Creates a pathway for **communication** between the **cerebrum** and **cerebellum**.
Midbrain: **Visual reflexes**.
Peripheral Nervous System: Contains **nerves**. There are **31 pairs** of **spinal nerves** that emerge from the spinal cord, and **12 pairs** of **cranial nerves** that emerge from the brain.
Cranial Nerves: Emerge from the brain, numbered via Roman numerals. Olfactory(I), Optic(II), Oculomotor(III), Trochlear(IV), Trigeminal(V), Abducens(VI), Facial(VII), Vestibulocochlear(VIII), Glossopharyngeal(IX), Vagus(X), Spinal Accessory(XI), Hypoglossal(XII)

Autonomic Nervous System: Responsible for maintenance of **homeostasis** within the body. There are two autonomic nervous responses in the body.
Sympathetic Response: Also called "**fight-or-flight**", when activated, increases **norepinephrine** in the body, **increasing** heart rate. It also **shuts down** digestive organs and pulls blood from them for use in the muscles.
Parasympathetic Response: Also called "**rest-and-digest**", when activated, **decreases** heart rate, brings blood into the digestive organs to stimulate **peristalsis**. Controlled by Cranial Nerve X, the **Vagus Nerve**.

Respiratory System:
Exchanges **oxygen** and **carbon dioxide** in blood, and aids in **eliminating waste** from the body.
Nose: Conducts and **warms air** coming in and exiting the body. **Filters** air via **mucous**.
Larynx: Tube at front of pharynx, strengthened by muscles. Contains the **epiglottis**, which prevents food from entering the larynx during swallowing. Allows **speech**.
Trachea: Cartilage inferior to the larynx, allows **passage of air** into lungs.
Bronchi: Split into right and left, divides into smaller branches as they move through the lungs. Smallest branches are called **bronchioles**. They secrete **mucous** to trap dirt and debris, which is then expelled from the lungs by **cilia**.
Alveoli: Air sacs at the end of bronchial tubes, connect to blood vessels. Responsible for **exchange** of oxygen and carbon dioxide.

Diaphragm: **Muscle** attached to base of rib cage and vertebrae, creates a vacuum to **bring air into the lungs** and **expel air from the lungs.** When the diaphragm **descends**, air **enters** the lungs. When the diaphragm **ascends**, air **exits** the lungs.

Skeletal System: Contains **bones**. Responsible for **protecting** the body, **creating blood cells**, providing **structure**, and giving muscles a **location to attach to** which **permits movement**.

Axial Skeleton: Consists of the **skull, vertebral column,** and **thoracic cage**.
Skull: Protects the brain. Contains the following bones: Frontal, occipital, parietal, temporal, mandible, maxilla, sphenoid, vomer, nasal, ethmoid, lacrimal, and zygomatic.
There are four main sutures of the cranium, holding the bones of the skull together. They are:
Sagittal Suture: Connects the two **parietal bones.**
Coronal Suture: Connects the **frontal bone** to the **parietal bones.**
Squamous Suture: Connects the **temporal bone** and **parietal bone.**
Lambdoid Suture: Connects the **occipital bone** and the **parietal bones.**

Vertebral Column: Protects the spinal cord. Contains **26** individual bones. **Seven cervical** vertebrae, **twelve thoracic** vertebrae, **five lumbar** vertebrae, **one sacral** vertebrae, **one coccygeal** vertebrae.
Thoracic Cage: Also called the **rib cage**, **protects** the organs inside the thorax. There are **twelve pairs** of ribs. The **superior seven** pairs are called **true ribs.** The **inferior five** pairs are called **false ribs. Ribs 11 and 12** are called **floating ribs**, and they do not attach to the sternum.

Appendicular Skeleton: Consists of the bones of the **upper** and **lower limbs**, and the **pectoral** and **pelvic girdles**.
Upper Limb: Contains the humerus, radius, ulna, carpals, metacarpals, and phalanges.
Carpals: Scaphoid, Lunate, Triquetrum, Pisiform, Trapezium, Trapezoid, Capitate, Hamate.
Lower Limb: Contains the femur, tibia, fibula, tarsals, metatarsals, and phalanges.

Tarsals: Calcaneus, Cuboid, Cuneiform I, Cuneiform II, Cuneiform III, Talus, Navicular.
Pectoral Girdle: Contains the clavicles and scapulae.
Pelvic Girdle: Contains the ilium, ischium, pubis, and sacrum.

Joint Classifications: Synarthrotic(non-movable), **Amphiarthrotic**(somewhat movable), **Diarthrotic**(freely movable)
There are **six** types of **synovial** joints:
Ball and Socket: Ball on the end of one bone fits into the **socket** on another.
Hinge: Allows only **flexion** and **extension**.
Pivot: Allows only **rotation**.
Plane/Gliding: Joints created by **flat** bone surfaces.
Saddle: Created by two **saddle-shaped** articulating bone surfaces.
Ellipsoid/Condyloid: Condyle of one bone fits into **elliptical** cavity of another.

Movements:
Flexion: Decreasing the **angle** of a joint.
Extension: Increasing the **angle** of a joint.
Adduction: Moving a structure **toward** the **midline**.
Abduction: Moving a structure **away** from the **midline**.
Protraction: Moving a structure **anteriorly**.
Retraction: Moving a structure **posteriorly**.
Inversion: Turning the sole of the foot in **toward** the **midline**.
Eversion: Turning the sole of the foot out **away** from the **midline**.
Elevation: Moving a structure **superiorly**.
Depression: Moving a structure **inferiorly**.
Supination: Rotating palm so it is facing **upwards**.
Pronation: Rotating palm so it is facing **downwards**.
Rotation: Turning a structure **around** its **long axis**.
Circumduction: Turning a structure around the **circumference** of a joint.
Opposition: Moving structures in **opposite** directions.
Lateral Deviation: Moving a structure from **side-to-side**.

Urinary System: Consists of the **kidneys, ureters, urinary bladder,** and **urethra**. Responsible for **elimination** of waste from the body, **reabsorption** of nutrients, and **pH regulation**.

Kidneys: **Filtrate** and **reabsorb** substances back into the body. Regulates the amount of **electrolytes** in the body. Inside each kidney, there are **one million nephrons**, which are responsible for reabsorbing vitamins, electrolytes, and water back into the blood stream.

Ureters: **Transport** urine from the kidneys to the bladder.

Urinary Bladder: **Stores** urine.

Urethra: **Transports** urine from the urinary bladder out of the body.

Medical Terminology

Medical terminology is widely used throughout the medical field, and is the primary way of communicating with other health-care professionals. Medical terminology has origins in Latin and Greek. A medical term consists of three parts: The word root, which is what the term is mainly talking about; the prefix, which comes at the beginning of the medical term; the suffix, which comes at the end of the word. Both the prefix and suffix help to further describe what may be happening in a certain medical condition.

Word Roots

Abdomin/o: Abdomen
Acr/o: Extremity
Aden/o: Gland
Adip/o: Fat
Angi/o: Vessel
Ankyl/o: Bent, crooked
Arteri/o: Artery
Arthr/o: Joint
Ather/o: Fatty plaque
Audi/o: Hearing
Aur/o: Ear
Bi/o: Life
Brachi/o: Arm

Bucc/o: Cheek
Carcin/o: Cancer
Cardi/o: Heart
Cephal/o: Head
Chlor/o: Green
Chol/e: Bile
Cholecyst/o: Gallbladder
Chondr/o: Cartilage
Cirrh/o: Yellow
Col/o: Large intestine
Corp/o: Body
Cost/o: Ribs
Cry/o: Cold

Cutane/o: Skin
Cyan/o: Blue
Cyst/o: Bladder
Dent/o: Teeth
Derm/o: Skin
Dist/o: Far
Dors/o: Back
Embol/o: Plug
Emphys/o: Inflate
Encephal/o: Brain
Enter/o: Small Intestine
Erythr/o: Red
Esophag/o: Esophagus
Gastr/o: Stomach
Gingiv/o: Gums
Gloss/o: Tongue
Gluc/o: Sugar
Hem/o: Blood
Hepat/o: Liver
Hist/o: Tissue
Home/o: Same
Hydr/o: Water
Hyster/o: Uterus
Inguin/o: Groin
Jaund/o: Yellow
Kerat/o: Hard
Kinesi/o: Movement
Kyph/o: Hill
Lact/o: Milk
Later/o: Side
Leuk/o: White
Lip/o: Fat

Lord/o: Curve
Mamm/o: Breast
Mast/o: Breast
Melan/o: Black
My/o: Muscle
Myel/o: Canal
Nas/o: Nose
Necr/o: Death
Nephr/o: Kidney
Neur/o: Nerve
Ocul/o: Eye
Onc/o: Tumor
Oophor/o: Ovary
Oste/o: Bone
Path/o: Disease
Ped/o: Foot
Phleb/o: Vein
Phren/o: Diaphragm
Pneum/o: Lung
Proxim/o: Near
Pulm/o: Lung
Pyr/o: Heat
Ren/o: Kidney
Rhin/o: Nose
Salping/o: Fallopian tube
Scler/o: Hard
Scoli/o: Crooked
Somat/o: Body
Spondyl/o: Vertebrae
Stomat/o: Mouth
Thorac/o: Chest
Ventr/o: Belly

Prefixes

a-: Without
ab-: Away from
ad-: Towards
af-: Towards
an-: Without
ana-: Against
ante-: Before
anti-: Against
auto-: Self
bi-: Two
brady-: Slow
circum-: Around
contra-: Against
di-: Double
dia-: Through
dys-: Bad, difficult
ef-: Away from
endo-: In
epi-: Above
exo-: Outside
homeo-: Same
hyper-: Excessive
hypo-: Below
infra-: Under

inter-: Between
intra-: Inside
iso-: Same
macro-: Large
mal-: Bad
meta-: Change
micro-: Small
mono-: One
multi-: Many
neo-: New
pan-: All
para-: Near
peri-: Around
poly-: Many
post-: After
pre-: Before
pseudo-: False
quadri-: Four
retro-: Behind
supra-: Above
syn-: Together
tachy-: Rapid
tri-: Three
uni-: One

Suffixes

-ac: Pertaining to
-al: Pertaining to
-algia: Pain
-ar: Pertaining to
-blast: Germ cell
-cision: Cutting
-clast: Break
-crine: Secrete
-cyte: Cell
-derma: Skin
-ectomy: Removal
-edema: Swelling
-emia: Blood condition
-esis: Condition
-ferent: To carry
-gen: Formation
-globin: Protein
-ic: Pertaining to
-ician: Specialist
-icle: Small

-ist: Specialist
-itis: Inflammation
-lysis: Dissolve
-oid: Resembling
-osis: Condition
-pathy: Disease
-phagia: Eating
-phasia: Speech
-physis: Growth
-plasia: Formation
-plegia: Paralysis
-pnea: Breathing
-poiesis: Formation
-rrhage: Bursting forth
-rrhea: Discharge
-stasis: Standing still
-tomy: Incision
-trophy: Nourishment
-uria: Urine

Pathology

Cardiovascular

Anemia: Decrease in **oxygen-carrying ability** of the blood, most commonly due to a lack of **erythrocytes**, **hemoglobin**, or both. Causes fatigue due to hypoxia.

    Massage is: Indicated.

Aneurysm: Bulging of a wall of an artery outward, caused by a weakened arterial wall. Most likely the result of **hypertension** putting strain on the arterial wall. May break open, resulting in severe **hemorrhaging** internally, which may be fatal.

    Massage is: Absolute contraindication.

Arteriosclerosis: Hardening of the walls of arteries, caused by a lack of **elasticity** in the arteries. Reduces circulation, which may lead to **hypertension**.

    Massage is: Absolute contraindication.

Atherosclerosis: Buildup of **fatty plaque**, or lipids, on the walls of the arteries, reducing blood flow. May result in **hypertension** and the formation of blood clots.

    Massage is: Absolute contraindication.

Embolism: A **blood clot** or bubble of gas freely moving throughout the circulatory system. May become lodged in the heart, lungs, or brain, resulting in lack of blood flow to those structures, causing **necrosis**.

    Massage is: Absolute contraindication.

Heart Murmur: Flow of blood **backwards** in the heart due to malfunctioning **valves**, typically the **bicuspid** or **mitral** valve. Formation of blood clots may occur, along with fatigue.

    Massage is: Absolute contraindication.

Hypertension: High blood pressure, 140/90 mm Hg. Results in inelasticity of the arterial walls, reducing circulation.

    Massage is: Indicated.

Migraine: Vascular headache. Caused by **dilation** of extracranial blood vessels, which puts substantial pressure upon the **meninges**, producing intense pain. May be caused by stress or smoke, among other things.

    Massage is: Indicated.

Myocardial Infarction: Death of heart tissue, usually caused by a blockage in the **coronary** arteries, which are responsible for supplying the myocardium with **blood**.

    Massage is: Indicated with physician approval.

Phlebitis: Inflammation of a **vein**, caused by trauma, pregnancy, prolonged periods of sitting or standing, and may present with **blood clots**.

    Massage is: Local contraindication.

Raynaud's Syndrome: Constriction of blood vessels in the hands and feet, which reduces **blood supply**. Caused by cigarette smoking, cold exposure, or stress.

    Massage is: Indicated.

Transient Ischemic Attack: Temporary cerebral dysfunction resulting from **ischemia** in part of the brain. Also known as a "mini-stroke", it can be a precursor to a more serious stroke in the future.

    Massage is: Indicated with physician approval.

Varicose Veins: Swollen veins, caused by dysfunction in the **valves** inside the veins, resulting in blood pooling down the legs and forcing the veins towards the surface of the body.

    Massage is: Local contraindication.

Digestive

Cholecystitis: Inflammation of the **gallbladder**, usually due to a blockage of the cystic duct, stopping the flow of **bile** into the duodenum. Blockages most commonly caused by **gallstones**.

    Massage is: Absolute contraindication.

Cirrhosis: Destruction of **liver** cells, resulting in the formation of adhesions and fibrous material in the **liver**, causing the **liver** to become a yellowish-orange color. **Liver** function is gradually impaired.

    Massage is: Absolute contraindication.

Crohn's Disease: Autoimmune disorder which affects the **gastrointestinal** tract, resulting in **inflammation** and **ulceration** of the mucous membranes, in which scar tissue can develop.

    Massage is: Absolute contraindication.

Diverticulosis: Development of small **pouches** that protrude from the walls of the **large intestine**, caused by weakening of the walls due to a lack of substances for the walls to press against.

    Massage is: Indicated.

Diverticulitis: Inflammation of diverticular pouches, which may become **abscessed** and develop **ulcers**.

    Massage is: Absolute contraindication.

Gastroenteritis: Inflammation of the lining of the **stomach** and **small intestine**, most commonly caused by food poisoning or emotional stress.

    Massage is: Absolute contraindication.

Hepatitis: Inflammation of the **liver** most commonly associated with a **viral** infection, which may be acute or chronic. Results in pain, nausea, fatigue, diarrhea, and jaundice in the acute stage of infection.

    Massage is: Absolute contraindication.

Hernia: Protrusion of an organ through the surrounding connective tissue membrane. May result in pain and impaired body function, depending on the location and herniated structures involved.

    Massage is: Local contraindication.

Endocrine

Addison's Disease: Autoimmune disorder which results in the degeneration of the **adrenal cortex**, causing a decrease in **adrenal** function.

    Massage is: Indicated.

Cushing's Disease: Overproduction of **corticosteroids**, resulting in increased **weight** and muscle **atrophy**.

    Massage is: Indicated.

Diabetes Mellitus: Increased levels of **glucose** in the blood stream. Diabetes Type I is caused by a decrease in **insulin** levels in the body, which restricts the breaking down of **glucose**, while Diabetes Type II is caused by the body being desensitized to **insulin**, which is then unable to break down **glucose**.

    Massage is: Indicated.

Goiter: Enlargement of the **thyroid** gland, commonly seen with **hyperthyroidism**, **hypothyroidism**, inflammation, or a lack of **iodine** in the diet.

    Massage is: Indicated.

Grave's Disease: Autoimmune disease resulting in **hyperthyroidism**, anxiety, trembling, and fatigue. May also result in protrusion of the **eyeballs**.

    Massage is: Indicated.

Hyperthyroidism: Increased **thyroid** function, results in a **goiter**, hypersensitivity to **heat**, increased appetite, and increased respiration.

    Massage is: Indicated.

Hypothyroidism: Lack of **thyroid** hormone in the body, results in **fatigue**, weight **gain**, edema, and sensitivity to **cold**.

Massage is: Indicated.

Integumentary

Acne: Bacterial infection of the **skin**, due to numerous factors, including **testosterone** production, stress, and hormonal imbalance.

Massage is: Local contraindication.

Athlete's Foot: Also called **Tinea Pedis**, it is a highly contagious **fungal** infection found on the **feet**, primarily between the **toes**, which may result in breaking of the skin and lead to bacterial infection.

Massage is: Local contraindication.

Basal Cell Carcinoma: Least serious, **slowest** growing, **most** common form of skin cancer, usually due to overexposure to sunlight.

Massage is: Local contraindication.

Burns: First degree burn – Most common, least serious. Most common form is a **sunburn**, affecting the epidermis, resulting in inflammation and irritation of the skin.
Second degree burn – Burn moves through the epidermis into the **dermis**, which leads to the development of **blisters** and swelling.
Third degree burn – Burn moves through the epidermis and the dermis, into the **subcutaneous** layer. Results in **necrosis** and **scarring** of the skin, and may lead to infection if not treated properly.

Massage is: First degree – Indicated. Second degree – Local contraindication. Third degree – Local contraindication.

Cellulitis: Acute infection caused by **staphylococci** or **streptococci** bacteria, which often enters the body through exposure to **wounds**, affecting nearby tissues. Presents with well-defined borders of inflammation.

    Massage is: Local contraindication.

Decubitus Ulcer: Also known as a **pressure** ulcer or **bed** sore, results in ulcerations caused by prolonged **pressure** placed on a part of the body, causing **ischemia** and ultimately **necrosis** of the affected tissue.

    Massage is: Local contraindication.

Eczema: Idiopathic disorder causing dry, red, itchy **patches** of skin. May be be either acute or chronic.

    Massage is: Local contraindication.

Herpes Simplex: Highly contagious chronic **viral** infection, resulting in **cold** sores around the mucous membranes.

    Massage is: Local contraindication.

Hives: Also known as **urticaria**, it is an inflammatory reaction in response to exposure to an **allergen** or **emotional stress**. May be either acute or chronic, depending on the cause.

    Massage is: Absolute contraindication.

Impetigo: Acute **bacterial** infection caused by **staphylococci** or **streptococci**, results in sores that form around the mouth, nose, and hands. Mostly seen in **children**, it is highly contagious.

    Massage is: Absolute contraindication.

Lice: Highly contagious **parasitic** infection, found in hair. Produce egg sacs called "**nits**".

    Massage is: Absolute contraindication.

Malignant Melanoma: Overproduction of **melanocytes**, resulting in formation of tumors that may **spread** to other regions of the body. A = **Asymmetrical**, B = **Border**, C = **Color**, D = **Diameter**, E = **Elevated**.

    Massage is: Absolute contraindication.

Mole: Benign skin **lesion**, resulting from an increased amount of **melanin** in an area.

    Massage is: Indicated.

Psoriasis: Autoimmune disorder in which the body's immune system attacks **epithelial** tissue. **Epithelial** cells quickly regenerate at a rate quicker than normal, which results in thick, dry, silvery patches of skin.

    Massage is: Indicated.

Ringworm: Also known as "**Tinea Corporis**", it is a **fungal** infection resulting in circular raised patches on the skin.

    Massage is: Local contraindication.

Scleroderma: An autoimmune disorder, resulting in excessive **collagen** production in the skin, causing the skin to become **hardened**. Can be a sign of organ failure.

    Massage is: If caused by organ failure, absolute contraindication. If not caused by organ failure, massage is indicated.

Sebaceous Cyst: Blockage of a **sebaceous** gland, resulting in the body forming a thick membrane of connective tissue around the gland, limiting tissue damage as a result of infection.

    Massage is: Local contraindication.

Squamous Cell Carcinoma: Form of **skin** cancer which develops into an area of **ulceration**, caused by overexposure to sunlight, or may be found in the mouth of a person who chews **tobacco** or smokes **cigarettes**.

    Massage is: Local contraindication.

Wart: Epidermal protrusion resulting from infection by the **Human Papilloma Virus**. Results in increased **keratin** production on the area of infection.

    Massage is: Local contraindication.

Lymphatic

Acquired Immunodeficiency Syndrome: **Viral infection**, caused by HIV, which destroys the body's **T-cells**, effectively disabling the **immune** system.

    Massage is: Indicated.

Allergies: **Hypersensitivity** of the body to agents which are normally harmless in most people.

    Massage is: Indicated.

Chronic Fatigue Syndrome: **Idiopathic** disease which results in symptoms such as **insomnia**, low-grade fever, and irritability.

    Massage is: Indicated.

Lymphedema: Increased amounts of **interstitial** fluid in a limb, resulting in **swelling**. Caused by inflammation, trauma, or blocked lymph channels.

    Massage is: Indicated.

Lupus: Autoimmune disorder affecting the **connective** tissues of the body, resulting in a rash across the **face**, scales on the skin, fatigue, fever, photosensitivity, and weight loss.

    Massage is: Absolute contraindication.

Mononucleosis: Viral infection, resulting in a high **fever**, fatigue, sore throat, and swollen **lymph nodes**.

    Massage is: Absolute contraindication.

Pitting Edema: Swollen area, leaves **pits** in the skin after applying **pressure**. May be a sign of organ failure.

    Massage is: Absolute contraindication.

Muscular

Adhesive Capsulitis: Formation of **adhesions** that stick the **joint** capsule to the head of the **humerus**, severely restricting the range of motion at the **shoulder** joint. May also be caused by hypertonicity of the **subscapularis**.

    Massage is: Indicated.

Atrophy: Loss of muscle **density** due to lack of **use** or malnourishment.

    Massage is: Indicated.

Fibromyalgia: Inflammatory disease affecting **muscles** and **connective tissue**, resulting in pain, numbness, tingling sensations in the limbs, and fatigue.

    Massage is: Indicated.

Golfer's Elbow: A form of **tendonitis**, results in inflammation and pain located at the **medial** epicondyle of the **humerus**. The **flexors** of the wrist are affected, as they originate on the **medial** epicondyle of the **humerus**.

    Massage is: Local contraindication.

Muscular Dystrophy: Autoimmune disorder, resulting in **degeneration** of muscles. Muscle **degeneration** leads to **atrophy** and lack of use, eventually resulting in **paralysis** and **deformity**.

    Massage is: Indicated.

Strain: An injury to a **muscle** or **tendon**, may be caused by overexertion or overstretching.

    Massage is: Local contraindication.

Tendonitis: Inflammation of a **tendon**, results from injury to either the **tenoperiosteal** or **musculotendinous** junction.

    Massage is: Local contraindication.

Tennis Elbow: A common form of **tendonitis**, results in inflammation and pain located at the **lateral** epicondyle of the **humerus**. The **extensors** of the wrist are affected, as they originate at the **lateral** epicondyle of the **humerus**.

    Massage is: Local contraindication.

Torticollis: Spasm of the **sternocleidomastoid** unilaterally, forcing the head to lean to **one side**. **Vertigo** may result.

Massage is: Indicated.

Whiplash: Straining or spraining of tendons, muscles, and ligaments in the **neck** due to violent forward motion of the **head** and **neck**. As a result, tendons, muscles and ligaments may be injured and weakened, with an increase in headaches, pain, and dizziness. Most commonly seen in **automobile accidents**.

Massage is: Local contraindication.

Nervous

Alzheimer's Disease: Progressive **degeneration** of brain tissue, resulting in loss of **memory**, **dementia**, confusion and disorientation.

Massage is: Indicated.

Bell's Palsy: Paralysis of one side of the **face** as a result of inflammation or compression of the **facial** nerve. May be permanent, or may subside.

Massage is: Indicated.

Carpal Tunnel Syndrome: Compression of the **median** nerve by the **transverse carpal ligament**, resulting in loss of function and sensation in the **hand**.

Massage is: Indicated.

Encephalitis: Inflammation of the **brain**, most commonly caused by a **viral** infection. The **virus** usually enters the body after contact with **mosquitoes**. Inflammation may result in necrotic brain tissue and death.

Massage is: Absolute contraindication.

Hemiplegia: Paralysis of one side of the **body**, usually as the result of a **stroke**, which may impair function to specific regions of the body.

Massage is: Indicated.

Meningitis: Inflammation of the **meninges**. **Bacterial** meningitis is the most severe form, which may result in death. Symptoms include nausea, vomiting, dizziness, and headache. Highly contagious.

Massage is: Absolute contraindication.

Multiple Sclerosis: Autoimmune disorder in which the immune system attacks the **myelin sheaths** surrounding axons in the **central** nervous system, causing degeneration of the **myelin**. Degeneration also results in scarring on the axons, which results in severe pain in acute stages.

Massage is: Absolute contraindication.

Paraplegia: Paralysis of the **lower limbs** due to an injury to the spinal cord anywhere below the **T1** segment. Loss of function results in muscle atrophy.

Massage is: Indicated.

Parkinson's Disease: Shaking or **trembling** due to reduced levels of the neurotransmitter **dopamine** in the body. Affects **fine** motor movements at first, then affects **larger** movements as the disease advances.

Massage is: Indicated.

Quadriplegia: Paralysis of the **arms** and **legs**, resulting from an injury to the spinal cord between **C5** and **T1**.

Massage is: Indicated.

Sciatica: Compression of the **sciatic** nerve by hypertonic muscles, most commonly the **piriformis**. Results in pain radiating down the **leg**, and may even reach the bottoms of the **feet**.

    Massage is: Indicated.

Trigeminal Neuralgia: Compression of the **trigeminal** nerve, resulting in severe pain around the **mouth**, **nose**, and **eyes**.

    Massage is: Indicated.

Respiratory

Apnea: Cessation of **breathing**, temporarily. Most commonly occurs during sleep, commonly caused by compression of airways by the tongue or pharynx.

    Massage is: Indicated.

Asthma: Spasm of **smooth** muscle in the bronchial tubes, which is a reaction to stimuli such as **allergens** or **emotional stress**. **Mucous** production is also increased, further reducing air intake, creating wheezing sounds upon inhalation.

    Massage is: Indicated.

Bronchitis: Inflammation of **bronchial** tubes, with additional **mucous** production. Acute bronchitis is the side effect of a primary infection such as **influenza**, while chronic bronchitis is the result of irritants entering the lungs over a long period of time, such as **cigarette smoke**.

    Massage is: Acute bronchitis – Absolute contraindication. Chronic bronchitis – Indicated.

Emphysema: Destruction of lung **alveoli** due to exposure to irritants such as cigarette smoke, reducing oxygen intake and carbon dioxide output.

    Massage is: Indicated.

Influenza: Acute **viral** infection, resulting in an inflamed pharynx and nasal cavity, increased mucous production, and fever.

    Massage is: Absolute contraindication.

Pneumonia: Streptococcal infection in the lungs, which fills the lung **alveoli** with fluid and waste products, reducing air intake.

    Massage is: Absolute contraindication.

Skeletal

Ankylosing Spondylitis: Progressive autoimmune disorder resulting in **degeneration** of intervertebral discs. Disc **degeneration** leads to loss of **curvature** of the spine, **fusion** of vertebrae together, and loss of motion at the site of bone fusion.

    Massage is: Indicated.

Baker's Cyst: Formation of a **sac** behind the knee as a result of **synovial** fluid leaking from the joint cavity.

    Massage is: Local contraindication.

Bursitis: Inflammation of a **bursa sac**, usually due to trauma to a **bursa**. Often presents with fluid buildup, restricting range of motion at the site if around a joint.

    Massage is: Local contraindication.

Dislocation: Displacement of a bone from its normal location, damaging tissues around the area. Severely weakens the joint following the dislocation, allowing for further dislocation to occur.

Massage is: Local contraindication.

Fracture: A **break** in a bone. A **simple** fracture remains inside the skin, while a **compound** fracture breaks through the skin.

Massage is: Local contraindication.

Gout: Excessive **uric acid** buildup in the body, resulting in a severely inflamed **big toe**, and may also be seen in the arms and hands as well. Caused by an inability of the body to eliminate **uric acid** normally.

Massage is: Local contraindication.

Herniated Disc: Protrusion of the gelatinous center of an intervertebral disc, known as the **nucleus pulposus**, through the tough cartilaginous portion of an intervertebral disc, known as the **annulus fibrosis**. Results in compression of spinal nerves, producing pain.

Massage is: Local contraindication.

Kyphosis: Hyper-curvature of the **thoracic** vertebrae, producing a hump-back appearance. Also known as **Dowager's Hump**. Can be caused by a tight **pectoralis minor**, weakened back muscles, or other conditions such as osteoporosis or ankylosing spondylitis.

Massage is: Indicated.

Lordosis: Hyper-curvature of the **lumbar** vertebrae, forcing the vertebrae anteriorly. Also known as **Swayback**. Can be caused by hypertonicity of the **psoas major**, or weakness in the **rectus abdominis**. May also result in overstretching of the hamstrings.

Massage is: Indicated.

Osteoarthritis: Erosion of the **hyaline** cartilage between articulating bones. Results in increased **friction** between the bones, causing pain and inflammation. Also known as **"wear and tear"** arthritis.

Massage is: Local contraindication.

Osteoporosis: Degeneration of bone tissue, due to a lack of **calcium** entering into the bones. Usually seen in **post-menopausal** women, due to a lack of **estrogen** production. Bones become thin and brittle, making them prone to injuries such as fracture.

Massage is: Indicated.

Rheumatoid Arthritis: Autoimmune disorder in which the body's immune system attacks **synovial** membranes surrounding joints. Upon degeneration, the membrane is replaced by **fibrous** tissue, which restricts range of motion in the joints. Usually takes place at the **metacarpophalangeal** joints of the hands. The fingers are turned to a **medial** position, making function difficult.

Massage is: Local contraindication.

Scoliosis: Lateral curvature of the vertebrae, most commonly in the **thoracic** vertebrae. Can be caused by severely hypertonic muscles, congenital deformities of the vertebral column, and poor posture.

Massage is: Indicated.

Sprain: Injury to a **ligament**, caused by overstretching or tearing of a **ligament**.

Grade 1: Stretching of a **ligament** without tearing.

Grade 2: Partial tearing of a **ligament** that presents with bruising and inflammation.

Grade 3: Complete rupture of a **ligament** which requires surgery to repair.

Massage is: Local contraindication.

Urinary

Cystitis: Bacterial infection of the urinary bladder, resulting in bloody urine, pain, and increased urination frequency.

Massage is: Indicated.

Pyelonephritis: Bacterial infection of the **kidneys**, usually results after obtaining **cystitis**.

Massage is: Absolute contraindication.

Uremia: Excessive amounts of **urea** in the **blood stream**, usually a sign of **renal** failure, caused by inability of the kidneys to filter properly.

Massage is: Indicated with physician approval.

Urinary Tract Infection: Bacterial infection typically affecting both the **urethra** and **urinary bladder**.

Massage is: Indicated.

Kinesiology

Bony Landmarks

Scapula: Acromion Process, Coracoid Process, Spine of Scapula, Supraspinous Fossa, Infraspinous Fossa, Superior Angle, Inferior Angle, Medial Border, Lateral Border, Glenoid Fossa, Supraglenoid Tubercle, Infraglenoid Tubercle, Subscapular Fossa.

Humerus: Head, Greater Tubercle, Lesser Tubercle, Intertubercular/Bicipital Groove, Deltoid Tuberosity, Radial Fossa, Coronoid Fossa, Medial Epicondyle, Lateral Epicondyle, Capitulum, Trochlea.

Radius: Head, Radial Tuberosity, Styloid Process.

Ulna: Olecranon Process, Coronoid Process, Ulnar Tuberosity, Head, Styloid Process.

Pelvis: Iliac Crest, Iliac Fossa, Anterior Superior Iliac Spine, Anterior Inferior Iliac Spine, Acetabulum, Obturator Foramen, Body of Pubis, Pubic Symphysis, Pubic Crest, Superior Ramus of Pubis, Inferior Ramus of Pubis, Ischial Tuberosity.

Femur: Head, Greater Trochanter, Lesser Trochanter, Gluteal Tuberosity, Linea Aspera, Adductor Tubercle, Medial Epicondyle, Lateral Epicondyle, Medial Condyle, Lateral Condyle.

Tibia: Tibial Plateau, Medial Condyle, Lateral Condyle, Tibial Tuberosity, Pes Anserinus, Medial Malleolus, Soleal Line.

Fibula: Styloid Process, Head, Lateral Malleolus.

Scapula (Anterior)

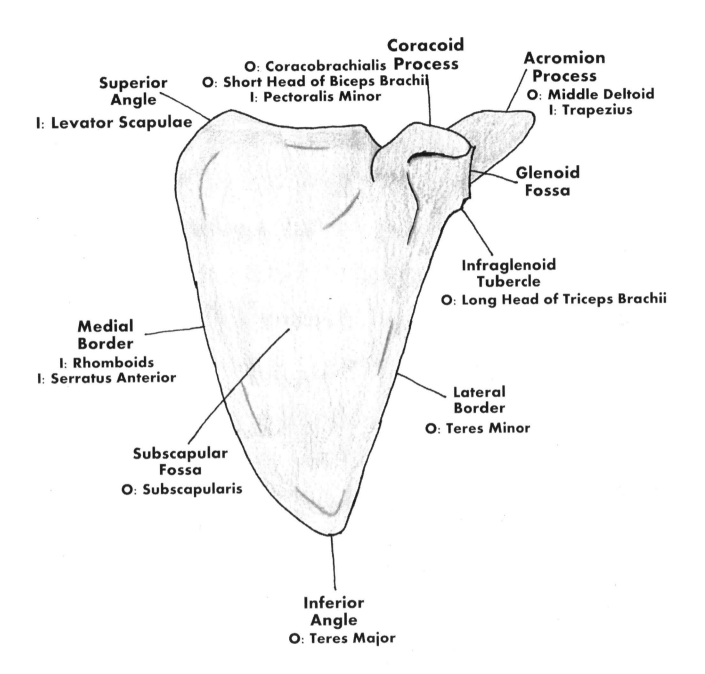

Scapula(Posterior)

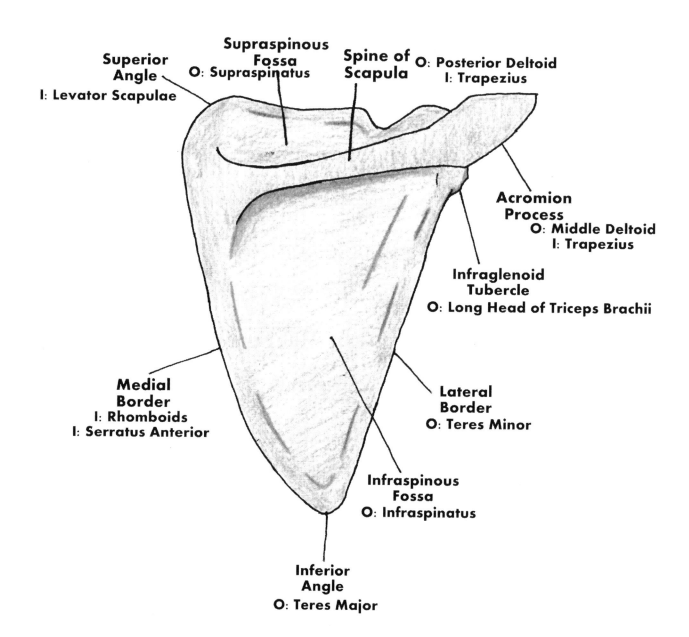

Humerus

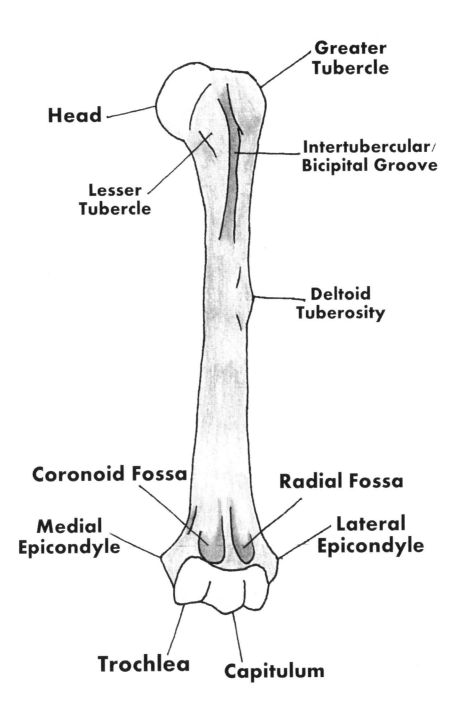

Radius

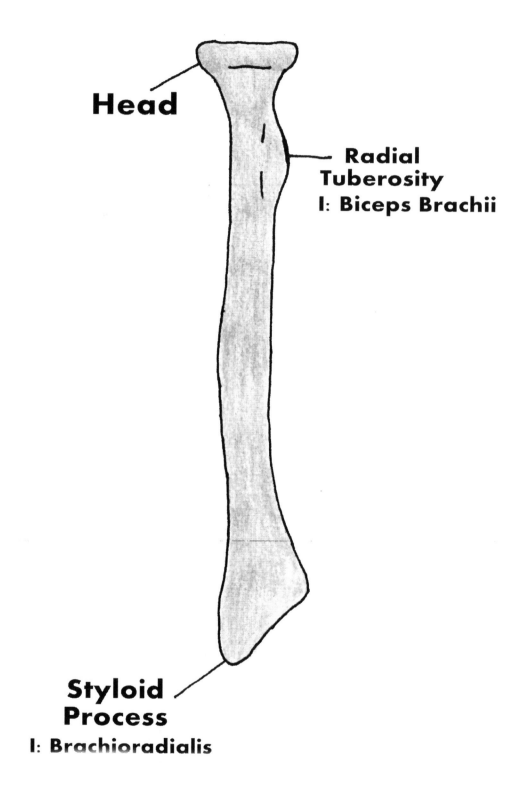

Ulna

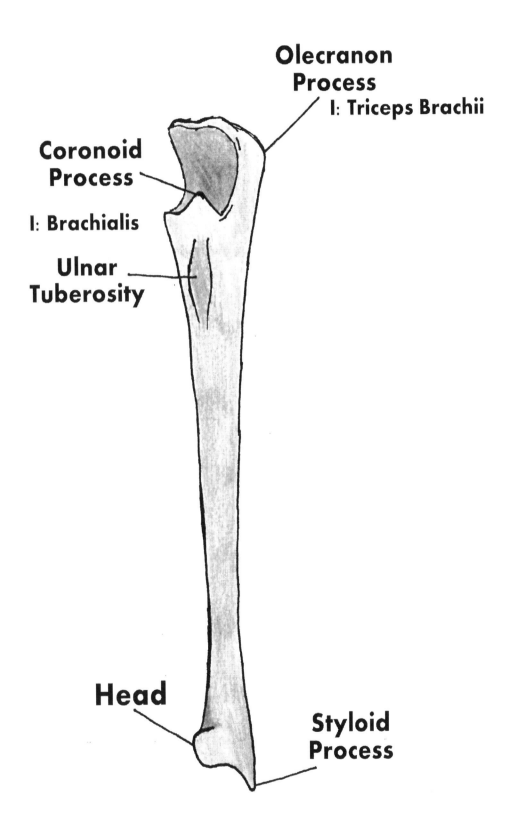

Pelvis

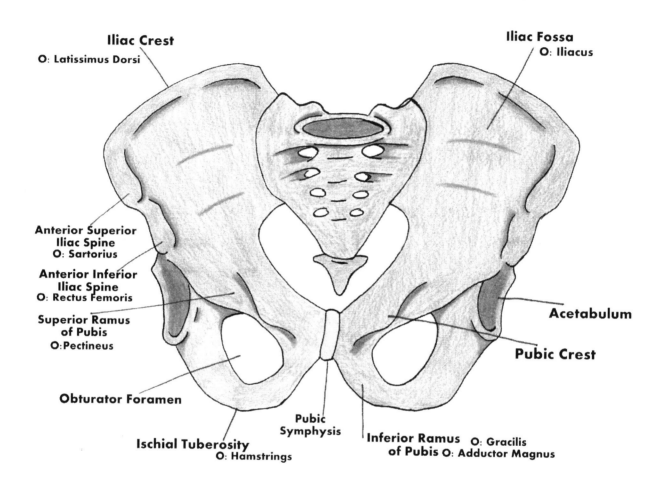

Femur

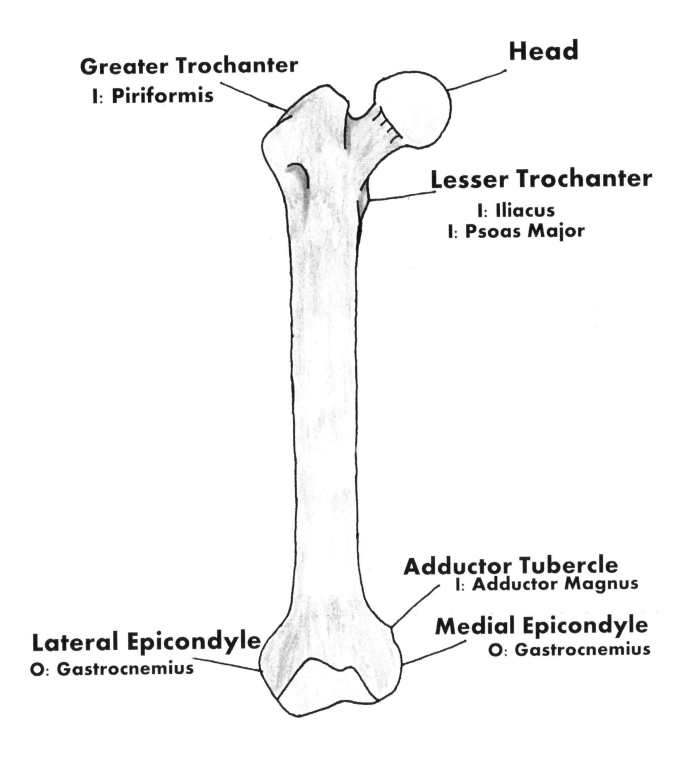

Tibia

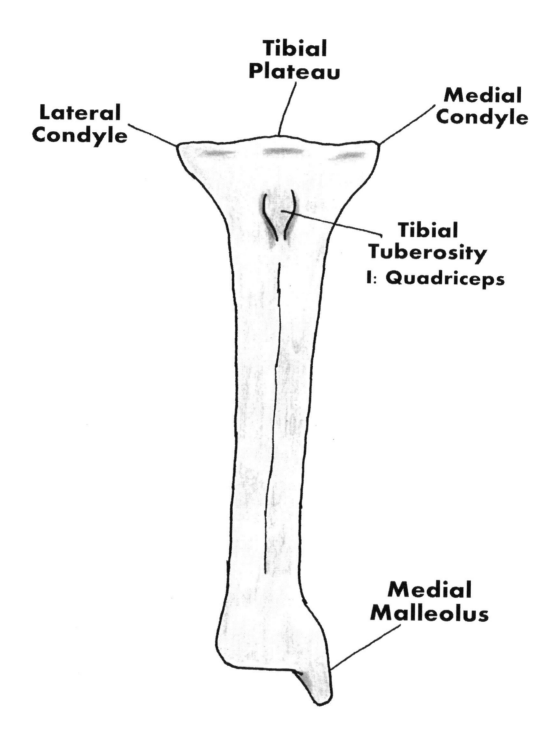

Fibula

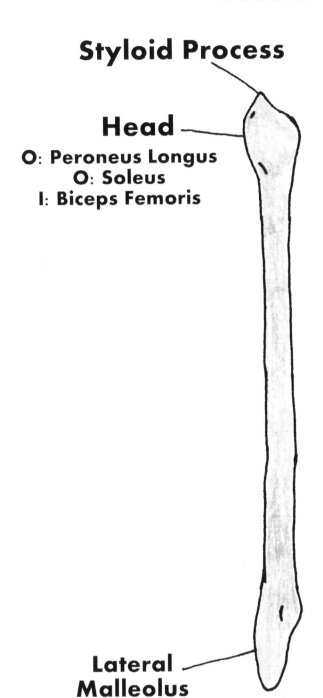

Muscles:

Origin: Proximal attachment point, the least-movable part of a muscle.

Insertion: Distal attachment point, the most-movable part of a muscle.

Action: Joint movement performed when a muscle contracts.

Innervation: Nerve that stimulates a muscle.

Synergist: A muscle that assists a prime mover in performing an action.

Antagonist: A muscle that performs the opposite action of an agonist.

In the space below this information, draw the muscle and attachment sites.

Levator Scapulae

Origin: Transverse processes of C1-C4

Insertion: Superior angle of the scapula

Action(s): Elevation of the scapula

Innervation: Cervical nerve, dorsal scapular nerve

Synergist(s): Upper fibers of trapezius

Antagonist(s): Lower fibers of trapezius

Draw the muscle and attachment sites:

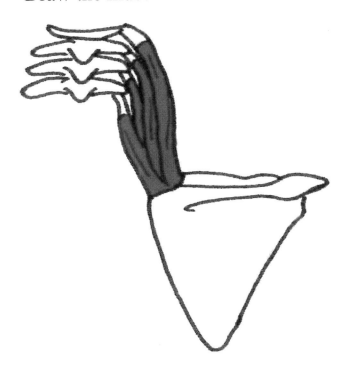

Trapezius

Origin: External occipital protuberance, spinous processes of T1-T12

Insertion: Clavicle, acromion process, spine of scapula

Action(s): Elevation, retraction/adduction, depression of scapula

Innervation: Accessory nerve

Synergist(s): Levator scapulae, rhomboids major and minor

Antagonist(s): Serratus anterior, pectoralis minor

Draw the muscle and attachment sites:

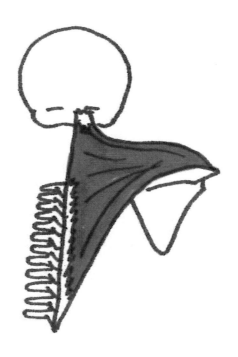

Anterior, Middle, and Posterior Deltoid

Origin: Lateral 1/3 of clavicle, acromion process, spine of scapula

Insertion: Deltoid tuberosity

Action(s): Flexion of the shoulder, abduction of the shoulder, extension of the shoulder

Innervation: Axillary nerve

Synergist(s): (A)Biceps brachii, pectoralis major, (M)supraspinatus, (P)latissimus dorsi

Antagonist(s): (A)Teres major, (M)latissimus dorsi, (P)Coracobrachialis

---

Draw the muscle and attachment sites:

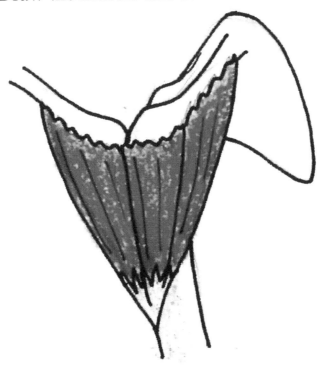

Rhomboid Major and Rhomboid Minor

Origin: Spinous processes of C7-T5

Insertion: Medial border of scapula

Action(s): Retraction/Adduction of scapula

Innervation: Dorsal scapular nerve

Synergist(s): Middle fibers of trapezius

Antagonist(s): Serratus anterior, pectoralis minor

Draw the muscle and attachment sites:

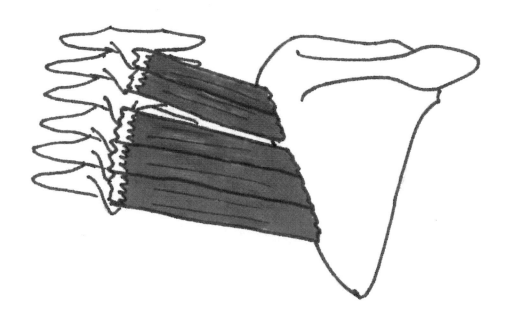

Supraspinatus

Origin: Supraspinous fossa

Insertion: Greater tubercle of humerus

Action(s): Abduction of shoulder

Innervation: Suprascapular nerve

Synergist(s): Deltoid

Antagonist(s): Latissimus dorsi, teres major

Draw the muscle and attachment sites:

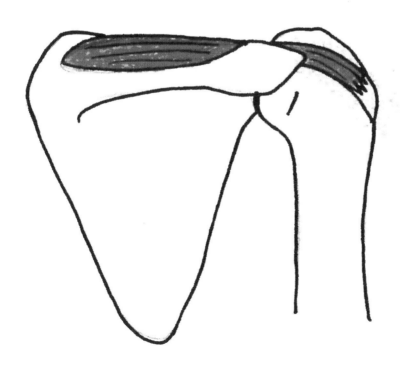

Infraspinatus

Origin: Infraspinous fossa

Insertion: Greater tubercle of humerus

Action(s): Lateral rotation and extension of shoulder

Innervation: Suprascapular nerve

Synergist(s): Teres minor

Antagonist(s): Pectoralis major

Draw the muscle and attachment sites:

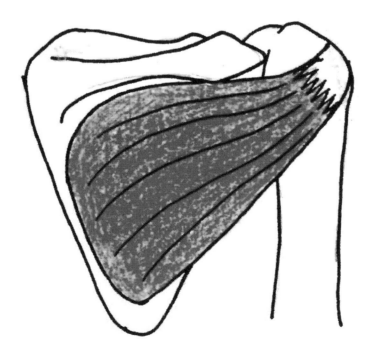

Teres Minor

Origin: Lateral border of scapula

Insertion: Greater tubercle of humerus

Action(s): Lateral rotation and extension of shoulder

Innervation: Axillary nerve

Synergist(s): Infraspinatus

Antagonist(s): Pectoralis major

Draw the muscle and attachment sites:

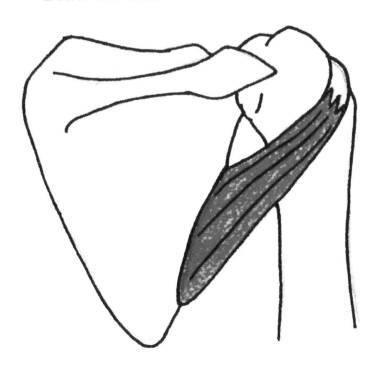

Subscapularis

Origin: Subscapular fossa

Insertion: Lesser tubercle of humerus

Action(s): Medial rotation and extension of shoulder

Innervation: Upper subscapular nerve, lower subscapular nerve

Synergist(s): Latissimus dorsi, teres major

Antagonist(s): Infraspinatus, coracobrachialis

Draw the muscle and attachment sites:

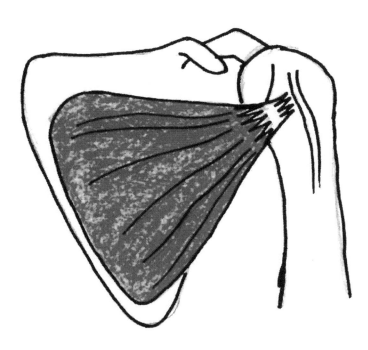

Latissimus Dorsi

Origin: Spinous processes of T7-L5, thoracolumbar aponeurosis, iliac crest

Insertion: Medial lip of intertubercular/bicipital groove

Action(s): Adduction, extension, medial rotation of shoulder

Innervation: Thoracodorsal nerve

Synergist(s): Teres major, subscapularis

Antagonist(s): Pectoralis major, deltoid

Draw the muscle and attachment sites:

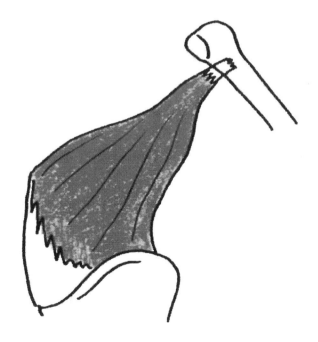

Teres Major

Origin: Inferior angle of scapula

Insertion: Medial lip of intertubercular/bicipital groove

Action(s): Adduction, extension, medial rotation of shoulder

Innervation: Lower subscapular nerve

Synergist(s): Latissimus dorsi, subscapularis

Antagonist(s): Pectoralis major, deltoid

Draw the muscle and attachment sites:

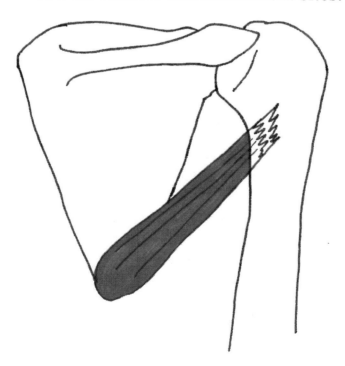

Pectoralis Major

Origin: Ribs, sternum, medial 2/3 of clavicle

Insertion: Lateral lip of intertubercular/bicipital groove

Action(s): Flexion, horizontal adduction, medial rotation, extension of shoulder

Innervation: Lateral pectoral nerve, medial pectoral nerve

Synergist(s): Biceps brachii, coracobrachialis, anterior deltoid, subscapularis

Antagonist(s): Latissimus dorsi, infraspinatus, teres minor, teres major

---

Draw the muscle and attachment sites:

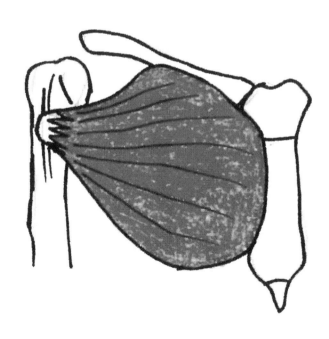

Pectoralis Minor

Origin: Ribs 3-5

Insertion: Coracoid process of scapula

Action(s): Abduction/protraction of scapula

Innervation: Medial pectoral nerve

Synergist(s): Serratus anterior

Antagonist(s): Rhomboid major and rhomboid minor

Draw the muscle and attachment sites:

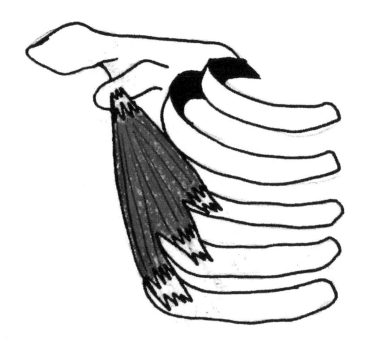

Serratus Anterior

Origin: Ribs 1-8 or 9

Insertion: Medial border of scapula on anterior surface

Action(s): Abduction/protraction of scapula

Innervation: Long thoracic nerve

Synergist(s): Pectoralis minor

Antagonist(s): Rhomboid major and rhomboid minor

Draw the muscle and attachment sites:

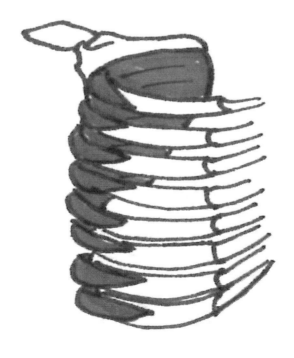

Biceps Brachii

Origin: Long Head: Supraglenoid tubercle
Short Head: Coracoid process

Insertion: Radial tuberosity

Action(s): Flexion of shoulder, flexion of elbow, supination of forearm

Innervation: Musculocutaneous nerve

Synergist(s): Coracobrachialis, brachialis, supinator

Antagonist(s): Infraspinatus, triceps brachii, pronator teres

---

Draw the muscle and attachment sites:

Coracobrachialis

Origin: Coracoid process

Insertion: Proximal medial shaft of humerus

Action(s): Flexion and horizontal adduction of shoulder

Innervation: Musculocutaneous nerve

Synergist(s): Biceps brachii, pectoralis major

Antagonist(s): Latissimus dorsi, infraspinatus

Draw the muscle and attachment sites:

Brachialis

Origin: Anterior distal shaft of humerus

Insertion: Coronoid process and ulnar tuberosity

Action(s): Flexion of elbow

Innervation: Musculocutaneous nerve

Synergist(s): Biceps brachii

Antagonist(s): Triceps brachii

Draw the muscle and attachment sites:

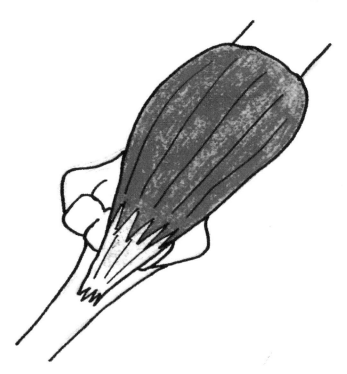

Brachioradialis

Origin: Lateral supracondylar ridge of humerus

Insertion: Styloid process of radius

Action(s): Flexion of elbow with hand in neutral position

Innervation: Radial nerve

Synergist(s): Brachialis

Antagonist(s): Triceps brachii

Draw the muscle and attachment sites:

Triceps Brachii

Origin: Long Head: Infraglenoid tubercle

Insertion: Olecranon process of ulna

Action(s): Extension of shoulder, extension of elbow

Innervation: Radial nerve

Synergist(s): Infraspinatus, anconeus

Antagonist(s): Biceps brachii, brachialis

Draw the muscle and attachment sites:

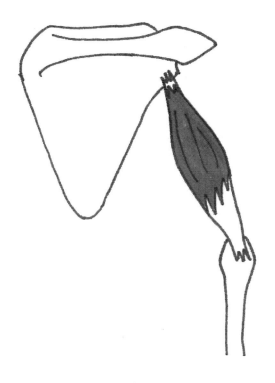

Pronator Teres

Origin: Medial epicondyle of humerus

Insertion: Lateral surface of middle radius

Action(s): Pronation of forearm, flexion of elbow

Innervation: Median nerve

Synergist(s): Brachialis

Antagonist(s): Biceps brachii, Supinator

Draw the muscle and attachment sites:

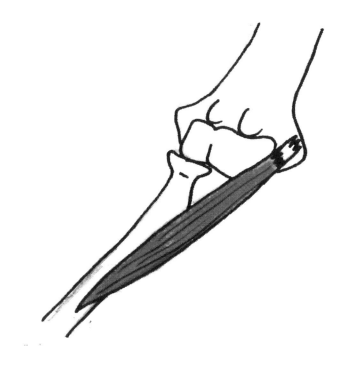

Psoas Major

Origin: Anterior surface of lumbar vertebrae

Insertion: Lesser trochanter of femur

Action(s): Flexion of hip, flexion of trunk

Innervation: Lumbosacral plexus

Synergist(s): Iliacus, rectus femoris

Antagonist(s): Biceps femoris

Draw the muscle and attachment sites:

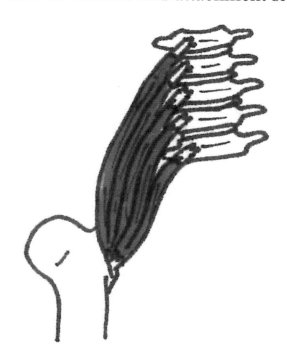

Iliacus

Origin: Iliac fossa

Insertion: Lesser trochanter of femur

Action(s): Flexion of hip

Innervation: Femoral nerve

Synergist(s): Psoas major, rectus femoris

Antagonist(s): Semimembranosus

Draw the muscle and attachment sites:

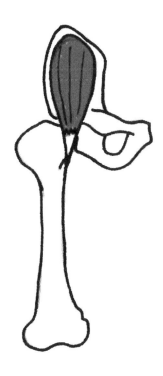

Piriformis

Origin: Anterior surface of sacrum

Insertion: Greater trochanter of femur

Action(s): Lateral rotation and extension of hip

Innervation: Nerve to the piriformis

Synergist(s): Gluteus maximus

Antagonist(s): Pectineus, rectus femoris

Draw the muscle and attachment sites:

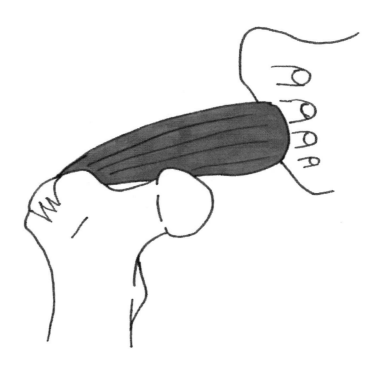

Gluteus Maximus

Origin: Gluteal surface of ilium, posterior sacrum

Insertion: Gluteal tuberosity, iliotibial band

Action(s): Abduction, lateral rotation, extension of hip

Innervation: Inferior gluteal nerve

Synergist(s): Piriformis, Biceps femoris

Antagonist(s): Rectus femoris, pectineus

Draw the muscle and attachment sites:

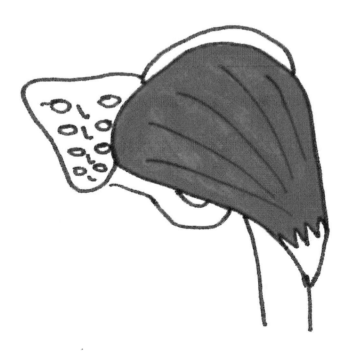

Rectus Femoris

Origin: Anterior Inferior Iliac Spine

Insertion: Tibial Tuberosity

Action(s): Flexion of hip, extension of knee

Innervation: Femoral nerve

Synergist(s): Iliacus, vastus medialis

Antagonist(s): Biceps femoris, semitendinosus

Draw the muscle and attachment sites:

Gracilis

Origin: Inferior ramus of pubis

Insertion: Pes anserinus

Action(s): Flexion and adduction of hip, flexion of knee

Innervation: Obturator nerve

Synergist(s): Adductor longus, gastrocnemius

Antagonist(s): Gluteus maximus, rectus femoris

Draw the muscle and attachment sites:

Pectineus

Origin: Superior ramus of pubis

Insertion: Pectineal line of linea aspera

Action(s): Flexion, medial rotation, and adduction of hip

Innervation: Femoral nerve

Synergist(s): Rectus femoris, adductor magnus

Antagonist(s): Piriformis

Draw the muscle and attachment sites:

Adductor Longus

Origin: Body of pubis

Insertion: Medial lip of linea aspera

Action(s): Flexion, adduction, medial rotation of hip

Innervation: Obturator nerve

Synergist(s): Gracilis, adductor magnus

Antagonist(s): Biceps femoris, gluteus maximus

Draw the muscle and attachment sites:

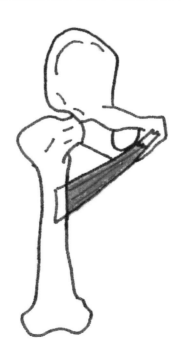

Adductor Magnus

Origin: Inferior ramus of pubis, ischial tuberosity

Insertion: Medial lip of linea aspera, adductor tubercle

Action(s): Flexion, adduction, extension of hip

Innervation: Obturator nerve, sciatic nerve

Synergist(s): Gracilis, Biceps femoris, Rectus femoris

Antagonist(s): Gluteus maximus, Semimembranosus, piriformis

Draw the muscle and attachment sites:

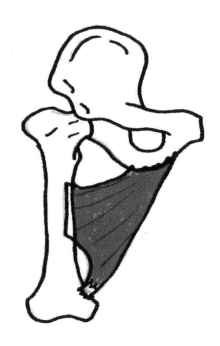

Sartorius

Origin: Anterior Superior Iliac Spine

Insertion: Pes anserinus

Action(s): Flexion, lateral rotation of hip, flexion of knee

Innervation: Femoral nerve

Synergist(s): Rectus femoris, gracilis

Antagonist(s): Biceps femoris, pectineus, rectus femoris

Draw the muscle and attachment sites:

Semimembranosus

Origin: Ischial tuberosity

Insertion: Posterior medial condyle of tibia

Action(s): Extension of hip, flexion of knee

Innervation: Sciatic nerve

Synergist(s): Biceps femoris, gastrocnemius

Antagonist(s): Rectus femoris

Draw the muscle and attachment sites:

Semitendinosus

Origin: Ischial tuberosity

Insertion: Pes anserinus

Action(s): Extension of hip, flexion of knee

Innervation: Sciatic nerve

Synergist(s): Semimembranosus, gastrocnemius

Antagonist(s): Rectus femoris

Draw the muscle and attachment sites:

Biceps Femoris

Origin: Long head: Ischial tuberosity

Insertion: Head of fibula

Action(s): Extension of hip, flexion of knee

Innervation: Sciatic nerve

Synergist(s): Semimembranosus, gastrocnemius

Antagonist(s): Rectus femoris

Draw the muscle and attachment sites:

Gastrocnemius and Soleus

Origin: Gastrocnemius: Posterior medial and lateral epicondyles of femur
Soleus: Soleal line and head of fibula

Insertion: Calcaneus via calcaneal tendon

Action(s): Gastrocnemius: Flexion of knee, plantarflexion of ankle
Soleus: Plantarflexion of ankle

Innervation: Tibial nerve

Synergist(s): Tibialis posterior, Biceps femoris

Antagonist(s): Tibialis anterior, Rectus femoris

Draw the muscle and attachment sites:

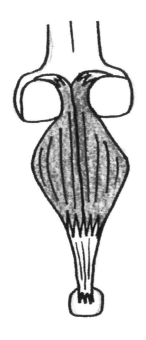

Peroneus Longus

Origin: Head and proximal shaft of fibula

Insertion: Base of first metatarsal

Action(s): Plantarflexion and eversion/pronation of ankle

Innervation: Superficial peroneal nerve

Synergist(s): Gastrocnemius, soleus

Antagonist(s): Tibialis anterior

Draw the muscle and attachment sites:

Tibialis Anterior

Origin: Lateral condyle, lateral shaft of tibia

Insertion: Base of first metatarsal

Action(s): Dorsiflexion, inversion/supination of ankle

Innervation: Deep peroneal nerve

Synergist(s): Extensor digitorum longus

Antagonist(s): Gastrocnemius, peroneus longus

Draw the muscle and attachment sites:

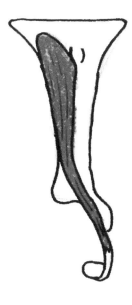

Muscles by Actions

In this section, we will review the major muscle actions, and the few muscles you should focus on studying that perform each action. You will find one muscle for each action that is bolded. This is the muscle you should spend 80-90% of your time studying for that specific action. Some muscles are easy to identify actions with, like the deltoid with abduction of the shoulder. Focusing instead on supraspinatus makes you more well-rounded, and increases your likelihood of getting any question about shoulder abduction correctly.

Just because you should spend the majority of your time focusing on one muscle doesn't mean you should ignore the others listed. Make sure you still study the other muscles that perform the action, not just the one that's bolded.

Remember, these are NOT the only actions that the body performs, and these are NOT the only muscles that perform each action! These are the muscle actions you're most likely to be tested on, and these are the muscles you're most likely to be asked about pertaining to the action. The flexors and extensors of the wrist have been left out because each of the muscles in those two groups tell you where they attach and what they do in their name. Example: Flexor digitorum longus. It attaches to the phalanges(digits), and flexes them. Pretty self-explanatory, if you ask me.

Shoulder:
Flexion: **Biceps Brachii**, Coracobrachialis, Pectoralis Major, Anterior Deltoid
Extension: Triceps Brachii, **Latissimus Dorsi**, Subscapularis, Teres Major
Abduction: Deltoid, **Supraspinatus**
Adduction: **Latissimus Dorsi**, Teres Major, Subscapularis
Medial Rotation: Pectoralis Major, **Latissimus Dorsi**, Teres Major, Subscapularis
Lateral Rotation: **Infraspinatus**, Teres Minor
Horiztonal Adduction: **Pectoralis Major**, Coracobrachialis
Horizontal Abduction: **Infraspinatus**, Teres Minor

Scapula:
Elevation: Levator Scapulae, **Trapezius**
Depression: **Trapezius**
Retraction/Adduction: **Rhomboids**, Trapezius
Protraction/Abduction: **Serratus Anterior**, Pectoralis Minor

Elbow:
Flexion: Biceps Brachii, Brachialis, **Brachioradialis**
Extension: Triceps Brachii, **Anconeus**

Forearm:
Supination: **Biceps Brachii**, Supinator
Pronation: **Pronator Teres**

Hip:
Flexion: **Rectus Femoris**, Iliacus, Psoas Major, Sartorius
Extension: **Semimembranosus, Semitendinosus, Biceps Femoris**, Gluteus Maximus
Adduction: Adductor Magnus, Adductor Longus, Adductor Brevis, **Gracilis**, Pectineus
Abduction: **Piriformis**, Gluteus Maximus

Knee:
Flexion: Semimembranosus, Semitendinosus, Biceps Femoris, **Gastrocnemius**
Extension: **Rectus Femoris**

Ankle:
Plantarflexion: Gastrocnemius, Soleus, **Peroneus Longus**
Dorsiflexion: **Tibialis Anterior**

Foot:
Eversion/Pronation: **Peroneus Longus**
Inversion/Supination: **Tibialis Anterior**

David's Easy Ways to Remember Things!

In this section, I will give you as many easy ways to remember information as possible. These have helped me learn information for years, and they really do work! Just remember, you don't have to use the same ways as I do to remember these pieces of information. If something doesn't stick, or doesn't look right, or doesn't make sense, don't be afraid to change it to something that works better for you. I've also included blank pages for you to write your own easy ways to remember things, so you have something to refer back to.

As you may notice, there aren't a lot to easy ways I have to remember information in Massage Therapy or Pathology. At this point, you should really understand everything about Massage Therapy backwards and forwards and not really need easy ways to remember that information. Pathology, however, is a little different. The absolute best thing you can do to help with remembering pathological conditions is to learn your medical terminology. Knowing your word roots, prefixes, and suffixes is the most helpful thing you can do to easily remember pathology.

If you have an easy way to remember something that I don't, please send an email and let me know what it is! Not only could it help me, but you could help other students learn the information! And honestly, who doesn't like helping others?

Without further adieu, let us begin!

Massage Therapy

Soft End Feel: Stoppage of range-of-motion caused by **soft** tissues(muscle).
Hard End Feel: Stoppage of range-of-motion caused by **hard** tissues(bone).
Absolute Contraindication: Massage cannot be performed at all.
Absolutely stay away from the client!

Anatomy and Physiology

Frontal/Coronal Plane: Splits the body into **front**(anterior) and back(posterior)
Types of Tissue: **M**uscular, **N**ervous, **E**pithelial, **C**onnective. **M**ust **N**ot **E**at **C**ake.
Epithelial Tissue: **P**rotects, **S**ecretes, **A**bsorbs. "Showing too much **skin** might require a **P**ublic **S**ervice **A**nnouncement."
Blast Cells: **B**last cells **b**uild.
Heart: Blood moves through the **a**tria, then the **v**entricles. **A** comes before **V** in the alphabet.
Arteries: **A**rteries take blood **a**way from the heart.
Small Intestine: Order of the small intestine: **D**uodenum, **J**ejunum, **I**leum. **D**avid **J**ogs **I**rregularly(side note: when I came up with this one with a student, she immediately said afterwards, "And that's why you're fat!" I was sad.)
Ovaries: Produce pr**o**gesterone.
Testes: Produce **test**osterone.
Pacinian Corpuscles: Detect deep pressure. The **Paci**fic Ocean is **deep**.
Nociceptors: Detect **pain**. "**No** pain, **no** gain."
Prime Mover/Agonist: The primary muscle performing an action. **Batman**.
Synergist: Assists the prime mover in performing an action. **Robin**.
Fixator: Stabilizes an area to allow an action to take place. **Alfred**.
Antagonist: The muscle that opposes the prive mover, performs the opposite action. **The Joker**.
Cerebellum: Responsible for muscle tone, balance, and coordination. Lifting a dumb**bell** gives you muscle tone.
Pons: Allows the cerebrum and cerebellum to communicate. Think of **pawns** on a chess board as messengers, allowing the two sides of the chess

board to communicate.
Carpals: **S**caphoid, **L**unate, **T**riquetrum, **P**isiform, **T**rapezium, **T**rapezoid, **C**apitate, **H**amate. To remember the order, remember this saying: **S**ome **L**overs **T**ry **P**ositions **T**hat **T**hey **C**an't **H**andle.
Lunate: Articulates with the **ulna**. Switch the L and U in "**Lu**nate" and it spells "**ul**na".
Joint Classifications: In order from least movable to most movable: **S**ynarthrotic, **A**mphiarthrotic, **D**iarthrotic. Remember **SAD**.
Supination: Your hand is in a position like you're holding a bowl of **soup**.
Pronation: You're **prone** to spilling the bowl of soup by turning your hand into pronation.
Inversion: The sole of the foot turns **in** towards the midline.

Pathology

Strain: Injury to a **tendon**.
Multiple Sclerosis: Degeneration of **myelin sheaths** in the central nervous system.
Lordosis: Hyper-curvature of the **lumbar** vertebrae.

Muscles

Levator Scapulae: **Elevates** the scapula.
Rotator Cuff Muscles: **S**upraspinatus, **I**nfraspinatus, **T**eres Minor, **S**ubscapularis. Remember "**SITS**".
Coracobrachialis: Originates on the **coracoid** process.
Biceps Femoris: Inserts onto the head of the **fibula**.
Pes Anserinus: Latin translation is "goose foot". Remember the saying "**SGT Goose Foot**" to remember the three muscles that insert onto the Pes Anserinus. **S**artorius, **G**racilis, Semi**t**endinosus.

Your Easy Ways to Remember Things

Massage Therapy Practice Test

Questions regarding massage therapy and business will primarily focus upon knowledge of Swedish massage strokes and techniques, ethics, the definition of specific modalities, and massage assessment and assessment techniques. Questions will also include information about business practice, communication, and law.

Questions regarding Massage Therapy will often be posed in a situational manner, in which you, the student, will need to be able to process a scenario and understand how to deal with specific situations. An example could be:

Q. Mr. Jones displays an active range-of-motion on the shoulder in pre-massage assessment. He experiences pain and difficulty upon flexion of the shoulder. The massage therapist would tailor their massage in which way
A. The therapist would avoid the affected joint
B. The therapist would assess hypertonicity of subscapularis
C. The therapist would apply a cold compress on the affected joint to alleviate pain
D. The therapist would recommend the client perform weight-bearing exercises to strengthen the joint

Not every question will be written in this way, but it is a good idea to understand how to dissect situational questions and which would be the most likely action needed to help with the given situation. When presented with these questions, just ask yourself, "How would I handle this situation?" When given an ethical question, just pick which answer is the best choice in a business setting. General rule of thumb for me with answers to ethics questions: If I were to do this action, would I get fired? If the answer is yes, don't pick that answer. Most likely, it's going to be common sense!

1. Plan information is
   A. Information the client shares about themselves
   B. Measurable information visible to the massage therapist
   C. Medical conditions the client has been assessed with
   D. Recommendations for future massage sessions

2. If a client experiences lower back pain due to a hypertonic psoas major while in the supine position, a bolster should be placed
   A. Under the knees
   B. Under the ankles
   C. Between the legs
   D. Under the hips

3. A bolster must be placed under the ankles when a client is laying in which position
   A. Prone
   B. Supine
   C. Side-lying
   D. Semi-reclining

4. Cryotherapy treatment used for an acute strain or sprain
   A. PPALM
   B. SOAP
   C. RICE
   D. CAR

5. Massage therapy may help to alleviate all of the following conditions except
   A. Headache
   B. Phlebitis
   C. Insomnia
   D. Hypertension

6. Polarity therapy was developed by
   A. Ida Rolf
   B. Johann Mezger
   C. Per Henrik Ling
   D. Randolph Stone

7. The most common substance used in body scrubs
   A. Salt
   B. Sugar
   C. Ground coffee
   D. Powdered milk

8. Technique primarily used to work on trigger points
   A. Wringing
   B. Ischemic compression
   C. Cross-fiber friction
   D. Myofascial release

9. Stoppage of range of motion due to trauma to an area
   A. Soft end feel
   B. Hard end feel
   C. Empty end feel
   D. Nervous end feel

10. Goals are
    A. Measurable or attainable accomplishments
    B. A generalized statement about the purpose of a business
    C. The theme of a business
    D. Business plans detailing projected income

11. A glove should be worn by the massage therapist if
    A. The client has an open wound on the back
    B. The client has an open wound on the arm
    C. The massage therapist has an open wound on the leg
    D. The massage therapist has an open wound on the hand

12. Massage has been practiced in India for
    A. 1000 years
    B. 300 years
    C. 3000 years
    D. 600 years

13. A pregnant client requests essential oils in her massage treatment. Of the following, which is an essential oil that would be appropriate to use
    A. Peppermint
    B. Ylang-ylang
    C. Ginger
    D. Rose

14. A certification is obtained via
    A. Passing a jurisprudence exam
    B. Paying a fee to a jurisdiction licensing agency
    C. Obtaining liability insurance to protect against malpractice
    D. Completing educational requirements in a school setting

15. An active stretch
    A. Client stretches into resistance without the help of a massage therapist
    B. Client stretches into resistance with the assistance of a massage therapist
    C. Massage therapist stretches the client into resistance with assistance from the client
    D. Massage therapist stretches the client into resistance without assistance from the client

16. Structural realignment therapy working on muscles and fascia over the course of ten sessions
   A. Rolfing
   B. Trager method
   C. Feldenkrais
   D. Myofascial release

17. Massage results in increased production of
   A. Cortisol
   B. Blood cells
   C. Pathogens
   D. Water retention

18. Information the client shares about themselves is documented under which section of SOAP notes
   A. Objective
   B. Subjective
   C. Assessment
   D. Plan

19. A massage therapist should wash their hands
   A. Only after using the restroom
   B. Before each massage
   C. After each massage
   D. Before and after each massage

20. Observable information the massage therapist can physically see is documented under what category in SOAP notes
   A. Subjective
   B. Objective
   C. Assessment
   D. Plan

21. Keeping a client covered while performing a massage
   A. Bolstering
   B. Draping
   C. Covering
   D. Wrapping

22. An active joint movement
   A. A client resists a movement being performed by a massage therapist
   B. A client moves the joint with the assistance of a massage therapist
   C. Client moves the joint without the assistance of a massage therapist
   D. A massage therapist moves a client's joint without the help of the client

23. Liabilities are
   A. Large companies free to operate independently
   B. Possessions owned by a business
   C. Raising the price of a product for sale
   D. Debts owed to a person or business

24. Percussion strokes, used to loosen phlegm in the respiratory tract and activate muscle spindle cells
   A. Petrissage
   B. Effleurage
   C. Friction
   D. Tapotement

25. Stimulation of tsubo points to stimulate nerves and increase circulation
   A. Shiatsu
   B. Reflexology
   C. Amma
   D. Ayurveda

26. Bindegewebsmassage focuses on massage of
   A. Blood vessels
   B. Lymphatic vessels
   C. Subcutaneous connective tissue
   D. Adhesions in fascia

27. Treatment mainly used to exfoliate dead skin cells from the body
   A. Body wrap
   B. Salt scrub
   C. Immersion bath
   D. Vichy shower

28. An end feel is
   A. Also known as a foot massage
   B. A very light massage stroke performed at the end of a massage
   C. Stoppage of range of motion due to factors such as muscle, bone, or an injury
   D. A passive joint mobilization performed by a massage therapist

29. A client moving a joint in the opposite direction that a massage therapist is moving it is an example of which joint movement
   A. Active
   B. Assistive
   C. Passive
   D. Resistive

30. The following is obtained after completing educational requirements and usually involves passing of an exam
   A. Certification
   B. License
   C. Insurance
   D. Scope of practice

31. Broadening of tendons, ligaments, and muscles which breaks down adhesions
   A. Deep transverse friction
   B. Sports massage
   C. Passive joint mobilization
   D. Bindegewebsmassage

32. The Swedish Movement Cure was introduced to the United States in
A. 1858
B. 1900
C. 1797
D. 1820

33. A license is obtained by a massage therapist in order to
A. Perform massage services but not receive monetary compensation
B. Perform massage services and receive monetary compensation
C. Protect the massage therapist against malpractice lawsuits
D. Perform diagnoses and prognoses of clients' medical conditions

34. Gliding movements are performed with
A. Petrissage
B. Effleurage
C. Tapotement
D. Friction

35. Contraindications for hydrotherapy include all of the following except
A. Contagious conditions
B. Hypertension
C. Acne
D. Skin rash

36. Massage may have all of the following psychological effects except
A. Increased relaxation
B. Decreased stress
C. Increased stress
D. Increased energy

37. Ancient massage technique involving kneading, tapotement, friction, popping the fingers and toes, and the use of scented perfumes
A. Tshanpau
B. Tsubo
C. Amma
D. Shiatsu

38. Application of hot and cold on the skin results in the blood vessels
A. Breaking down and building up
B. Constricting and closing
C. Dilating and opening
D. Dilating and constricting

39. ABMP and AMTA offer
A. Business plans
B. Massage licensure
C. Massage certification
D. Liability insurance

40. Stimulating massage strokes include all of the following except
A. Friction
B. Effleurage
C. Tapotement
D. Vibration

41. Insect bites may be aided in treatment by use of the following essential oil
A. Peppermint
B. Tea tree
C. Lavender
D. Sandalwood

42. To take pressure off the lower back of a client laying supine, a bolster should be placed
A. Between the legs
B. Under the ankles
C. Under the knees
D. Under the hips

43. If an independent contractor makes less than $600 in a year, they are not required to file the following tax form
A. Schedule C
B. W-2
C. 1040
D. 1099

44. A massage table which is controlled by motors to adjust the height is called
A. Hydraulic
B. Adjustable
C. Pressurized
D. Portable

45. Sharing of feelings and emotions on the part of the client is known as
A. Self-disclosure
B. Transference
C. Confidentiality
D. Counter-transference

46. Friction
A. Light gliding strokes towards the heart, used to increase circulation and apply lubricant
B. Strokes that move across tissue, used to break up adhesions
C. Kneading strokes, used to release adhesions and increase circulation
D. Percussion strokes, used to stimulate muscle spindle cells

47. Long gliding stroke in which the hands are held just above the body, not touching
A. Nerve stroke
B. Effleurage
C. Aura stroke
D. Feather stroke

48. Turkish bath
A. Also known as a hot tub
B. Steam room focusing on every part of the body but the head
C. Sauna inside a large stone building
D. Also known as a cold tub

49. Using the same linen between two separate clients is known as
A. Common sheet
B. Same linen
C. Common towel
D. Same towel

50. Reciprocity
A. A license from one jurisdiction being valid in a second jurisdiction
B. A massage therapist and client both benefiting from a session
C. A certification allowing for licensure to take place
D. Massage therapist obtaining more than one certification

51. Massage developed by Elizabeth Dicke which focuses on subcutaneous connective tissue
A. Myofascial release
B. Lymphatic drainage
C. Rolfing
D. Bindegewebsmassage

52. Effleurage
A. Kneading strokes, used to release adhesions and increase circulation
B. Strokes that move across tissue, used to break up adhesions
C. Light gliding strokes towards the heart, used to increase circulation and apply lubricant
D. Percussion strokes, used to stimulate muscle spindle cells

53. Points of manipulation similar to Amma, developed in Japan
A. Shiatsu
B. Tsubo
C. Ayurveda
D. Tshanpau

54. Keeping a client's information private and protected
A. Ethics
B. Confidentiality
C. Self-disclosure
D. Transference

55. Stoppage of a range of motion due to certain factors is known as
A. Static stretch
B. Resistance
C. End feel
D. Proprioceptive neuromuscular facilitation

56. Decor in a massage establishment should be all of the following except
A. Relaxing
B. Professional
C. Comfortable
D. Septic

57. Universal precautions
A. Controlling infectious agents to prevent the spread of disease
B. Understanding contraindications for massage therapy
C. Preventing injuries to the client due to faulty equipment
D. Being aware of any faulty body mechanics

58. Localized ischemia can be produced by application of which massage stroke
A. Friction
B. Effleurage
C. Petrissage
D. Vibration

59. Lomi Lomi is a massage which originated in
A. Thailand
B. Hawaii
C. Japan
D. China

60. Cross-fiber friction is also known as
A. Longitudinal friction
B. Transverse friction
C. Compression
D. Circular friction

61. Stance used to perform massage strokes such as petrissage, friction, and tapotement
A. Bow
B. Archer
C. Warrior
D. Swimmer

62. The "S" of "SOAP" stands for
A. Standard
B. Sustained
C. Superficial
D. Subjective

63. A passive stretch
A. Client stretches into resistance without the help of a massage therapist
B. Client stretches into resistance with the assistance of a massage therapist
C. Massage therapist stretches the client into resistance with assistance from the client
D. Massage therapist stretches the client into resistance without assistance from the client

64. Parts of the body targeted in reflexology include all of the following except
A. Abdomen
B. Hands
C. Feet
D. Ears

65. Records of massage have been dated as far back as
A. The 1800's
B. 3000 BC
C. The Dark Ages
D. 600 AD

66. Massage therapy increases the production of
A. Cortisol
B. Urine
C. Hypertension
D. Bacteria

67. Amma is a massage technique developed in
A. Japan
B. China
C. India
D. Sweden

68. Chair massage became popularized in the 1980's due to the work of
A. Per Henrik Ling
B. James Cyriax
C. David Palmer
D. Lawrence Jones

69. Reciprocal inhibition should be utilized if a client suffers from
A. Cramping
B. Seizures
C. Headaches
D. Sciatica

70. Realignment of muscle and connective tissue to return the body to a vertical axis
A. Reiki
B. Myofascial release
C. Thai massage
D. Rolfing

71. Massage stroke best utilized to break up adhesions in tissue
A. Petrissage
B. Effleurage
C. Friction
D. Tapotement

72. Client files should be kept for IRS purposes for up to
A. Two years
B. Six years
C. One year
D. Five years

73. The proper temperature to keep a massage room should be around
A. 65 degrees
B. 75 degrees
C. 80 degrees
D. 60 degrees

74. Very light form of effleurage performed at the end of a massage session
A. Petrissage
B. Friction
C. Nerve stroke
D. Tapotement

75. Proprioceptive Neuromuscular Facilitation may also be known as
A. Positional release
B. Myofascial Release
C. Strain-counter strain
D. Muscle Energy Technique

76. Water, telephone, and linen service are all
A. Business assets
B. Business expenses
C. Business arrangements
D. Business property

77. Confidentiality
A. Protecting client information
B. Allowing only a client's spouse to view information
C. Disregarding a client's right to privacy
D. Allowing a client to discuss other client's treatments

78. Massage technique developed by the Chinese which involves locating points on the body which might benefit from rubbing, pressing, and pulling
A. Shiatsu
B. Amma
C. Tsubo
D. Ayurveda

79. A massage therapist is unable to diagnose any medical condition. Performing a diagnosis is not within the massage therapist's
A. Scope of practice
B. Liability
C. Certification
D. Capabilities

80. A client stretching themselves into resistance with the assistance of a massage therapist
A. Passive stretch
B. Active stretch
C. Active assistive stretch
D. Resistive stretch

81. Shower utilizing sixteen shower heads that pinpoint specific regions of the body
A. Vichy shower
B. Turkish bath
C. Swiss shower
D. Russian bath

82. Light touch massage used to increase the flow of cerebrospinal fluid from the base of the vertebral column to the skull, which aids in treatment of many medical conditions
A. Osteosymmetry
B. Orthobionomy
C. Craniosacral Therapy
D. Cryotherapy

83. Re-educating the body to move more effectively and efficiently is a primary component of
A. Trager Method
B. Craniosacral Therapy
C. Yoga
D. Feldenkrais

84. The "O" of "SOAP" stands for
A. Objective
B. Olfaction
C. Olecranon
D. Outer

85. The Travell Method is a form of treatment designed for
A. Stretching
B. Structural realignment
C. Trigger points
D. Awareness of movement

86. David Palmer helped to popularize
A. Energy work
B. Reflexology
C. Chair massage
D. Prenatal massage

87. Massage designed to aid in athletic performance
A. Rolfing
B. Sports massage
C. Trager method
D. Feldenkrais

88. The "P" of "SOAP" stands for
A. Plan
B. Palpation
C. Protrusion
D. Palm

89. A client demonstrating range of motion is an example of which joint movement
A. Active
B. Assistive
C. Passive
D. Resistive

90. Johann Mezger was responsible for
A. Popularizing the word "massage" in America
B. Developing Swedish Gymnastics
C. Introducing Swedish massage to the US
D. Developing the terms for the massage strokes, based in French

91. Examples of moist heat include all of the following except
A. Immersion bath
B. Heating pad
C. Steam room
D. Hot tub

92. Ayurveda means
A. Push-pull
B. Massage
C. Life energy
D. Art of life

93. Massage performed by two massage therapists on one client using synchronized movements
A. Four arm massage
B. Four hand massage
C. Two head massage
D. Four leg massage

94. Sports massage is primarily used to increase
A. Respiration
B. Circulation
C. Inhalation
D. Excretion

95. Form filled out post-massage by the massage therapist, detailing work done, areas of concern for the next treatment, and any information the client shared about themselves
A. SOAP notes
B. Intake form
C. Liability form
D. Insurance form

96. Reiki, Jin Shin Do, and Polarity Therapy are all forms of
A. Kinesiology techniques
B. Movement techniques
C. Manipulative techniques
D. Energy techniques

97. Proper body mechanics include all of the following except
A. Keep back straight
B. Bend knees slightly
C. Keep wrists locked
D. Keep table at proper height

98. Form of friction in which the therapist moves the stroke perpendicular to the direction of muscle fibers
A. Compression
B. Circular friction
C. Cross-fiber friction
D. Superficial friction

99. A pregnant client would need to be placed in
A. Side-lying position
B. Supine position
C. Prone position
D. A massage chair

100. Which of the following essential oils does not have antiseptic properties
A. Eucalyptus
B. Lavender
C. Tea tree
D. Lemon

101. If a client suffers from menopause, an ideal essential oil to use during treatment is
A. Lemon
B. Peppermint
C. Ginger
D. Lavender

102. Hand washing, wearing gloves, and placing contaminated linen in biohazard bags are all forms of
A. Universal precautions
B. Sanitation
C. Sterilization
D. Housekeeping

103. Medical history may be filled out by the client as part of the
A. Assessment form
B. Intake form
C. SOAP notes
D. PPALM form

104. Gross income minus expenses deducted results in
A. Net worth
B. Net income
C. State income
D. Federal income

105. A bolster placed under the knees is used in which position
A. Prone
B. Supine
C. Side-lying
D. Chair

106. Cryotherapy is the use of
A. Cold
B. Heat
C. Water
D. Body wraps

107. Cupping, hacking, and tapping all are forms of
A. Petrissage
B. Effleurage
C. Friction
D. Tapotement

108. Evaluation of how a person holds their body while standing is
A. Pathological analysis
B. Gait analysis
C. Ergonomic analysis
D. Posture analysis

109. Percussion strokes, used to loosen phlegm in the respiratory tract and activate muscle spindle cells
A. Petrissage
B. Effleurage
C. Friction
D. Tapotement

110. Wrapping a client in a cocoon-like structure is known as
A. Diaper draping
B. Top cover draping
C. Full sheet draping
D. Scrub draping

111. Controlling infectious agents to prevent the spread of disease
A. Universal precautions
B. Sanitization
C. Contraindications
D. Disinfection

112. James Cyriax is responsible for popularizing
A. Deep transverse friction
B. Lymphatic drainage
C. Sports massage
D. Osteosymmetry

113. The "C" in RICE stands for
A. Compensation
B. Compression
C. Contraction
D. Concentric

114. RICE is used to treat injuries to
A. Bone
B. Hard tissue
C. Soft tissue
D. Lungs

115. Stance in which the feet run perpendicular to the massage table
A. Archer
B. Warrior
C. Bow
D. Swimmer

116. Book-keeping and taxes for a massage business may be handled by a massage therapist or
A. Client
B. Insurer
C. Practitioner
D. Accountant

117. Areas of the body in which caution is advised during massage of a pregnant client include all of the following except
A. Face
B. Abdomen
C. Ankles
D. Lumbar

118. A partnership is a business owned by
A. One person
B. Two or more people
C. No people
D. The government

119. Pressing of tsubo points to increase the flow of Ki
A. Amma
B. Shiatsu
C. Ayurveda
D. Tshanpau

120. A wage and tax statement detailing income and withheld taxes from the previous year for an employee
A. W-2
B. 1040
C. Schedule K1
D. 1099

121. A client stretching themselves into resistance without the assistance of a massage therapist
A. Passive stretch
B. Active stretch
C. Active assistive stretch
D. Resistive stretch

122. Inflammation may be reduced with the application of
A. Hot packs
B. Hydrotherapy
C. Lymphatic drainage
D. Cryotherapy

123. Form most commonly used to document work performed during a massage session
A. Intake form
B. SOAP notes
C. Assessment form
D. Massage notes

124. The "R" in RICE stands for
A. Rest
B. Resist
C. Reflex
D. Regain

125. Effects of massage that produce involuntary responses of the body
A. Mechanical effects
B. Emotional effects
C. Reflex effects
D. Sensory effects

126. CRAC is a form of
A. SOAP
B. RICE
C. MET
D. CAR

127. All of the following are end feels except
A. Soft end feel
B. Hard end feel
C. Empty end feel
D. Nervous end feel

128. Lymphatic drainage massage stimulates increased lymph circulation directed
A. Medially
B. Distally
C. Proximally
D. Laterally

129. Stimulation of specific points on the hands, feet, and ears that may correspond to tissues and organs throughout the body
A. Reflexology
B. Reiki
C. Rolfing
D. Polarity

130. RICE, the primary treatment utilized for a strain or sprain, stands for
A. Resist, Increase, Contract, Elongate
B. Rest, Ice, Compression, Elevation
C. Relax, Immersion, Cold, Exertion
D. Relax, Inflammation, Contraction, Elevation

131. Sauna inside of a large stone building
A. Swedish bath
B. Russian bath
C. Swiss bath
D. Turkish bath

132. "Would you like your neck massaged?" is an example of
A. Listening question
B. Open-ended question
C. Feedback question
D. Closed-ended question

133. Of the following, which is a form of assessment not normally used in massage
A. Blood pressure reading
B. Palpation
C. Gait analysis
D. Ergonomic analysis

134. To take pressure off the lower back of a client laying prone, a bolster should be placed
A. Under the knees
B. Under the ankles
C. Between the legs
D. Under the hips

135. During the course of a massage, a client discloses he has pain in his shoulders and mid-back. This information would be documented under which section of SOAP notes
A. Assessment
B. Subjective
C. Objective
D. Plan

136. Ida Rolf developed the following massage modality
A. Feldenkrais
B. Trager
C. Rolfing
D. Deep transverse friction

137. During a side-lying massage, a bolster must be placed
A. Between the legs and arms, and under the head
B. Under the ankles and neck
C. Under the knees and ankles
D. Under the head only

138. Effleurage, petrissage, and tapotement are terms developed by
A. Charles Mills
B. Per Henrik Ling
C. Douglas Graham
D. Johann Mezger

139. A business that has only one owner is known as
A. Limited liability corporation
B. Partnership
C. Sole proprietorship
D. S Corporation

140. If a client experiences lower back pain due to a hypertonic psoas major while in the prone position, a bolster should be placed
A. Under the knees
B. Under the ankles
C. Between the legs
D. Under the hips

141. The Taylor Brothers were responsible for
A. Popularizing the word "massage" in America
B. Developing Swedish Gymnastics
C. Introducing Swedish massage to the US
D. Developing the terms for the massage strokes, based in French

142. Modern term for Chinese massage
A. Tui-na
B. Watsu
C. Ayurveda
D. Shiatsu

143. The application of cold packs or ice is known as
A. Cryotherapy
B. Immersion bath
C. Infrared treatment
D. Hydrotherapy

144. "How are you today?" is an example of
A. Closed-ended question
B. Open-ended question
C. Abrupt question
D. Feedback question

145. An independent contractor must do what to work for a person or company
A. Agree to commission-based pay
B. Rent a massage room
C. Sign a contract
D. Own their own business

146. The type of massage technique and strokes being performed by the massage therapist, along with areas of the body being massaged, is documented under which category on SOAP notes
A. Subjective
B. Objective
C. Assessment
D. Plan

147. Keeping client information private and protected
A. Self-disclosure
B. Assurance
C. Confidentiality
D. Closed-ended

148. Phenol, bleach, and alcohol are all examples of
A. Disinfectants
B. Soap
C. Hand sanitizers
D. Oil removers

149. Form of friction in which the massage therapist presses tissue down against deeper tissue to broaden or flatten the tissue
A. Circular friction
B. Cross-fiber friction
C. Compression
D. Superficial friction

150. Disinfecting agents include all of the following except
A. Rubbing alcohol
B. Water
C. Bleach
D. Ammonia

151. During the course of a massage, the client requests that the massage therapist pop their wrist joint. If the massage therapist were to comply with the request, it would be a violation of
A. Scope of practice
B. Licensing
C. Malpractice
D. Certification

152. Licensing regulations detail the activities a massage therapist may engage in for their practice. These are known as
A. Scope of practice
B. Business standards
C. Regulations
D. Liabilities

153. Endangerment sites
A. Structures that may be massaged freely
B. Areas of the body that must not be massaged
C. Areas of the body that warrant caution
D. Areas of the body the massage therapist may only massage with gloves

154. Effleurage, petrissage, friction, and tapotement are all strokes found in the following type of massage
A. Trager
B. Lymphatic drainage
C. Shiatsu
D. Swedish

155. The intake form may detail all of the following information except
A. Health history
B. Hobbies
C. Occupation
D. Income

156. A person who signs a contract to work for a person or company is known as
A. Partner
B. Employee
C. Sole proprietor
D. Independent contractor

157. During the course of a massage, a massage therapist discovers a client's right scapula is slightly elevated in relation to the left scapula. This information would be documented under which section of SOAP notes
A. Subjective
B. Objective
C. Assessment
D. Plan

158. The use of water in any form during a massage session, or by itself, is known as
A. Hydrotherapy
B. Cryotherapy
C. Orthobionomy
D. Osteosymmetry

159. Feldenkrias, Trager Mentastics, and Aston Patterning are all forms of
A. Energy techniques
B. Movement techniques
C. Manipulative techniques
D. Kinesiology techniques

160. A common area used to assess a client with jaundice is
A. Teeth
B. Tongue
C. Eyes
D. Hair

161. Reddening and increased heat of the skin as the result of a massage is known as
A. Varicose veins
B. Anemia
C. Hyperemia
D. Phlebitis

162. A pre-event sports massage may be performed up to
  A. One hour before an event
  B. Thirty minutes before an event
  C. Fifteen minutes before an event
  D. One day before an event

163. A 1099 must be filed how often
  A. Monthly
  B. Annually
  C. Bi-monthly
  D. Quarterly

164. Lifting and squeezing tissue is a part of
  A. Friction
  B. Effleurage
  C. Tapotement
  D. Petrissage

165. Pain resulting from a trigger point being felt in a different region of the body is known as
  A. Latent pain
  B. Contagious pain
  C. Contracted pain
  D. Referred pain

166. Massage stroke designed to stimulate muscle spindle activity, especially useful in pre-event sports massage
  A. Tapotement
  B. Friction
  C. Effleurage
  D. Petrissage

167. Essential oils are mainly used in which type of treatment
  A. Hydrotherapy
  B. Aromatherapy
  C. Body wraps
  D. Body scrubs

168. Centripetal massage strokes are directed
  A. Away from the heart
  B. Towards the heart
  C. Down the legs
  D. Around the abdomen

169. An accountant may handle all of the following except
  A. Book-keeping
  B. Taxes
  C. Accounting
  D. Advertising

170. A massage therapist should wash their hands before and after each massage using
  A. Cold water
  B. Bleach
  C. Rubbing alcohol
  D. Anti-bacterial soap

171. A question asked that is used for feedback from a client
  A. Open-ended
  B. Close-ended
  C. Confidential
  D. Tactful

172. Shiatsu involves
  A. Stimulating tsubo points to increase Ki flow
  B. Pulling of limbs to increase range of motion
  C. Channeling universal energy throughout the client's body without touching
  D. Cupping movements to stimulate circulation

173. A feather stroke is also known as
  A. Aura stroke
  B. Nerve stroke
  C. Deep gliding stroke
  D. Vibration

174. A short general statement detailing the goal of a business
  A. Public image
  B. Purpose
  C. Mission statement
  D. Business plan

175. Massage stroke directed toward the heart used to increase circulation, transition between strokes, and apply massage lubricant
  A. Friction
  B. Petrissage
  C. Effleurage
  D. Vibration

176. Reiki originated in
  A. Japan
  B. China
  C. India
  D. America

177. Massage strokes directed towards the heart are called
  A. Centrifugal
  B. Centripetal
  C. Chucking
  D. Superficial

178. A body out of vertical alignment might most benefit from the following treatment
A. Swedish massage
B. Lymphatic drainage
C. Rolfing
D. Thai massage

179. Self-disclosure
A. The client sharing feelings and emotions during a massage session
B. The massage therapist sharing their feelings and emotions during a massage session
C. A massage therapist disclosing their scope of practice
D. A client viewing a massage therapist as they would a significant person in their early life

180. A sitz bath is a bath in which the client immerses their body up to
A. The knees
B. The chest
C. The neck
D. The hips

181. Jasmine, sandalwood, and grapefruit are all examples of
A. Massage table materials
B. Gemstones
C. Essential oils
D. Perfumes

182. An empty end feel is felt at the end of a range of motion due to
A. Tight muscle
B. Bone
C. Trauma to a joint
D. Resistance

183. A massage table, chair, and music source are located in
A. Massage room
B. Business area
C. Changing room
D. Bathroom

184. Lymphatic drainage massage involves light strokes and
A. Application of heat
B. Deep strokes
C. Tapotement
D. Pumping actions

185. Process by which essential oils are made
A. Filtering
B. Distilling
C. Blending
D. Brewing

186. Transference
A. Keeping a client's information private and protected
B. The massage therapist bringing their own unresolved issues into the therapeutic relationship
C. The client viewing a massage therapist as a significant person in their early life
D. Relocating from one office to another

187. Shaking or trembling movements used to sedate or stimulate a specific part of the body
A. Petrissage
B. Vibration
C. Friction
D. Tapotement

188. Polarity therapy helps clients to balance
A. Mind and soul
B. Hips and shoulders
C. Knees and ankles
D. Body and mind

189. Massage technique used during a pre-event sports massage, but not during an inter or post-event sports massage
A. Friction
B. Tapotement
C. Petrissage
D. Effleurage

190. Nerve stroke
A. Light gliding strokes towards the heart, used to increase circulation and apply lubricant
B. Very light strokes, used at the end of a massage
C. Kneading strokes, used to release adhesions and increase circulation
D. Percussion strokes, used to stimulate muscle spindle cells

191. Most common form of linens used in a massage treatment
A. Sheets
B. Towels
C. Blankets
D. Pillows

192. The Ayur-Veda was written around
A. 1800 BC
B. 2000 BC
C. 600 AD
D. 1000 AD

193. Feldenkrais is a movement system designed to
A. Relax major muscle groups via positional release
B. Increase the flow of cerebrospinal fluid from the cranium to the sacrum
C. Re-educate the body to move more efficiently
D. Stretch hypertonic muscles with the use of proprioceptive neuromuscular facilitation

194. In a business setting, a massage therapist's credentials must be
A. Posted in visibility of all clients
B. Kept in a secure location away from sight
C. Kept in the massage room, in a drawer
D. Posted beneath the massage table

195. A massage therapist stretching a client into resistance without assistance from the client
A. Active assistive stretch
B. Active stretch
C. Passive stretch
D. Resistive stretch

196. Stance in which the feet run perpendicular to the massage table
A. Bow
B. Archer
C. Horse
D. Swimmer

197. Client records, consultations, and transactions occur in the
A. Changing room
B. Massage room
C. Bathroom
D. Business area

198. Which of the following massage strokes is best in increasing venous circulation
A. Tapotement
B. Friction
C. Effleurage
D. Petrissage

199. Roman who wrote De Medicina, which details the use of massage, bathing, and exercise
A. Celsus
B. Galen
C. Constantine
D. Hippocrates

200. Massage stroke best utilized to sedate an area
A. Petrissage
B. Vibration
C. Friction
D. Tapotement

201. The sheet or towel used to cover a client while performing a massage
A. Top cover
B. Full sheet
C. Diaper
D. Full towel

202. An active assistive stretch
A. Client stretches into resistance without the help of a massage therapist
B. Client stretches into resistance with the assistance of a massage therapist
C. Massage therapist stretches the client into resistance with assistance from the client
D. Massage therapist stretches the client into resistance without assistance from the client

203. Abrupt stoppage of range of motion due to structures such as bone
A. Soft end feel
B. Hard end feel
C. Empty end feel
D. Nervous end feel

204. Deep transverse friction was developed by
A. James Cyriax
B. Elizabeth Dicke
C. Johann Mezger
D. Emil Vodder

205. A question asked that is used when asking for a yes or no response
A. Open-ended
B. Close-ended
C. Confidential
D. Tactful

206. A system of movements performed in specific ways to achieve certain results is known as
A. Stroke
B. Process
C. Modality
D. Treatment

207. The Hawaiian word "lomi" means
A. Relax
B. Stretch
C. Massage
D. Ocean

208. An assessment is performed
A. Only before and after a massage
B. Only before a massage
C. Only after a massage
D. Before, during, and after the massage

209. Petrissage
A. Light gliding strokes towards the heart, used to increase circulation and apply lubricant
B. Strokes that move across tissue, used to break up adhesions
C. Kneading strokes, used to release adhesions and increase circulation
D. Percussion strokes, used to stimulate muscle spindle cells

210. Greek physician who combined massage and exercise and founded the first gymnasium
A. Hippocrates
B. Aesculpius
C. Socrates
D. Per Henrik Ling

211. A question that requires only a yes or no response
A. Open-ended question
B. Closed-ended question
C. Feedback question
D. Abrupt question

212. Destroying any living organism on a surface is known as
A. Washing
B. Disinfection
C. Sanitation
D. Sterilization

213. Assessment information is
A. Information the client shares about themselves
B. Measurable information visible to the massage therapist
C. Medical conditions the client has been assessed with
D. Recommendations for future massage sessions

214. Massage technique developed by the Chinese
A. Amma
B. Shiatsu
C. Ayurveda
D. Tsubo

215. Counter-transference
A. The client viewing a massage therapist as a significant person in their early life
B. The massage therapist bringing their own unresolved issues into the therapeutic relationship
C. Keeping a client's information private and protected
D. Relocating from one office to another

216. A client performing an action with the help of the massage therapist is an example of which joint movement
A. Active
B. Resistive
C. Passive
D. Assistive

217. A massage table that is able to be folded and transported easily from one location to another
A. Hydraulic
B. Adjustable
C. Pressurized
D. Portable

218. Stoppage of a range of motion due to muscle and other soft tissues
A. Soft end feel
B. Hard end feel
C. Empty end feel
D. Nervous end feel

219. Compression is a form of
A. Petrissage
B. Effleurage
C. Friction
D. Tapotement

220. Top cover
A. Towel or sheet used to cover the client
B. Wrapping a client in a cocoon-like structure
C. Uncovering a part of the body to massage
D. Only covering parts of the body not being worked on

221. Cross-fiber, circular, and compression are all forms of
A. Petrissage
B. Effleurage
C. Friction
D. Tapotement

222. Per Henrik Ling was responsible for
A. Popularizing the word "massage" in America
B. Developing Swedish Gymnastics
C. Introducing Swedish massage to the US
D. Developing the terms for the massage strokes, based in French

223. Massage technique in which substantial pressure is applied to the body to affect deeper body structures
A. Deep tissue
B. Muscle Energy Technique
C. Swedish massage
D. Connective Tissue Massage

224. Gentle rhythmic massage designed to increase lymph circulation
A. Lymphatic drainage
B. Swedish massage
C. Sports massage
D. Orthobionomy

225. An ideal massage lubricant should be
A. Perfume scented
B. Mineral-based
C. Petroleum-based
D. Hypoallergenic

226. Massage stroke consisting of kneading strokes, used to break up adhesions between tissues and increase local circulation
A. Tapotement
B. Effleurage
C. Friction
D. Petrissage

227. A massage room should contain all of the following except
A. A music source
B. A bathroom
C. Subdued lighting
D. Comfortable temperature

228. One of the best ways to assess a client is by
A. Looking
B. Palpating
C. Listening
D. Smelling

229. Lomi Lomi, Craniosacral Therapy, and Rolfing are all forms of
A. Energy techniques
B. Movement techniques
C. Manipulative techniques
D. Kinesiology techniques

230. Fulling is a form of
A. Petrissage
B. Effleurage
C. Tapotement
D. Friction

231. Universal precautions should be followed with
A. Clients with allergies
B. Only clients with contagious conditions
C. Every client
D. Clients with no previous medical conditions

232. Medical conditions the client has been assessed with are documented on which section of SOAP notes
A. Subjective
B. Objective
C. Assessment
D. Plan

233. Contrast baths utilize
A. Warm and lukewarm water
B. Hot and cold water
C. Hot and warm water
D. Cold water and ice

234. A client is looking for structural realignment therapy. The type of massage they are requesting is
A. Myofascial release
B. Feldenkrais
C. Rolfing
D. Sports massage

235. Cinnamon essential oil should be avoided in clients who are
A. Pregnant
B. Elderly
C. Allergic to nuts
D. Bulemic

236. Questions asked in a pre-massage interview should be
A. Forced
B. Open-ended
C. Abrupt
D. Closed-ended

237. Treatment utilizing heated stones placed or rubbed on the body
A. Turkish bath
B. Aromatherapy
C. Hot stone
D. Vichy shower

238. Essential oil commonly used to aid in treatment of insomnia and chronic fatigue syndrome
A. Eucalyptus
B. Sweet orange
C. Lavender
D. Rosemary

239. Massage stroke focusing on moving layers of tissue across one another and separating tissues
A. Petrissage
B. Effleurage
C. Friction
D. Tapotement

240. A pre-event sports massage requires the following kinds of strokes to be performed
A. Relaxing
B. Invigorating
C. Slow
D. Light

241. Hydrotherapy treatment utilizing a device with multiple shower heads, performed on a water-proof table
A. Vichy shower
B. Swiss shower
C. Swedish shower
D. Russian shower

242. A trigger point that results in pain only when being palpated
A. Acute
B. Active
C. Passive
D. Latent

243. Feather stroke
A. Light gliding strokes towards the heart, used to increase circulation and apply lubricant
B. Very light strokes, used at the end of a massage
C. Kneading strokes, used to release adhesions and increase circulation
D. Shaking or trembling movements, used to sedate or stimulate

244. Lighting in a massage room should be
A. Confined to a candle
B. Bright
C. Off
D. Subdued

245. An area of the body that warrants consideration due to underlying structures
A. Fractures
B. Contraindications
C. Endangerment sites
D. Dermatomes

246. A mission statement is
A. A generalized statement detailing the focus of a business
B. The theme of a business
C. Attainable accomplishments designated by the owner
D. A positive self-image

247. Contrast baths should always end with immersion in
A. Cold
B. Hot
C. Warm
D. Lukewarm

248. Tax form required to be submitted by sole proprietors
A. 1099
B. Schedule K1
C. 1040
D. Schedule C

249. Celsus wrote the following book, which details the importance of massage, bathing, and exercise
A. The Ayur-Veda
B. De Medicina
C. The San-Tsai-Tou-Hoei
D. The Cong Fou

250. After a massage, the massage therapist notifies the client of stretches that the therapist thinks might help with a client's range-of-motion. This information would be documented under which section of SOAP notes
A. Subjective
B. Objective
C. Assessment
D. Plan

251. The primary goal of a massage performed after a sporting event is
A. Move metabolic waste out of tissues
B. Increase circulation
C. Stimulate muscle fibers
D. Break up adhesions between tissues

252. Longitudinal friction goes in which direction to muscle fibers
A. Diagonal
B. Opposite direction
C. Same direction
D. Away from

253. The "A" of "SOAP" stands for
A. Alleviate
B. Assessment
C. Arrangement
D. Alignment

254. Massage may reduce all of the following except
A. Pain
B. Cortisol
C. Stress
D. Adhesions

255. A sole proprietorship is a business that has how many owners
A. More than ten
B. Two
C. Four
D. One

256. A massage therapist moving a joint through its range of motion with the client completely relaxed is an example of which joint movement
A. Active
B. Assistive
C. Passive
D. Resistive

257. Massage involving deep structural realignment, usually taking place over ten sessions
A. Lomi Lomi
B. Rolfing
C. Feldenkrais
D. Myofascial release

258. A proper dilution of bleach is
 A. One part water to one part bleach
 B. Ten parts bleach to one part water
 C. Ten parts bleach to ten parts water
 D. Ten parts water to one part bleach

259. Form of friction in which the therapist utilizes small movements that go in a circular pattern through the tissue in order to loosen adhesions
 A. Cross-fiber friction
 B. Compression
 C. Circular friction
 D. Superficial friction

260. Part of the body used to perform tapping
 A. Fingertips
 B. Palms
 C. Forearms
 D. Sides of palms

261. The massage table height should be determined by
 A. The height of the massage therapist
 B. The height of the client
 C. The weight of the client
 D. The size of the bolsters

262. Examples of dry heat include all of the following except
 A. Heating pad
 B. Steam
 C. Infrared sauna
 D. Sauna

263. An asset is
 A. Untaxable income
 B. A weakness in a company's business model
 C. A business with no liabilities
 D. A possession of a business

264. All of the following companies provide liability insurance for massage therapists except
 A. NCBMTB
 B. ABMP
 C. AMTA
 D. NAMT

265. Gentle, rhythmic massage strokes may be
 A. Centrifugal
 B. Stimulating
 C. Sedative
 D. Deep

266. The pattern or design of a massage treatment is known as
 A. Deliberation
 B. Process
 C. Sequence
 D. Contact

267. With a client laying prone, a bolster must be placed
 A. Between the legs and arms, and under the head
 B. Under the ankles
 C. Under the knees and neck
 D. Under the head only

268. Lymphatic drainage was developed by
 A. Per Henrik Ling
 B. James Cyriax
 C. Emil Vodder
 D. Elizabeth Dicke

269. Massage strokes directed away from the heart are called
 A. Centripetal
 B. Centrifugal
 C. Chucking
 D. Superficial

270. All of the following are stimulating essential oils except
 A. Lavender
 B. Lemongrass
 C. Grapefruit
 D. Peppermint

271. Aromatherapy uses the following to restore and heal the body
 A. Mud
 B. Bath salts
 C. Essential oils
 D. Paraffin wax

272. Technique used to treat adhesions found between fascia and muscles
 A. Rolfing
 B. Myofascial release
 C. Deep tissue
 D. Osteosymmetry

273. Massage focused on connective tissue beneath the skin, affecting vascular reflexes related to pathological conditions
 A. Deep transverse friction massage
 B. Rolfing
 C. Lymphatic drainage
 D. Bindegewebsmassage

274. Stance used to perform long, gliding strokes
 A. Horse
 B. Archer
 C. Warrior
 D. Swimmer

275. Business expenses include all of the following except
A. Massages
B. Advertising
C. Electricity
D. Credit card fees

276. Slightly bent knees, straight back, and limp wrists are all examples of
A. Proper massage techniques
B. Improper body mechanics
C. Proper body mechanics
D. Improper massage modalities

277. Which of the following is an essential oil that has a calming effect
A. Eucalyptus
B. Lemon
C. Ginger
D. Tangerine

278. Full-body steam bath used to increase activity of sudoriferous glands
A. Swiss bath
B. Russian bath
C. Swedish shower
D. Vichy shower

279. Which of the following massage strokes is best in releasing metabolic waste from tissues
A. Tapotement
B. Effleurage
C. Friction
D. Petrissage

280. Sheets or towels are also known as
A. Bolsters
B. Drapes
C. Blankets
D. Linens

281. Vibration
A. Light gliding strokes towards the heart, used to increase circulation and apply lubricant
B. Very light strokes, used at the end of a massage
C. Kneading strokes, used to release adhesions and increase circulation
D. Shaking or trembling movements, used to sedate or stimulate

282. All of the following are appropriate massage lubricants except
A. Almond oil
B. Mineral oil
C. Coconut oil
D. Grapeseed oil

283. Stance in which the feet are placed parallel to the table
A. Warrior
B. Horse
C. Archer
D. Swimmer

284. An employee receives the following tax form detailing income and tax information
A. W-2
B. 1040
C. Schedule K1
D. 1099

285. An essential oil to avoid using on a pregnant client
A. Eucalyptus
B. Lavender
C. Ylang-ylang
D. Peppermint

286. Massage has the following affect on blood vessels
A. Constriction
B. Dilation
C. Toning
D. Formation

287. If a client is unable to withstand any amount of pressure during a massage, a treatment the therapist might recommend would be
A. Reiki
B. Rolfing
C. Myofascial release
D. Lymphatic drainage

288. Massage technique designed to release blockages in the flow of fluid from the sacrum to the cranium
A. Craniosacral Therapy
B. Trager Method
C. Feldenkrais
D. Muscle Energy Technique

289. The "I" in RICE stands for
A. Immersion
B. Ice
C. Inflammation
D. Increase

290. Superficial friction results in the following condition of the skin
A. Regeneration
B. Hypoemia
C. Atrophy
D. Hyperemia

291. A resistive joint movement
 A. Client moves the joint without the assistance of a massage therapist
 B. A client moves the joint with the assistance of a massage therapist
 C. A client resists a movement being performed by a massage therapist
 D. A massage therapist moves a client's joint without the help of the client

292. A question used when asking for feedback from a client
 A. Open-ended question
 B. Closed-ended question
 C. Feedback question
 D. Applied question

293. Subjective information is
 A. Medical conditions the client has been assessed with
 B. Measurable information visible to the massage therapist
 C. Information the client shares about themselves
 D. Recommendations for future massage sessions

294. An aura stroke is a massage stroke in which
 A. The hands are pressed firmly into the body
 B. The hands are touching the body very lightly
 C. The hands are held just above the body
 D. The hands are placed on the body without substantial pressure

295. An active assistive joint movement
 A. Client moves the joint without the assistance of a massage therapist
 B. A client moves the joint with the assistance of a massage therapist
 C. A client resists a movement being performed by a massage therapist
 D. A massage therapist moves a client's joint without the help of the client

296. Essential oil commonly used to aid in relaxation of smooth muscles in the respiratory tract
 A. Eucalyptus
 B. Lavender
 C. Lemongrass
 D. Peppermint

297. Aura strokes may be especially useful in which modality
 A. Reflexology
 B. Reiki
 C. Rolfing
 D. Lomi Lomi

298. Soap is essential in
 A. Bleaching
 B. Disinfection
 C. Sterilization
 D. Sanitation

299. Hawaiian massage similar to Swedish massage, utilizing rhythmic massage strokes that flow freely up and down the body
 A. Watsu
 B. Thai Massage
 C. Amma
 D. Lomi Lomi

300. Manual manipulation of the body's soft tissues
 A. Massage
 B. Chiropractic
 C. Movement
 D. MET

301. Skin rolling is a form of
 A. Petrissage
 B. Effleurage
 C. Tapotement
 D. Friction

302. The "E" in RICE stands for
 A. Exertion
 B. Elevation
 C. Energy
 D. Eccentric

303. A massage establishment should contain all of the following areas except
 A. Changing room
 B. Massage room
 C. Business area
 D. Bathroom

304. Douglas Graham was responsible for
 A. Introducing Swedish massage to the US
 B. Developing Swedish Gymnastics
 C. Popularizing the word "massage" in America
 D. Developing the terms for the massage strokes, based in French

305. Which of the following is obtained to allow a massage therapist to perform massage and receive monetary compensation
 A. Certification
 B. License
 C. Scope of practice
 D. Liability insurance

306. Protection from accidents and malpractice is gained by obtaining
A. Limited Liability Corporation
B. Massage certification
C. Licensure
D. Liability insurance

307. Lavender may aid in treatment of all of the following conditions except
A. Anxiety
B. Chronic fatigue syndrome
C. Insomnia
D. Chronic bronchitis

308. A massage license from one jurisdiction being recognized as valid in another jurisdiction
A. Reciprocity
B. Certification
C. Liability
D. Malpractice

309. Vigorous massage strokes are
A. Sedative
B. Stimulating
C. Relaxing
D. Centrifugal

310. Liability insurance protects the massage therapist in instances such as
A. Overbooking
B. Unsatisfied clients
C. Malpractice
D. Repetitive strain injuries

311. Physical possessions owned by a business are known as
A. Accounts
B. Liabilities
C. Assets
D. Trade

312. A passive joint movement
A. Client moves the joint without the assistance of a massage therapist
B. A client moves the joint with the assistance of a massage therapist
C. A client resists a movement being performed by a massage therapist
D. A massage therapist moves a client's joint without the help of the client

313. An independent contractor does not receive
A. Benefits
B. Pay
C. Compensation
D. Gratuity

314. Gentle shaking and rocking movements to improve range of motion
A. Polarity therapy
B. Trager method
C. Sports massage
D. Rolfing

315. Pre-massage interview used to determine the treatment to be performed, areas of concern, and contraindications
A. Consultation
B. Evaluation
C. Documentation
D. Intake

316. Massage modality which operates under the premise of balancing both the body and mind
A. Lomi Lomi
B. Orthobionomy
C. Polarity therapy
D. Deep transverse friction

317. A 1099 must be filed by an independent contractor unless they make less than
A. $1000 per year
B. $5000 per year
C. $600 per year
D. $2500 per year

318. Physical effects of massage therapy are called
A. Emotional effects
B. Mechanical effects
C. Reflex effects
D. Sensory effects

319. Massage technique targeting reflex points on the hands, feet, and ears to stimulate organs and tissue throughout the body
A. Mentastics
B. Reiki
C. Trager method
D. Reflexology

320. A bolster is placed between the legs and arms and under the head in which position
A. Slightly elevated
B. Supine
C. Prone
D. Side-lying

321. Swedish massage is based on the Western principals of
A. Anatomy and physiology
B. Energy
C. Life force
D. Chi

322. Rolfing aligns major body segments, known as
A. Structural realignment
B. Somatic holding pattern
C. Mentastics
D. Balance of body and mind

323. Stretch technique in which a muscle is stretched to resistance, followed by an isometric contraction by the client, then the muscle stretched further after the contraction
A. Active static stretch
B. Proprioceptive neuromuscular facilitation
C. Strain counter-strain
D. Myofascial release

324. A set of guiding moral principles is known as
A. Regulations
B. Scope of practice
C. Ethics
D. Reputation

325. Stance used to perform massage strokes such as petrissage, friction, and tapotement
A. Archer
B. Horse
C. Bow
D. Swimmer

326. Suggestions for future treatments by the massage therapist would be documented under which section of SOAP notes
A. Subjective
B. Objective
C. Assessment
D. Plan

327. Form used to detail tax return information for individuals
A. 1040
B. W-2
C. 1099
D. 990

328. Good body mechanics are important to
A. Perform a shorter massage
B. Prevent injuries to the therapist
C. Massage the head and neck
D. Prevent injuries to the client

329. Movement of a joint through the entire extent of its action is known as
A. Stretching
B. Range of motion
C. Traction
D. Active movement

330. With a client laying supine, a bolster must be placed
A. Between the legs and arms, and under the head
B. Under the ankles and neck
C. Under the knees
D. Under the head only

331. Mentastics was developed by
A. Randolph Stone
B. Moshe Feldenkrais
C. Ida Rolf
D. Milton Trager

332. The term "massage" became popularized in America by
A. Johann Mezger
B. The Taylor Brothers
C. Douglas Graham
D. Per Henrik Ling

333. A soft end feel is felt at the end of a range of motion due to
A. Tight muscle
B. Bone
C. Injuries
D. Resistance

334. Ability to perform services legally according to occupational standards and licensing
A. Certification
B. Scope of practice
C. Reciprocity
D. Regulations

335. An independent contractor is responsible for filing which tax form
A. Schedule K1
B. W2
C. 1099
D. Schedule C

336. Full sheet
A. Towel or sheet used to cover the client
B. Wrapping a client in a cocoon-like structure
C. Uncovering a part of the body to massage
D. Only covering parts of the body not being worked on

337. Cryotherapy is used to reduce
A. Inflammation
B. Frostbite
C. Hypoxia
D. Edema

338. Massage produces what affect on blood vessels
A. Breaks down blood vessel walls
B. Decreases the size of blood vessel lumen
C. Develops new blood vessels
D. Increases the size of blood vessel lumen

339. Most questions asked by the massage therapist towards the client during a massage session should be
A. Closed-ended
B. Open-ended
C. Informative
D. Assessment related

340. MET is also known as
A. Massage Elongation Trigger
B. Massage Extremity using Tapotement
C. Myofascial Elasticity Technique
D. Muscle Energy Technique

341. Chucking and wringing are forms of
A. Effleurage
B. Petrissage
C. Tapotement
D. Friction

342. A trigger point that causes pain without palpation
A. Acute
B. Latent
C. Active
D. Chronic

343. Form of compression in which a muscle fiber is compressed between the thumb and fingers
A. Pincer compression
B. Transverse compression
C. Cross-fiber compression
D. Longitudinal compression

344. A client that may not benefit from specific essential oils is someone who might suffer from
A. Allergies
B. Insomnia
C. Acquired Immuno Deficiency Syndrome
D. Cellulitis

345. Gait analysis is observation and interpretation of a person's
A. Walking pattern
B. Somatic holding pattern
C. Sitting pattern
D. Range of motion

346. Objective information is
A. Information the client shares about themselves
B. Measurable information visible to the massage therapist
C. Medical conditions the client has been assessed with
D. Recommendations for future massage sessions

347. Tapotement
A. Light gliding strokes towards the heart, used to increase circulation and apply lubricant
B. Strokes that move across tissue, used to break up adhesions
C. Kneading strokes, used to release adhesions and increase circulation
D. Percussion strokes, used to stimulate muscle spindle cells

348. Which of the following massage strokes is best in aiding lung decongestion
A. Tapotement
B. Effleurage
C. Friction
D. Petrissage

349. A massage therapist bringing their own unresolved issues into the therapeutic relationship
A. Self-disclosure
B. Transference
C. Counter-transference
D. Ethics

350. Centrifugal massage strokes are directed
A. Around the abdomen
B. Towards the heart
C. Away from the heart
D. On the scalp

Massage Therapy Answer Key

01.D	41.B	81.C	121.B	161.C
02.A	42.C	82.C	122.D	162.C
03.A	43.D	83.D	123.B	163.D
04.C	44.A	84.A	124.A	164.D
05.B	45.A	85.C	125.C	165.D
06.D	46.B	86.C	126.C	166.A
07.A	47.C	87.B	127.D	167.B
08.B	48.C	88.A	128.C	168.B
09.C	49.C	89.A	129.A	169.D
10.A	50.A	90.D	130.B	170.D
11.D	51.D	91.B	131.D	171.A
12.C	52.C	92.D	132.D	172.A
13.B	53.B	93.B	133.A	173.B
14.D	54.B	94.B	134.B	174.C
15.A	55.C	95.A	135.B	175.C
16.A	56.D	96.D	136.C	176.A
17.B	57.A	97.C	137.A	177.B
18.B	58.A	98.C	138.D	178.C
19.D	59.B	99.A	139.C	179.A
20.B	60.B	100.B	140.B	180.D
21.B	61.C	101.D	141.C	181.C
22.C	62.D	102.A	142.A	182.C
23.D	63.D	103.B	143.A	183.A
24.D	64.A	104.B	144.B	184.D
25.A	65.B	105.B	145.C	185.B
26.C	66.B	106.A	146.B	186.C
27.B	67.B	107.D	147.C	187.B
28.C	68.C	108.D	148.A	188.D
29.D	69.A	109.D	149.C	189.B
30.A	70.D	110.C	150.B	190.B
31.A	71.C	111.A	151.A	191.A
32.A	72.B	112.A	152.A	192.A
33.B	73.B	113.B	153.C	193.C
34.B	74.C	114.C	154.D	194.A
35.C	75.D	115.B	155.D	195.C
36.C	76.B	116.D	156.D	196.C
37.A	77.A	117.A	157.B	197.D
38.D	78.B	118.B	158.A	198.C
39.D	79.A	119.B	159.B	199.A
40.B	80.C	120.A	160.C	200.B

201.A	246.A	291.C	336.B
202.B	247.A	292.A	337.A
203.B	248.D	293.C	338.D
204.A	249.B	294.C	339.B
205.B	250.D	295.B	340.D
206.C	251.A	296.A	341.D
207.C	252.C	297.B	342.C
208.D	253.B	298.D	343.A
209.C	254.B	299.D	344.D
210.B	255.D	300.A	345.A
211.B	256.C	301.A	346.B
212.D	257.B	302.B	347.D
213.C	258.D	303.A	348.A
214.A	259.C	304.C	349.C
215.B	260.A	305.B	350.C
216.D	261.A	306.D	
217.D	262.B	307.D	
218.A	263.D	308.A	
219.C	264.A	309.B	
220.A	265.C	310.C	
221.C	266.C	311.C	
222.B	267.B	312.D	
223.A	268.C	313.A	
224.A	269.B	314.B	
225.D	270.A	315.A	
226.D	271.C	316.C	
227.B	272.B	317.C	
228.C	273.D	318.B	
229.C	274.B	319.D	
230.A	275.A	320.D	
231.C	276.C	321.A	
232.C	277.A	322.A	
233.B	278.B	323.B	
234.C	279.D	324.C	
235.A	280.D	325.B	
236.D	281.D	326.D	
237.C	282.B	327.A	
238.C	283.C	328.B	
239.C	284.A	329.B	
240.B	285.D	330.C	
241.A	286.B	331.D	
242.D	287.A	332.C	
243.B	288.A	333.A	
244.D	289.B	334.B	
245.C	290.D	335.C	

Anatomy and Physiology Practice Test

Questions about anatomy and physiology will focus on all of the specific structures of the body and their functions. Questions will primarily focus on the body systems, the parts of each system, and what each system does.

Other questions may involve organelles and their functions, the different types of tissue, their functions and what structures they make, and other structural information.

Many of the structures in the body are connected, and therefore, may be easily remembered. Try mnemonics to remember certain aspects of anatomy, such as the following: My Elephant Never Cries. If you remember this phrase, you will remember how many types of tissue are in the body, and what the name of each tissue starts with: M, E, N, C.

Connecting certain aspects of anatomy is another way to easily remember information. An example could be, there are twelve thoracic vertebrae, twelve pairs of ribs, and twelve pairs of cranial nerves. Associate all three of those anatomical structures together, and it would make remembering them much easier!

1. The sympathetic nervous system is also referred to as
A. Housekeeping
B. Rest and digest
C. Fight or flight
D. Central

2. A hair follicle contains which portion of a strand of hair
A. Root
B. Shaft
C. Arrector pili
D. Medullary cavity

3. The longest vein in the body, located on the medial aspect of the leg and thigh
A. Great saphenous
B. Femoral
C. External iliac
D. Brachial

4. The pituitary gland produces all of the following hormones except
A. Growth hormone
B. Testosterone
C. Follicle stimulating hormone
D. Prolactin

5. Perirenal fat is found surrounding the
A. Rectum
B. Bladder
C. Liver
D. Kidneys

6. Primary function of a gland
A. Secretion
B. Protection
C. Absorption
D. Contraction

7. Branching muscle tissue is also called
A. Smooth
B. Skeletal
C. Cardiac
D. Striated

8. Production of fibrin in the blood aids in which process
A. Red blood cell formation
B. Coagulation
C. Phagocytosis
D. Leukopoiesis

9. Mastication is more commonly known as
A. Chewing
B. Swallowing
C. Sneezing
D. Defecating

10. The pulmonary arteries carry blood from the right ventricle to
A. Left atrium
B. Rest of the body
C. Aorta
D. Lungs

11. Sodium and chloride ions allow conduction of electricity. They are examples of
A. Metabolics
B. Calcium
C. Urine
D. Electrolytes

12. Growth hormone, prolactin, and follicle-stimulating hormone are all produced by the
A. Thalamus
B. Pituitary
C. Testes
D. Thyroid

13. T lymphocytes are produced by which gland
A. Thymus
B. Thalamus
C. Pituitary
D. Pineal

14. Stratum granulosum lies directly superficial to
A. Stratum corneum
B. Stratum lucidum
C. Stratum spinosum
D. Stratum basale

15. The phrenic nerve emerges from the
A. Neck
B. Chest
C. Lumbar
D. Brain

16. Another name for a leukocyte is
A. Thrombocyte
B. Red blood cell
C. Platelet
D. White blood cell

17. The cervical plexus emerges from which sets of vertebrae
A. C1-C7
B. C1-C4
C. T1-T6
D. L1-S4

18. There are seven vertebrae in which region of the vertebral column
A. Thoracic
B. Cervical
C. Lumbar
D. Coccygeal

19. Erythrocytes
A. Carry oxygen and carbon dioxide throughout the body
B. Are also called neutrophils and perform phagocytosis
C. Produce thrombi at an area of trauma
D. Allow transport of blood cells throughout the body

20. Beta waves are produced when a person is in the following mental state
A. Hungry
B. Asleep
C. Relaxed
D. Alert

21. Absorption of nutrients primarily takes place in what part of the small intestine
A. Jejunum
B. Ileum
C. Duodenum
D. Cecum

22. All of the following are types of leukocytes except
A. Thrombocytes
B. Neutrophil
C. Basophils
D. Lymphocyte

23. The largest of the salivary glands
A. Subbuccal
B. Sublingual
C. Submandibular
D. Parotid

24. Peristalsis is controlled by which of the following types of muscle
A. Cardiac
B. Skeletal
C. Smooth
D. Striated

25. Vitamin D is produced in the following organ
A. Liver
B. Skin
C. Pancreas
D. Spleen

26. Cell clusters in the pancreas that produce insulin
A. Medullary cells
B. Islets of Langerhans
C. Nephrons
D. Inlets of Longmire

27. Part of the respiratory passage that divides into the left and right bronchus
A. Larynx
B. Pharynx
C. Trachea
D. Epiglottis

28. The pancreatic duct joins with the bile duct to enter the duodenum at the
A. Hepatopancreatic ampulla
B. Cystopancreatic ampulla
C. Gastrointestinal ampulla
D. Islets of Langerhans

29. Function of red blood cells
A. Clot to prevent hemorrhage
B. Fight diseases and eat dead cells
C. Transport oxygen and carbon dioxide
D. Transport blood cells throughout the body

30. Cells in the peripheral nervous system can perform an action that cells in the central nervous system cannot. What is this action
A. Die
B. Regenerate
C. Produce neurotransmitters
D. Communicate with one another

31. The esophagus passes through the following structure on its way to the stomach
A. Peritoneum
B. Liver
C. Pericardium
D. Diaphragm

32. The primary somatosensory area is located in which of the following lobes
A. Occipital
B. Temporal
C. Parietal
D. Frontal

33. The functional unit of tissue is called
A. Cell
B. Nerve
C. Blood
D. Muscle

34. Most superior portion of the sternum
A. Costal cartilage
B. Body
C. Xiphoid process
D. Manubrium

35. Which of the following molecules attaches to hemoglobin
A. Nitrogen
B. Oxygen
C. Helium
D. Argon

36. Breaking down food, absorption of nutrients, and elimination of waste is the function of which body system
A. Urinary
B. Digestive
C. Cardiovascular
D. Lymphatic

37. Non-striated muscle is
A. Involuntary
B. Voluntary
C. Controlled easily
D. Controlled by concentration

38. Connective tissue connecting bone to bone
A. Fascia
B. Tendon
C. Ligament
D. Dermis

39. The right kidney lies where in relation to the position of the left kidney
A. Superior
B. Inferior
C. Anterior
D. Posterior

40. All of the following carry blood away from the heart except
A. Capillaries
B. Arteries
C. Arterioles
D. Veins

41. Protein fiber that gives bone its strength
A. Cartilate
B. Elastin
C. Collagen
D. Periosteum

42. Nerves are categorized as being from which division of the nervous system
A. Central
B. Peripheral
C. Autonomic
D. Sympathetic

43. When reading blood pressure, the lower number represents
A. Diastolic pressure
B. Systolic pressure
C. Venous pressure
D. Pulmonary pressure

44. The adrenal glands are located atop which organs
A. Large intestine
B. Small intestine
C. Kidneys
D. Ureters

45. Dopamine is an example of a
A. Neurotransmitter
B. Synapse
C. Neuron
D. Dendrite

46. A vertebral curvature positioned anteriorly is called
A. Lordotic
B. Kyphotic
C. Scoliotic
D. Amniotic

47. When inhaling, the diaphragm moves in which direction
A. Inferiorly
B. Superiorly
C. Anteriorly
D. Posteriorly

48. Which of the following is not a structure in the digestive system
A. Gallbladder
B. Spleen
C. Liver
D. Pancreas

49. The trachea lies directly inferior to the
A. Lungs
B. Pharynx
C. Bronchus
D. Larynx

50. Pepsin is located in the
A. Stomach
B. Small intestine
C. Pancreas
D. Gallbladder

51. The cardiac sphincter is located in which body system
A. Urinary
B. Cardiovascular
C. Nervous
D. Digestive

52. Most anterior lobe in the cerebrum
A. Parietal
B. Temporal
C. Frontal
D. Occipital

53. Bone found in the region of the forearm
A. Radius
B. Humerus
C. Fibula
D. Hamate

54. Water is absorbed by the
A. Large intestine
B. Stomach
C. Esophagus
D. Liver

55. Which of the following is an example of cardiac muscle
A. Orbicularis oris
B. Biceps femoris
C. Arrector pili
D. Papillary muscle

56. Which of the following is an example of an exocrine gland
A. Hypothalamus
B. Thymus
C. Adrenal
D. Sudoriferous

57. The hypoglossal, vagus, glossopharangeal, and accessory nerves are all cranial nerves that emerge from the
A. Pons
B. Cerebrum
C. Medulla oblongata
D. Cerebellum

58. Which of the following is not a type of bone cell
A. Osteoprogenitor
B. Periosteum
C. Osteocyte
D. Osteoclast

59. Coronary arteries
A. Supply blood to the abdomen
B. Supply blood to the head and neck
C. Supply blood to the myocardium
D. Supply blood to the arm and forearm

60. Which of the following is the only bone in the body that is part of both the axial and appendicular skeletons
A. Sacrum
B. Clavicle
C. Sternum
D. Atlas

61. Tendons
A. Connect ligaments to muscles to prevent friction
B. Connect bones to bones to provide stability
C. Connect muscles to muscles to allow synergists
D. Connect bones and muscles to allow movement

62. Cerumen is also known as
A. Ear wax
B. Mucous
C. Cilia
D. Tears

63. Blood cell responsible for regulation of the body's immune system
A. Thrombocytes
B. Leukocytes
C. Erythrocytes
D. Platelets

64. The pineal gland is located
A. In the neck
B. In the chest
C. In the abdomen
D. In the skull

65. All of the following are hormones produced by the anterior pituitary except
A. Oxytocin
B. Growth hormone
C. Prolactin
D. Melanocyte-stimulating hormone

66. Expression of emotion is strongly linked to the following structure in the limbic system
A. Amygdala
B. Hippocampus
C. Hypothalamus
D. Septal area

67. Structure located inside the right atrium
A. Chordae tendinae
B. Bicuspid valve
C. Sinoatrial node
D. Papillary muscles

68. Which bone is not part of the pelvic girdle
A. Coccyx
B. Sacrum
C. Ilium
D. Ischium

69. Bronchial tubes branch out into smaller tubes called
A. Larynx
B. Alveoli
C. Trachea
D. Bronchioles

70. Blood passes from the right atrium through the tricuspid valve into the
A. Left ventricle
B. Left atrium
C. Right ventricle
D. Pulmonary artery

71. How many bones form the pectoral girdle
A. Four
B. Two
C. Three
D. Five

72. Balancing electrolyte and acid levels in the body is regulated by
A. Stomach
B. Bladder
C. Large intestine
D. Kidneys

73. Vibration of air produces speech, which is the responsibility of
A. Larynx
B. Pharynx
C. Trachea
D. Epiglottis

74. The auricle, external acoustic meatus, and tympanic membrane are all parts of the
A. Ear
B. Eye
C. Esophagus
D. Small intestine

75. Type of gland that secretes its substances directly into the blood stream
A. Exocrine
B. Endocrine
C. Eccrine
D. Sebaceous

76. Valve found between the left atrium and left ventricle
A. Pulmonary
B. Tricuspid
C. Aortic
D. Bicuspid

77. Salivary glands are considered which type of gland
A. Sebaceous
B. Endocrine
C. Eccrine
D. Exocrine

78. Epinephrine and norepinephrine are produced by which glands
A. Adrenal
B. Pituitary
C. Pineal
D. Ovaries

79. Baroreceptors, nociceptors, and proprioceptors are all examples of
A. Motor nerves
B. Nerve roots
C. Sensory receptors
D. Neurons

80. Endocrine glands create what substance for the body
A. Sweat
B. Hormones
C. Oil
D. Milk

81. Type of cell broken down inside the spleen
A. Osteocyte
B. Leukocyte
C. Thrombocyte
D. Erythrocyte

82. Vein running from the medial surface of the foot to the inguinal region
A. Great saphenous vein
B. Femoral vein
C. Obturator vein
D. Superficial tibial vein

83. Bones are held together via
A. Cartilage
B. Tendons
C. Ligaments
D. Periosteum

84. Insulin is created in the pancreas by
A. Leukocytes
B. Alpha cells
C. Beta cells
D. Lymph

85. The largest artery in the body
A. Aorta
B. Brachial
C. External iliac
D. Femoral

86. The adrenal glands are located
A. Inside the spleen
B. On the underside of the liver
C. Beside the pancreas
D. On top of the kidneys

87. Alpha cells are responsible for production of
A. Glucagon
B. Insulin
C. Bile
D. Melanin

88. Vomiting, breathing, sneezing, and other vital functions are controlled by
A. Cerebrum
B. Pons
C. Medulla oblongata
D. Frontal lobe

89. Chyme comes into contact with bile in the
A. Duodenum
B. Jejunum
C. Ileum
D. Liver

90. Brain waves that occur only during sleep
A. Delta
B. Alpha
C. Beta
D. Theta

91. The sternal angle is located between the site of fusion for which two bones of the sternum
A. Xiphoid process and body
B. Body and xiphoid process
C. Xiphoid process and manubrium
D. Manubrium and body

92. Organ covering the body that provides protection and heat regulation
A. Skin
B. Liver
C. Subcuntaneous fat
D. Urethra

93. Upon reaching tissue, oxygen attached to hemoglobin is exchanged with which other substance, a waste product
A. Alcohol
B. Carbon monoxide
C. Carbon dioxide
D. Uria

94. Nervous tissue
A. Protects the body from entry of microorganisms
B. Transmits electrical signals throughout the body
C. Secretes substances into the blood stream
D. Contracts and creates heat

95. Type of lymphocyte that fights viruses, cancerous cells, and fungus
A. Monocyte
B. B cells
C. Neutrophil
D. T cells

96. Red blood cells are also known as
A. Erythrocytes
B. Leukocytes
C. Thrombocytes
D. Plasma

97. Pleural membranes surround
A. Intestines
B. Heart
C. Lungs
D. Liver

98. All of the following are functions of the digestive system except
A. Elimination of feces
B. Absorption of nutrients
C. Break-down of food
D. Elimination of urine

99. The sense of smell is detected by which cranial nerve
A. Hypoglossal
B. Optic
C. Accessory
D. Olfactory

100. Most posterior lobe of the cerebrum
A. Temporal
B. Occipital
C. Cerebellum
D. Frontal

101. The carotid arteries carry blood to
A. Arm and forearm
B. Head and neck
C. Thigh and leg
D. Chest and abdomen

102. How many vertebrae are in the vertebral column
A. 24
B. 26
C. 31
D. 12

103. Release of insulin and glucagon is inhibited by
A. Hydrochloric acid
B. Bile
C. Somatostatin
D. Pepsin

104. How many bones fuse together to form the sacrum
A. Three
B. One
C. Five
D. Four

105. The left and right hemispheres of the cerebrum are connected via the
A. Brain stem
B. Diencephalon
C. Cerebellum
D. Corpus callosum

106. A vertebral curvature positioned posteriorly is called
A. Lordotic
B. Kyphotic
C. Scoliotic
D. Amniotic

107. Rapid breathing and enlargement of the pupils are a sign the body is in which nervous response
A. Rest and digest
B. Parasympathetic
C. Sympathetic
D. Peripheral

108. The thyroid cartilage sits in front of the
A. Larynx
B. Uvula
C. Trachea
D. Epiglottis

109. Digestive enzyme produced by the liver, which enters the duodenum at the hepatopancreatic ampulla
A. Pepsin
B. Insulin
C. Glucagon
D. Bile

110. Epithelial tissue is avascular, which means it has
A. No nerve supply
B. A rich blood supply
C. No blood supply
D. A rich nerve supply

111. Homeostasis
A. Maintaining a constant internal environment
B. Secretion of hormones
C. Nervous impulses traveling from the skin to the brain
D. Creating heat via smooth muscle contraction

112. The hepatic portal vein collects blood from all of the following structures except
A. Pancreas
B. Stomach
C. Spleen
D. Liver

113. Which of the following is not a reaction of the body upon stimulation of the sympathetic nervous response
A. Increased blood sugar
B. Increased heart rate
C. Peristalsis
D. Enlarged pupils

114. The radial artery provides blood to the
A. Forearm and hand
B. Arm and axilla
C. Head and shoulder
D. Arm and forearm

115. A sudoriferous gland is a type of exocrine gland that produces what substance
A. Oil
B. Sweat
C. Testosterone
D. Milk

116. The end of the stomach that joins with the duodenum
A. Pylorus
B. Fundus
C. Cardia
D. Cecum

117. Taste receptors in the tongue are located in what part of the tongue
A. Epiglottis
B. Muscle
C. Incisors
D. Papillae

118. The right lung contains how many lobes
A. Three
B. Two
C. Four
D. One

119. Pericardium
A. Surrounds the brain and spinal cord to protect
B. Surrounds the lungs to prevent collapse
C. Surrounds the heart to reduce friction
D. Surrounds the abdominal wall to separate organs from muscle

120. The optic nerve is a cranial nerve that sends which inputs to the brain
A. Voluntary facial movement
B. Scent
C. Taste
D. Visual

121. The anterior cruciate ligament
A. Is found at the pelvis and holds the sacrum and ilium together
B. Is found at the knee and holds the fibula and tibia together
C. Is found at the elbow and holds the radius and ulna together
D. Is found in the knee and holds the tibia and femur together

122. The porta hepatis contains all of the following structures except
A. Cystic duct
B. Pancreatic duct
C. Hepatic duct
D. Bile duct

123. Adipose tissue
A. Is a form of epithelial tissue that absorbs nutrients into the body
B. Is a form of muscle tissue that creates heat
C. Is a form of connective tissue that protects and insulates the body
D. Is a form of nervous tissue surrounding axons to insulate them

124. Chemical messenger primarily responsible for the beginning stages of the inflammatory response
A. Histamine
B. Dopamine
C. Phagocytes
D. Platelets

125. Which type of muscle is responsible for peristalsis
A. Striated
B. Cardiac
C. Skeletal
D. Smooth

126. In a blood pressure reading, the higher number represents
A. Heart rate
B. Diastolic pressure
C. Arterial contraction
D. Systolic pressure

127. What part of a long bone is the epiphysis
A. Growth plate
B. Shaft
C. Ends
D. Articular cartilage

128. The definition of anatomy is
A. Study of the structure of the body
B. Study of the function of the body
C. Study of disease
D. Study of movement

129. The medulla oblongata
A. Is part of the meninges and provides protection for the brain
B. Is part of the cerebrum and regulates emotions and aggression
C. Is part of the cerebellum and regulates balance
D. Is part of the brain stem and regulates the vital functions of the body

130. Control of the muscles responsible for mastication is provided by which cranial nerve
A. Facial
B. Trigeminal
C. Olfactory
D. Vagus

131. Protein secreted by the stomach which allows absorption of vitamin B12 in the ileum
A. Pepsin
B. Amylase
C. Intrinsic factor
D. Hydrochloric acid

132. Substance absorbed by the large intestine
A. Sodium
B. Bile
C. Protein
D. Water

133. What part of the body is being studied in anatomy
A. Structure
B. Function
C. Diseases
D. Movement

134. Dilation of the ventricles causes
A. Contraction
B. Systole
C. Diastole
D. Circulation

135. Coagulation is also known as
A. Clotting
B. Absorption
C. Cell division
D. Scar tissue formation

136. The aortic valve
A. Allows blood to move from the left ventricle into the aorta
B. Allows blood to move from the right ventricle into the aorta
C. Allows blood to move from the left ventricle to the lungs
D. Allows blood to move from the right ventricle to the lungs

137. Beta cells produce
A. Bile
B. Glucagon
C. Somatostatin
D. Insulin

138. Function of the floating ribs
A. Protecting kidneys
B. Trunk extension
C. Allows stomach expansion
D. Protecting urinary bladder

139. Where two bones come together
A. Fracture
B. Articulation
C. Contracture
D. Ellipsoid

140. Which of the following is considered avascular
A. Muscle
B. Ligament
C. Dermis
D. Bone

141. Connective tissue covering the shaft of long bones
A. Hyaline
B. Pericardium
C. Periosteum
D. Articular cartilage

142. Light pressure is detected by
A. Nociceptors
B. Pacinian corpuscles
C. Merkel discs
D. Meissner's corpuscles

143. Cardiac muscle is found in what organ of the body
A. Lungs
B. Small intestine
C. Spleen
D. Heart

144. Survival instincts are regulated by the
A. Limbic system
B. Frontal lobe
C. Cerebellum
D. Parietal lobe

145. There are five bones in which region of the vertebral column
A. Thoracic
B. Cervical
C. Lumbar
D. Sacral

146. The pancreas
A. Produces insulin and glucagon and empties these substances into the duodenum
B. Produces hydrochloric acid and pepsin and empties these substances into the stomach
C. Filters glucose from the blood stream and absorbs insulin into the stomach
D. Digests food into usable parts for the small intestine to allow absorption

147. The medulla of the kidney contains
A. Glomeruli
B. Adrenal glands
C. Renal pyramids
D. Tubules

148. The stratum spinosum lies superficial to the
A. Stratum corneum
B. Stratum granulosum
C. Stratum lucidum
D. Stratum germinativum

149. The cardiac sphincter is found between the
A. Esophagus and stomach
B. Left atrium and left ventricle
C. Stomach and small intestine
D. Right atrium and right ventricle

150. The aortic valve is found between the aorta and
A. Right atrium
B. Left atrium
C. Left ventricle
D. Right ventricle

151. Clotting of the blood is the responsibility of
A. Leukocytes
B. Thrombocytes
C. Erythrocytes
D. Plasma

152. Photoreceptors are located in the following structure, located in the back of the eye
A. Retina
B. Iris
C. Sclera
D. Cornea

153. Storage of bile is controlled by the
A. Gallbladder
B. Liver
C. Small intestine
D. Stomach

154. Motor axons help control
A. Movement
B. Sensation
C. Olfactory input
D. Visual input

155. From superficial to deep, the order of the meninges
A. Pia mater, dura mater, arachnoid
B. Pia mater, arachnoid, dura mater
C. Arachnoid, dura mater, pia mater
D. Dura mater, arachnoid, pia mater

156. Which of the following is not a part of a nerve cell
A. Dendrite
B. Nucleus
C. Myelin sheath
D. Axon

157. Gland sitting in front of the cartilage atop the larynx
A. Pituitary
B. Thymus
C. Thyroid
D. Adrenal

158. Cartilage found between the vertebrae
A. Hyaline cartilage
B. Intervertebral discs
C. Vertebral symphysis
D. Vertebral facets

159. Bile secreted by the liver is stored in the
A. Duodenum
B. Gallbladder
C. Pancreas
D. Spleen

160. Pain is relayed to the brain via the
A. Thalamus
B. Thymus
C. Parathyroid
D. Diencephalon

161. Function of the pons
A. Controls the functions of cranial nerves
B. Allows the medulla oblongata and the cerebellum to communicate
C. Allows the cerebrum and cerebellum to communicate
D. Produces hormones responsible for growth and maturation

162. Contraction of smooth muscle in the uterus is controlled by
A. Estrogen
B. Vagus nerve
C. Phrenic nerve
D. Oxytocin

163. Glucagon is produced by
A. Delta cells
B. Beta cells
C. Alpha cells
D. Theta cells

164. Which of the following is processed by the temporal lobe
A. Pain
B. Vision
C. Memory
D. Mood

165. Part of the brain that contributes in control of the autonomic nervous system
A. Parietal lobe
B. Frontal lobe
C. Corpus callosum
D. Hypothalamus

166. The peritoneal membrane
A. Is found in the thorax and lines the thoracic cavity
B. Is found in the abdomen and lines the abdominal cavity
C. Is found in the thorax and surrounds the heart
D. Is found in the dorsal cavity and surrounds the brain and spinal cord

167. Type of epithelium that forms glands
A. Stratified epithelium
B. Squamous epithelium
C. Glandular epithelium
D. Neural epithelium

168. Glands located atop the kidneys
A. Adrenal
B. Parathyroids
C. Thalamus
D. Pituitary

169. The layer of epidermis lying immediately superior to the stratum granulosum
A. Stratum germinativum
B. Stratum spinosum
C. Stratum corneum
D. Stratum lucidum

170. Sensory axons carry nerve impulses
A. Away from the muscle
B. Away from the brain
C. Towards the nerve
D. Towards the brain

171. Alpha cells in the pancreas produce
A. Glycogen
B. Insulin
C. Glucagon
D. Bile

172. Arteries carry blood in which direction
A. Between the heart chambers
B. Towards the heart
C. Away from the heart
D. Between the heart valves

173. The olfactory nerve detects the following sense and sends an impulse to the brain for interpretation
A. Smell
B. Taste
C. Vision
D. Touch

174. The white of the eye is also called the
A. Cornea
B. Lens
C. Retina
D. Sclera

175. Brain waves most commonly seen in children
A. Alpha
B. Theta
C. Beta
D. Delta

176. Lacrimal glands produce
A. Ear wax
B. Sweat
C. Tears
D. Hormones

177. The entrance to the kidney is also called the
A. Cortex
B. Renal artery
C. Renal pyramid
D. Hilum

178. Function of dendrites
A. Communicate nerve impulses to muscles
B. Send action potentials to other neurons
C. Receive action potentials from axons
D. Transmit electrical signals from the nucleus to the axon

179. All of the following are examples of exocrine glands except
A. Sudoriferous
B. Mammary
C. Sebaceous
D. Pituitary

180. The superior seven pairs of ribs are also called
A. Inferior ribs
B. False ribs
C. Superior ribs
D. True ribs

181. Sphincter located between the pharynx and esophagus
A. Esophageal
B. Cardiac
C. Pyloric
D. Ileocecal

182. The stratum lucidum lies deep to the
A. Stratum basale
B. Stratum granulosum
C. Stratum corneum
D. Stratum spinosum

183. Which of the following is a nerve cell process that emerges from the cell body
A. Cytoplasm
B. Nucleus
C. Axon
D. Mitochondria

184. Most cells in the body are surrounded by
A. Cell membrane
B. Cytoplasm
C. Nucleus
D. Ribosome

185. Carbohydrates are broken down into the following substance via digestive enzymes
A. Amino acids
B. Protein
C. Glucose
D. Glycerol

186. Smooth muscle can be found in all of the following parts of the body except
A. Eyes
B. Heart
C. Skin
D. Esophagus

187. Sensory receptor responsible for detecting the sense of hearing
A. Chemoreceptors
B. Baroreceptors
C. Photoreceptors
D. Mechanoreceptors

188. Blood found in the right atrium is low in oxygen and has an abundance of
A. Hormones
B. Carbon monoxide
C. Sodium
D. Carbon dioxide

189. Cartilage located between the epiphysis and diaphysis where growth in the bone takes place
A. Metaphysis
B. Hyaline
C. Periosteum
D. Osteoprogenitor

190. Waste moves through the large intestine in the following order
A. Transverse colon, ascending colon, sigmoid colon, descending colon
B. Sigmoid colon, descending colon, transverse colon, ascending colon
C. Ascending colon, transverse colon, descending colon, sigmoid colon
D. Descending colon, ascending colon, transverse colon, sigmoid colon

191. Main type of cell that creates nervous tissue
A. Axon
B. Neuron
C. Dendrite
D. Astrocyte

192. There are how many pairs of ribs in the body
A. Twenty-four
B. Ten
C. Twelve
D. Seven

193. Air sacs located at the end of bronchial tubes
A. Alveoli
B. Bronchioles
C. Cilia
D. Epiglottis

194. Muscles found in the ventricles of the heart responsible for preventing prolapse of a valve
A. Papillary muscles
B. Cardiopulmonary muscles
C. Atrioventricular muscles
D. Septal muscles

195. Oxytocin stimulates contraction of smooth muscle in the following organ
A. Small intestine
B. Stomach
C. Uterus
D. Esophagus

196. Mesentery is found in the following body region
A. Chest
B. Abdomen
C. Cranium
D. Vertebral column

197. Which of the following is made of connective tissue
A. Heart
B. Bone
C. Skin
D. Brain

198. The sense of smell is detected by
A. Chemoreceptors
B. Nociceptors
C. Baroreceptors
D. Photoreceptors

199. The kidneys lie immediately beneath which glands
A. Parathyroids
B. Adrenal
C. Thymus
D. Pancreas

200. Which of the following is not one of the four types of tissue
A. Nervous
B. Connective
C. Epithelial
D. Skeletal

201. Proprioceptor responsible for detecting deep pressure
A. Meissner's corpuscles
B. Golgi tendon organ
C. Spindle cell
D. Pacinian corpuscles

202. The jejunum is responsible for
A. Absorption of nutrients into the blood stream
B. Digestion and excretion of waste
C. Filtration of electrolytes into the kidneys
D. Mastication of food in the alimentary canal

203. The fight or flight response is also known as
A. Sympathetic
B. Parasympathetic
C. Autonomic
D. Peripheral

204. Another name for a nerve cell
A. Neuron
B. Axon
C. Neuroglia
D. Brain

205. The skeletal system
A. Absorbs substances into the blood stream
B. Connects tissues together
C. Protects organs and creates blood cells
D. Circulates blood throughout the body

206. Which of the following is not made of connective tissue
A. Adipose
B. Epidermis
C. Blood
D. Cartilage

207. The epidermis contains how many layers
A. Two
B. Three
C. Four
D. Five

208. An area of skin innervated by a specific nerve is called a
A. Dermatitis
B. Synapse
C. Dermatome
D. Reflex

209. Deoxygenated blood enters the heart into which chamber
A. Right ventricle
B. Right atrium
C. Left atrium
D. Left ventricle

210. Tissue that forms the endocrine glands
A. Muscular
B. Connective
C. Epithelial
D. Nervous

211. Hematopoiesis
A. Occurs inside the bones in the medullary cavity
B. Breaking down of infectious agents inside the body
C. Formation of scar tissue
D. Creation of the amniotic sac

212. The submandibular, sublingual, and parotid glands are all examples of
A. Sudoriferous glands
B. Sebaceous glands
C. Salivary glands
D. Eccrine glands

213. Fiber emerging from a neuron cell body which sends action potentials away from the neuron
A. Nucleus
B. Schwann cells
C. Dendrite
D. Axon

214. Arteries carrying blood to the head and neck
A. Coronary
B. Carotid
C. Jugular
D. Subclavian

215. The most superficial layer of epidermis
A. Stratum corneum
B. Stratum lucidum
C. Stratum basale
D. Stratum granulosum

216. The parasympathetic nervous system takes what action on the heart
A. No change in heart rate
B. Increase heart rate
C. Decrease heart rate
D. Tachycardia

217. Schwann cells produce
A. Neuroglia
B. Neurons
C. Axons
D. Myelin

218. The retina contains
A. Sclera
B. Cones
C. Iris
D. Pupil

219. Function of the corpus callosum
A. Allows transport of nutrients through the brain
B. Allows communication between the two hemispheres of the cerebrum
C. Allows communication between the cerebrum and cerebellum
D. Allows secretion of growth hormone

220. The largest internal organ in the body
A. Liver
B. Stomach
C. Brain
D. Spleen

221. Alternate name for the right atrioventricular valve
A. Aortic valve
B. Mitral valve
C. Bicuspid valve
D. Tricuspid valve

222. Enzyme located in the saliva which aids in digestion of carbohydrates
A. Epinephrine
B. Prolactin
C. Amylase
D. Parotid

223. The diaphragm separates which body cavities from each other
A. Abdominal and pelvic
B. Thoracic and abdominal
C. Pelvic and thoracic
D. Dorsal and ventral

224. The bones of the wrist are also called
A. Carpals
B. Tarsals
C. Metacarpals
D. Phalanges

225. Vitamin synthesized by bacteria in the large intestine
A. Vitamin D
B. Vitamin A
C. Vitamin K
D. Vitamin B12

226. All of the following are forms of connective tissue except
A. Bone
B. Epidermis
C. Adipose
D. Cartilage

227. The epidermis lies where in relation to the dermis
A. Inferior
B. Deep
C. Superior
D. Superficial

228. Concentric contraction
A. Muscle tension remains constant and muscle length increases
B. Muscle tension increases and muscle length decreases
C. Muscle tension increases and muscle tension increases
D. Muscle tension increases and muscle length remains constant

229. Saliva contains amylase, which aids in digestion of
A. Lipids
B. Proteins
C. Carbohydrates
D. Amino acids

230. Increase of calcium in the blood stream is achieved by secretion of the following hormone
A. Parathyroid hormone
B. Prolactin
C. Oxytocin
D. Epinephrine

231. Growth hormone, prolactin, and follicle-stimulating hormone are all produced by the
A. Thyroid
B. Testes
C. Thalamus
D. Pituitary

232. Artery supplying blood to the lower limbs which emerges from the abdominal aorta
A. Popliteal
B. Femoral
C. Great saphenous
D. External iliac

233. Glucose is converted to glycogen in the
A. Stomach
B. Liver
C. Spleen
D. Small intestine

234. Electromyographs measure
A. Brain wave activity
B. Heart activity
C. Muscle activity
D. Hearing ability

235. Part of the brain controlling motivation, aggression, mood, and social behavior
A. Cerebellum
B. Temporal lobe
C. Frontal lobe
D. Hypothalamus

236. Insulin is produced by which organ
A. Pancreas
B. Liver
C. Gallbladder
D. Stomach

237. Order of the parts of the sternum from inferior to superior
A. Xiphoid process, manubrium, body
B. Manubrium, body, xiphoid process
C. Body, xiphoid process, manubrium
D. Xiphoid process, body, manubrium

238. Absorption of glucose into the body's cells is produced by
A. Progesterone
B. Insulin
C. Lactose
D. Melatonin

239. Each hand contains how many phalanges
A. Five
B. Fifteen
C. Fourteen
D. Four

240. The tricuspid valve
A. Forces blood from the left atrium to the left ventricle
B. Allows blood to move through the right ventricle into the right atrium
C. Found between the right atrium and right ventricle
D. Keeps blood from moving backwards from the aorta into the ventricle

241. Blood in the right ventricle is
A. Oxygenated
B. Deoxygenated
C. Clotted
D. Going backwards

242. Afferent impulses are carried along which type of axon
A. Sensory
B. Motor
C. Efferent
D. Ocular

243. Primary function of sudoriferous glands
A. Production of protein
B. Hormone release
C. Protection of skin
D. Help control body temperature

244. The dorsal body cavity
A. Protects the digestive organs in the abdomen
B. Surrounds the heart and lungs
C. Protects the brain and spinal cord
D. Houses internal reproductive organs

245. The right and left sides of the heart are separated by the
A. Pulmonary veins
B. Tricuspid valve
C. Bicuspid valve
D. Septum

246. The large intestine converts chyme into
A. Bolus
B. Feces
C. Water
D. Bile

247. Semicircular canals and otolith organs in the ear provide which sense for the body
A. Coordination
B. Balance
C. Hearing
D. Vision

248. Cartilage
A. Found on articular surface of bones to prevent friction
B. Connects muscles to bones to allow movement
C. Holds bones to bones to provide structural support
D. Surrounds organs in the abdomen to prevent friction

249. Visual interpretation is controlled by the following lobe of the cerebrum
A. Occipital
B. Temporal
C. Frontal
D. Parietal

250. Which of the following is interpreted by the occipital lobe
A. Olfactory
B. Language
C. Memory
D. Vision

251. The space between the pia mater and arachnoid is filled with
A. Cerebrospinal fluid
B. Craniosacral energy
C. Blood
D. Mucous

252. Sudoriferous and sebaceous glands are both located in which region of the body
A. Skin
B. Respiratory passages
C. Kidneys
D. Stomach lining

253. Emulsification of lipids in the duodenum is controlled by
A. Glucagon
B. Insulin
C. Bile
D. Amylase

254. The brain and spinal cord are found in the following division of the nervous system
A. Peripheral
B. Central
C. Somatic
D. Autonomic

255. Which ribs are located just lateral to the sternal angle of the sternum
A. Sixth
B. First
C. Fifth
D. Second

256. Cell mitosis takes place in the following part of the epidermis
A. Stratum basale
B. Stratum lucidum
C. Stratum granulosum
D. Stratum spinosum

257. Epidermal layer lying deep to the stratum spinosum
A. Stratum granulosum
B. Stratum corneum
C. Stratum germinativum
D. Stratum lucidum

258. Tissue specializing in protection, absorption, and secretion
A. Muscular
B. Connective
C. Nervous
D. Epithelial

259. Heat creation is produced by which type of muscle tissue
A. Smooth
B. Cardiac
C. Skeletal
D. Adipose

260. The meninges
A. Surround the brain and spinal cord to provide protection
B. Surround the heart and lungs to provide protection
C. Are inside the small and large intestine to allow absorption of nutrients and water
D. Are found in the dermis to hold subcutaneous fat to the dermis

261. Intermediate layer of the meninges
A. Brain
B. Dura mater
C. Pia mater
D. Arachnoid

262. Nociceptors detect
A. Pain
B. Temperature
C. Chemical concentration
D. Body position

263. Mammary glands produce what substance
A. Oil
B. Sweat
C. Milk
D. Testosterone

264. The thoracic and sacral vertebrae are curved in which way
A. Lordotic
B. Kyphotic
C. Scoliotic
D. Amniotic

265. The mitral valve is located between
A. Left ventricle and aorta
B. Right ventricle and pulmonary artery
C. Right atrium and right ventricle
D. Left atrium and left ventricle

266. Which of the following is not a stage in the cell cycle
A. Growth stage
B. Synthetic stage
C. Death stage
D. Second growth stage

267. Cartilage sitting in front of the larynx
A. Oropharynx cartilage
B. Thymus cartilage
C. Trachea cartilage
D. Thyroid cartilage

268. Movement of the limbs is controlled by which type of muscle tissue
A. Cardiac
B. Skeletal
C. Smooth
D. Hyaline

269. Periodontal ligaments connect
A. Head to neck
B. Jaw to jaw
C. Teeth to gums
D. Teeth to jaw

270. Site of communication between nerve cells via neurotransmitters
A. Dendrite
B. Axon
C. Synapse
D. Nucleus

271. The brain stem includes all of the following except
A. Medulla oblongata
B. Cerebellum
C. Pons
D. Midbrain

272. White blood cells are also known as
A. Erythrocytes
B. Leukocytes
C. Thrombocytes
D. Platelets

273. The descending order of the small intestine is
A. Duodenum, ileum, jejunum
B. Ileum, jejunum, duodenum
C. Duodenum, jejunum, ileum
D. Jejunum, duodenum, ileum

274. The thoracic vertebrae contains how many bones
A. Twelve
B. Seven
C. Five
D. Eleven

275. There are how many pairs of spinal nerves in the peripheral nervous system
A. 24
B. 12
C. 18
D. 31

276. Vein found in the region of the armpit
A. Inguinal vein
B. Brachial vein
C. Femoral vein
D. Axillary vein

277. The brachial plexus emerges from which region of the vertebral column
A. T7-T12
B. C5-T1
C. L1-S4
D. C1-C4

278. Type of muscle tissue that is involuntary
A. Striated
B. Skeletal
C. Cardiac
D. Epithelial

279. Veins carry blood in which direction
A. Towards the heart
B. Away from the heart
C. To the organs
D. Towards the limbs

280. The jugular notch is located on top of which bone of the sternum
A. Sternal angle
B. Body
C. Xiphoid process
D. Manubrium

281. The pulmonary veins carry blood from the lungs to
A. The aorta
B. The body
C. The vena cava
D. The heart

282. Islets of Langerhans are found in which glandular organ
A. Kidneys
B. Pancreas
C. Liver
D. Spleen

283. Sensory receptors responsible for detecting changes in chemical concentration in the body
A. Chemoreceptors
B. Baroreceptors
C. Nociceptors
D. Thermoreceptors

284. Brain wave activity is measured using the following instrument
A. Electroencephalogram
B. Electrocardiogram
C. Ophthalmoscope
D. Audiometer

285. Each kidney contains roughly how many nephrons
A. One hundred
B. One thousand
C. Ten thousand
D. One million

286. The heaviest organ in the body is the
A. Brain
B. Stomach
C. Liver
D. Heart

287. Pepsin is a digestive enzyme located in the stomach. Another digestive enzyme in the stomach is
A. Hydrochloric acid
B. Insulin
C. Glucagon
D. Bile

288. The ovaries and testes are examples of
A. Exocrine glands
B. Digestive organs
C. Endocrine glands
D. Cardiovascular vessels

289. Baroreceptors detect
A. Pressure in large blood vessels
B. Changes in chemical concentration
C. Pain
D. Different temperatures

290. Blood passes from the left atrium to the left ventricle through the following valve
A. Aortic
B. Mitral
C. Tricuspid
D. Pulmonary

291. The majority of the neural tissue in the body is found in which region of the body
A. Arms
B. Legs
C. Intestines
D. Brain

292. Leukocytes
A. Provide protection against pathogens and remove dead cells and debris
B. Transport oxygen and carbon dioxide throughout the body
C. Allow transport of blood cells throughout the body
D. Clot the blood in an area of trauma

293. Blood pressure is measured using which medical instrument
A. AED
B. Colonoscopy
C. Thermometer
D. Sphygmomanometer

294. Function of smooth muscle found in the skin
A. Secreting oil
B. Standing hair up
C. Contracting skin
D. Shivering

295. Stratum germinativum is located in the
A. Epidermis
B. Dermis
C. Liver
D. Bone

296. Motor axons carry nerve impulses
A. Towards the spinal cord
B. Towards the brain
C. Away from the brain
D. Away from muscle

297. Structure of the limbic system, essential in the formation of new memories
A. Septal area
B. Hypothalamus
C. Amygdala
D. Hippocampus

298. The second cervical vertebrae is also called the
A. Occiput
B. Atlas
C. Axis
D. Dens

299. When a person is in a relaxed and awake state, the brain waves they are exhibiting are
A. Beta waves
B. Alpha waves
C. Theta waves
D. Delta waves

300. Muscle tissue responsible for pumping blood throughout the body
A. Skeletal
B. Cardiac
C. Smooth
D. Striated

301. Cilia contain glands that secrete
A. Sebum
B. Mucous
C. Sweat
D. Ear wax

302. Which type of gland is found in the skin
A. Adrenal
B. Mammary
C. Pineal
D. Sebaceous

303. The alimentary canal
A. Is also known as the circulatory system
B. Contains the brain and spinal cord
C. Consists of the mouth, esophagus, stomach, and intestines
D. Brings blood from the heart to the lungs and back to the heart

304. Order of the epidermal layers from deep to superficial
A. Granulosum, lucidum, corneum, germinativum, spinosum
B. Corneum, lucidum, granulosum, spinosum, germinativum
C. Lucidum, spinosum, granulosum, germinativum, corneum
D. Germinativum, spinosum, granulosum, lucidum, corneum

305. The great saphenous vein
A. Located in the medial leg and thigh
B. Carries blood to the heart from the pelvis to the inferior vena cava
C. Takes blood and lymph into the thoracic duct
D. Supplies oxygen to the lower limbs

306. Sweat is produced by which type of gland
A. Sebaceous
B. Sudoriferous
C. Mammary
D. Eccrine

307. Hormone stimulating the bones to increase in size and length
A. Follicle-stimulating hormone
B. Luteinizing hormone
C. Growth hormone
D. Progesterone

308. The windpipe is also called the
A. Bronchus
B. Pharynx
C. Larynx
D. Trachea

309. The femoral artery wraps around the thigh to the back of the knee to become the
A. Peroneal artery
B. Tibial artery
C. Popliteal artery
D. Patellar artery

310. The ampulla of Vater connects the
A. Small intestine to large intestine
B. Gallbladder to liver
C. Pancreas to small intestine
D. Pharynx to esophagus

311. Perception of your own body parts and position of your body
A. Integration
B. Proprioception
C. Reflexes
D. Nociceptor

312. The spinal cord is formed by which type of tissue
A. Epithelial
B. Connective
C. Muscular
D. Nervous

313. Chyme moves from the stomach into the small intestine through which sphincter
A. Ileocecal
B. Cardiac
C. Pyloric
D. Esophageal

314. Oxygen enters the blood and carbon dioxide exits the blood through
A. Alveoli
B. Trachea
C. Bronchioles
D. Larynx

315. Albumin is synthesized by the
A. Gallbladder
B. Pancreas
C. Liver
D. Spleen

316. The four regions of the upper limb include
A. Shoulder, elbow, wrist, phalanges
B. Hand, forearm, shoulder, elbow
C. Arm, forearm, wrist, hand
D. Humerus, radius, scaphoid, metacarpal

317. The mitral valve
A. Allows blood to flow from the left ventricle into the aorta
B. Keeps blood from flowing from the right atrium into the right ventricle
C. Allows blood to move from the left atrium into the left ventricle
D. Keeps blood from flowing into the pulmonary artery from the right ventricle

318. Peristalsis is controlled by which nervous system
A. Sympathetic
B. Parasympathetic
C. Autonomic
D. Peripheral

319. Order of the epidermal layers from superficial to deep
A. Germinativum, spinosum, granulosum, lucidum, corneum
B. Corneum, lucidum, granulosum, spinosum, germinativum
C. Spinosum, granulosum, lucidum, corneum, germinativum
D. Corneum, granulosum, lucidum, spinosum, germinativum

320. A monocyte is what type of cell
A. Osteocyte
B. Epithelial
C. Leukocyte
D. Stratified

321. Blood flowing from the heart to the lungs and back to the heart is called
A. SA node circulation
B. Cardiac circulation
C. Somatic circulation
D. Pulmonary circulation

322. Another name for the parasympathetic nervous system
A. Rest and digest
B. Sympathetic
C. Fight or flight
D. Autonomic

323. Platelets are also called
A. Erythrocytes
B. Leukocytes
C. Thrombocytes
D. Osteocytes

324. The teeth, tongue, and salivary glands are all structures located in the
A. Pharynx
B. Nasal cavity
C. Oral cavity
D. Esophagus

325. Arteries supplying blood to the kidneys to aid in filtration of the blood
A. Hepatic arteries
B. Renal arteries
C. Gastric arteries
D. Cystic arteries

326. What type of contraction is the smooth muscle in the digestive tract responsible for
A. Irregular
B. Voluntary
C. Ventricular
D. Rhythmic

327. The left lung contains how many lobes
A. Five
B. Three
C. Four
D. Two

328. Epithelial tissue
A. Holds tissue together and separates tissues
B. Provides protection, secretes substances, and absorbs substances
C. Is found inside joints and helps to lubricate joints
D. Allows nerve impulses to be transmitted from the brain to muscles

329. Antibodies are produced by the following cells
A. Erythrocytes
B. Lymphocytes
C. Thrombocytes
D. Osteocytes

330. Blood is routed to the myocardium via the following arteries
A. Carotid
B. Cardiac
C. Coronary
D. Jugular

331. Study of the structure of the human body
A. Pathology
B. Anatomy
C. Physiology
D. Kinesiology

332. Bone is made of what type of tissue
A. Nervous
B. Epithelial
C. Muscular
D. Connective

333. Artery supplying blood to the forearm and hand
A. Radial artery
B. Humeral artery
C. Tibial artery
D. Brachial artery

334. Type of lymphocyte that is effective against bacteria
A. T cell
B. Macrophage
C. Natural killer cell
D. B cell

335. Production of growth hormone is controlled by which gland
A. Testes
B. Adrenal
C. Pituitary
D. Thymus

336. The tympanic membrane is also known as
A. Epiglottis
B. Eardrum
C. Larynx
D. Iris

337. Structure preventing food and water from entering into the lungs
A. Trachea
B. Pharynx
C. Uvula
D. Larynx

338. Keratin is produced by
A. Stratum germinativum
B. Stratum granulosum
C. Stratum lucidum
D. Stratum spinosum

339. The largest veins in the body, responsible for returning deoxygenated blood to the heart
A. Aorta
B. Vena Cava
C. Pulmonary arteries
D. Pulmonary veins

340. Pressure felt in the walls of arteries when blood is not passing through them
A. Dilation
B. Systolic
C. Diastolic
D. Arteriole

341. The cecum is located in the
A. Spleen
B. Small intestine
C. Stomach
D. Large intestine

342. The external iliac artery
A. Supplies blood to the thigh and leg
B. Supplies blood to the internal reproductive organs
C. Emerges from the femoral artery
D. Brings blood to the inferior vena cava from the lower limbs

343. Organ that stores bile and empties bile into the duodenum
A. Gallbladder
B. Pancreas
C. Liver
D. Stomach

344. Most sensations are processed in which of the following lobes of the cerebrum
A. Frontal
B. Occipital
C. Parietal
D. Temporal

345. The deepest layer of the epidermis
A. Stratum granulosum
B. Stratum germinativum
C. Stratum lucidum
D. Stratum spinosum

346. Delta cells in the pancreas secrete
A. Glucagon
B. Insulin
C. Bile
D. Somatostatin

347. The sensation of balance is provided by which structure
A. Nociceptor
B. Occipital lobe
C. Optic nerve
D. Semicircular canal

348. Primary functions of epithelial tissue
A. Absorption, heat creation
B. Protection, secretion, absorption
C. Protection, absorption, sensory reception
D. Contraction, secretion

349. Types of glands that secrete their substances onto a surface are known as
A. Eccrine
B. Endocrine
C. Exocrine
D. Pituitary

350. The jugular notch is located between which two bones
A. Clavicles
B. Ribs
C. Scapulae
D. Manubrium and sternal body

351. Central nervous system
A. Contains the brachial, cervical, and lumbosacral plexus
B. Contains the spinal nerves and allows sensation to be detected
C. Contains the cranial nerves and allows sensation to be detected
D. Contains the brain and spinal cord and allows mental activity

352. How many different types of tissue are found in the body
A. Two
B. Three
C. Four
D. One

353. The brain is formed by which type of tissue
A. Muscular
B. Nervous
C. Epithelial
D. Connective

354. Capillaries located in the kidneys, allowing waste products to be filtered from the blood for elimination
A. Adrenal
B. Renal arteries
C. Nephron
D. Glomeruli

355. Blood located in the left atrium is low in carbon dioxide but rich in
A. Carbon monoxide
B. Oxygen
C. Hormones
D. Calcium

356. Paired organs include all of the following except
A. Gallbladder
B. Lung
C. Kidney
D. Ureter

357. Digestive enzymes that help to break down fat are produced by the following type of cell located in the stomach
A. Pyloric
B. Parietal
C. Oxyntic
D. Zymogen

358. The true ribs connect to the sternum via
A. Costal tendons
B. Costal cartilage
C. Costal ligaments
D. Costal bones

359. Valve found between the left ventricle and aorta
A. Tricuspid
B. Bicuspid
C. Mitral
D. Aortic

360. Annulus fibrosis is located
A. Between vertebrae
B. In bone
C. In the lungs
D. Between ribs

361. Protein found inside of red blood cells, responsible for transporting oxygen and carbon dioxide throughout the body
A. Mitochondria
B. Hemoglobin
C. Hemophilia
D. Leukocyte

362. Sight is detected by
A. Nociceptors
B. Baroreceptors
C. Photoreceptors
D. Mechanoreceptors

363. Which of the following organs plays an important role in the body's immune response
A. Large intestine
B. Esophagus
C. Spleen
D. Urinary bladder

364. How many bones fuse together to form the coccyx
A. Five
B. Four
C. Two
D. Three

365. The spinal nerve plexus that emerges from C1-C4
A. Cervical plexus
B. Brachial plexus
C. Lumbar plexus
D. Sacral plexus

366. Exocrine glands are
A. Structures that create various substances and secrete them onto a surface
B. Structures that create hormones and secrete them into the blood
C. Structures that absorb substances and filter them into the blood
D. Structures that create leukocytes and secrete them into the oral cavity

367. The vagus nerve controls which autonomic nervous system
A. Fight or flight
B. Sympathetic
C. Autonomic
D. Parasympathetic

368. Growth hormone is produced by the
A. Pituitary gland
B. Thymus
C. Adrenal gland
D. Testes

369. What substance passes through the pyloric sphincter
A. Insulin
B. Feces
C. Bolus
D. Chyme

370. Which of the following is an example of skeletal muscle
A. Papillary muscle
B. Quadratus lumborum
C. Arrector pili
D. Smooth endoplasmic reticulum

371. Sensory receptor that helps detect movement in joints and muscles
A. Baroreceptors
B. Nociceptors
C. Proprioceptors
D. Chemoreceptors

372. The hepatic artery brings blood to the liver from the
A. Inferior vena cava
B. Abdomen
C. Brain
D. Aorta

373. Contraction of cardiac muscle in the right ventricle sends blood
A. To the right atrium
B. To the body
C. To the aorta
D. To the lungs

374. Ligaments hold what structures together
A. Tendons to muscles
B. Muscles to bones
C. Bones to bones
D. Bones to tendons

375. Descending order of the urinary tract
A. Urethra, bladder, ureters, kidneys
B. Kidneys, ureters, bladder, urethra
C. Kidneys, bladder, ureters, urethra
D. Bladder, ureters, kidneys, urethra

376. Structure responsible for closing the entry to the larynx during swallowing
A. Vocal cords
B. Tongue
C. Epiglottis
D. Trachea

377. Bone found in the region of the arm
A. Humerus
B. Radius
C. Ulna
D. Lunate

378. The esophagus, aorta, and inferior vena cava all pass through the
A. Pleural cavity
B. Peritoneal membrane
C. Pericardium
D. Diaphragm

379. The longest vein in the body
A. Brachial vein
B. Femoral vein
C. Great saphenous vein
D. Inferior vena cava

380. Valve located between the right atrium and right ventricle
A. Bicuspid
B. Aortic
C. Tricuspid
D. Mitral

381. Muscular tissue
A. Connects and separates tissues
B. Contracts and produces heat
C. Produces hormones and secretes them
D. Absorbs substances into the body

382. The cervical and lumbar vertebrae are curved in which way
A. Scoliotic
B. Kyphotic
C. Lordotic
D. Amniotic

383. Function of serous membranes
A. Secreting sebum
B. Connect organs
C. Creating blood
D. Separate organs

384. Connective tissue responsible for transport of leukocytes to areas of inflammation
A. Blood
B. Bone
C. Cartilage
D. Fascia

385. Epidermis
A. Is located deep to the dermis and allows water to move in and out of the body
B. Is vascular and provides protection for the body from microorganisms and trauma
C. Is avascular and provides protection for the body from microorganisms and trauma
D. Contains sensory receptors that detect pressure, pain, and temperature

386. A cell body of a neuron is also called
A. Glial cell
B. Perikaryon
C. Schwann cell
D. Node of ranvier

387. Follicle-stimulating hormone stimulates production of
A. Milk
B. Oocytes
C. Epinephrine
D. Norepinephrine

388. The larynx is located between
A. Tongue and uvula
B. Trachea and bronchus
C. Epiglottis and pharynx
D. Pharynx and trachea

389. The first cervical vertebrae is also called the
A. Occiput
B. Axis
C. Atlas
D. Dens

390. Melanocytes produce
A. Hair
B. Skin pigment
C. Bone
D. Sweat glands

391. Which of the following is not a function of epithelial tissue
A. Absorption
B. Protection
C. Heat production
D. Secretion

392. The true ribs connect to which bone
A. Scapula
B. Humerus
C. Sternum
D. Clavicle

393. Zymogen cells produce digestive enzymes that help to digest
A. Fat
B. Carbohydrates
C. Glucose
D. Insulin

394. Oxyntic cells produce
A. Saliva
B. Pepsin
C. Bile
D. Hydrochloric acid

395. The stratum granulosum lies deep to the
A. Stratum lucidum
B. Stratum spinosum
C. Stratum germinativum
D. Stratum basale

396. All of the following are structures that pass through the diaphragm except
A. Inferior vena cava
B. Esophagus
C. Abdominal aorta
D. Stomach

397. The cerebellum
A. Responsible for emotions
B. Responsible for coordination and balance
C. Responsible for visual reflexes
D. Responsible for olfaction and memory input

398. Which is the only organ in the body that contains both endocrine and exocrine glands
A. Liver
B. Pancreas
C. Stomach
D. Lungs

399. Glomeruli and tubules are found in which portion of a kidney
A. Medulla
B. Cortex
C. Adrenal
D. Nephron

400. Sphincters in the digestive tract are responsible for
A. Preventing food from moving backwards
B. Secreting digestive enzymes
C. Absorbing nutrients
D. Preventing blood flow into the organs

401. Adipose is considered which type of connective tissue
A. Cartilage
B. Dense connective tissue
C. Loose connective tissue
D. Bone

402. There are how many pairs of cranial nerves in the peripheral nervous system
A. 12
B. 31
C. 24
D. 18

403. Lymph
A. Creates red blood cells to allow transport of oxygen
B. Contains blood to help fight disease
C. Provides inflammation upon trauma to tissue
D. Contains interstitial fluid to help filter blood

404. Dermatomes are innervated by which type of nerve
A. Cranial nerve
B. Spinal nerve
C. Optic nerve
D. Accessory nerve

405. Food that has been swallowed and entered the pharynx has become
A. Carbohydrates
B. Chyme
C. Feces
D. Bolus

406. Production of egg cells and sperm is maintained by the following hormone, produced by the pituitary gland
A. Follicle-stimulating hormone
B. Prolactin
C. Lactogenic hormone
D. Epinephrine

407. Brain wave activity is recorded by using the following device
A. Electroencephalogram
B. Sphygmomanometer
C. Centrifuge
D. Mammogram

408. Ligaments have no blood supply. This makes them
A. Avascular
B. Vascular
C. Serous
D. Elastic

409. Ribs eleven and twelve are also known as
A. True ribs
B. Floating ribs
C. Superior ribs
D. Levitating ribs

410. Mammary glands
A. Endocrine glands that produce and secrete milk
B. Exocrine glands that produce and secrete sebum
C. Exocrine glands that produce and secrete milk
D. Endocrine glands that produce and secrete sebum

411. Cartilaginous portion of an intervertebral disc
A. Annulus fibrosis
B. Nucleus pulposus
C. Dens
D. Vertebral facet

412. Part of the small intestine that attaches to the stomach via the pyloric sphincter
A. Cecum
B. Jejunum
C. Ileum
D. Duodenum

413. Rhythmic contractions occurring in the esophagus, stomach, small intestine, and large intestine, helping to move food through the alimentary canal
A. Peristalsis
B. Tetanus
C. Isotonic
D. Concentric

414. Spinal nerve plexus emerging from L1-S4
A. Brachial plexus
B. Cervical plexus
C. Lumbosacral plexus
D. Thoracic plexus

415. The limbic system controls the body's
A. Mood
B. Survival behaviors
C. Memory
D. Visual input

416. Ligaments
A. Connect bones to other bones to stabilize a joint
B. Connect muscles to bones to provide movement
C. Connect cartilage to muscles to provide protection
D. Connect muscles to tendons to prevent injuries

417. Last structure of the digestive tract, located anteriorly to the sacrum
A. Urethra
B. Rectum
C. Anus
D. Sigmoid colon

418. Muscle tone, coordination and balance is controlled by
A. Cerebrum
B. Pons
C. Cerebellum
D. Medulla oblongata

419. Structures located in the duodenum and jejunum that increase surface area, allowing for more abundant absorption of nutrients
A. Intestinal villi
B. Intestinal cilia
C. Duodenal fold
D. Circular folds

420. Cilia are hairlike structures located in the lining of the
A. Trachea
B. Alveoli
C. Stomach
D. Small intestine

421. The gallbladder
A. Filters out dead or dying red blood cells from the blood stream
B. Stores bilirubin and supplies bilirubin to the liver
C. Secretes insulin and glucagon into the duodenum
D. Stores bile and empties bile into the duodenum

422. Reception, conduction, transmission, and response are all responses when the body produces a
A. Bone
B. Contraction
C. Thought
D. Reflex

423. A neuron is what type of cell
A. Nerve
B. Skin
C. Muscle
D. Bone

424. Digestive enzyme produced by the liver, responsible for emulsification of lipids in the small intestine
A. Glucagon
B. Insulin
C. Bile
D. Amylase

425. The gallbladder is responsible for
A. Creating glucagon and emptying glucagon into the liver
B. Creating bile and emptying bile into the stomach
C. Storing insulin and emptying insulin into the duodenum
D. Storing bile and emptying bile into the duodenum

426. Photoreceptors detect
A. Taste
B. Smell
C. Sight
D. Sound

427. Skeletal muscle is controlled
A. Voluntarily
B. Involuntarily
C. Autonomically
D. Sympathetically

428. Primary functions of nervous tissue include all of the following except
A. Mental activity
B. Sensory reception
C. Stimulating muscle
D. Pumping blood

429. The circadian rhythm is regulated by
A. Prolactin
B. Melatonin
C. Estrogen
D. Testosterone

430. Loop of Henle is located in which part of the kidney
A. Cortex
B. Adrenal glands
C. Nephron
D. Renal papilla

431. Melatonin is produced by the
A. Pineal gland
B. Pituitary gland
C. Adrenal gland
D. Thalamus

432. There are how many bones in the ankle
A. Eight
B. Two
C. Seven
D. Five

433. The largest part of the brain is also known as
A. Cerebellum
B. Cerebrum
C. Spinal cord
D. Diencephalon

434. The stratum lucidum lies immediately superior to the
A. Stratum germinativum
B. Stratum corneum
C. Stratum spinosum
D. Stratum granulosum

435. Rods and cones are located in the
A. Iris
B. Cornea
C. Retina
D. Sclera

436. Blood passes from the right atrium into which chamber
A. Left ventricle
B. Left atrium
C. Right ventricle
D. Aorta

437. Arrector pili muscles attach to
A. Walls of intestines
B. Hair follicles
C. Hair shafts
D. Bronchial tubes

438. Which of the following is a function of connective tissue
A. Protection
B. Secretion
C. Absorption
D. Contraction

439. Renal pyramids are located in which portion of the kidney
A. Nephron
B. Cortex
C. Adrenal
D. Medulla

440. Upon opening, the esophageal sphincter allows food to move between the
A. Small intestine and large intestine
B. Esophagus and stomach
C. Stomach and small intestine
D. Pharynx and esophagus

441. The ACL, PCL, LCL, and MCL are all ligaments of the
A. Elbow
B. Ankle
C. Shoulder
D. Knee

442. Dead cells in the epidermis are located in which layer
A. Stratum basale
B. Stratum corneum
C. Stratum granulosum
D. Stratum spinosum

443. All of the following are cranial nerves that assist in movement of the eyeball and eyelids except
A. Oculomotor
B. Optic
C. Trochlear
D. Abducens

444. Sebum
A. Produced by salivary glands that empty into the oral cavity
B. Produced by sudoriferous glands that empty directly onto the skin
C. Produced by sebaceous glands that attach to hair
D. Produced by ceruminous glands that create ear wax

445. The dura mater is located directly superior to the
A. Brain
B. Pia mater
C. Cranium
D. Arachnoid

446. The cystic duct carries bile from the gallbladder to the
A. Pancreatic duct
B. Common bile duct
C. Jejunum
D. Ileum

447. The liver
A. Detoxifies harmful substances from the blood stream and secretes bile into the gallbladder
B. Produces insulin and regulates the amount of sugar in the blood stream
C. Produces pepsin and hydrochloric acid to aid in digestion of bolus
D. Absorbs water and nutrients into the blood stream

448. Release of urine from the bladder is controlled by which nervous system
A. Sympathetic
B. Parasympathetic
C. Fight or flight
D. Autonomic

449. Ligament connecting teeth to the mandible and maxilla
A. Periodontal
B. Cementum
C. Maxillary
D. Gingiva

450. Erythrocytes are also called
A. White blood cells
B. Red blood cells
C. Platelets
D. Plasma

451. Hair is made of which type of tissue
A. Muscular
B. Connective
C. Epithelial
D. Nervous

452. Another term for a blood clot within a blood vessel
A. Thrombus
B. Embolus
C. Aneurysm
D. Fibrin

453. Cranial nerve responsible for sending visual inputs to the brain
A. Optic
B. Oculomotor
C. Trigeminal
D. Olfactory

454. The trigeminal nerve branches into three divisions. These divisions are
A. Zygomatic, maxillary, optic
B. Mandibular, optic, nasal
C. Maxillary, mandibular, zygomatic
D. Maxillary, ophthalmic, mandibular

455. All of the following are formed by nervous tissue except
A. Brain
B. Spine
C. Spinal cord
D. Cerebellum

456. Thermoreceptors detect
A. Changes in chemical concentration
B. Pressure in blood vessels
C. Changes in temperature
D. Pain

457. An audiometer measures a person's ability to
A. Feel
B. Hear
C. Taste
D. See

458. Stimulation of the parasympathetic nervous system has what action on the digestive tract
A. Increases peristalsis
B. Shuts down peristalsis
C. Decreases absorption
D. Increases lymph circulation

459. Glucagon is a digestive enzyme produced by the pancreas responsible for
A. Decreasing glucose levels in the blood
B. Increasing glucose levels in the blood
C. Increasing potassium levels in the blood
D. Decreasing potassium levels in the blood

460. Sex cells are produced by which type of cell division
A. Fertilization
B. Mitosis
C. Meiosis
D. Zygote

461. The outer portion of a kidney is known as its
A. Medulla
B. Cortex
C. Cavity
D. Adrenal

462. Skeletal muscle is responsible for which actions
A. Protection and secretion
B. Beating the heart and transporting nutrients
C. Peristalsis and absorption
D. Moving the limbs and creating heat

463. The subclavian vein arises from the
A. Superior vena cava
B. Brachial vein
C. Aorta
D. Axillary vein

464. The anterior cruciate ligament connects the following bones
A. Ulna and humerus
B. Femur and fibula
C. Humerus and radius
D. Tibia and femur

465. The sclera is found in which part of the body
A. Eye
B. Ear
C. Oral cavity
D. Appendix

466. Myelin in the peripheral nervous system is produced by
A. Nodes of ranvier
B. Schwann cells
C. Axons
D. Neurons

467. Digestive enzyme responsible for increasing glucose levels in the blood
A. Bile
B. Insulin
C. Glucagon
D. Pepsin

468. Which of the following is not a type of lymphocyte
A. Natural killer cell
B. Neutrophil
C. T cell
D. B cell

469. Intermediate portion of the sternum, directly inferior to the manubrium
A. Body
B. Xiphoid process
C. Jugular notch
D. Costal cartilage

470. The medulla oblongata controls heart rate, blood vessel diameter, and
A. Release of growth hormone
B. Balance
C. Coordination
D. Sneezing

471. Glucagon is a digestive enzyme produced in the pancreas by
A. Alpha cells
B. Beta cells
C. Lymphatic tissue
D. Erythrocytes

472. Pressure felt in walls of arteries as blood passes through them
A. Arteriole
B. Diastolic
C. Systolic
D. Veinous

473. There are twelve bones in which region of the vertebral column
A. Sacral
B. Lumbar
C. Cervical
D. Thoracic

474. Involuntary reaction in response to a stimulus
A. Withdrawal
B. Contraction
C. Reflex
D. Regeneration

475. The heart contains how many chambers
A. Four
B. Two
C. Three
D. Five

476. The thymus produces
A. Thyroid hormones
B. T lymphocytes
C. Parathyroid hormones
D. Growth hormones

477. Major artery found in the anterior region of the thigh
A. External iliac
B. Great saphenous
C. Brachial
D. Femoral

478. Beta cells are responsible for creation of
A. Glucagon
B. Insulin
C. Bile
D. Keratin

479. Process that carries nerve impulses away from the neuron
A. Dendrite
B. Axon
C. Nucleus
D. Golgi apparatus

480. Blood returns to the heart from the trunk and lower limbs via the
A. Aorta
B. Superior vena cava
C. Inferior vena cava
D. Pulmonary vein

481. The nucleus pulposus of an intervertebral disc is surrounded by the
A. Vertebral body
B. Annulus fibrosis
C. Intervertebral ligaments
D. Dens

482. Vitamin B12 is primarily absorbed into the bloodstream by the
A. Duodenum
B. Jejunum
C. Ileum
D. Cecum

483. Layer of the meninges most responsible for protection of the brain and spinal cord
A. Epidural
B. Pia mater
C. Arachnoid
D. Dura mater

484. Which of the following is not a bone of the cranium
A. Mandible
B. Parietal
C. Occipital
D. Frontal

485. The jejunum connects to the liver via the
A. Renal artery
B. Hepatic portal vein
C. Gastric aorta
D. Pyloric sphincter

486. Cranial nerve connecting the eyeballs to the occipital lobe
A. Trochlear
B. Olfactory
C. Oculomotor
D. Optic

487. A callus is formed by the following layer of the epidermis
A. Stratum spinosum
B. Stratum granulosum
C. Stratum lucidum
D. Stratum basale

488. The primary ion in intercellular fluid is
A. Calcium
B. Sodium
C. Iron
D. Potassium

489. Prolactin, produced by the anterior pituitary, produces
A. Insulin
B. Milk
C. Glucagon
D. Estrogen

490. The cerebellum is formed by which type of tissue
A. Connective
B. Nervous
C. Epithelial
D. Muscular

491. Connective tissue holding bones together
A. Tendon
B. Ligament
C. Cartilage
D. Periosteum

492. Melanin
A. Provides pigmentation to the skin
B. Allows protection by producing a thickened area of skin
C. Waterproofs the skin
D. Allows absorption of water into the skin

493. The outer most membrane of a serous membrane is called
A. Peritoneal membrane
B. Visceral serous membrane
C. Temporal serous membrane
D. Parietal serous membrane

494. The definition of physiology is
A. Studying movement
B. Studying the structure of the body
C. Studying the cause of disease
D. Studying the function of the body

495. Structure bringing air into the lungs
A. Larynx
B. Pharynx
C. Trachea
D. Uvula

496. The ovaries produce
A. Luteinizing hormone
B. Testosterone
C. Progesterone
D. Melatonin

497. The inferior five pairs of ribs are also called
A. True ribs
B. False ribs
C. Superior ribs
D. Inferior ribs

498. Which part of a long bone is the diaphysis
A. Shaft
B. End
C. Articular surface
D. Growth plate

499. The lumbar region contains how many vertebrae
A. Seven
B. Twelve
C. Five
D. One

500. The urinary bladder is found in which body cavity
A. Cranial
B. Abdominal
C. Thoracic
D. Pelvic

501. Peristalsis takes place in all of the following organs except
A. Esophagus
B. Liver
C. Stomach
D. Large intestine

502. The phrenic nerve
A. Originates in the chest and innervates the digestive tract to allow peristalsis
B. Originates in the neck and innervates the heart to reduce heart rhythm
C. Originates in the neck and innervates the diaphragm to allow breathing
D. Originates in the head and innervates the tongue to allow speech

503. Most internal layer of a serous membrane
A. Deep serous membrane
B. Parietal serous membrane
C. Elastic serous membrane
D. Visceral serous membrane

504. Study of the function of the human body
A. Anatomy
B. Physiology
C. Pathology
D. Etiology

505. Amylase is located in the
A. Saliva
B. Stomach
C. Small intestine
D. Pancreas

506. Fatty material coating axons, assisting in quick transport of nerve impulses
A. Adipose
B. Dendrite
C. Cytoplasm
D. Myelin

507. Vitamin responsible for absorption of calcium by the bones
A. Vitamin D
B. Vitamin A
C. Vitamin C
D. Vitamin B2

508. The nerve primarily responsible for control of the parasympathetic nervous system is
A. Hypoglossal
B. Trigeminal
C. Vagus
D. Phrenic

509. The pancreatic duct enters the following structure to aid in digestion
A. Duodenum
B. Jejunum
C. Stomach
D. Gallbladder

510. Vein returning blood to the heart from the head and upper limbs
A. Superior vena cava
B. Inferior vena cava
C. Aorta
D. Pulmonary vein

511. Digestive enzyme responsible for lowering blood glucose levels
A. Glucagon
B. Insulin
C. Bile
D. Pepsin

512. Heart activity is detected via an
A. Ophthalmoscope
B. Electroencephalogram
C. Audiometer
D. Electrocardiogram

513. All of the following are regulated by the temporal lobe except
A. Hearing
B. Smell
C. Vision
D. Memory

514. An electroencephalogram measures
A. Headaches
B. Blood pressure
C. Muscle tension
D. Brain wave activity

515. Vein found in the region of the arm
A. Femoral vein
B. Brachial vein
C. Great saphenous vein
D. Axillary vein

516. The shaft of a long bone is also called
A. Periosteum
B. Epiphysis
C. Metaphysis
D. Diaphysis

517. Substance found in erythrocytes which attaches to oxygen and carbon dioxide, allowing transport of these molecules to parts of the body
A. Platelets
B. Leukocyte
C. Anemia
D. Hemoglobin

518. Structure in a nephron responsible for reabsorption of electrolytes
A. Renal tubules
B. Collecting duct
C. Adrenal glands
D. Cortex

519. The frontal lobe is responsible for controlling and interpreting
A. Motivation
B. Vision
C. Balance
D. Memory

520. Muscle found in the skin is also known as
A. Interdermal muscle
B. Epidermal muscle
C. Arrector pili
D. Papillary muscle

521. Function of non-striated muscle in the digestive tract
A. Contracting skeletal muscle
B. Absorbing nutrients
C. Transporting blood
D. Peristalsis

522. Ureters connect which two structures together
A. Liver and gallbladder
B. Bladder and urethra
C. Small intestine and pancreas
D. Kidneys and bladder

523. The sympathetic nervous response causes an increase in heart rate, which is caused by an increase in which hormone in the body
A. Dopamine
B. Norepinephrine
C. Melatonin
D. Epinephrine

524. Cranial nerve which branches into the ophthalmic, maxillary, and mandibular divisions
A. Vagus
B. Facial
C. Vestibulocochlear
D. Trigeminal

525. The inner portion of a kidney is called
A. Medulla
B. Cortex
C. Oblongata
D. Adrenal

526. Mesentery is part of which serous membrane
A. Pleural
B. Pericardium
C. Peritoneal
D. Meninges

527. Gelatinous center of an intervertebral disc
A. Dens
B. Annulus fibrosis
C. Nucleus pulposus
D. Vertebral canal

528. Type of tissue that forms exocrine glands
A. Connective
B. Epithelial
C. Nervous
D. Muscular

529. Location of the sinoatrial node
A. Left ventricle
B. Right ventricle
C. Left atrium
D. Right atrium

530. A neutrophil is what type of cell
A. Leukocyte
B. Osteocyte
C. Squamous cell
D. Epithelium

531. Meissner's corpuscles detect
A. Smell
B. Deep pressure
C. Pain
D. Light pressure

532. Urea and ammonia are filtered from the blood by the
A. Large intestine
B. Bladder
C. Kidneys
D. Spleen

533. Which of the following is not regulated by the frontal lobe
A. Aggression
B. Olfactory reception
C. Visual input
D. Language

534. Alpha waves are seen in a person who is
A. Awake and unconscious
B. Awake and relaxed
C. Asleep and conscious
D. Asleep and unconscious

535. Bile is produced by the
A. Gallbladder
B. Liver
C. Stomach
D. Pancreas

536. Function of the kidneys
A. Regulation of electrolytes
B. Absorption of nutrients from food
C. Eliminating waste
D. Excretion of carbon dioxide

537. Oxygen, upon entering the bloodstream, attaches to an iron compound known as
A. Leukocyte
B. Plasma
C. Thrombocyte
D. Hemoglobin

538. Theta waves are typically only seen in
A. Elderly
B. Adults
C. Cats
D. Children

539. The tricuspid valve is located between which two structures
A. Left ventricle and aorta
B. Left atrium and left ventricle
C. Stomach and esophagus
D. Right atrium and right ventricle

540. Tubes that connect the kidneys to the urinary bladder
A. Ureters
B. Urethra
C. Biliary duct
D. Collecting duct

541. A bolus is found in all of the following parts of the digestive tract except
A. Pharynx
B. Large intestine
C. Stomach
D. Esophagus

542. The hypothalamus controls which other important gland in the body
A. Pituitary
B. Adrenal
C. Thymus
D. Parathyroids

543. Secretion is performed by which structures in the body
A. Muscles
B. Bones
C. Glands
D. Nerves

544. Relaxation of cardiac muscle results in which pressure felt in arterial walls
A. Pulmonary
B. Systolic
C. Venous
D. Diastolic

545. Part of the brain stem that allows communication between the cerebrum and cerebellum
A. Midbrain
B. Pons
C. Medulla oblongata
D. Diencephalon

546. Chyme moves from the stomach through the pyloric sphincter into the
A. Ileum
B. Jejunum
C. Duodenum
D. Cecum

547. The large intestine
A. Digests and breaks down food
B. Absorbs nutrients from chyme
C. Eliminates waste and absorbs water from fecal matter
D. Reabsorbs electrolytes into the blood stream

548. The sublingual salivary glands are located beneath the
A. Ears
B. Tongue
C. Nose
D. Mandible

549. Which of the following is a characteristic of muscle tissue
A. Sensibility
B. Protectability
C. Elasticity
D. Absorbability

550. Milk is produced by the mammary glands, which are stimulated by
A. Estrogen
B. Prolactin
C. Testosterone
D. Growth hormone

551. Another name for thrombocytes is
A. Red blood cells
B. Platelets
C. White blood cells
D. Plasma

552. Upon stimulation of the sympathetic nervous response, the following reaction takes place in the heart
A. No change
B. Decreased heart rate
C. Increased heart rate
D. Cardiac arrest

553. Folds of the peritoneum that provide organs in the abdomen with nerve and blood supply
A. Smooth muscle
B. Diaphragm
C. Mesentery
D. Pericardium

554. Epidermal layer lying superficial to the stratum spinosum
A. Stratum granulosum
B. Stratum basale
C. Stratum lucidum
D. Stratum germinativum

555. Pacinian corpuscles are proprioceptors that detect
A. Deep pressure
B. Light pressure
C. Pain
D. Temperature

556. The pulmonary arteries carry
A. Deoxygenated blood
B. Oxygenated blood
C. Clotted blood
D. No blood

557. Contraction of the cardiac muscle in the following chamber sends blood out of the heart to the rest of the body
A. Left atrium
B. Right ventricle
C. Right atrium
D. Left ventricle

558. The sacrum articulates with which bone of the pelvis
A. Pubis
B. Ischium
C. Ilium
D. Femur

559. Red blood cells contain hemoglobin. Hemoglobin is made of
A. Iron
B. Calcium
C. Sodium
D. Potassium

560. Epinephrine and norepinephrine are produced by the
A. Thalamus
B. Pineal gland
C. Pituitary gland
D. Adrenal glands

561. The organization of a structure in the body
A. Organ → Tissue → Cell
B. Cell → Tissue → Organ
C. Cell → Organ → Tissue
D. Tissue → Cell → Organ

562. Epithelial tissue is found in all of the following parts of the body except
A. Skin
B. Lungs
C. Heart
D. Intestines

563. The most abundant type of cell in blood
A. Leukocytes
B. Erythrocytes
C. Thrombocytes
D. Platelets

564. Another name for smooth muscle is
A. Non-striated
B. Striated
C. Branching
D. Skeletal

565. Bone located in the thigh
A. Tibia
B. Femur
C. Fibula
D. Talus

566. Lipids are broken down into the following due to digestive enzymes
A. Glycerol
B. Amino acids
C. Fructose
D. Galactose

567. The most superficial and thickest layer of the meninges which comes into contact with the cranium
A. Dura mater
B. Pia mater
C. Arachnoid
D. Dermis

568. Bone located in the leg
A. Fibula
B. Femur
C. Navicular
D. Hallux

569. The liver produces and stores
A. Epinephrine
B. Hemoglobin
C. Vitamin B12
D. Vitamin A

570. Which of the following type of muscle tissue is found in the heart
A. Skeletal
B. Cardiac
C. Smooth
D. Pyloric

571. Endocrine glands are
A. Structures that create and secrete saliva into the oral cavity
B. Structures that create and secrete sweat onto the skin
C. Structures that create and secrete hormones into the blood
D. Structures that create and secrete sebum onto hair and skin

572. The epidermis lies immediately superficial to the
A. Subcutaneous layer
B. Hair
C. Dermis
D. Bone

573. Skeletal muscle is also called
A. Striated
B. Branching
C. Non-striated
D. Smooth

574. Proteins are broken down into the following via digestive enzymes
A. Glucose
B. Amino acids
C. Lipids
D. Fructose

575. Bacteria and the toxins produced by bacteria are destroyed by which of the following types of lymphocyte after they secrete antibodies to fight the infection
A. Eosinophils
B. T cells
C. Natural killer cells
D. B cells

576. Protein found in plasma, synthesized in the liver
A. T cell
B. Iron
C. Albumin
D. Fibrin

577. Blood that enters the left atrium from the pulmonary veins contains an abundance of
A. Hormones
B. Carbon dioxide
C. Oxygen
D. Calcium

578. Sensory receptor that detects pain
A. Baroreceptor
B. Nociceptor
C. Chemoreceptor
D. Proprioceptor

579. Most inferior portion of the sternum
A. Manubrium
B. Body
C. Xiphoid process
D. Jugular notch

580. Pennate and spiral are both types of
A. Muscles
B. Nerves
C. Organs
D. Connective tissue

581. Type of tissue containing very little extracellular material
A. Nervous
B. Muscular
C. Connective
D. Epithelial

582. Part of the brain split into two hemispheres
A. Cerebellum
B. Cerebrum
C. Brain stem
D. Diencephalon

583. Structure located between the pharynx and trachea
A. Uvula
B. Larynx
C. Tongue
D. Bronchus

584. The four regions of the lower limb
A. Femur, tibia, calcaneus, hallux
B. Thigh, leg, ankle, foot
C. Thigh, shin, ankle, foot
D. Leg, calf, ankle, foot

585. Blood passes from the right ventricle into the following blood vessel on its way to the lungs for oxygenation
A. Aorta
B. Pulmonary veins
C. Vena cava
D. Pulmonary arteries

586. Sphincter located between the small intestine and large intestine
A. Ileocecal
B. Pyloric
C. Cardiac
D. Esophageal

587. Gland controlled by the hypothalamus, which it lies beneath
A. Thymus
B. Pineal
C. Pituitary
D. Parathyroids

588. Mast cells release what substance into an area of injury or infection
A. Hormones
B. Histamine
C. Neutrophil
D. Eosinophil

589. T lymphocytes are produced by the
A. Hypothalamus
B. Thymus
C. Thyroid
D. Pituitary

590. Nutrients are mainly absorbed into the blood stream and lymphatic vessels in the following part of the small intestine
A. Duodenum
B. Ileum
C. Jejunum
D. Cecum

591. Sebum is produced by which type of gland
A. Mammary
B. Sudoriferous
C. Adrenal
D. Sebaceous

592. The left ventricle is located directly inferior to
A. Bicuspid valve
B. Tricuspid valve
C. Right atrium
D. Right ventricle

593. The central nervous system contains all of the following structures except
A. Spinal cord
B. Brain
C. Nerves
D. Medulla oblongata

594. Rods and cones are examples of
A. Mechanoreceptors
B. Photoreceptors
C. Thermoreceptors
D. Chemoreceptors

595. Food moves from the small intestine into the following part of the large intestine
A. Sigmoid colon
B. Ascending colon
C. Cecum
D. Transverse colon

596. What substance moves through the ileocecal sphincter
A. Bile
B. Feces
C. Bolus
D. Chyme

597. Skeletal muscle attaches to what structures in the body
A. Cartilage
B. Ligaments
C. Bones
D. Skin

598. Certain leukocytes perform phagocytosis, which is when cells perform what action
A. Eat substances
B. Absorb nutrients
C. Move from an area of high concentration to an area of low concentration
D. Transportation of oxygen and carbon dioxide

599. Substance found in erythrocytes, made of iron
A. Plasma
B. Hemoglobin
C. Platelets
D. Thrombocytes

600. Another name for cardiac muscle is
A. Smooth
B. Striated
C. Non-striated
D. Branching

601. The cervical vertebrae contains how many bones
A. Twelve
B. Seven
C. Five
D. One

602. Serous membranes
A. Secrete synovial fluid into a joint cavity to lubricate a joint
B. Are filled with interstitial fluid to fight disease
C. Separate organs to prevent friction
D. Surround fasciculi in muscle tissue

603. Functions of muscle tissue include all of the following except
A. Diffusion
B. Heat production
C. Movement
D. Transportation

604. Peripheral nervous system
A. Contains the medulla oblongata which regulates the vital functions of the body
B. Contains the cerebellum which provides balance and coordination
C. Contains the spinal cord which allows nerves to communicate with the brain
D. Contains spinal nerves that innervate muscles

605. The skin produces the following type of vitamin
A. Vitamin K
B. Vitamin A
C. Vitamin D
D. Vitamin B12

606. Type of lymphocyte that can recognize pathogens
A. B cell
B. T cell
C. Natural killer cell
D. Monocyte

607. Intrinsic factor is secreted by the
A. Liver
B. Pancreas
C. Stomach
D. Gallbladder

608. The epiglottis
A. Allows food to move from the mouth into the pharynx
B. Allows food to move from the pharynx into the esophagus
C. Prevents food from moving from the pharynx into the nasal sinus
D. Prevents food and liquid from moving into the larynx upon swallowing

609. The pyloric sphincter is located between which two structures
A. Stomach and small intestine
B. Stomach and esophagus
C. Pancreas and small intestine
D. Small intestine and large intestine

610. Spinal nerve plexus emerging from C5-T1
A. Lumbar plexus
B. Cervical plexus
C. Brachial plexus
D. Sacral plexus

611. Function of cardiac muscle
A. Movement
B. Heat creation
C. Peristalsis
D. Transportation

612. The four bones that make up the pelvic girdle are
A. Ilium, femur, pubis, sacrum
B. Ilium, ischium, pubis, sacrum
C. Sacrum, coccyx, ilium, ischium
D. Pubis, ischium, sacrum, coccyx

613. Arrector pili muscle is located where
A. Stomach
B. Eyes
C. Skin
D. Large intestine

614. Non-striated muscle tissue is also called
A. Smooth
B. Skeletal
C. Cardiac
D. Branching

615. An eosinophil is a type of
A. Erythrocyte
B. Leukocyte
C. Monocyte
D. Osteocyte

616. A synapse is
A. Where two or more neurons meet
B. Where the brain meets the cerebellum
C. Where a dendrite meets a cell body
D. Where a nerve cell body meets an axon

617. The thymus produces what
A. Growth hormone
B. Adrenaline
C. Estrogen
D. T lymphocytes

618. The rest and digest response is also known as
A. Peripheral
B. Sympathetic
C. Parasympathetic
D. Fight or flight

619. Contraction of the ventricles of the heart results in which type of pressure felt in the walls of arteries
A. Systolic
B. Diastolic
C. Venous
D. Pulmonary

620. Antibodies play what role in the body's defense against pathogens
A. Destroy foreign substances
B. Engulf particles
C. Carrier cells for immunity
D. Create leukocytes

621. Which of the following structures is formed by epithelial tissue
A. Cerebellum
B. Skeletal muscle
C. Tendon
D. Epidermis

622. Parathyroid hormone increases concentration of what substance in the bloodstream
A. Sodium
B. Calcium
C. Magnesium
D. Potassium

623. Storage of urine is found in the
A. Kidneys
B. Gallbladder
C. Bladder
D. Urethra

624. Sebaceous glands connect to
A. Arrector pili
B. Hair follicles
C. Skin openings
D. Kidneys

625. Duct connecting the gallbladder to the liver
A. Bile duct
B. Hepatocystic duct
C. Pancreatic duct
D. Pyloric duct

626. Which type of muscle tissue is controlled voluntarily
A. Epithelial
B. Cardiac
C. Smooth
D. Skeletal

627. Pain is detected by
A. Photoreceptors
B. Baroreceptors
C. Mechanoreceptors
D. Nociceptors

628. Substance produced by the liver which aids in the digestion of lipids
A. Bile
B. Vitamin A
C. Insulin
D. Glucagon

629. Structure in the throat providing vibration of air to produce voice
A. Trachea
B. Pharynx
C. Esophagus
D. Larynx

630. Layer of the epidermis that contains keratin
A. Stratum spinosum
B. Stratum germinativum
C. Stratum lucidum
D. Stratum corneum

631. Urea, ammonia, and creatinine are filtered from the body and form
A. Urine
B. Sweat
C. Oil
D. Feces

632. Another name for cell division
A. Contracture
B. Splitting
C. Meiosis
D. Mitosis

633. Food passes from the stomach into the small intestine through which structure
A. Cardiac sphincter
B. Pyloric sphincter
C. Esophageal sphincter
D. Ileocecal sphincter

634. Parasympathetic nervous system
A. Is involuntary and allows digestion of food
B. Is voluntary and decreases heart rate and blood pressure
C. Is involuntary and increases heart rate and blood pressure
D. Is voluntary and decreases food digestion

635. Layer of epidermis primarily responsible for protecting the body against bacteria
A. Stratum corneum
B. Stratum germinativum
C. Stratum spinosum
D. Stratum granulosum

636. All of the following are nerves that emerge from the medulla oblongata except
A. Accessory
B. Vagus
C. Trigeminal
D. Glossopharangeal

637. An eletroencephalogram measures
A. Muscle contractions
B. Heart rhythm
C. Blood pressure
D. Brain wave activity

638. Digestive enzymes break down the following into glucose, fructose, and galactose
A. Carbohydrates
B. Amino acids
C. Protein
D. Lipids

639. Spinal nerves and cranial nerves are both part of which division of the nervous system
A. Parasympathetic
B. Central
C. Sympathetic
D. Peripheral

640. The primary electrolyte in extracellular fluid is
A. Sodium
B. Calcium
C. Potassium
D. Iron

641. Endocrine glands secrete their substances where
A. Into the respiratory passages
B. Onto a surface
C. Into the blood
D. Into the digestive organs

642. From deep to superficial, the order of the meninges
A. Dura mater, pia mater, arachnoid
B. Dura mater, arachnoid, pia mater
C. Arachnoid, pia mater, dura mater
D. Pia mater, arachnoid, dura mater

643. Pulmonary veins carry
A. Carbon dioxide
B. Deoxygenated blood
C. Oxygenated blood
D. Hormones

644. Upon exhalation, the diaphragm moves in which direction
A. Inferiorly
B. Superiorly
C. Anteriorly
D. Posteriorly

645. The superior angle of the stomach is known as the
A. Fundus
B. Cardia
C. Pylorus
D. Antrum

646. The inferior chambers of the heart are known as
A. Atria
B. Ventricles
C. Vena Cava
D. Aorta

647. A bolus moves from the mouth to the esophagus through the
A. Trachea
B. Pharynx
C. Larynx
D. Stomach

648. Hormone responsible for increasing heart rate and moving blood from digestive organs into the muscles
A. Aldosterone
B. Oxytocin
C. Growth hormone
D. Norepinephrine

649. Ceruminous glands secrete
A. Sweat
B. Ear wax
C. Oil
D. Hormones

650. Periosteum
A. Surrounds the heart
B. Surrounds the epiphysis of a long bone
C. Covers articular surface of bones to prevent friction
D. Surrounds the shaft of long bones

651. When a person is in a mentally alert state, the brain waves being exhibited are
A. Alpha waves
B. Beta waves
C. Theta waves
D. Delta waves

652. The most abundant form of connective tissue found in the body
A. Fascia
B. Bone
C. Cartilage
D. Blood

653. Sudoriferous glands
A. Produce ear wax
B. Protect the body from microorganisms
C. Regulate temperature within the body
D. Aid in digestion by producing saliva

654. Contraction of the ventricles causes
A. Systole
B. Diastole
C. Dilation
D. Embolism

655. The pancreas empties its secretions into the duodenum and they mix with
A. Feces
B. Bolus
C. Chyme
D. Water

656. Hormone produced by the adrenal gland
A. Luteinizing hormone
B. Norepinephrine
C. Estrogen
D. Testosterone

657. An egg cell and sperm cell, when joined together, form what
A. DNA
B. Zygote
C. RNA
D. Nucleus

658. The hippocampus
A. Stimulates the hypothalamus to control the pituitary gland
B. Controls the interpretation of smell
C. Receives visual input
D. Helps to form new memories

659. The left atrium receives blood from the
A. Pulmonary arteries
B. Pulmonary veins
C. Superior vena cava
D. Inferior vena cava

660. Hair is made of
A. Melanin
B. Epidermis
C. Keratin
D. Sebum

661. The trachea is also known as
A. Windpipe
B. Lung
C. Throat
D. Voice box

662. Perirenal fat surrounds
A. Gallbladder
B. Liver
C. Spleen
D. Kidneys

663. Food moves through the large intestine in the following order
A. Sigmoid colon, descending colon, transverse colon, ascending colon, cecum
B. Ascending colon, transverse colon, descending colon, sigmoid colon, cecum
C. Descending colon, ascending colon, cecum, sigmoid colon, transverse colon
D. Cecum, ascending colon, transverse colon, descending colon, sigmoid colon

664. Function of insulin
A. Digestion of glucose
B. Absorption of glucose
C. Absorption of lipids
D. Elimination of wastes

665. Clotting factors produced by the liver include
A. Prothrombin and fibrinogen
B. Fibrinogen and hemoglobin
C. Hemoglobin and prothrombin
D. Fibrinogen and plasma

666. The oculomotor, trochlear, and abducens nerves all help to control the movement of the
A. Eyes
B. Nose
C. Tongue
D. Ears

667. Aged red blood cells are destroyed in the following organ
A. Liver
B. Stomach
C. Pancreas
D. Spleen

668. Pressure felt in the walls of arteries when blood is not passing through
A. Systolic
B. Diastolic
C. Venous
D. Cardiac

669. Synovial fluid is secreted into a joint by
A. Articular cartilage
B. Joint capsule
C. Synovial membrane
D. Bone

670. The femur connects to the tibia via the
A. Anterior cruciate ligament
B. Meniscus
C. Articular cartilage
D. Interosseous membrane

671. Efferent impulses are carried along which type of axon
A. Afferent
B. Sensory
C. Motor
D. Ocular

672. Order of the structures of the respiratory passage from superior to inferior
A. Bronchus, larynx, trachea, pharynx
B. Pharynx, larynx, trachea, bronchus
C. Larynx, pharynx, trachea, bronchus
D. Trachea, pharynx, larynx, bronchus

673. Photoreceptors send visual input to the
A. Optic nerve
B. Trigeminal nerve
C. Oculomotor nerve
D. Abducens nerve

674. During the fight or flight response, what body function shuts down
A. Movement
B. Circulation
C. Respiration
D. Digestion

675. Of the following types of leukocytes, which arrives at the site of bacterial infection first
A. Neutrophils
B. Eosinophils
C. Monocytes
D. Basophils

676. Nociceptors detect which sensation
A. Temperature
B. Pain
C. Light pressure
D. Deep pressure

677. Stratum granulosum is responsible for production of
A. Keratin
B. Melanin
C. Pigment
D. Oil

678. Type of metal vital in the formation of hemoglobin
A. Tin
B. Aluminum
C. Iron
D. Steel

679. Pressure felt as blood passes through an artery
A. Diastolic
B. Systolic
C. Venous
D. Cardiac

680. Bile aids in the digestion of
A. Lipids
B. Glucose
C. Carbohydrates
D. Protein

681. The pylorus is found at the exit of what organ
A. Small intestine
B. Stomach
C. Large intestine
D. Esophagus

682. Sympathetic nervous system
A. Is voluntary and increases heart rate and blood pressure
B. Is involuntary and increases heart rate and blood pressure
C. Is involuntary and decreases heart rate and blood pressure
D. Is voluntary and decreases heart rate and blood pressure

683. Lungs and kidneys are both examples of
A. Paired organs
B. Digestive organs
C. Respiratory organs
D. Urinary organs

684. Tissue responsible for separating tissues from each other
A. Nervous
B. Epithelial
C. Muscular
D. Connective

685. Cerebrospinal fluid is located between which two layers of the meninges
A. Dura mater and pia mater
B. Arachnoid and pia mater
C. Dura mater and arachnoid
D. Pia mater and dura mater

686. The three types of muscle tissue are
A. Striated, dense, cardiac
B. Skeletal, cardiac, epithelial
C. Epithelial, smooth, branching
D. Skeletal, cardiac, smooth

687. Hemoglobin is a substance made of iron, located where
A. Erythrocytes
B. Leukocytes
C. Lymph
D. Thrombocytes

688. All of the following are organs of the digestive system except
A. Pancreas
B. Stomach
C. Liver
D. Kidneys

689. Type of muscle tissue attaching to bones
A. Elastic
B. Branching
C. Striated
D. Smooth

690. The oral cavity contains all of the following structures except
A. Epiglottis
B. Tongue
C. Teeth
D. Salivary glands

691. Eccentric contraction
A. Muscle length decreases and muscle tension increases
B. Muscle length increases and muscle tension remains constant
C. Muscle length remains constant and muscle tension increases
D. Muscle length decreases and muscle tension remains constant

692. Luteinizing hormone stimulates the production of what substance
A. Progesterone
B. Epinephrine
C. Norepinephrine
D. Melatonin

693. Hormones produced by endocrine glands primarily affect which body system
A. Nervous
B. Digestive
C. Integumentary
D. Lymphatic

694. Pressure felt in large blood vessels is detected by
A. Thermoreceptors
B. Chemoreceptors
C. Baroreceptors
D. Nociceptors

695. Cerumen is located in the
A. Ear
B. Nose
C. Gallbladder
D. Liver

696. Order of the brain stem from superior to inferior
A. Midbrain, medulla oblongata, pons
B. Medulla oblongata, pons, midbrain
C. Pons, medulla oblongata, midbrain
D. Midbrain, pons, medulla oblongata

697. Cartilage found covering the surface of articulating bones
A. Dense
B. Elastic
C. Hyaline
D. Loose

698. A ring-like band of muscle found in the digestive tract between organs
A. Sphincter
B. Cardiac
C. Valve
D. Skeletal

699. The superior heart chambers are known as
A. Ventricles
B. Atria
C. Vena Cava
D. Aorta

700. The aorta carries blood to the liver via the
A. Carotid artery
B. Renal artery
C. Hepatic artery
D. Pulmonary artery

701. Fibrinogen and prothrombin are produced by
A. Gallbladder
B. Spleen
C. Liver
D. Appendix

702. Ligament connecting the anterior superior iliac spine to the pubis
A. Inguinal ligament
B. Sacrotuberous ligament
C. Iliolumbar ligament
D. Sacroiliac ligament

703. Glands are made of which type of tissue
A. Nervous
B. Connective
C. Muscular
D. Epithelial

704. Layer of epidermis lying immediately deep to the stratum corneum
A. Stratum granulosum
B. Stratum basale
C. Stratum spinosum
D. Stratum lucidum

705. Apocrine sweat glands
A. Are located in areas such as the armpits and groin
B. Are located in the dermis and attach to hair shafts
C. Are located in the ear canal and produce ear wax
D. Are located in the head and produce saliva

706. Ureters transport what substance
A. Blood
B. Urine
C. Lymph
D. Feces

707. Order of the parts of the sternum from superior to inferior
A. Body, manubrium, xiphoid process
B. Xiphoid process, body, manubrium
C. Manubrium, body, xiphoid process
D. Manubrium, xiphoid process, body

708. The lungs
A. Exchange oxygen and carbon monoxide in the blood
B. Exchange sodium and potassium in the blood
C. Exchange oxygen and carbon dioxide in the blood
D. Exchange nitrogen and carbon monoxide in the blood

709. Type of gland found in the skin that produces sweat
A. Sudoriferous
B. Sebaceous
C. Mammary
D. Thymus

710. The superior vena cava returns blood to the heart from which location
A. Legs
B. Head
C. Trunk
D. Groin

711. An ophthalmoscope is used to view the inside of a person's
A. Eyeball
B. Large intestine
C. Mouth
D. Ear

712. The nucleus pulposus is located in
A. Stratum germinativum
B. Vertebral bodies
C. Squamous epithelium
D. Intervertebral discs

713. Monocytes, when entering into an area of infection, become
A. Basophils
B. Macrophages
C. Neutrophils
D. T cells

714. The four types of tissue found in the body are
A. Muscular, smooth, skeletal, cardiac
B. Epithelial, connective, nervous, muscular
C. Epithelial, skeletal, connective, nervous
D. Connective, epithelial, nervous, smooth

715. The hepatic portal vein brings blood to the liver from the
A. Brain
B. Heart
C. Lungs
D. Abdomen

716. Blood cell responsible for transport of oxygen and carbon dioxide throughout the body
A. Leukocyte
B. Erythrocyte
C. Thrombocyte
D. Plasma

717. Glomeruli are responsible for
A. Excreting waste from the body
B. Secreting hormones into the blood
C. Filtering waste into the kidneys
D. Eliminating waste via the lungs

718. Glands located in the lateral superior edge of the orbital socket
A. Lacrimal glands
B. Parotid glands
C. Sublingual glands
D. Eccrine glands

719. Digestive enzyme located in the stomach that aids in breaking down food into usable parts for absorption
A. Insulin
B. Bile
C. Bilirubin
D. Pepsin

720. Histamine is released by which of the following cells
A. Neutrophils
B. Mast cells
C. Monocytes
D. B cells

721. Which of the following types of muscle is involuntary
A. Epithelial
B. Skeletal
C. Striated
D. Non-striated

722. Vitamin A is produced and stored by the
A. Gallbladder
B. Liver
C. Spleen
D. Small intestine

723. The three parts of the brain stem
A. Medulla oblongata, pons, midbrain
B. Midbrain, cerebellum, pons
C. Medulla oblongata, cerebellum, midbrain
D. Pons, medulla oblongata, cerebrum

724. The most inferior portion of the brain stem
A. Midbrain
B. Pons
C. Medulla oblongata
D. Diencephalon

725. Which of the following is not a main group of food
A. Lipids
B. Protein
C. Carbohydrates
D. Insulin

726. Which of the following is a function of connective tissue
A. Absorb nutrients
B. Hold structures together
C. Sensory input
D. Regulation of hormones

727. Sebaceous glands produce what substance
A. Oil
B. Sweat
C. Milk
D. Epinephrine

728. The smallest type of blood vessel
A. Capillary
B. Artery
C. Vein
D. Arteriole

729. Secretion of testosterone is controlled by
A. Luteinizing hormone
B. Estrogen
C. Growth hormone
D. Antidiuretic hormone

730. Urine flows from the kidneys through the ureters on its way to the
A. Urethra
B. Bladder
C. Bloodstream
D. Liver

731. Structure attached to the ileum
A. Cardia
B. Pylorus
C. Cecum
D. Duodenum

732. Neutrophils perform
A. Attack tumors
B. Pinocytosis
C. Histamine release
D. Phagocytosis

733. Which of the following is considered one of the four types of tissue in the body
A. Nervous
B. Smooth
C. Skeletal
D. Hair

734. Avascular tissue responsible for protection, secretion, and absorption
A. Muscular
B. Connective
C. Epithelium
D. Nervous

735. Which of the following is not a function of glial cells
A. Transport of cerebrospinal fluid
B. Electrolyte maintenance between nerve cells
C. Protection from microorganisms
D. Creation of myelin

736. Tears are produced by
A. Lacrimal glands
B. Salivary glands
C. Sudoriferous glands
D. Eccrine glands

737. Estrogen and progesterone are produced by the
A. Testes
B. Hypothalamus
C. Adrenal glands
D. Ovaries

738. Connective tissue
A. Transmits electrical impulses throughout the body
B. Contracts and produces heat
C. Separates tissues from each other
D. Absorbs substances and protects against microorganisms

739. The kidneys
A. Reabsorbs urea into the blood stream and removes water
B. Eliminates waste from the bladder
C. Filter waste from the blood and reabsorb substances into the body
D. Produces norepinephrine to assist with the sympathetic nervous response

740. Action potentials are
A. Neurotransmitters
B. Hormones
C. Sensory receptors
D. Electric impulses

741. The pulmonary valve
A. Allows blood to move from the left ventricle into the pulmonary artery
B. Allows blood to move from the right ventricle into the pulmonary artery
C. Allows blood to move from the right ventricle into the aorta
D. Allows blood to move from the left ventricle into the aorta

742. The thoracic body cavity
A. Contains the liver, stomach, small intestine, large intestine, pancreas, spleen, and gallbladder
B. Is separated from the dorsal body cavity via the diaphragm
C. Contains the lungs, heart, and major blood vessels
D. Holds the spleen against the stomach to prevent rupture of the spleen

743. Exocrine glands secrete their substances where
A. Onto a surface
B. Into the blood
C. Onto the brain
D. Inside the ear

744. Ligament connecting the sacrum to the ischial tuberosity
A. Iliolumbar ligament
B. Sacrotuberous ligament
C. Supraspinous ligament
D. Sacrospinous ligament

745. Phagocytosis is performed by
A. Basophils
B. Neutrophils
C. Histamines
D. T cells

746. Delta waves occur when a person is in what mental state
A. Nervous
B. Alert
C. Relaxed
D. Asleep

747. The small intestine
A. Breaks down food into usable parts for absorption
B. Absorbs water from feces and eliminates waste
C. Absorbs nutrients from chyme into the blood
D. Transports food from the mouth to the stomach

748. A sphygmomanometer measures
A. Muscle cramping
B. Blood pressure
C. Tidal volume
D. Circulation

749. The metaphysis is located between the diaphysis and
A. Periosteum
B. Articular cartilage
C. Epiphyseal plate
D. Epiphysis

750. The center of an intervertebral disc is known as
A. Nucleus pulposus
B. Annulus fibrosis
C. Intervertebral facet
D. Gelatinous nucleus

751. The pyloric sphinter connects the small intestine to the
A. Gallbladder
B. Pancreas
C. Stomach
D. Large intestine

752. Layer of the meninges immediately deep to the arachnoid
A. Dermis
B. Dura mater
C. Cranium
D. Pia mater

753. Prolactin is a hormone that affects which glands
A. Adrenal
B. Mammary
C. Sebaceous
D. Parathyroids

754. Which of the following part of blood is responsible for clotting of the blood in response to physical trauma
A. White blood cells
B. Red blood cells
C. Platelets
D. Plasma

755. The liver converts glucose into
A. Glycogen
B. Insulin
C. Glucagon
D. Carbohydrates

756. The emotion of fear is regulated by the
A. Hypothalamus
B. Amygdala
C. Occipital lobe
D. Hippocampus

757. Branching processes emerging from a cell body of a neuron
A. Schwann cells
B. Axon
C. Nucleus
D. Dendrites

758. Striated muscle is also called
A. Skeletal
B. Cardiac
C. Smooth
D. Branching

759. Alveoli are located at the ends of
A. Pulmonary veins
B. Bronchial tubes
C. Bronchioles
D. Trachea

760. Before entering an area of infection, mast cells are known as
A. Neutrophils
B. Basophils
C. Monocytes
D. Lymphocytes

761. The bones of the ankle are also called
A. Tibia and fibula
B. Carpals
C. Metatarsals
D. Tarsals

762. Sphincter located between the esophagus and stomach
A. Pyloric
B. Esophageal
C. Cardiac
D. Ileocecal

763. Melatonin levels in the body fluctuate in response to the
A. Circadian rhythm
B. Heart rhythm
C. Circulatory system
D. Lymphatic system

764. The ileocecal sphincter is located between which two structures
A. Stomach and esophagus
B. Small intestine and stomach
C. Small intestine and large intestine
D. Large intestine and rectum

765. Insulin is secreted by the following
A. Alpha cells
B. Beta cells
C. Delta cells
D. Theta cells

766. Wernicke's area, located at the junction of the temporal and parietal lobes, is responsible for
A. Jealousy
B. Visual input
C. Olfactory reception
D. Interpretation of language

767. The stomach
A. Absorbs nutrients into the blood stream via papillae
B. Digests and breaks down food via contraction of smooth muscle and digestive enzymes
C. Performs mastication
D. Absorbs water from feces and eliminates waste from the body

768. A natural killer cell is a type of
A. Lymphocyte
B. Monocyte
C. Macrophage
D. Basophil

769. Muscle separating the thoracic cavity from the abdominal cavity
A. Transverse obliques
B. Rectus abdominis
C. Latissimus dorsi
D. Diaphragm

770. The hypothalamus, hippocampus, amygdala, and septal area are all part of the
A. Diencephalon
B. Limbic system
C. Cerebellum
D. Parietal lobe

771. Thin connective tissue surrounding the brain and spinal cord, primarily responsible for providing protection
A. Pericardium
B. Serous membrane
C. Meninges
D. Peritoneal membrane

772. The vagus nerve
A. Innervates the heart and digestive organs and is the primary nerve in the parasympathetic response
B. Innervates the diaphragm and allows the action of breathing to take place
C. Innervates the brain and allows mental activity to occur
D. Innervates the muscles of the arm and forearm and allows many movements such as elbow flexion and supination

773. Most internal layer of meninges which sits atop the brain
A. Arachnoid
B. Pia mater
C. Dura mater
D. Cerebellum

774. The end of a long bone is called
A. Metaphysis
B. Diaphysis
C. Epiphysis
D. Periosteum

775. Lobe responsible for interpretation of memory, smell, and hearing
A. Occipital
B. Frontal
C. Temporal
D. Parietal

776. The function of the mouth
A. Absorption
B. Mastication
C. Excretion
D. Secretion

777. The layer of the epidermis that lies immediately superficial to the stratum basale
A. Stratum spinosum
B. Stratum germinativum
C. Stratum corneum
D. Stratum granulosum

778. Which of the following is not a part of the axial skeleton
A. Sacrum
B. Ribs
C. Skull
D. Clavicle

779. Changes in temperature can be detected by
A. Chemoreceptors
B. Thermoreceptors
C. Nociceptors
D. Baroreceptors

780. Cells in the walls of alveoli secrete the following substance, which reduces surface tension on the walls of the alveoli
A. Cilia
B. Mucous
C. Sebum
D. Surfactant

781. Hydrochloric acid is produced by the following types of cell in the stomach
A. Oxyntic
B. Mucous
C. Pyloric
D. Zymogen

782. Nephrons are responsible for reabsorption of
A. Water
B. Urea
C. Vitamins
D. Lactic acid

783. Somatostatin is secreted by
A. Beta cells
B. Alpha cells
C. Delta cells
D. Theta cells

784. The cricoid is cartilage that helps to make the
A. Knee
B. Pharynx
C. Trachea
D. Larynx

785. Follicle-stimulating hormone, produced by the pituitary gland, affects what other structure in the body
A. Ovaries
B. Testes
C. Pancreas
D. Thyroid

786. Of the following, which is not an endocrine gland
A. Adrenal gland
B. Sudoriferous gland
C. Pituitary gland
D. Pineal gland

787. Insulin is a digestive enzyme secreted by the pancreas, responsible for
A. Lowering iron levels in the blood
B. Increasing glucose levels in the blood
C. Lowering glucose levels in the blood
D. Increasing iron levels in the blood

788. Nerve primarily responsible for initiating the release of stomach acid during digestion
A. Phrenic
B. Vagus
C. Gastric
D. Trigeminal

789. The femoral artery arises from the
A. Tibial artery
B. Internal iliac artery
C. Abdominal aorta
D. External iliac artery

790. How many bones are located in the wrist
A. Eight
B. Seven
C. Two
D. Five

791. Fat surrounding the kidneys is known as
A. Pericardial fat
B. Perirenal fat
C. Perihepatic fat
D. Pericystic fat

792. Reflexes are processed and interpreted in which part of the body
A. Muscle
B. Brain
C. Spinal cord
D. Axon

793. Which type of gland plays an important role in maintaining body temperature
A. Eccrine
B. Sebaceous
C. Sudoriferous
D. Adrenal

794. Which of the following is not a characteristic of muscle tissue
A. Extensibility
B. Protectability
C. Contractility
D. Elasticity

795. Which type of gland has no ducts
A. Endocrine
B. Exocrine
C. Eccrine
D. Mammary

796. Which of the following is not a function of connective tissue
A. Insulating the body
B. Protection
C. Separating tissues
D. Hormone release

797. Natural pacemaker of the body, responsible for contracting the right and left ventricles
A. Phrenic nerve
B. Papillary muscles
C. SA node
D. Coronary arteries

798. Part of the stomach extending from the fundus to the pylorus
A. Cardia
B. Body
C. Pyloric sphincter
D. Lesser curvature

799. Periosteum is a form of which type of tissue
A. Nervous
B. Connective
C. Epithelial
D. Muscular

800. Bile acids are absorbed into the bloodstream from the ileum to aid in
A. Water absorption
B. Protein synthesis
C. Waste elimination
D. Digestion of fat

Anatomy and Physiology Answer Key

1. C	41. C	81. D	121. D	161. C
2. A	42. B	82. A	122. B	162. D
3. A	43. A	83. C	123. C	163. C
4. B	44. C	84. C	124. A	164. C
5. D	45. A	85. A	125. D	165. D
6. A	46. A	86. D	126. D	166. B
7. C	47. A	87. A	127. C	167. C
8. B	48. B	88. C	128. A	168. A
9. A	49. D	89. A	129. D	169. D
10. D	50. A	90. A	130. B	170. D
11. D	51. D	91. D	131. C	171. C
12. B	52. C	92. A	132. D	172. C
13. A	53. A	93. C	133. A	173. A
14. C	54. A	94. B	134. C	174. D
15. A	55. D	95. D	135. A	175. B
16. D	56. D	96. A	136. A	176. C
17. B	57. C	97. C	137. D	177. D
18. B	58. B	98. D	138. A	178. C
19. A	59. C	99. D	139. B	179. D
20. D	60. A	100. B	140. B	180. D
21. A	61. D	101. B	141. C	181. A
22. A	62. A	102. B	142. D	182. C
23. D	63. B	103. C	143. D	183. C
24. C	64. D	104. C	144. A	184. A
25. B	65. A	105. D	145. C	185. C
26. B	66. C	106. B	146. A	186. B
27. C	67. C	107. C	147. B	187. D
28. A	68. A	108. A	148. D	188. D
29. C	69. D	109. D	149. A	189. A
30. B	70. C	110. C	150. C	190. C
31. D	71. A	111. A	151. B	191. B
32. C	72. D	112. D	152. A	192. C
33. A	73. A	113. C	153. A	193. A
34. D	74. A	114. A	154. A	194. A
35. B	75. B	115. B	155. D	195. C
36. B	76. D	116. A	156. C	196. B
37. A	77. D	117. D	157. C	197. B
38. C	78. A	118. A	158. A	198. A
39. B	79. C	119. C	159. B	199. B
40. D	80. B	120. D	160. A	200. D

201. D	246. B	291. D	336. B	381. B
202. A	247. B	292. A	337. D	382. C
203. A	248. A	293. D	338. B	383. D
204. A	249. A	294. B	339. B	384. A
205. C	250. D	295. A	340. C	385. C
206. B	251. A	296. C	341. D	386. B
207. D	252. A	297. D	342. A	387. B
208. C	253. C	298. C	343. A	388. D
209. B	254. B	299. B	344. C	389. C
210. C	255. D	300. B	345. B	390. B
211. A	256. A	301. B	346. D	391. C
212. C	257. C	302. D	347. D	392. C
213. D	258. D	303. C	348. B	393. A
214. B	259. C	304. D	349. C	394. D
215. A	260. A	305. A	350. A	395. A
216. C	261. D	306. B	351. D	396. D
217. D	262. A	307. C	352. C	397. B
218. B	263. C	308. D	353. B	398. B
219. B	264. B	309. C	354. D	399. B
220. A	265. D	310. C	355. B	400. A
221. D	266. C	311. B	356. A	401. C
222. C	267. D	312. D	357. D	402. A
223. B	268. B	313. C	358. B	403. D
224. A	269. D	314. A	359. D	404. B
225. C	270. C	315. C	360. A	405. D
226. B	271. B	316. C	361. B	406. A
227. D	272. B	317. C	362. C	407. A
228. B	273. C	318. B	363. C	408. A
229. C	274. A	319. B	364. B	409. B
230. A	275. D	320. C	365. A	410. C
231. D	276. D	321. D	366. A	411. A
232. D	277. B	322. A	367. D	412. D
233. B	278. C	323. C	368. A	413. A
234. C	279. A	324. C	369. D	414. C
235. C	280. D	325. B	370. B	415. B
236. A	281. D	326. D	371. C	416. A
237. D	282. B	327. D	372. D	417. C
238. B	283. A	328. B	373. D	418. C
239. C	284. A	329. B	374. C	419. A
240. C	285. D	330. C	375. B	420. A
241. B	286. C	331. B	376. C	421. D
242. A	287. A	332. D	377. A	422. D
243. D	288. C	333. A	378. D	423. A
244. C	289. A	334. D	379. C	424. C
245. D	290. B	335. C	380. C	425. D

426. C	471. A	516. D	561. B	606. B
427. A	472. C	517. D	562. C	607. C
428. D	473. D	518. B	563. B	608. D
429. B	474. C	519. A	564. A	609. A
430. C	475. A	520. C	565. B	610. C
431. A	476. B	521. D	566. A	611. D
432. C	477. D	522. D	567. A	612. B
433. B	478. B	523. B	568. A	613. C
434. D	479. B	524. D	569. D	614. A
435. C	480. C	525. A	570. B	615. B
436. C	481. B	526. C	571. C	616. A
437. B	482. C	527. C	572. C	617. D
438. A	483. D	528. B	573. A	618. C
439. D	484. A	529. D	574. B	619. A
440. D	485. B	530. A	575. D	620. A
441. D	486. D	531. D	576. C	621. D
442. B	487. C	532. C	577. C	622. B
443. B	488. D	533. C	578. B	623. C
444. C	489. B	534. B	579. C	624. B
445. D	490. B	535. B	580. A	625. A
446. B	491. B	536. A	581. D	626. D
447. A	492. A	537. D	582. B	627. D
448. B	493. D	538. D	583. B	628. A
449. A	494. D	539. D	584. B	629. D
450. B	495. C	540. A	585. D	630. C
451. C	496. C	541. B	586. A	631. A
452. A	497. B	542. A	587. C	632. D
453. A	498. A	543. C	588. B	633. B
454. D	499. C	544. D	589. B	634. A
455. B	500. D	545. B	590. C	635. A
456. C	501. B	546. C	591. D	636. C
457. B	502. C	547. C	592. A	637. D
458. A	503. D	548. B	593. C	638. B
459. B	504. B	549. C	594. B	639. D
460. C	505. A	550. B	595. C	640. A
461. B	506. D	551. B	596. D	641. C
462. D	507. A	552. C	597. C	642. D
463. D	508. C	553. C	598. A	643. C
464. D	509. A	554. A	599. B	644. B
465. A	510. A	555. A	600. D	645. A
466. B	511. B	556. A	601. B	646. B
467. C	512. D	557. D	602. C	647. B
468. B	513. C	558. C	603. A	648. D
469. A	514. D	559. A	604. D	649. B
470. D	515. B	560. D	605. C	650. D

651. B	681. B	711. A	741. B	771. C
652. D	682. B	712. D	742. C	772. A
653. C	683. A	713. B	743. A	773. B
654. A	684. D	714. B	744. B	774. C
655. C	685. B	715. D	745. B	775. C
656. B	686. D	716. B	746. D	776. B
657. B	687. A	717. C	747. C	777. A
658. D	688. D	718. A	748. B	778. D
659. B	689. C	719. D	749. D	779. B
660. C	690. A	720. B	750. A	780. D
661. A	691. B	721. D	751. C	781. A
662. D	692. A	722. B	752. D	782. C
663. D	693. A	723. A	753. B	783. C
664. B	694. C	724. C	754. C	784. D
665. A	695. A	725. D	755. A	785. A
666. A	696. D	726. B	756. B	786. B
667. D	697. C	727. A	757. D	787. C
668. B	698. A	728. A	758. A	788. B
669. C	699. B	729. A	759. C	789. D
670. A	700. C	730. B	760. B	790. A
671. C	701. C	731. C	761. D	791. B
672. B	702. A	732. D	762. C	792. C
673. A	703. D	733. A	763. A	793. C
674. D	704. D	734. C	764. C	794. B
675. A	705. A	735. D	765. B	795. A
676. B	706. B	736. A	766. D	796. D
677. A	707. C	737. D	767. B	797. C
678. C	708. C	738. C	768. A	798. B
679. B	709. A	739. C	769. D	799. B
680. A	710. B	740. D	770. B	800. D

Pathology Practice Test

Questions regarding pathology could include information on the following: What a disease specifically is, what causes a disease, any contraindications for the disease, and even questions on the definition of medical terms, although unlikely.

Questions in pathology could be similar to questions in Massage Therapy, where they will be asked in a situational manner. Questions could involve a client presenting with a specific condition, and will ask how a therapist would approach the situation. This also falls under assessment.

Make sure you know your medical terminology! Not only might you have questions asking the definition of terms, medical terminology can also assist you in breaking down the names of medical conditions, which is an easy way to figure out what something is, even without knowing what the disease is beforehand! An example could be, Arteriosclerosis. You can break down this term into three parts: "Arterio" would refer to "artery", "scler" would refer to "hard", and "osis" would refer to "condition". Thus, "Arteriosclerosis" would mean "Condition of hard arteries"!

Not only can medical terminology help you with pathology, but it can also help you with other areas, such as anatomy and physiology! An example: "Nephr/o" means "kidney". If you know the term for kidney, you can easily identify the location of nephrons, just by looking at the name!

1. Most common form of arthritis
A. Rheumatoid arthritis
B. Gouty arthritis
C. Osteoarthritis
D. Periostitis

2. The leading cause of lung, oral, and esophageal cancer
A. Industrial dust
B. Cigarette smoking
C. Asbestos
D. Cystic fibrosis

3. Cellulitis
A. Bacterial infection resulting in yellow scabs around the nose
B. Viral infection resulting in yellow scabs around the mouth
C. Bacterial infection involving the skin and surrounding tissues
D. Viral infection causing cold sores to appear around the mouth

4. Aneurysm
A. Bulge in an artery wall, usually caused by a weakened artery due to a condition such as hypertension
B. Inflammation of a vein due to trauma, resulting in blood clot formation
C. Blood clot in the blood stream becoming lodged in the heart, lungs, or brain, resulting in death of tissue
D. Ischemia in the myocardium due to a blockage in the coronary arteries, resulting in myocardial infarction

5. The most common form of papilloma
A. Wart
B. Acne
C. Psoriasis
D. Cyst

6. A second degree burn is considered
A. Not a contraindication
B. An absolute contraindication
C. An endangerment site
D. A local contraindication

7. Baker's cyst is considered
A. A local contraindication
B. An absolute contraindication
C. An endangerment site
D. Not a contraindication

8. The definition of "nephr/o" is
A. Liver
B. Body
C. Brain
D. Kidney

9. Decrease in oxygen traveling throughout the body
A. Hypoplasia
B. Hypoglycemia
C. Hypoxia
D. Hyperplasia

10. Achilles tendonitis can be caused by a strain to the
A. Pes anserinus
B. Patellar tendon
C. Calcaneal tendon
D. Ischial tuberosity tendon

11. Subacute osteoarthritis is considered
A. A local contraindication
B. An absolute contraindication
C. An endangerment site
D. Not a contraindication

12. The most common site of sprain
A. Shoulder
B. Knee
C. Elbow
D. Ankle

13. Nausea, vomiting, and fatigue with yellowing of the skin may be the result of
A. Hepatitis
B. Food poisoning
C. Diarrhea
D. Meningitis

14. Spasm of capillaries in the fingers and toes, restricting circulation
A. Cyanosis
B. Raynaud's syndrome
C. Emphysema
D. Diabetes mellitus

15. If left untreated, septicemia may result in
A. New blood formation
B. Death
C. Malignancy
D. Amputation

16. Squamous cell carcinoma is what type of tumor
A. Benign
B. Malignant
C. Idiopathic
D. Lymphatic

17. Crohn's disease
A. Inflammation of diverticular pouches, resulting in abscesses and ulcerations, causing severe septicemia
B. Irritation of the stomach, resulting in inflammation of the stomach, forcing pepsin through the cardiac sphincter
C. Formation of pouches in the large intestine as a result of contractions of smooth muscle in the large intestine without substances to press against
D. Autoimmune disorder resulting in inflammation of the inner linings of the small intestine and large intestine

18. Ischemia may ultimately result in
A. Phlebitis
B. Arteriosclerosis
C. Necrosis
D. Varicose veins

19. Gradual degeneration of parts of the adrenal glands
A. Adrenal hyperplasia
B. Grave's disease
C. Cushing's syndrome
D. Addison's disease

20. The definition of the prefix "an-" is
A. Without
B. Against
C. Bad
D. One

21. Reduction of swelling and emptying of mucous from the nasal cavity can be accomplished by use of
A. Decongestants
B. Expectorants
C. Statins
D. Antihistamines

22. Inflammation of a bursa sac, usually present due to trauma
A. Synovitis
B. Bursitis
C. Osteoarthritis
D. Bruxism

23. Medication prescribed to fight off bacterial infections
A. Anti-inflammatory
B. Antivenoms
C. Antipyretics
D. Antibiotics

24. The definition of "my/o" is
A. Bone
B. Vessel
C. Muscle
D. Heart

25. Inflammation of the urethra, a condition usually accompanied by cystitis or prostatitis
A. Salpingitis
B. Nephritis
C. Epididymitis
D. Urethritis

26. Excessive death of myocardium results in
A. Arrhythmia
B. Stroke
C. Myocardial infarction
D. Heart murmur

27. Grade 3 sprain
A. Complete rupture of a ligament
B. Partial tearing of a tendon
C. Complete rupture of a tendon
D. Partial tearing of a ligament

28. Acne is considered
A. An absolute contraindication
B. A local contraindication
C. An endangerment site
D. Not a contraindication

29. Due to having a shorter urethra, women are more prone to developing the following condition than men
A. Prostatitis
B. Nephritis
C. Cystitis
D. Cholecystitis

30. In a client with lordosis, the following muscle might be weakened, resulting in an exaggerated anterior tilt of the pelvis
A. Psoas major
B. Latissimus dorsi
C. Quadratus lumborum
D. Rectus abdominis

31. Hives are usually the result of
A. Exposure to an allergen or emotional stress
B. Exposure to the herpes simplex virus
C. Exposure to tinea pedis
D. Exposure to mites that burrow under the skin

32. Increased accumulation of fluid in the lungs
A. Pulmonary aneurysm
B. Pulmonary edema
C. Pulmonary embolism
D. Pulmonary degeneration

33. The definition of "kerat/o" is
A. Death
B. Tissue
C. Nose
D. Hard

34. A blood pressure reading of 140/90 results in a person being diagnosed with
A. Hypertension
B. Hypotension
C. Hyperemia
D. Myocardial infarction

35. The most common type of diabetes
A. Insulin-dependent diabetes
B. Diabetes type I
C. Juvenile diabetes
D. Diabetes type II

36. The definition of "chol/e" is
A. Insulin
B. Bile
C. Pancreas
D. Glucose

37. The floating ribs are considered
A. A local contraindication
B. An absolute contraindication
C. An endangerment site
D. Not a contraindication

38. Pyelonephritis is considered
A. A local contraindication
B. An absolute contraindication
C. An endangerment site
D. Not a contraindication

39. Uncontrolled hypertension is considered
A. A local contraindication
B. An absolute contraindication
C. An endangerment site
D. Not a contraindication

40. Meningitis
A. Inflammation of the meninges, resulting in pressure being placed on the brain
B. Inflammation of the brain, causing increased pressure placed on the cranium
C. Degeneration of brain tissue, resulting in loss of memory
D. Paralysis of one side of the body due to infection of the Herpes Simplex virus

41. The definition of the suffix "-rrhea" is
A. Discharge
B. Bursting forth
C. Growth
D. Urine

42. The definition of the suffix "-ician" is
A. Breathing
B. Formation
C. Specialist
D. Condition

43. Paralysis of the lower limbs
A. Quadriplegia
B. Hemiplegia
C. Paraplegia
D. Triplegia

44. Muscular dystrophy
A. Muscle tissue losing density due only to lack of use
B. Hereditary condition causing degeneration and atrophy of muscle tissue
C. Painful tender spots in muscles causing fatigue and numbness
D. Inflammation of muscle tissue caused by trauma

45. A common treatment for bursitis
A. Lymphatic drainage
B. Heat and compression
C. Rest and ice
D. Cold compress and friction

46. Phlebitis is considered
A. An absolute contraindication
B. A local contraindication
C. An endangerment site
D. Not a contraindication

47. Analgesics are used to combat
A. Pain
B. Obesity
C. Inflammation
D. Gout

48. Asbestos is considered
A. An occupational carcinogen
B. A hereditary carcinogen
C. An anti-inflammatory disease
D. A type of malignant skin cancer

49. Genetic disorder leading to muscular degeneration and atrophy
A. Multiple sclerosis
B. Strain
C. Muscular dystrophy
D. Fibromyalgia

50. A ventricular contraction exerting over 140 mmHg may be a sign of
A. Myocardial infarction
B. Hypotension
C. Hyperemia
D. Hypertension

51. The definition of "leuk/o" is
A. Yellow
B. Green
C. Red
D. White

52. Medication used to treat stroke, myocardial infarction, and embolism
A. Statin
B. Antihistamine
C. Anticoagulant
D. Decongestant

53. Malignant melanoma
A. Most common, least serious, slowest growing form of skin cancer
B. Least common, most serious, fastest growing form of skin cancer
C. Most common, most serious, fastest growing form of skin cancer
D. Least common, least serious, slowest growing form of skin cancer

54. In a typical healthy adult, the most common site of pus formation is
A. In the armpits
B. In the mouth
C. Under the skin
D. In the bones

55. The definition of "somat/o" is
A. Gland
B. Fatty plaque
C. Cancer
D. Body

56. Athlete's foot is considered
A. A local contraindication
B. An absolute contraindication
C. An endangerment site
D. Not a contraindication

57. Tightness in the piriformis may result in
A. Osteomyelitis
B. Sciatica
C. Ankylosing spondylitis
D. Contracture

58. Sciatica
A. Injury to the tibial nerve, causing decreased ability to extend the digits
B. Compression of the sciatic nerve by the piriformis, resulting in pain radiating down the lower limb
C. Compression of the facial nerve, resulting in loss of function of one side of the face
D. An injury to the spinal cord at L1, resulting in paraplegia

59. A thrombus is also known as
A. Aneurysm
B. Embolus
C. Blood clot
D. Platelet

60. Acute cholecystitis is considered
A. A local contraindication
B. An absolute contraindication
C. An endangerment site
D. Not a contraindication

61. The definition of "hepat/o" is
A. Liver
B. Blood
C. Brain
D. Kidney

62. Hypertension
A. Inflammation of veins caused by non-functioning valves
B. Increased accumulation of lipids attached to the walls of arteries
C. Fatty plaque deposits inside the arteries
D. Excessive pressure placed on walls of arteries

63. Cramping and abdominal pain, associated with rectal bleeding, may be a sign of
A. Hiatal hernia
B. Crohn's disease
C. Diverticulosis
D. Ulcerative colitis

64. Fungal infection affecting the finger or toenails
A. Tinea capitis
B. Tinea unguium
C. Tinea cruris
D. Tinea pedis

65. Hemiplegia
A. Paralysis of only the legs
B. Paralysis of one side of the body
C. Paralysis of all four limbs
D. Paralysis of one side of the face

66. Loss of density in bone, caused by a decrease in the hormone estrogen in the body
A. Osteomyelitis
B. Menopause
C. Osteoporosis
D. Scoliosis

67. Medications helpful in breaking up phlegm and mucous in the respiratory passages
A. Expectorants
B. Decongestants
C. Bronchodilators
D. Anticoagulants

68. A client who suffers from rosacea would be referred to which doctor
A. Dermatologist
B. Nephrologist
C. Cardiologist
D. Gastroenterologist

69. Buildup of plaque on teeth could result in
A. Gastritis
B. Tonsilitis
C. Stomatitis
D. Periodontitis

70. Infectious pharyngitis is considered
A. A local contraindication
B. An absolute contraindication
C. An endangerment site
D. Not a contraindication

71. Pathology is the study of
A. Body structure
B. Disease
C. Body function
D. Cause of disease

72. The study of tumors
A. Pathology
B. Etiology
C. Cardiology
D. Oncology

73. Degeneration of myelin sheaths in the central nervous system
A. Multiple sclerosis
B. Myasthenia gravis
C. Parkinson's disease
D. Alzheimer's disease

74. Progressive wasting of muscle tissue
A. Muscle atrophy
B. Fibromyalgia
C. Torticollis
D. Muscular dystrophy

75. Bone spurs in a joint may be the result of
A. Myeloma
B. Osteoarthritis
C. Rheumatoid arthritis
D. Ankylosing spondylitis

76. Pus includes all of the following except
A. Dead tissue
B. Bacteria
C. Edematic tissue
D. Dead white blood cells

77. Pain felt at the medial epicondyle of the humerus is associated with
A. Tennis elbow
B. Golfer's elbow
C. Carpal tunnel syndrome
D. Synovitis

78. A client who suffers from eczema would be referred to which doctor
A. Cardiologist
B. Nephrologist
C. Dermatologist
D. Gastroenterologist

79. TMJ dysfunction is considered
A. A local contraindication
B. An absolute contraindication
C. An endangerment site
D. Not a contraindication

80. Impetigo may be the result of which of the following
A. Staphylococcus
B. Herpes simplex
C. Autoimmune attacks
D. Thrush

81. Bradycardia is a form of
A. Aneurysm
B. Heart murmur
C. Infarction
D. Arrhythmia

82. Bell's palsy results in paralysis of
A. Only the legs
B. The arms and legs
C. One side of the body
D. One side of the face

83. Bacterial infection resulting in honeycomb sores around the mouth and nose
A. Boil
B. Impetigo
C. Psoriasis
D. Meningitis

84. Discoloration of the skin due to breakage of blood vessels under the skin
A. Contusion
B. Concussion
C. Urticaria
D. Keloid

85. Histamines increase dilation of blood vessels to allow more blood to enter into an area. This is called
A. Swelling
B. Inflammation
C. Hypoxia
D. Anemia

86. The most common form of hernia
A. Inguinal
B. Umbilical
C. Hiatal
D. Intestinal

87. Sun spots are also known as
A. Melanoma
B. Mole
C. Lentigo
D. Carcinoma

88. While at work, Chris falls and lands on his back, injuring it. The next day, he calls to make a massage appointment, hoping the massage will help with his pain. The appropriate response would be
A. Reschedule the massage and refer the client to a physician
B. Perform the massage and do compression onto the back
C. Perform the massage and apply heat to the affected area
D. Perform the massage and do passive joint mobilization on the vertebrae

89. Injury to a muscle or tendon
A. Synovitis
B. Sprain
C. Strain
D. Bursitis

90. The definition of the prefix "micro-" is
A. Around
B. Large
C. Small
D. Eating

91. Bell's palsy is considered
A. A local contraindication
B. An absolute contraindication
C. An endangerment site
D. Not a contraindication

92. The definition of "mamm/o" is
A. Breast
B. Milk
C. Tear
D. Uterus

93. Discoloration of skin, turning the skin and mucous membranes blue
A. Diabetes mellitus
B. Raynaud's syndrome
C. Cyanosis
D. Atherosclerosis

94. Tinea capitis is a fungal infection found on the
A. Feet
B. Scalp
C. Groin
D. Fingernails

95. Autoimmune disorder resulting in degeneration of the adrenal cortex
A. Grave's disease
B. Cushing's syndrome
C. Adrenal hyperplasia
D. Addison's disease

96. Lordosis is also known as
A. Swayback
B. Dowager's hump
C. Scoliosis
D. Bamboo spine

97. Influenza is considered
A. A local contraindication
B. An absolute contraindication
C. An endangerment site
D. Not a contraindication

98. Constipation is considered
A. A local contraindication
B. An absolute contraindication
C. An endangerment site
D. Not a contraindication

99. Dysphasia
A. An injury to the brain resulting in impairment of speech
B. An injury to the face causing paralysis of one side of the face
C. An injury to the spinal cord resulting in paralysis
D. An injury to the lungs causing air bubbles in the thoracic cavity

100. An adenoma is a tumor usually found in which structures
A. Bones
B. Lymph nodes
C. Glands
D. Joints

101. Acute wear and tear arthritis is considered
A. An absolute contraindication
B. A local contraindication
C. An endangerment site
D. Not a contraindication

102. A nephrologist would be the type of specialist referred to in all of the following conditions except
A. Lupus
B. Pitting edema
C. Pyelonephritis
D. Uremia

103. Swelling of a vein as a result of valves inside the vein malfunctioning, allowing blood to move backwards
A. Phlebitis
B. Varicose veins
C. Varicose ulcer
D. Deep vein thrombosis

104. Overstretching of a ligament that does not result in tearing
A. Grade 2 strain
B. Grade 1 strain
C. Grade 2 sprain
D. Grade 1 sprain

105. Subacute sprains are considered
A. A local contraindication
B. An absolute contraindication
C. An endangerment site
D. Not a contraindication

106. The definition of the suffix "-oid" is
A. Discharge
B. Bursting forth
C. Growth
D. Resembling

107. Medial epicondylitis is more commonly known as
A. Tennis elbow
B. Golfer's elbow
C. Football shoulder
D. Soccer knee

108. Chronic form of hepatitis
A. Hepatitis A
B. Hepatitis C
C. Hepatitis D
D. Hepatitis B

109. Signs of inflammation include
A. Heat, pain, redness, coldness
B. Pain, edema, swelling, redness
C. Swelling, heat, redness, pain
D. Redness, pain, heat, dehydration

110. A client who suffers from pitting edema would be referred to which doctor
A. Dermatologist
B. Nephrologist
C. Cardiologist
D. Gastroenterologist

111. Infectious laryngitis is considered
A. A local contraindication
B. An absolute contraindication
C. An endangerment site
D. Not a contraindication

112. The definition of the prefix "homeo-" is
A. Different
B. Same
C. Behind
D. Difficult

113. Inflammation of diverticular pouches, resulting in severe abdominal pain
A. Diverticulitis
B. Diverticulosis
C. Crohn's disease
D. Ulcerative colitis

114. Crohn's disease in the sub-acute stage is considered
A. A local contraindication
B. An absolute contraindication
C. An endangerment site
D. Not a contraindication

115. Chronic heart burn is known as
A. Gastroesophageal reflux disease
B. Achalasia
C. Gastritis
D. Gastroenteritis

116. Alzheimer's disease is considered
A. A local contraindication
B. An absolute contraindication
C. An endangerment site
D. Not a contraindication

117. Golfer's elbow is also known as
A. Lateral epicondylitis
B. Medial epicondylitis
C. Tuberculitis
D. Olecranon bursitis

118. A benign tumor made of fatty tissue
A. Lipoma
B. Melanoma
C. Keratosis
D. Xanthoma

119. Anticoagulants are medications that prevent
A. Blood vessel dilation
B. Inflammation
C. Mucous production
D. Blood clotting

120. The definition of the prefix "pan-" is
A. Before
B. Near
C. New
D. All

121. Jumper's knee affects the
A. Patellar tendon
B. Flexors of the wrist
C. Extensors of the wrist
D. Pes anserinus

122. Plantar warts are located
A. On the bottom of the foot
B. On the top of the hands
C. On the back of the legs
D. On thee front of the arms

123. Dowager's hump is considered
A. A local contraindication
B. An absolute contraindication
C. An endangerment site
D. Not a contraindication

124. The definition of "kyph/o" is
A. Gums
B. Hill
C. Sugar
D. Muscle

125. The definition of the suffix "-algia" is
A. Paralysis
B. Inflammation
C. Secrete
D. Pain

126. Mesothelioma, a form of lung cancer, results from exposure to
A. Asbestos
B. Dust
C. Cigarette smoke
D. Staphylococci bacteria

127. Unconsciousness immediately following a blow to the head
A. Aneurysm
B. Contusion
C. Concussion
D. Neuralgia

128. Inflammatory disease affecting the lining of the alimentary canal, which may result in ulcerations and severe diarrhea
A. Diverticulitis
B. Diverticulosis
C. Crohn's disease
D. Celiac disease

129. Concussion
A. Increased blood flow to an area following trauma
B. Trauma to an area, resulting in internal bleeding
C. A blow to the head, resulting in unconsciousness
D. Inflammation of the brain, resulting in death of nervous tissue

130. Ringworm is a form of
A. Fungus
B. Bacteria
C. Virus
D. Parasite

131. The definition of "arteri/o" is
A. Heart
B. Joints
C. Lung
D. Artery

132. Paralysis of the arms and legs is a condition known as
A. Paraplegia
B. Quadriplegia
C. Hemiplegia
D. Semiplegia

133. Atherosclerosis
A. Hardening of the walls of the arteries
B. Fatty plaque buildup in the arteries
C. Bulging of an arterial wall
D. Inflammation of a vein

134. The definition of the prefix "multi-" is
A. New
B. Near
C. Many
D. All

135. Trigeminal neuralgia is considered
A. A local contraindication
B. An absolute contraindication
C. An endangerment site
D. Not a contraindication

136. Fracture of the lateral malleolus as a result of forceful turning of the ankle outwards
A. Pott's fracture
B. Colles fracture
C. Compound fracture
D. Spiral fracture

137. Form of lupus which forms thick red patches across the face most common in middle-aged women
A. Dermatomyositis
B. Systemic lupus erythematosus
C. Discoid lupus erythematosus
D. Polymyositis

138. Varicose veins
A. Inflammation of a vein due to trauma to a vein
B. Swelling of veins as a result of valve incompetence, causing blood to flow backwards
C. Swelling of a vein due to excessive lymph fluid in a limb
D. Inflammation of a vein due to immobility as a result of surgery

139. Arteriosclerosis
A. Hardening of the walls of the arteries
B. Fatty plaque buildup in the arteries
C. Bulging of an arterial wall
D. Inflammation of a vein

140. All of the following are contagious conditions except
A. Mononucleosis
B. Cellulitis
C. Psoriasis
D. Osteomyelitis

141. The definition of the prefix "a-" is
A. Against
B. Without
C. Bad
D. One

142. Antiarrhythmics
A. Medication that controls rate of heart contraction
B. Medication that reduces the amount on inflammation in an area
C. Medication that controls the cholesterol levels in the blood
D. Medication that controls the size of blood vessel lumen

143. Diverticulitis
A. Autoimmune disorder resulting in inflammation of the inner linings of the small intestine and large intestine
B. Irritation of the stomach, resulting in inflammation of the stomach, forcing pepsin through the cardiac sphincter
C. Formation of pouches in the large intestine as a result of contractions of smooth muscle in the large intestine without substances to press against
D. Inflammation of diverticular pouches, resulting in abscesses and ulcerations, which may cause severe septicemia

144. The definition of "aden/o" is
A. Body
B. Fatty plaque
C. Cancer
D. Gland

145. Medication that may result in asthma attacks
A. Vasodilators
B. Beta-blockers
C. Antihistamines
D. Statins

146. Phlebitis
A. Swelling of veins as a result of valve incompetence, causing blood to flow backwards
B. Inflammation of a vein due to trauma to a vein
C. Swelling of a vein due to excessive lymph fluid in a limb
D. Inflammation of an artery due to immobility as a result of surgery

147. Infection of mammary glands may result in
A. Mastitis
B. Angina pectoris
C. Cystic fibrosis
D. Pneumonia

148. The definition of "embol/o" is
A. Inflate
B. Plug
C. Ear
D. Hearing

149. A cerebral embolism may result in
A. Alzheimer's disease
B. Thrombosis
C. Cardiac arrest
D. Stroke

150. Blockage of a pore may result in the development of
A. Melanoma
B. Wart
C. Lupus
D. Acne

151. A pustule is a common symptom of
A. Acne
B. Cellulitis
C. Rosacea
D. Lupus

152. Psoriasis is considered
A. A local contraindication
B. An absolute contraindication
C. An endangerment site
D. Not a contraindication

153. Acute hepatitis is considered
A. A local contraindication
B. An absolute contraindication
C. An endangerment site
D. Not a contraindication

154. Muscular dystrophy is considered
A. A local contraindication
B. An absolute contraindication
C. An endangerment site
D. Not a contraindication

155. Dilation of blood vessels during the inflammatory stage is controlled by
A. Histamines
B. Leukocytes
C. Neutrophils
D. Fibrosis

156. Psoriasis
A. Inflammation of skin resulting in skin coming into contact with an irritant
B. Autoimmune disorder resulting in thick, dry, silvery patches of skin
C. Blockage of sebaceous glands, resulting in pustules
D. Skin irritation caused by exposure to cold, affecting blood vessels and hair follicles

157. A patient with severe bradycardia would most likely need a pacemaker implanted into their body to regulate
A. Embolism formation
B. Lipid accumulation
C. Heart rhythm
D. Phlebitis

158. Body temperature below 90 degrees results in
A. Hypothermia
B. Heat stroke
C. Heat cramps
D. Frostbite

159. The definition of "ather/o" is
A. Gland
B. Fatty plaque
C. Cancer
D. Body

160. The definition of "neur/o" is
A. Muscle
B. Pain
C. Death
D. Nerve

161. The first stage of the inflammatory response is release of histamine in the area, in order to
A. Constrict blood vessels to decrease erythrocyte activity in the area
B. Constrict blood vessels to decrease blood circulation into the area
C. Dilate blood vessels to increase erythrocyte activity in the area
D. Dilate blood vessels to increase neutrophil activity in the area

162. Osteoporosis is considered
A. A local contraindication
B. An absolute contraindication
C. An endangerment site
D. Not a contraindication

163. Blood in the urine, usually a result of renal failure
A. Hyperemia
B. Pyelonephritis
C. Cystitis
D. Uremia

164. The definition of the suffix "-blast" is
A. Germ cell
B. Inflammation
C. Secrete
D. Pain

165. Adhesive capsulitis
A. Adhesions forming in the liver, causing decreased bile production and blood detoxification
B. Joint capsule surrounding the glenohumeral joint adhering to the head of the humerus, reducing movement
C. Tearing of fascia along the medial tibia, causing increased pain upon walking
D. Autoimmune disorder causing degeneration of myelin sheaths in the central nervous system, resulting in scarring of an axon

166. A client who suffers from psoriasis schedules a massage. An appropriate treatment modification would be
A. Performing vigorous friction on the patches to exfoliate dead skin
B. Avoiding the affected pouches to not worsen them
C. Working on the dry patches if pain is not present
D. Reschedule the massage as psoriasis is contagious

167. The definition of the suffix "-itis" is
A. Paralysis
B. Inflammation
C. Secrete
D. Swelling

168. Amoxycillin and methicillin are forms of
A. Macrolides
B. Penicillin
C. Cephalosporins
D. Tetracyclines

169. Drug used to treat acute asthma
A. Bronchodilator
B. Expectorant
C. Decongestant
D. Anticoagulant

170. The definition of the prefix "circum-" is
A. Above
B. Through
C. Around
D. Eating

171. The definition of "ocul/o" is
A. Ovary
B. Groin
C. Ear
D. Eye

172. The definition of "onc/o" is
A. Cancer
B. Blood
C. Tumor
D. Heart

173. A Pott's fracture is a breakage of the
A. Lateral malleolus
B. Medial malleolus
C. Styloid process
D. Talus

174. Virus resulting in the development of warts
A. Herpes simplex
B. Human papilloma virus
C. Epstein-Barr virus
D. Urticaria

175. Bronchodilators are helpful in treating which condition in an acute episode
A. Cystic fibrosis
B. Asthma
C. Emphysema
D. Tuberculosis

176. Quadriplegia is considered
A. A local contraindication
B. An absolute contraindication
C. An endangerment site
D. Not a contraindication

177. Encephalitis
A. Inflammation of the brain caused by a viral infection
B. Aneurysm in the cerebrum causing brain damage
C. Blockage of a coronary artery, resulting in necrosis of myocardium
D. Inflammation of the meninges, leading to migraine headaches

178. Cellulitis is usually caused by infection of the following
A. Adipose
B. Staphylococcus
C. Herpes simplex
D. Streptococcus

179. Bacterial infection which involves the periosteum and can enter into the medullary cavity of a bone
A. Osteoporosis
B. Osteomyelitis
C. Ankylosing spondylitis
D. Subluxation

180. Subacute Golfer's Elbow is considered
A. A local contraindication
B. An absolute contraindication
C. An endangerment site
D. Not a contraindication

181. Acute viral infection affecting the respiratory tract
A. Influenza
B. Pneumonia
C. Pneumothorax
D. Bronchitis

182. Ischemia
A. Narrowing of blood vessels in the fingers and toes, restricting blood flow
B. Hardening of the walls of arteries, producing hypertension
C. Inflammation of veins, resulting in thrombus formation
D. Lack of oxygen entering into a tissue, which may result in necrosis

183. Pacemakers are commonly implanted in patients who suffer from
A. Arrhythmia
B. Emphysema
C. Angina pectoris
D. Heart murmur

184. The definition of the suffix "-stasis" is
A. Pertaining to
B. Standing still
C. Nourishment
D. Environment

185. Failure of an organ or specific tissue to properly develop is known as
A. Dermaplasia
B. Hyperplasia
C. Hypoplasia
D. Hepatoplasia

186. The definition of the prefix "mal-" is
A. Without
B. Against
C. Bad
D. One

187. Generally, people in good health heal how quickly compared to those in poor health
A. Quicker
B. Slower
C. The same
D. Equally

188. A client with gingivitis would be referred to the following doctor
A. Gastrologist
B. Neurologist
C. Dentist
D. Urologist

189. An injury to a ligament
A. Sprain
B. Strain
C. Fracture
D. Dislocation

190. Raynaud's syndrome
A. Vasodilation of blood vessels in the cranium, resulting in migraine headaches
B. Vasoconstriction of blood vessels in fingers and toes, restricting circulation
C. Vasoconstriction of coronary arteries, leading to ischemia of myocardium
D. Vasodilation of meninges, restriction flow of cerebrospinal fluid

191. The definition of the suffix "-icle" is
A. Skin
B. Small
C. Growth
D. Resembling

192. Dermabrasion helps to reduce
A. Keratin buildup
B. Scar tissue
C. Skin tags
D. Cellulitis

193. Compared to a benign tumor, a malignant tumor is
A. More serious
B. Less serious
C. Equally as serious
D. Not serious

194. Vertigo
A. Abnormal lateral curvature of the cervical vertebrae
B. Bacterial infection of the mucous membranes
C. Ringing in the ears
D. Dizziness

195. The definition of the prefix "ante-" is
A. Away
B. Self
C. Before
D. Against

196. Low blood pressure is also referred to as
A. Hypotension
B. Hypertension
C. Phlebitis
D. Arteriosclerosis

197. Hypoxia can be caused by an increase of what substance in the body
A. Nitrogen
B. Oxygen
C. Carbon monoxide
D. Helium

198. Cystic fibrosis is what type of disorder
A. Autoimmune
B. Genetic
C. Idiopathic
D. Sickle cell

199. Tendonitis is often what type of injury
A. Repetitive strain
B. Repetitive sprain
C. Atrophic
D. Autoimmune

200. The definition of "thorac/o" is
A. Back
B. Belly
C. Leg
D. Chest

201. Cancer of connective tissue is known as
A. Sarcoma
B. Melanoma
C. Carcinoma
D. Lymphoma

202. A contusion is considered
A. A local contraindication
B. An absolute contraindication
C. An endangerment site
D. Not a contraindication

203. Loss of voice due to inflammation of the voice box
A. Bronchitis
B. Pharyngitis
C. Tonsilitis
D. Laryngitis

204. The definition of the prefix "epi-" is
A. Through
B. Above
C. Around
D. Eating

205. Shingles is considered
A. A local contraindication
B. An absolute contraindication
C. An endangerment site
D. Not a contraindication

206. The definition of "ren/o" is
A. Water
B. Cold
C. Kidney
D. Heat

207. The definition of "esophag/o" is
A. Small intestine
B. Stomach
C. Esophagus
D. Bladder

208. A client who suffers from arthritis would be referred to which doctor
A. Dermatologist
B. Nephrologist
C. Cardiologist
D. Rheumatologist

209. Hardening of the walls of the arteries
A. Arteriosclerosis
B. Atherosclerosis
C. Phlebitis
D. Varicose veins

210. Cysts found in the liver, formed by larvae of dog tapeworm
A. Hydatid cysts
B. Ganglion cysts
C. Sebaceous cysts
D. Renal cysts

211. The formation of scar tissue
A. Hypoplasia
B. Hyperplasia
C. Fibrosis
D. Inflammatory response

212. Backing up of urine in the kidneys due to blockage of the ureters by an object such as a kidney stone
A. Pyelonephritis
B. Cystitis
C. Uremia
D. Hydronephritis

213. A person that bruises easily may suffer from
A. Hemophilia
B. Porphyria
C. Muscular dystrophy
D. Atrophy

214. Inflammation of a joint
A. Osteoporosis
B. Arthritis
C. Dislocation
D. Subluxation

215. The definition of the prefix "peri-" is
A. Above
B. Large
C. Around
D. Eating

216. The definition of "cirrh/o" is
A. Yellow
B. Green
C. Red
D. Black

217. An acute sore caused by herpes simplex is considered
A. Not a contraindication
B. An absolute contraindication
C. An endangerment site
D. A local contraindication

218. A lack of hemoglobin in erythrocytes may result in
A. Decreased immune response
B. Raynaud's syndrome
C. Myocardial infarction
D. Anemia

219. Hiatal hernia
A. A portion of the small intestine protrudes through the peritoneum into the umbilicus
B. A portion of the stomach protrudes through the cardiac sphincter into the esophagus
C. A portion of the stomach protrudes through the diaphragm
D. A portion of the small intestine protrudes through the peritoneum into the groin

220. The body's natural response to tissue damage
A. Inflammation
B. Edema
C. Cellular mitosis
D. Hypoplasia

221. Cystitis is most common in
A. Elderly
B. Men
C. Children
D. Women

222. Displacement of bone from its usual location
A. Dislocation
B. Simple fracture
C. Arthritis
D. Ankylosing spondylitis

223. Osgood-Schlatter disease is considered
A. An endangerment site
B. An absolute contraindication
C. A local contraindication
D. Not a contraindication

224. Urticaria is also known as
A. Psoriasis
B. Herpes
C. Hives
D. Warts

225. A tumor is also called a
A. Abscess
B. Mole
C. Neoplasm
D. Cyst

226. Form of tendonitis affecting the extensors of the wrist
A. Golfer's elbow
B. Tennis elbow
C. Patellar tendonitis
D. Frozen shoulder

227. A lice infestation is considered
A. A local contraindication
B. An absolute contraindication
C. An endangerment site
D. Not a contraindication

228. A diet with consumption of salt in high quantities may result in
A. Hypertension
B. Hypotension
C. Hyperemia
D. Myocardial infarction

229. Influenza is a
A. Virus
B. Bacteria
C. Fungus
D. Parasite

230. The definition of the suffix "-cyte" is
A. Germ cell
B. Inflammation
C. Cell
D. Pain

231. The definition of the prefix "neo-" is
A. Before
B. Near
C. New
D. Disease

232. Inflammation of gums that may lead to infection and deterioration of ligaments holding teeth to the jaw
A. Stomatitis
B. Tonsilitis
C. Periodontitis
D. Glossitis

233. Of the following, which condition is contagious
A. Ankylosing spondylitis
B. Osteoporosis
C. Trigeminal neuralgia
D. Mononucleosis

234. Viral or bacterial infection resulting in severe increases of fluids in the lungs
A. Pneumonia
B. Asthma
C. Bronchitis
D. Emphysema

235. A wart is caused by
A. Parasite
B. Bacteria
C. Fungus
D. Virus

236. Histamines
A. Constrict blood vessels to decrease circulation in the inflammatory response
B. Dilate blood vessels to increase circulation in the inflammatory response
C. Increase lymph circulation in the inflammatory response
D. Decrease lymph circulation in the inflammatory response

237. Bursitis is considered
A. An absolute contraindication
B. A local contraindication
C. An endangerment site
D. Not a contraindication

238. Fracture of the lateral malleolus of the fibula
A. Colles fracture
B. Compound fracture
C. Pott's fracture
D. Greenstick fracture

239. A body temperature over 104 degrees can lead to
A. Heat stroke
B. Hypothermia
C. Frostbite
D. Myocardial infarction

240. The definition of "inguin/o" is
A. Pelvis
B. Groin
C. Tongue
D. Armpit

241. Scabies
A. Infection of the human papilloma virus resulting in the formation of verrucae
B. Infection of the herpes zoster virus causing burning sores
C. Infestation of mites that burrow under the skin causing severe itching
D. Infection of fungus on the skin causing a ring-like rash

242. Statins are used to combat
A. Arrhythmia
B. Allergies
C. Trauma
D. Hypertension

243. Gastroesophageal reflux disease is considered
A. A local contraindication
B. An absolute contraindication
C. An endangerment site
D. Not a contraindication

244. A concussion is considered
A. A local contraindication
B. An absolute contraindication
C. An endangerment site
D. Not a contraindication

245. Medications that aid the function of coughing
A. Decongestants
B. Expectorants
C. Antihistamines
D. Bronchodilators

246. Uremia is considered
A. A local contraindication
B. An absolute contraindication
C. An endangerment site
D. Not a contraindication

247. Alzheimer's disease
A. Brain tissue degeneration, resulting in dementia and loss of memory
B. Decrease in dopamine levels in the body, resulting in decreased motor function control
C. Inflammation of the brain, resulting in brain damage and loss of function
D. Degeneration of myelin in the central nervous system, exposing axons

248. Deterioration of blood vessels supplying the limbs with blood and oxygen
A. Peripheral vascular disease
B. Raynaud's syndrome
C. Diabetes mellitus
D. Hypoxia

249. Histamine release as a result of exposure to an allergen results in
A. Warts
B. Shingles
C. Urticaria
D. Ichthyosis

250. An avulsion is considered
A. A local contraindication
B. An absolute contraindication
C. An endangerment site
D. Not a contraindication

251. Aspirin is a form of
A. Expectorant
B. Anticoagulant
C. Statin
D. Beta-blocker

252. Anemia results in
A. Varicose veins
B. Myocardial infarction
C. Lack of oxygen traveling through the body
D. Increased lipid content in the blood

253. The definition of "dors/o" is
A. Back
B. Belly
C. Leg
D. Chest

254. HIV targets which specific cell
A. Erythrocytes
B. Neutrophils
C. T lymphocytes
D. Monocytes

255. Periodontitis
A. Inflammation of gums resulting in degeneration of periodontal ligaments
B. Inflammation of the mouth resulting in degeneration of mucous membranes
C. Inflammation of tonsils resulting in abscesses and ulcerations on the tonsils
D. Inflammation of the epiglottis resulting in reduced inhalation

256. Aneurysm
A. Hardening of the walls of the arteries
B. Fatty plaque buildup in the arteries
C. Bulging of an arterial wall
D. Inflammation of a vein

257. The definition of the suffix "-ac" is
A. Inflammation
B. Pertaining to
C. Cell
D. Pain

258. Form of skin cancer commonly seen in late-stage AIDS
A. Squamous cell carcinoma
B. Malignant melanoma
C. Basal cell carcinoma
D. Kaposi's sarcoma

259. Cirrhosis of the liver results in
A. Overproduction of bile, which restricts the ability of the body to emulsify fats
B. Death of liver tissue, which is replaced by fibrous tissue
C. Decrease in the production of bilirubin, which causes the skin to become yellow
D. Reformation of liver cells, restoring natural liver function

260. A cardiologist is a doctor who specializes in the
A. Lungs
B. Heart
C. Liver
D. Bladder

261. Melanoma tumors are commonly all of the following except
A. Flat
B. Elevated
C. Asymmetrical
D. Black

262. Rapid production of epithelial cells resulting in thick silvery patches, caused by an autoimmune response
A. Papilloma
B. Melanoma
C. Rosacea
D. Psoriasis

263. A patient with severe tachycardia would most likely need a pacemaker implanted into their body to regulate
A. Phlebitis
B. Lipid accumulation
C. Embolism formation
D. Heart rhythm

264. Dopamine is a neurotransmitter which helps to stabilize the body in specific movements. A lack of dopamine in the body would result in
A. Anemia
B. Alzheimer's disease
C. Parkinson's disease
D. Sleep apnea

265. Basal cell carcinoma develops a tumor that most commonly appears on
A. Neck
B. Arms
C. Face
D. Legs

266. Hepatitis
A. Inflammation of the pancreas
B. Inflammation of the kidneys
C. Inflammation of the stomach
D. Inflammation of the liver

267. Form of tendonitis affecting the flexors of the wrist
A. Golfer's elbow
B. Tennis elbow
C. Patellar tendonitis
D. Frozen shoulder

268. The definition of the prefix "dia-" is
A. Between
B. Through
C. Below
D. False

269. Bradycardia, a form of arrhythmia, results in
A. Slow heart beat
B. Rapid heart beat
C. Heart murmur
D. Angina pectoris

270. Inflammation of the inner lining of the heart
A. Myocarditis
B. Pericarditis
C. Phlebitis
D. Endocarditis

271. Emphysema
A. Spasm of smooth muscle surrounding bronchial tubes, reducing inhalation
B. Inflammation of bronchial tubes due to inhalation of smoke from cigarette smoking
C. Destruction of alveoli, resulting in decreased oxygen intake
D. Bacterial infection of the lungs, reducing carbon dioxide output

272. Subdural hematoma
A. A blood clot on top of the brain beneath the dura mater following head trauma
B. Inflammation of the meninges following a bacterial infection
C. Paralysis of the spinal cord due to injections common in childbirth
D. Brain damage arising from stroke

273. Statins are medications that help to reduce what substance in the body
A. Epinephrine
B. Cholesterol
C. Histamine
D. Calcium

274. Constipation is the result of insufficient amounts of the following substance in fecal matter
A. Bile
B. Water
C. Plasma
D. Lymph

275. Acute asthma is considered
A. A local contraindication
B. An absolute contraindication
C. An endangerment site
D. Not a contraindication

276. The definition of the prefix "auto-" is
A. Outside
B. Self
C. Before
D. Against

277. An idiopathic disease is
A. A disease in which the cause is unknown
B. A disease which is cancerous
C. A disease which is autoimmune in nature
D. A disease which results in bacterial infection

278. Non-infectious pleurisy is considered
A. A local contraindication
B. An absolute contraindication
C. An endangerment site
D. Not a contraindication

279. Head trauma may result in the formation of a blood clot between the brain and dura mater, also called
A. Subdural hematoma
B. Meningitis
C. Migraine
D. Epidural hematoma

280. The definition of the prefix "tri-" is
A. Valve
B. Above
C. Three
D. Below

281. Osteoporosis
A. Bacterial infection involving the periosteum and medullary cavity
B. Overabundance of calcium, making bones strong
C. Insufficient calcium entering into bone tissue, resulting in brittle bones
D. A lateral curvature of the thoracic vertebrae

282. Diverticulitis is considered
A. A local contraindication
B. An absolute contraindication
C. An endangerment site
D. Not a contraindication

283. Gout
A. Inflammation of joints caused by increased amounts of uric acid
B. Bacterial infection that enters the periosteum and bone canal
C. Cancer of bone that enters the medullary cavity
D. Inflammation of joints caused by increased amounts of sodium chloride

284. Fibromyalgia is considered
A. A local contraindication
B. An absolute contraindication
C. An endangerment site
D. Not a contraindication

285. Paralysis of one half of the face, caused by stimulation of the Herpes Simplex virus, which affects the Facial nerve
A. Graves disease
B. Cerebral palsy
C. Trigeminal neuralgia
D. Bell's palsy

286. The definition of the suffix "-emia" is
A. Nourishment
B. Blood condition
C. Pertaining to
D. Standing still

287. Multiple sclerosis affects the
A. Brain and spinal cord
B. Median nerve
C. Cranial nerves
D. Lumbosacral plexus

288. A client notifies a massage therapist that they have a small area of skin affected by cellulitis. The appropriate response by the massage therapist would be
A. Apply heat to the affected area to allow increased circulation to enter the area
B. Work on the affected area to help break up fat deposits under the skin
C. Avoid the affected area but continue massaging the rest of the body
D. Reschedule the massage until the cellulitis has completely cleared up

289. The definition of the suffix "-osis" is
A. Skin
B. Small
C. Growth
D. Condition

290. Autoimmune disease which results in attack of the body's connective tissues
A. Still's disease
B. Lupus erythematosus
C. Dermatomyositis
D. Myasthenia gravis

291. Enlargement of lymph nodes in the groin, neck, and axilla may be a sign of
A. Non-Hodgkins lymphoma
B. Malignant melanoma
C. Leukemia
D. Myeloma

292. Excessive bilirubin in the blood stream results in
A. Jaundice
B. Hepatitis
C. Encephalitis
D. Cyanosis

293. A blockage of a blood vessel may result in
A. Phlebitis
B. Arrhythmia
C. Ischemia
D. Hyperemia

294. A massage therapist is working on a client's back, when they come upon severe acne, including whiteheads. The proper course of action for the massage therapist to take
A. Reschedule the massage until the acne has subsided
B. Continue the massage, avoiding the affected area
C. Massage vigorously over the pustules
D. Perform friction on the affected area

295. The definition of the prefix "retro-" is
A. Before
B. Same
C. Behind
D. Difficult

296. Tightness in the following muscle may result in pain shooting down the lower limb into the plantar surface of the feet
A. Latissimus dorsi
B. Rectus femoris
C. Piriformis
D. Psoas major

297. The definition of the prefix "hyper-" is
A. Rapid
B. Slow
C. Excessive
D. Below

298. The definition of "hist/o" is
A. Tissue
B. Uterus
C. Vagina
D. Liver

299. Meningitis can be caused by all of the following except
A. Parasite
B. Fungus
C. Bacteria
D. Stroke

300. Increased levels of bilirubin in the blood stream results in
A. Jaundice
B. Hepatitis
C. Nephritis
D. Anemia

301. The definition of the prefix "contra-" is
A. Without
B. Against
C. Bad
D. One

302. Varicose veins are a form of
A. Phlebitis
B. Arteriosclerosis
C. Atherosclerosis
D. Raynaud's disease

303. Multiple sclerosis is most common in
A. Elderly
B. Men
C. Children
D. Women

304. Acute rheumatoid arthritis is considered
A. An endangerment site
B. An absolute contraindication
C. A local contraindication
D. Not a contraindication

305. The definition of "emphys/o" is
A. Plug
B. Inflate
C. Ear
D. Hearing

306. Acute bronchitis is considered
A. A local contraindication
B. An absolute contraindication
C. An endangerment site
D. Not a contraindication

307. Juvenile diabetes
A. The body creates too much glucagon
B. The body produces too much insulin
C. The body lacks sufficient glucagon
D. The body lacks sufficient insulin

308. The definition of "hemat/o" is
A. Liver
B. Blood
C. Tumor
D. Kidney

309. A headache is considered
A. A local contraindication
B. An absolute contraindication
C. An endangerment site
D. Not a contraindication

310. The definition of the suffix "-ic" is
A. Pertaining to
B. Formation
C. Specialist
D. Dissolve

311. Ringworm
A. Parasitic infection resulting in severe weight loss
B. Bacterial infection resulting in yellow scabs around the mouth
C. Viral infection resulting in circular ulcers on the skin
D. Fungal infection resulting in a circular rash on the skin

312. A cold sore around the mouth of a client would affect a massage in what way
A. Massage around the mouth is indicated
B. Massage around the mouth is contraindicated
C. Massage would not be performed at all until the cold sore clears up
D. Massage around the mouth would be beneficial to speed healing of the sore

313. The definition of the suffix "-al" is
A. Pertaining to
B. Inflammation
C. Cell
D. Pain

314. The definition of "gluc/o" is
A. Gums
B. Pancreas
C. Sugar
D. Muscle

315. Penicillin is used to fight the following type of infection
A. Viral
B. Bacterial
C. Fungal
D. Parasitic

316. Hemiplegia is considered
A. A local contraindication
B. An absolute contraindication
C. An endangerment site
D. Not a contraindication

317. Adhesive capsulitis is considered
A. A local contraindication
B. An absolute contraindication
C. An endangerment site
D. Not a contraindication

318. The definition of the prefix "hypo-" is
A. Rapid
B. Slow
C. Excessive
D. Below

319. Chronic bronchitis
A. Spasm of smooth muscle surrounding bronchial tubes, reducing inhalation
B. Inflammation of bronchial tubes due to inhalation of smoke from cigarette smoking
C. Destruction of alveoli, resulting in decreased oxygen intake
D. Bacterial infection of the lungs, reducing carbon dioxide output

320. Beta-blockers are medications that disable the functions of
A. Epinephrine
B. Histamine
C. Calcium
D. Parathyroid hormone

321. Urethritis may be accompanied by inflammation of the
A. Bladder
B. Kidney
C. Testicles
D. Uterus

322. All of the following are caused by an infection of the staphylococci bacteria except
A. Impetigo
B. Cellulitis
C. Sebaceous cyst
D. Osteomyelitis

323. Chronic inflammation located at the tibial tuberosity, caused by overuse of the quadriceps
A. Osgood-Schlatter disease
B. Grave's disease
C. Raynaud's disease
D. Knock-knee

324. Histamines dilate blood vessels to
A. Decrease lymph circulation to an area of trauma
B. Decrease blood flow to an area of trauma
C. Increase lymph circulation to an area of trauma
D. Increase blood flow to an area of trauma

325. The definition of the prefix "uni-" is
A. Two
B. Disease
C. Bad
D. One

326. Non-infectious laryngitis is considered
A. A local contraindication
B. An absolute contraindication
C. An endangerment site
D. Not a contraindication

327. Electrocardiogram may detect the presence of
A. Angina pectoris
B. Heart murmur
C. Tachycardia
D. Bradycardia

328. The definition of "dent/o" is
A. Crooked
B. Cheek
C. Teeth
D. Tongue

329. Inflammation of a joint
A. Arthritis
B. Articulation
C. Atherosclerosis
D. Arteriosclerosis

330. Trigeminal neuralgia involves the following cranial nerve
A. Cranial nerve X
B. Cranial nerve V
C. Cranial nerve VII
D. Cranial nerve XII

331. Paralysis of the legs is a condition known as
A. Paraplegia
B. Quadriplegia
C. Hemiplegia
D. Semiplegia

332. Varicose veins may result in the formation of
A. Edematic tissue
B. Inflammation
C. Blood clots
D. Adhesions

333. The definition of "carcin/o" is
A. Gland
B. Fatty plaque
C. Cancer
D. Body

334. Of the following, which condition is contagious
A. Cerebral palsy
B. Arrhythmia
C. Angina pectoris
D. Herpes simplex

335. Acute hives are considered
A. A local contraindication
B. An absolute contraindication
C. An endangerment site
D. Not a contraindication

336. The definition of "jaund/o" is
A. Green
B. Yellow
C. Red
D. Black

337. Diverticulosis may be a result of a diet lacking in sufficient
A. Fiber
B. Fat
C. Protein
D. Potassium

338. The definition of "home/o" is
A. Same
B. Different
C. Balance
D. Other

339. Hypoplasia
A. Reduction in the amount of oxygen traveling throughout the body
B. Extreme formation of an organ or tissue resulting in tumors
C. Lack of proper formation of an organ or tissue
D. Rapid regeneration of damaged tissue

340. Asthma
A. Bacterial infection of the lungs, reducing carbon dioxide output
B. Inflammation of bronchial tubes due to cigarette smoking
C. Destruction of alveoli, resulting in decreased oxygen intake
D. Spasm of smooth muscle surrounding bronchial tubes, reducing inhalation

341. Ringing in the ears as the result of exposure to loud noise or old age
A. Vertigo
B. Tinnitus
C. Torticollis
D. Mastoiditis

342. Damage to the brain resulting in impaired speech
A. Dysphasia
B. Apnea
C. Arrhythmia
D. Encephalitis

343. Inflammation is the body's response to
A. Cell division
B. Tissue damage
C. Increased interstitial fluid
D. Edema

344. Hypoadrenalism is considered
A. A local contraindication
B. An absolute contraindication
C. An endangerment site
D. Not a contraindication

345. All of the following are local contraindications except
A. Skin rash
B. Phlebitis
C. Cyst
D. Endocarditis

346. Bacteria, testosterone production, and hormonal imbalance may all result in the development of
A. Acne
B. Warts
C. Impetigo
D. Facial hair

347. Frozen shoulder is considered
A. A local contraindication
B. An absolute contraindication
C. An endangerment site
D. Not a contraindication

348. Subacute rheumatoid arthritis is considered
A. A local contraindication
B. An absolute contraindication
C. An endangerment site
D. Not a contraindication

349. Blood poisoning is also referred to as
A. Septicemia
B. Anemia
C. Arthritis
D. Myalgia

350. A lesion visible to the naked eye is called
A. Epidermal lesion
B. Dermal lesion
C. Gross lesion
D. Keratin lesion

351. Painkillers are known as
A. Analgesics
B. Antipyretics
C. Anti-inflammatories
D. Antidiuretics

352. Hypertension may lead to the development of
A. Varicose veins
B. Atherosclerosis
C. Phlebitis
D. Heart murmur

353. The study of tissue
A. Pathology
B. Etiology
C. Histology
D. Oncology

354. The definition of "cephal/o" is
A. Crooked
B. Cheek
C. Teeth
D. Head

355. The definition of "chondr/o" is
A. Ribs
B. Cartilage
C. Large intestine
D. Vertebrae

356. Acute tendonitis is considered
A. A local contraindication
B. An absolute contraindication
C. An endangerment site
D. Not a contraindication

357. Subacute tendonitis is considered
A. A local contraindication
B. An absolute contraindication
C. An endangerment site
D. Not a contraindication

358. The anterior compartment of the neck is considered
A. A local contraindication
B. An absolute contraindication
C. An endangerment site
D. Not a contraindication

359. Phlebitis
A. Hardening of the walls of the arteries
B. Fatty plaque buildup in the arteries
C. Bulging of an arterial wall
D. Inflammation of a vein

360. Hypertension is also known as
A. Chest pain
B. Heart attack
C. High blood pressure
D. Blood clot

361. Gout is considered
A. An absolute contraindication
B. A local contraindication
C. An endangerment site
D. Not a contraindication

362. Cerebral infarction results in
A. Angina pectoris
B. Heart attack
C. Arrhythmia
D. Stroke

363. Wheezing accompanied by progressive loss of function due to alveolar degeneration in the lungs may be a sign of
A. Emphysema
B. Asthma
C. Acute bronchitis
D. Pleurisy

364. The inability of the heart to maintain a steady rhythm may result in implantation of a
A. Pacemaker
B. Arterial stent
C. Dialysis
D. Defibrillator

365. Tumor made of glandular tissue, usually benign
A. Carcinoma
B. Melanoma
C. Adenoma
D. Lymphoma

366. The definition of the suffix "-ist" is
A. Breathing
B. Formation
C. Specialist
D. Condition

367. Osteoarthritis
A. Inflammation of a joint caused by increased uric acid
B. Destruction of synovial membranes with formation of fibrous tissue
C. Destruction of articular cartilage increasing friction between bones
D. Inflammation of periosteum surrounding diaphyses

368. Sores produced by urticaria are known as
A. Wheals
B. Warts
C. Scabs
D. Acne

369. Warts located on the bottom of the foot
A. Dorsal warts
B. Plantar warts
C. Ankle warts
D. Tarsal warts

370. Golfer's elbow
A. Affects the extensors of the wrist, resulting in pain at the lateral epicondyle of the humerus
B. Affects the flexors of the wrist, resulting in pain at the medial epicondyle of the humerus
C. Affects the adductors of the thigh, resulting in pain at the inguinal region
D. Affects the flexors of the shoulder, resulting in pain at the acromion process

371. Antihistamines are used to control the body's response to
A. Medication
B. Stress
C. Allergies
D. Bruising

372. Formation of a blood clot inside of a blood vessel is known as
A. Thrombosis
B. Embolism
C. Aneurysm
D. Infarction

373. Appendicitis
A. Inflammation of an aneurysm
B. Inflammation of the alimentary canal
C. Inflammation of the aponeurosis
D. Inflammation of the appendix

374. The definition of "necr/o" is
A. Hard
B. Tissue
C. Nose
D. Death

375. Erosion of hyaline cartilage between articulating bones, increasing friction between the bones
A. Pyelonephritis
B. Rheumatoid arthritis
C. Osteoarthritis
D. Osteoporosis

376. The study of disease
A. Pathology
B. Etiology
C. Cardiology
D. Oncology

377. Muscle atrophy is considered
A. A local contraindication
B. An absolute contraindication
C. An endangerment site
D. Not a contraindication

378. Lack of blood flow into the fingers and toes, often a result of exposure to cold
A. Rheumatoid arthritis
B. Raynaud's syndrome
C. Vasodilation
D. Diabetes mellitus

379. Varicose veins most often occur in
A. Legs
B. Arms
C. Thighs
D. Ankles

380. Arthritis
A. Displacement of bone from its normal location
B. Bacterial infection of bone
C. Destruction of periosteum
D. Inflammation of joints

381. Cancer involving bone is known as
A. Sarcoma
B. Carcinoma
C. Melanoma
D. Lymphoma

382. A myocardial infarction is also known as
A. Aneurysm
B. Heart attack
C. Coronary bypass
D. Chest pain

383. Viral infection resulting in inflammation of the liver
A. Nephritis
B. Hepatitis
C. Mononucleosis
D. Encephalitis

384. An acute herpes zoster infection is considered
A. A local contraindication
B. An absolute contraindication
C. An endangerment site
D. Not a contraindication

385. Acute whiplash is considered
A. A local contraindication
B. An absolute contraindication
C. An endangerment site
D. Not a contraindication

386. Scars are considered
A. A local contraindication
B. An absolute contraindication
C. An endangerment site
D. Not a contraindication

387. All of the following are local contraindications except
A. Decubitus ulcer
B. Acne
C. Cellulitis
D. Psoriasis

388. If a client shows signs of pitting edema, which specialist should they be referred to
A. Oncologist
B. Cardiologist
C. Dermatologist
D. Nephrologist

389. The definition of the prefix "meta-" is
A. Change
B. Excessive
C. Inside
D. False

390. What is the most common form of hepatitis
A. Hepatitis A
B. Hepatitis B
C. Hepatitis C
D. Hepatitis D

391. Fungal infection affecting the groin
A. Tinea capitis
B. Tinea corporis
C. Tinea cruris
D. Tinea pedis

392. Pericarditis is considered
A. A local contraindication
B. An absolute contraindication
C. An endangerment site
D. Not a contraindication

393. The definition of "derm/o" is
A. Life
B. Cold
C. Skin
D. Same

394. Sarcoma is a cancer of
A. Connective tissue
B. Epithelial tissue
C. Muscular tissue
D. Nervous tissue

395. Development of crystals in tissues caused by excessive uric acid production
A. Osteomalacia
B. Gout
C. Rheumatoid arthritis
D. Osteoarthritis

396. The definition of "nas/o" is
A. Death
B. Tissue
C. Nose
D. Hard

397. A neurologist is a doctor that specializes in
A. Stomach
B. Heart
C. Brain
D. Lungs

398. A ganglion cyst is considered
A. An endangerment site
B. An absolute contraindication
C. A local contraindication
D. Not a contraindication

399. Hypothyroidism leads to an increased sensitivity to
A. Heat
B. Cold
C. Light touch
D. Deep pressure

400. Nephritis
A. Inflammation of the kidneys
B. Inflammation of the liver
C. Inflammation of the small intestine
D. Inflammation of the urinary bladder

401. Bruxism is the leading cause of
A. TMJ disorder
B. Congestive heart failure
C. Bursitis
D. Diverticulosis

402. Portion of an intervertebral disc that protrudes through the annulus fibrosis during a disc herniation
A. Spinal cord
B. Annulus pulposus
C. Facet cartilage
D. Nucleus pulposus

403. Pain in the chest most commonly resulting from exercise
A. Angina pectoris
B. Myocardial infarction
C. Mastitis
D. Atherosclerosis

404. Degeneration of intervertebral discs in the cervical region results in
A. Torticollis
B. Whiplash
C. Spondylitis
D. Kyphosis

405. Anemia is considered
A. A local contraindication
B. An absolute contraindication
C. An endangerment site
D. Not a contraindication

406. Hypothermia
A. Causes increased sweating to decrease body temperature
B. Caused by a body temperature that drops below 90 degrees
C. Results in severe headache and nausea with an increase in heart rate
D. Results in localized ischemia

407. Rheumatoid arthritis
A. Destruction of joints caused by increase in uric acid
B. Destruction of hyaline cartilage located between articulating bones
C. Destruction of intervertebral discs between vertebral bodies
D. Destruction of synovial membrane surrounding diarthrotic joints

408. A client who suffers from arrhythmia would be referred to which doctor
A. Dermatologist
B. Nephrologist
C. Cardiologist
D. Gastroenterologist

409. HIV may be transmitted through all of the following means except
A. Saliva contact
B. Blood contact
C. Sexual contact
D. Milk contact

410. Hemorrhoids are considered
A. A local contraindication
B. An absolute contraindication
C. An endangerment site
D. Not a contraindication

411. During the course of a massage, the massage therapist notices a pre-existing contusion on the client's leg. The massage therapist should
A. Avoid the contusion, notify the client where the contusion is located, and document the contusion in SOAP notes
B. Work over the contusion to help break up potential blood clots that may have formed during the course of healing
C. Apply a cold compress to the affected contusion to reduce blood flow to the contusion
D. Reschedule the massage until the contusion has resolved, as contusions are absolute contraindications

412. Primary muscle involved in adhesive capsulitis which tightens and restricts range of motion
A. Pectoralis major
B. Supraspinatus
C. Subscapularis
D. Trapezius

413. Loss of function of a limb is the result of
A. Neuralgia
B. Tremor
C. Paralysis
D. Neuritis

414. Autoimmune disorder affecting myelin sheaths in the central nervous system
A. Multiple sclerosis
B. Myasthenia gravis
C. Parkinson's disease
D. Alzheimer's disease

415. Sac-like structure surrounding liquid that should not be in the body
A. Gland
B. Cyst
C. Heart
D. Mediastinum

416. Histology
A. Study of disease
B. Study of cause of disease
C. Study of tumors
D. Study of tissue

417. The definition of the suffix "-edema" is
A. Paralysis
B. Inside
C. Inflammation
D. Swelling

418. The definition of the suffix "-crine" is
A. Paralysis
B. Inside
C. Secrete
D. Swelling

419. Autoimmune disorder resulting in increased epithelial production, producing thick scaly patches of skin
A. Psoriasis
B. Rosacea
C. Wart
D. Lupus

420. Ibuprofen is an example of
A. Non-steroidal anti-inflammatory drug
B. Statin
C. Bronchodilator
D. Expectorant

421. Scleroderma
A. Hardening of the skin often seen with Raynaud's syndrome
B. Hypothermia causing decreased oxygen to the brain
C. Fatty plaque forming in the walls of arteries
D. Acne in the skin, resulting in a bacterial infection such as cellulitis

422. Herpes simplex is a
A. Bacteria
B. Virus
C. Fungus
D. Parasite

423. Lateral curvature of the thoracic vertebrae
A. Swayback
B. Dowager's hump
C. Scoliosis
D. Bamboo spine

424. If systolic pressure measures 140 or higher, a person may be diagnosed with
A. Hypotension
B. Hypertension
C. Hyperemia
D. Myocardial infarction

425. A podiatrist is a doctor that specializes in the
A. Ears
B. Mouth
C. Feet
D. Bladder

426. Encephalitis is considered
A. A local contraindication
B. An absolute contraindication
C. An endangerment site
D. Not a contraindication

427. Inflammation of the bronchi as a result of a secondary infection, such as pneumonia
A. Asthma
B. Chronic bronchitis
C. Acute bronchitis
D. Influenza

428. Anemia can result in
A. Hypoxia
B. Hypothermia
C. Raynaud's syndrome
D. Frostbite

429. Scabies is considered
A. A local contraindication
B. An absolute contraindication
C. An endangerment site
D. Not a contraindication

430. Paralysis of one side of the body is a condition known as
A. Paraplegia
B. Quadriplegia
C. Hemiplegia
D. Semiplegia

431. A heart rate of 140-220 beats per minute resulting from abnormal electrical impulses stimulating the ventricles to contract rapidly
A. Atrial fibrillation
B. Bradycardia
C. Heart murmur
D. Tachycardia

432. A first degree burn that does not hurt is considered
A. A local contraindication
B. An absolute contraindication
C. An endangerment site
D. Not a contraindication

433. Oncology
A. Study of disease
B. Study of cause of disease
C. Study of tumors
D. Study of tissue

434. Gingivitis
A. Inflammation of gums
B. Inflammation of stomach
C. Inflammation of tongue
D. Inflammation of tonsils

435. Cyanosis
A. Bluish discoloration of skin and mucous membranes
B. Reddish discoloration of skin and mucous membranes
C. Yellowish discoloration of skin and mucous membranes
D. Orange discoloration of skin and mucous membranes

436. The definition of the suffix "-esis" is
A. Skin
B. Small
C. Growth
D. Condition

437. A person suffering from the flu, common cold, or sinusitis might benefit from use of which medications
A. Anticoagulants
B. Decongestants
C. Vasodilators
D. Beta-blockers

438. A deep cut is known as
A. Avulsion
B. Laceration
C. Puncture
D. Fracture

439. A complete ACL tear is which grade sprain
A. Grade 0
B. Grade 1
C. Grade 2
D. Grade 3

440. A strain is an injury to
A. Tendon
B. Ligament
C. Bone
D. Periosteum

441. Scarring of myelin sheaths in the central nervous system is the result of
A. Parkinson's disease
B. Myasthenia gravis
C. Multiple sclerosis
D. Alzheimer's disease

442. Parkinson's disease
A. Drop in dopamine levels in the body, resulting in gradual increase of shaking or trembling, specifically during fine motor actions
B. Degeneration of brain tissue, resulting in loss of memory
C. Inflammation of the brain, resulting in brain damage and loss of function
D. Compression of the facial nerve, resulting in paralysis of one side of the face

443. Fungal infection affecting the epidermis, resulting in a circular rash
A. Cordyceps
B. Athlete's foot
C. Ringworm
D. Whitlow

444. Degeneration of brain tissue, ultimately resulting in loss of memory and often dementia
A. Parkinson's disease
B. Cerebral palsy
C. Alzheimer's disease
D. Stroke

445. The definition of "lact/o" is
A. Breast
B. Milk
C. Tear
D. Uterus

446. An abundance of scar tissue grown in one location
A. Keloid
B. Adhesion
C. Sclerosis
D. Osteoblast

447. The definition of "adip/o" is
A. Body
B. Fat
C. Brain
D. Kidney

448. The definition of the suffix "-ar" is
A. Pain
B. Inflammation
C. Cell
D. Pertaining to

449. Irregular heart beat
A. Myocardial infarction
B. Heart murmur
C. Arrhythmia
D. Angina pectoris

450. The definition of "audi/o" is
A. Inflate
B. Plug
C. Ear
D. Hearing

451. Pathology
A. Study of disease
B. Study of cause of disease
C. Study of tumors
D. Study of tissue

452. The definition of the prefix "brady-" is
A. Rapid
B. Slow
C. Excessive
D. Below

453. A client who suffers from acne would be referred to which doctor
A. Nephrologist
B. Dermatologist
C. Cardiologist
D. Gastroenterologist

454. Inflammation of the skin of the face caused by irritation of hair follicles
A. Rosacea
B. Eczema
C. Lupus
D. Hyperemia

455. Angina pectoris is considered
A. A local contraindication
B. An absolute contraindication
C. An endangerment site
D. Not a contraindication

456. Progressive weakness of skeletal muscle may be a sign of
A. Discoid lupus erythematosus
B. Still's disease
C. Dermatomyositis
D. Myasthenia gravis

457. Acute lupus erythematosus is considered
A. A local contraindication
B. An absolute contraindication
C. An endangerment site
D. Not a contraindication

458. All of the following are contagious conditions except
A. Rosacea
B. Cellulitis
C. Influenza
D. Scabies

459. Cystic fibrosis is considered
A. A local contraindication
B. An absolute contraindication
C. An endangerment site
D. Not a contraindication

460. Malignancy is also known as
A. Cancer
B. Cyst
C. Edema
D. Inflammation

461. Cystic fibrosis is passed on through genes. This makes it
A. Autoimmune
B. Contagious
C. Hereditary
D. Inflammatory

462. The definition of the suffix "-uria" is
A. Discharge
B. Flow
C. Growth
D. Urine

463. Involuntary painful contraction of a muscle caused by lack of oxygen or dehydration
A. Cramp
B. Spasm
C. Twitch
D. Strain

464. Basal cell carcinoma is most often caused by
A. Sunlight exposure
B. Overproduction of melanocytes
C. Autoimmune attacks on the epithelium
D. Exposure to cold

465. Atopic dermatitis is considered
A. A local contraindication
B. An absolute contraindication
C. An endangerment site
D. Not a contraindication

466. The definition of the prefix "supra-" is
A. Eating
B. Through
C. Below
D. Above

467. Ulceration may occur in the fingers and toes in severe forms of
A. Emphysema
B. Cyanosis
C. Raynaud's syndrome
D. Paraplegia

468. Acute gastritis is considered
A. A local contraindication
B. An absolute contraindication
C. An endangerment site
D. Not a contraindication

469. Chronic degeneration of alveolar sacs, reducing the exchange of carbon dioxide and oxygen in and out of the blood
A. Emphysema
B. Asthma
C. Pneumonia
D. Bronchitis

470. Tendonitis
A. Inflammation of a bone
B. Inflammation of a ligament
C. Inflammation of a muscle
D. Inflammation of a tendon

471. Inflammation of heart muscle
A. Pericarditis
B. Myocarditis
C. Phlebitis
D. Endocarditis

472. Heat stroke
A. A person's internal body temperature remains over 104 degrees
B. A person's internal body temperature drops below 98.6 degrees
C. A person's internal body temperature remains over 90 degrees
D. A person's internal body temperature drops below 104 degrees

473. Swelling of the thyroid gland results in
A. Abscess
B. Goiter
C. Cyst
D. Gout

474. Multiple sclerosis affects all of the following structures except
A. Spinal cord
B. Cerebellum
C. Cerebrum
D. Peripheral nerves

475. Degeneration of intervertebral discs over a long period of time, reducing space between vertebrae, which ultimately results in vertebral fusion
A. Scoliosis
B. Ankylosing spondylitis
C. Rheumatoid arthritis
D. Osteoarthritis

476. Quadriplegia
A. Paralysis of only the legs
B. Paralysis of one side of the body
C. Paralysis of all four limbs
D. Paralysis of one side of the face

477. Itching of the scalp may be a sign of
A. Lice
B. Ringworm
C. Scabies
D. Scurvy

478. The second most common form of skin cancer
A. Kaposi's sarcoma
B. Malignant melanoma
C. Basal cell carcinoma
D. Squamous cell carcinoma

479. Nerve running deep to the flexor retinaculum of the wrist, which may be compressed, resulting in loss of sensation in the hand
A. Radial
B. Ulnar
C. Median
D. Tibial

480. Controlled hypertension is considered
A. A local contraindication
B. An absolute contraindication
C. An endangerment site
D. Not a contraindication

481. Contraction of hepatitis B is most likely due to exposure to
A. Blood
B. Feces
C. Saliva
D. Semen

482. Chronic irritation of skin resulting in red, dry, burning patches
A. Eczema
B. Stasis dermatitis
C. Contact dermatitis
D. Acne

483. Partial tearing of a ligament caused by overstretching
A. Grade 1 sprain
B. Grade 2 sprain
C. Grade 3 sprain
D. Grade 1 strain

484. The definition of "gloss/o" is
A. Pelvis
B. Groin
C. Tongue
D. Armpit

485. The definition of the suffix "-physis" is
A. Discharge
B. Bursting forth
C. Growth
D. Urine

486. Stomach acid flowing from the stomach into the esophagus is a result of the following structure not functioning properly
A. Pyloric sphincter
B. Esophageal sphincter
C. Cardiac sphincter
D. Ileocecal sphincter

487. Cigarette smoking may lead to
A. Oral cancer
B. Cerebral aneurysms
C. Pulmonary valve prolapse
D. Hemorrhoids

488. Cushing's syndrome
A. Overproduction in thyroid hormone, resulting in bulging of the eyes
B. Degeneration of the adrenal glands due to an autoimmune response
C. Protrusion of the small intestine through the abdominal peritoneum into the umbilicus
D. Excess use of synthetic corticosteroids, resulting in weight gain, muscle atrophy, and hypertension

489. Hypotension is also referred to as
A. Low blood pressure
B. High blood pressure
C. Arrhythmia
D. Varicose veins

490. The definition of the suffix "-ectomy" is
A. Cutting
B. Blood condition
C. To carry
D. Removal

491. Acute sprains are considered
A. An absolute contraindication
B. A local contraindication
C. An endangerment site
D. Not a contraindication

492. Hypertonicity of pectoralis minor may result in
A. Swayback
B. Dowager's hump
C. Scoliosis
D. Bamboo spine

493. Heart murmurs are considered
A. A local contraindication
B. An absolute contraindication
C. An endangerment site
D. Not a contraindication

494. A nephrologist is a specialist who works with
A. Kidneys
B. Heart
C. Liver
D. Stomach

495. Cerebral palsy is considered
A. A local contraindication
B. An absolute contraindication
C. An endangerment site
D. Not a contraindication

496. Form of tendonitis affecting the patellar tendon
A. Golfer's elbow
B. Tennis elbow
C. Jumper's knee
D. Croquette wrist

497. Insulin dependent diabetes, in which the body lacks an appropriate amount of insulin, is also known as
A. Diabetes type I
B. Diabetes type II
C. Diabetes insipidous
D. Non insulin-dependent diabetes

498. Basal cell carcinoma is what type of tumor
A. Idiopathic
B. Malignant
C. Benign
D. Lymphatic

499. A client who suffers from Crohn's disease would be referred to which doctor
A. Dermatologist
B. Nephrologist
C. Cardiologist
D. Gastroenterologist

500. Acquired immunodeficiency syndrome is also known as
A. HIV
B. AIDS
C. Sarcoidosis
D. Leukemia

501. The study of the cause of disease
A. Pathology
B. Etiology
C. Radiology
D. Idiopathology

502. The definition of "rhin/o" is
A. Death
B. Tissue
C. Nose
D. Hard

503. Overstretching of a ligament results in
A. Sprain
B. Strain
C. Fracture
D. Tendonitis

504. Inflammation of a tendon
A. Myelitis
B. Fibromyalgia
C. Carpal tunnel syndrome
D. Tendonitis

505. A burning sensation during urination may be a sign of
A. Cholecystitis
B. Nephritis
C. Prostatitis
D. Cystitis

506. Ringworm is considered
A. A local contraindication
B. An absolute contraindication
C. An endangerment site
D. Not a contraindication

507. Food poisoning, ingestion of bacterial or viral agents, results in
A. Gastroenteritis
B. Crohn's disease
C. Ulcerative colitis
D. Diverticulosis

508. Chronic or acute ringing in the ears
A. Tinnitus
B. Vertigo
C. Lentigo
D. Otitis media

509. Benign tumors grow
A. Quickly
B. Slowly
C. Outward
D. Towards the lymph

510. Acquired Immunodeficiency syndrome is considered
A. A local contraindication
B. An absolute contraindication
C. An endangerment site
D. Not a contraindication

511. Varicose veins are considered
A. A local contraindication
B. An absolute contraindication
C. An endangerment site
D. Not a contraindication

512. Metastasizing is
A. Swallowing
B. Chewing
C. Spreading of cancer
D. Growth of bone at the metaphysis

513. Trauma to an area may result in
A. Hemopoiesis
B. Hemiplegia
C. Hemorrhage
D. Hypoxia

514. Exposure to asbestos may result in
A. Mesothelioma
B. Pericarditis
C. Pleurisy
D. Pneumonia

515. Excessive use of synthetic corticosteroids may result in the following condition
A. Addison's disease
B. Cushing's syndrome
C. Hepatitis
D. Grave's disease

516. Torticollis is considered
A. A local contraindication
B. An absolute contraindication
C. An endangerment site
D. Not a contraindication

517. A client would be referred to a dermatologist for all of the following conditions except
A. Cellulitis
B. Lupus
C. Warts
D. Sebaceous cyst

518. The axilla is considered
A. A local contraindication
B. An absolute contraindication
C. An endangerment site
D. Not a contraindication

519. Diverticulosis
A. Autoimmune disorder resulting in inflammation of the inner linings of the small intestine and large intestine
B. Irritation of the stomach, resulting in inflammation of the stomach, forcing pepsin through the cardiac sphincter
C. Formation of pouches in the large intestine as a result of contractions of smooth muscle in the large intestine without substances to press against
D. Inflammation of diverticular pouches, resulting in abscesses and ulcerations, causing severe septicemia

520. The definition of "scler/o" is
A. Crooked
B. Spine
C. Skin
D. Hard

521. Carpal tunnel syndrome affects which nerve of the brachial plexus
A. Median
B. Radial
C. Axillary
D. Femoral

522. Pus is formed by
A. Dead white blood cells
B. Dead red blood cells
C. Bacteria waste
D. Plasma

523. An abnormal growth of tissue results in the formation of a
A. Tumor
B. Mole
C. Callus
D. Mucous membrane

524. A goiter is considered
A. An absolute contraindication
B. A local contraindication
C. An endangerment site
D. Not a contraindication

525. A secondary tumor
A. Forms into a primary tumor
B. Is the original tumor of a malignant cancer
C. Is made of epithelial cells
D. Is also called a metastasis

526. The definition of the suffix "-globin" is
A. Pertaining to
B. Standing still
C. Nourishment
D. Protein

527. Chris has recently recovered from a severe pneumonia infection. A massage technique that may aid in lung decongestion would be
A. Vibration
B. Effleurage
C. Tapotement
D. Friction

528. Leukemia
A. Malignant cancer of white blood cells, resulting in a decrease in functioning leukocytes in the body
B. Cancer of lymph nodes and ducts causing tumors in and around the armpits and neck
C. Tumors arising from bone tissue, causing an increase in the susceptibility to fracture at the site of tumor growth
D. Cancer of melanocytes, spreading to other organs throughout the body via lymph ducts

529. Laryngitis
A. Inflammation of the throat
B. Inflammation of the voice box
C. Inflammation of bronchial tubes
D. Inflammation of tonsils

530. Medical device implanted into patients with uncontrolled arrhythmia
A. Angioplasty
B. Electrocardiogram
C. Arterial stent
D. Pacemaker

531. Benign tumors
A. Spread to other parts of the body through lymph
B. Do not spread to other locations in the body
C. Spread to other parts of the body through blood
D. Spread to other parts of the body through interstitial fluid

532. Paraplegia
A. Paralysis of the legs due to an injury to the spinal cord below T1
B. Paralysis of the arms and legs due to an injury to the spinal cord between C5 and T1
C. Paralysis of one side of the body due to transient ischemic attack, resulting in brain damage
D. Paralysis of one side of the face due to an injury to cranial nerve VII

533. Hydatid cysts in humans occur most often in which organ
A. Brain
B. Liver
C. Kidneys
D. Bladder

534. The definition of "abdomin/o" is
A. Stomach
B. Abdomen
C. Intestines
D. Bladder

535. Blood clot formation in a vein, resulting in vein inflammation
A. Thrombophlebitis
B. Atherosclerosis
C. Iron-deficient anemia
D. Varicose veins

536. Leukemia is a malignant form of cancer arising from
A. Bone marrow
B. Red blood cells
C. Plasma
D. White blood cells

537. Cephalosporin is a type of
A. Antigen
B. Antifungal
C. Antiviral
D. Antibiotic

538. Sleep apnea is considered
A. A local contraindication
B. An absolute contraindication
C. An endangerment site
D. Not a contraindication

539. A client presents with warts on the bottom of the foot. An appropriate response would be
A. Perform the massage, avoiding the affected area
B. Perform the massage, performing cross-fiber friction over the affected area
C. Reschedule the massage and refer the client to a dermatologist
D. Perform the massage and apply wart removing cream to the affected area

540. Medications that specifically control heart rhythm are known as
A. Antihistamines
B. Beta-blockers
C. Antiarrhythmics
D. Vasodilators

541. Overproduction in melanocytes results in a tumor known as
A. Sarcoma
B. Carcinoma
C. Melanoma
D. Lymphoma

542. An acute dislocation is considered
A. An endangerment site
B. An absolute contraindication
C. A local contraindication
D. Not a contraindication

543. Emphysema is considered
A. A local contraindication
B. An absolute contraindication
C. An endangerment site
D. Not a contraindication

544. Decreased hemoglobin in erythrocytes may be caused by
A. Iron deficient anemia
B. Sickle cell anemia
C. Lymphedema
D. Arteriosclerosis

545. Pneumothorax is the presence of a bubble of air in the
A. Pleural membrane
B. Alveoli
C. Bronchial tubes
D. Trachea

546. Cirrhosis of the liver is considered
A. A local contraindication
B. An absolute contraindication
C. An endangerment site
D. Not a contraindication

547. Quadriplegia
A. Paralysis of the legs due to an injury to the spinal cord below T1
B. Paralysis of the arms and legs due to an injury to the spinal cord between C5 and T1
C. Paralysis of one side of the body due to transient ischemic attack, resulting in brain damage
D. Paralysis of one side of the face due to an injury to cranial nerve VII

548. The definition of "erythr/o" is
A. Yellow
B. Green
C. Red
D. White

549. A high ankle sprain results in tearing of the
A. Interosseous ligament
B. Meniscus
C. Anterior cruciate ligament
D. Medial collateral ligament

550. Achilles tendonitis is especially common in people who perform the following action
A. Swimming
B. Jumping
C. Running
D. Walking

551. Periostitis
A. Infection of periosteum
B. Degeneration of periosteum
C. Overproduction of periosteum
D. Inflammation of periosteum

552. The definition of "angi/o" is
A. Artery
B. Vessel
C. Muscle
D. Heart

553. Muscular dystrophy is
A. A genetic disorder
B. A sexually transmitted disease
C. A viral infection
D. Degeneration of bone after menopause

554. The definition of "later/o" is
A. Curve
B. Far
C. Side
D. Near

555. A feeling of well-being, accompanied by an increase of heart rate and breathing rate, could be a sign of
A. Hyperlordosis
B. Hypoxia
C. Thrombus
D. Ankylosing spondylitis

556. A diet high in iron is helpful in prevention of a specific form of
A. Varicose veins
B. Leukemia
C. Lymphedema
D. Anemia

557. Bamboo spine is considered
A. A local contraindication
B. An absolute contraindication
C. An endangerment site
D. Not a contraindication

558. Lice, scabies, and ticks are all types of
A. Parasites
B. Bacterium
C. Fungi
D. Viruses

559. Inability of the body to properly clot
A. Hemorrhage
B. Hemophilia
C. Hemopoiesis
D. Cystic fibrosis

560. In Parkinson's disease, what happens to dopamine
A. Dopamine converts to cortisol
B. Dopamine levels increase
C. Dopamine levels stay the same
D. Dopamine levels drop

561. Expectorants help in
A. Thinning mucous
B. Draining sinuses
C. Blocking histamines
D. Dilating respiratory passages

562. Raynaud's disease is considered
A. A local contraindication
B. An absolute contraindication
C. An endangerment site
D. Not a contraindication

563. The definition of "col/o" is
A. Ribs
B. Cartilage
C. Large intestine
D. Vertebrae

564. The definition of the prefix "ab-" is
A. Towards
B. Away
C. Before
D. Against

565. Paraplegia is considered
A. A local contraindication
B. An absolute contraindication
C. An endangerment site
D. Not a contraindication

566. The definition of "pyr/o" is
A. Water
B. Cold
C. Kidney
D. Heat

567. All of the following are local contraindications except
A. Raynaud's syndrome
B. Phlebitis
C. Fracture
D. Acne

568. The definition of the prefix "infra-" is
A. Above
B. Through
C. Below
D. False

569. Swayback is considered
A. A local contraindication
B. An absolute contraindication
C. An endangerment site
D. Not a contraindication

570. In a herniated disc, the nucleus pulposus protrudes through the
A. Annulus fibrosis
B. Vertebral body
C. Intervertebral facet
D. Sacral foramina

571. Pins and needles is a sensation known as
A. Parasthesia
B. Anaesthesia
C. Paralysis
D. Paraplegia

572. Rosacea is considered
A. A local contraindication
B. An absolute contraindication
C. An endangerment site
D. Not a contraindication

573. Boil
A. Bacterial infection of hair follicles
B. Bacterial infection of mucous membranes
C. Viral infection of mucous membranes
D. Bacterial infection of bone

574. Medication that destroys bacteria or prevents further bacterial growth
A. Antipsychotic
B. Antibiotic
C. Expectorant
D. Antiviral

575. The most fatal form of tumor is
A. Cystic
B. Benign
C. Malignant
D. Gangrenous

576. Bacterial infection spreading upwards from the urethra results in
A. Cholecystitis
B. Nephritis
C. Prostatitis
D. Cystitis

577. Thickening of arterial walls, leading to conditions such as hypertension
A. Arteriosclerosis
B. Angina pectoris
C. Scleroderma
D. Phlebitis

578. Hemodialysis involves filtering of
A. Feces
B. Urine
C. Blood
D. Water

579. Inflammation of a vein which may result from immobilization or trauma
A. Hepatitis
B. Arteriosclerosis
C. Phlebitis
D. Nephritis

580. The definition of "oophor/o" is
A. Uterus
B. Ovary
C. Fallopian tube
D. Eye

581. Rheumatoid arthritis is what type of disorder
A. Sarcoma
B. Viral
C. Bacterial
D. Autoimmune

582. The definition of "bucc/o" is
A. Crooked
B. Cheek
C. Teeth
D. Tongue

583. Lack of sufficient water in feces may result in
A. Diarrhea
B. Constipation
C. Diverticulosis
D. Crohn's disease

584. The definition of the suffix "-trophy" is
A. Pertaining to
B. Standing still
C. Nourishment
D. Protein

585. Digitalis and quinidine are both forms of
A. Antihistamine drugs
B. Antiarrhythmic drugs
C. Statins
D. Vasodilators

586. Hyper-curvature in the lumbar region
A. Bamboo spine
B. Dowager's hump
C. Scoliosis
D. Swayback

587. An abrasion is considered
A. An absolute contraindication
B. A local contraindication
C. An endangerment site
D. Not a contraindication

588. Bluish tinting of the skin
A. Cyanosis
B. Raynaud's syndrome
C. Diabetes mellitus
D. Atherosclerosis

589. Vitamin D insufficiency, resulting in softening of bone tissue
A. Osteomalacia
B. Dowager's hump
C. Lordosis
D. Paget's disease

590. All of the following are local contraindications except
A. Contusion
B. High ankle sprain
C. Bell's palsy
D. Bursitis

591. Carcinoma is a type of cancer affecting
A. Bone
B. Lymph
C. Epithelium
D. Blood

592. Third stage of the inflammatory response
A. Phagocytosis
B. Tissue repair
C. Pinocytosis
D. Histamine release

593. Tennis elbow
A. Affects the flexors of the wrist, resulting in pain at the medial epicondyle of the humerus
B. Affects the extensors of the wrist, resulting in pain at the lateral epicondyle of the humerus
C. Affects the adductors of the thigh, resulting in pain at the inguinal region
D. Affects the flexors of the shoulder, resulting in pain at the acromion process

594. Cranial nerve VII is involved in
A. Bell's palsy
B. Cerebral palsy
C. Trigeminal neuralgia
D. Hemotaxis

595. Gradual destruction of synovial membranes surrounding joints with an increase in formation of fibrous tissue
A. Gouty arthritis
B. Osteoarthritis
C. Ankylosing spondylitis
D. Rheumatoid arthritis

596. Highly contagious bacterial infection of mucous membranes, most common in children
A. Impetigo
B. Herpes simplex
C. Psoriasis
D. Boil

597. A lateral ankle sprain is the result of the ankle being forced into which position
A. Plantarflexion
B. Eversion
C. Dorsiflexion
D. Inversion

598. Contraction of hepatitis A is most likely due to exposure to
A. Blood
B. Feces
C. Saliva
D. Semen

599. Temporary obstruction of a blood vessel leading to the brain results in
A. Myocardial infarction
B. Transient ischemic attack
C. Cerebral aneurysm
D. Pulmonary embolism

600. The most common form of malignancy in children
A. Leukemia
B. Anemia
C. Melanoma
D. Non-Hodgkins Lymphoma

601. Hyperthyroidism leads to an increased sensitivity to
A. Heat
B. Cold
C. Light touch
D. Deep pressure

602. Carbon monoxide attaches to red blood cells and prevents the transport of oxygen throughout the body, resulting in
A. Hypothermia
B. Hypoxia
C. Raynaud's syndrome
D. Frostbite

603. Acute Tennis Elbow is considered
A. An endangerment site
B. An absolute contraindication
C. A local contraindication
D. Not a contraindication

604. Thrombophlebitis is considered
A. A local contraindication
B. An absolute contraindication
C. An endangerment site
D. Not a contraindication

605. Migraine headaches are also known as
A. Trigeminal headaches
B. Muscular tension headaches
C. Glycemic headaches
D. Vascular headaches

606. Each of the following are contagious conditions except
A. Mononucleosis
B. Cellulitis
C. Meningitis
D. Lupus

607. A ganglion cyst is primarily located
A. On the legs and thighs
B. On the hands, wrists, and feet
C. On the back and neck
D. On the chest, abdomen, and pelvis

608. Appendicitis is considered
A. A local contraindication
B. An absolute contraindication
C. An endangerment site
D. Not a contraindication

609. The definition of the prefix "exo-" is
A. Outside
B. Self
C. Inside
D. Against

610. The definition of the prefix "ad-" is
A. Away
B. Towards
C. Front
D. Self

611. A dermatologist is a doctor who specializes in the
A. Heart
B. Kidneys
C. Skin
D. Brain

612. Penicillin is a form of
A. Antiviral
B. Anti-inflammatory
C. Antibiotic
D. Antifungal

613. The definition of "aur/o" is
A. Ovary
B. Groin
C. Ear
D. Eye

614. Wear and tear arthritis, resulting in destruction of hyaline cartilage between articulating bones, increasing friction
A. Osteoarthritis
B. Rheumatoid arthritis
C. Gouty arthritis
D. Arthralgia

615. A client with Bell's palsy would be referred to which doctor
A. Cardiologist
B. Neurologist
C. Rheumatologist
D. Dermatologist

616. Hyper-curvature in the thoracic region, forcing the vertebrae laterally
A. Lordosis
B. Kyphosis
C. Scoliosis
D. Spondylitis

617. Connective tissue surrounding substances in the body, such as an infection
A. Pleurisy
B. Serous membrane
C. Peritoneal membrane
D. Cyst

618. The definition of "ped/o" is
A. Curve
B. Disease
C. Side
D. Foot

619. Influenza
A. Viral infection affecting the respiratory tract
B. Viral infection affecting the endocrine system
C. Bacterial infection affecting the respiratory tract
D. Bacterial infection affecting the digestive system

620. Acute osteoarthritis is considered
A. An endangerment site
B. An absolute contraindication
C. A local contraindication
D. Not a contraindication

621. The definition of "phleb/o" is
A. Artery
B. Blood
C. Lung
D. Vein

622. Hyper-curvature in the lumbar region
A. Kyphosis
B. Lordosis
C. Scoliosis
D. Spondylitis

623. Type of cell that typically does not regenerate
A. Stratum germinativum
B. Epithelial
C. Nervous
D. Muscular

624. An example of a superficial lesion is
A. Birthmark
B. Abscess
C. Pimple
D. Wart

625. Cessation of breathing during sleep
A. Narcolepsy
B. Dyspnea
C. Sleep apnea
D. Insomnia

626. Carpal tunnel syndrome is considered
A. A local contraindication
B. An absolute contraindication
C. An endangerment site
D. Not a contraindication

627. Multiple sclerosis during remission is considered
A. A local contraindication
B. An absolute contraindication
C. An endangerment site
D. Not a contraindication

628. The leading cause of cancerous death
A. Skin cancer
B. Heart cancer
C. Lung cancer
D. Prostate cancer

629. A protrusion of the nucleus pulposus from its normal location through the annulus fibrosis
A. Hiatal hernia
B. Subluxation
C. Herniated disc
D. Spondylitis

630. Hemiplegia
A. Paralysis of the legs due to an injury to the spinal cord below T1
B. Paralysis of the arms and legs due to an injury to the spinal cord between C5 and T1
C. Paralysis of one side of the body due to transient ischemic attack, resulting in brain damage
D. Paralysis of one side of the face due to an injury to cranial nerve VII

631. West Nile virus often results in
A. Encephalitis
B. Meningitis
C. Impetigo
D. Lymphoma

632. The definition of the prefix "post-" is
A. Before
B. Near
C. Behind
D. After

633. Nerve pain resulting in sudden, sharp stabbing sensations
A. Neuritis
B. Neuralgia
C. Dermatitis
D. Myalgia

634. Severe scleroderma is considered
A. Not a contraindication
B. An absolute contraindication
C. An endangerment site
D. A local contraindication

635. Lack of blood flow to an area results in
A. Hyperemia
B. Arrhythmia
C. Phlebitis
D. Ischemia

636. A red-ringed rash is found in
A. Tinea pedis
B. Ringworm
C. Shingles
D. Psoriasis

637. The definition of the prefix "di-" is
A. Two
B. Life
C. Head
D. One

638. Idiopathic condition resulting in pain in muscles
A. Bell's palsy
B. Muscular dystrophy
C. Tendonitis
D. Fibromyalgia

639. Inflammation of the gums
A. Tonsilitis
B. Gastritis
C. Stomatitis
D. Gingivitis

640. Gradual degeneration of parts of the adrenal glands
A. Grave's disease
B. Addison's disease
C. Cushing's syndrome
D. Adrenal hyperplasia

641. A metastasis is also known as
A. A secondary tumor
B. A primary tumor
C. Chewing
D. Epiphyseal plate

642. The definition of "bi/o" is
A. Skin
B. Two
C. Life
D. Same

643. Thoracic outlet syndrome is considered
A. A local contraindication
B. An absolute contraindication
C. An endangerment site
D. Not a contraindication

644. Ankylosing spondylitis
A. Protrusion of the gelatinous center of an intervertebral disc through the cartilaginous portion
B. Vertebrae moving out of place, resulting in pinching of spinal nerves
C. Degeneration of intervertebral discs, resulting in fusion of vertebrae and loss of natural curvature of the spine
D. Hyper-curvature of the vertebrae, forcing the vertebrae laterally

645. Angina pectoris, hypertension, and migraines may all be treated with
A. Vasodilators
B. Antihistamines
C. Beta-blockers
D. Corticosteroids

646. Resistance to insulin in the blood stream leads to
A. Diabetes type II
B. Diabetes type I
C. Juvenile diabetes
D. Hypoglycemia

647. Chronic gastritis is considered
A. A local contraindication
B. An absolute contraindication
C. An endangerment site
D. Not a contraindication

648. Allergic reaction to gluten in the diet
A. Celiac disease
B. Crohn's disease
C. Lactose intolerance
D. Colic

649. Stasis dermatitis
A. Inflammation of the skin caused by irritants coming in contact with the epidermis
B. Inflammation of the skin caused by blockages of the sebaceous glands
C. Inflammation of the skin caused by fluid buildup beneath the skin
D. Inflammation of the skin caused by exposure to cold

650. Adhesions forming between the head of the humerus and glenoid fossa, severely restricting range of motion in the shoulder
A. Multiple sclerosis
B. Adhesive capsulitis
C. Osteoarthritis
D. Synovitis

651. A tumor that does not spread throughout the body
A. Malignant
B. Benign
C. Melanoma
D. Basal

652. A primary tumor
A. Is the site of lymphatic drainage into a tumor
B. Is the site of spreading tumors in malignant cancer
C. Is the site of the original tumor in malignant cancer
D. Is derived from a secondary tumor

653. Tumors of the lymph nodes, most commonly seen in the neck and axilla
A. Malignant melanoma
B. Leukemia
C. Myeloma
D. Non-Hodgkin's lymphoma

654. Hookworm, ascariasis, and pinworm are all forms of
A. Parasite
B. Virus
C. Bacteria
D. Fungus

655. Inflammation of the brain
A. Meningitis
B. Encephalitis
C. Endocarditis
D. Osteomyelitis

656. Pancreatitis is considered
A. A local contraindication
B. An absolute contraindication
C. An endangerment site
D. Not a contraindication

657. Phlebitis
A. Bulge in an artery wall, usually caused by a weakened artery due to a condition such as hypertension
B. Inflammation of a vein due to trauma, resulting in blood clot formation
C. Blood clot in the blood stream becoming lodged in the heart, lungs, or brain, resulting in death of tissue
D. Ischemia in the myocardium due to a blockage in the coronary arteries, resulting in myocardial infarction

658. Tinea cruris is considered
A. A local contraindication
B. An absolute contraindication
C. An endangerment site
D. Not a contraindication

659. Pneumonia is considered
A. A local contraindication
B. An absolute contraindication
C. An endangerment site
D. Not a contraindication

660. Diarrhea is most often caused by
A. Consumption of spicy foods
B. Lack of water in feces
C. Bacterial infection of the large intestine
D. Overabundance of water in feces

661. Trauma to the skin may result in
A. Urticaria
B. Edema
C. Bruising
D. Melanoma

662. Of the following, which condition is contagious
A. Impetigo
B. Bradycardia
C. Tendonitis
D. Lordosis

663. Pleurisy
A. Inflammation of pleural membrane resulting in chest pain
B. Inflammation of bronchial tubes with increased mucous production
C. Spasm of smooth muscle surrounding bronchial tubes, reducing oxygen intake
D. Bacterial infection resulting in increased fluid in the lungs

664. Damage to the brain resulting in impairment of motor functions
A. Glaucoma
B. Bell's palsy
C. Trigeminal neuralgia
D. Cerebral palsy

665. The definition of the suffix "-ferent" is
A. Nourishment
B. Blood condition
C. To carry
D. Standing still

666. Lack of oxygen entering into a tissue, which may result in necrosis
A. Arrhythmia
B. Phlebitis
C. Ischemia
D. Hypertension

667. An injury to the spinal cord below T1 may result in
A. Cerebral palsy
B. Quadriplegia
C. Bell's palsy
D. Paraplegia

668. The definition of "ventr/o" is
A. Back
B. Belly
C. Leg
D. Chest

669. Pneumonia, impetigo, and cellulitis are all the result of
A. Viral infection
B. Fungal infection
C. Bacterial infection
D. Parasitic infection

670. Autoimmune disorder in which the small and large intestines are attacked by the body's immune system, resulting in inflammation of the inner linings of the intestines
A. Ulcerative colitis
B. Celiac disease
C. Diverticulosis
D. Crohn's disease

671. The definition of "myel/o" is
A. Movement
B. Hill
C. Canal
D. Muscle

672. Medical procedure used to remove waste products and toxic substances from the blood when the kidneys are unable to function properly
A. Dialysis
B. Electrolysis
C. Paracentesis
D. Transfusion

673. High-density lipoprotein is also known as
A. Bad cholesterol
B. Good cholesterol
C. Neutral cholesterol
D. Cystic cholesterol

674. The definition of "lip/o" is
A. Abdomen
B. Mouth
C. Lips
D. Fat

675. Tinea pedis and ringworm are both caused by
A. Fungus
B. Bacteria
C. Virus
D. Parasite

676. High fever and malaise may be a sign of
A. Arrhythmia
B. Septicemia
C. Anemia
D. Myocardial ischemia

677. Blockages in the following arteries may result in myocardial infarction
A. Coronary
B. Carotid
C. Brachial
D. Subclavian

678. Blood flowing backwards in the heart between chambers due to decrease in function of valves
A. Arrhythmia
B. Heart murmur
C. Bradycardia
D. Ventricular septal defect

679. Melanoma tumors are usually
A. The same size throughout
B. Symmetrical
C. Brown in color
D. Raised off the skin

680. A hernia is considered
A. Not a contraindication
B. An absolute contraindication
C. An endangerment site
D. A local contraindication

681. The definition of the suffix "-lysis" is
A. Breathing
B. Formation
C. Specialist
D. Dissolve

682. Cerebral palsy
A. Impairment of motor functions due to damage to specific areas of the brain
B. Paralysis of one side of the face due to stimulation of the Herpes Simplex virus
C. Loss of function of part of the face due to an injury to the facial nerve
D. Pain in the face due to compression placed on cranial nerve V

683. Fungal infection affecting the scalp
A. Tinea cruris
B. Tinea corporis
C. Tinea capitis
D. Tinea pedis

684. All of the following are contagious conditions except
A. Osteomyelitis
B. Rheumatoid arthritis
C. Influenza
D. Mononucleosis

685. Lentigo
A. Benign skin lesion with increased production of melanin
B. Rapid formation of melanocytes resulting in a cancerous tumor
C. Form of skin cancer that grows slowly and is easily detectable
D. Also known as sun spots, usually form during senescence

686. Eczema is considered
A. A local contraindication
B. An absolute contraindication
C. An endangerment site
D. Not a contraindication

687. The four signs of inflammation
A. Pain, swelling, redness, heat
B. Pain, swelling, inflammation, heat
C. Pain, inflammation, cyanosis, heat
D. Pain, inflammation, redness, sweat

688. Cushing's disease is considered
A. A local contraindication
B. An absolute contraindication
C. An endangerment site
D. Not a contraindication

689. TIA is also known as
A. Transient ischemic attack
B. Temporoinguinal angle
C. Tubercular interosseous attachment
D. Thyroid immunity ailment

690. All of the following are local contraindications except
A. Wart
B. Sprain
C. Osteomyelitis
D. Head lice

691. Decreased absorption of iron into the body may result in
A. Scurvy
B. Anemia
C. Scabies
D. Atherosclerosis

692. Edematic tissue is composed primarily of
A. Synovial fluid
B. Blood
C. Lymph
D. Serous fluid

693. Lipoma
A. Tumor formed by melanocyte production
B. Tumor formed by sebaceous glands
C. Tumor of fatty tissue
D. Malignant tumor on the lips

694. The definition of "scoli/o" is
A. Crooked
B. Spine
C. Lumbar
D. Swayback

695. A thrombus in the cerebrum restricting circulation may result in
A. Angina pectoris
B. Heart attack
C. Arrhythmia
D. Stroke

696. Fever is considered
A. A local contraindication
B. An absolute contraindication
C. An endangerment site
D. Not a contraindication

697. Which of the following conditions would a client be referred to a nephrologist for
A. Pitting edema
B. Cellulitis
C. Hepatitis
D. Neuralgia

698. A client with thoracic outlet syndrome would be referred to which doctor
A. Neurologist
B. Cardiologist
C. Rheumatologist
D. Dermatologist

699. Generalized myalgia, localized muscle pain, and trouble sleeping could be the result of
A. Carpal tunnel syndrome
B. Fibromyalgia
C. Muscular dystrophy
D. Tendonitis

700. The definition of the suffix "-plasia" is
A. Speech
B. Eating
C. Formation
D. Removal

701. Sebaceous cyst
A. Formation of connective tissue surrounding oil gland
B. Formation of connective tissue containing fatty tissue
C. Formation of connective tissue attached to tendon sheaths
D. Formation of connective tissue spreading to other parts of the body

702. Fungal infection affecting the foot
A. Tinea capitis
B. Tinea corporis
C. Tinea cruris
D. Tinea pedis

703. An example of an occupational carcinogen
A. Asbestos
B. Cigarette smoking
C. Mineral oil
D. Aluminum exposure

704. Tinnitus
A. Dizziness and nausea
B. Ringing in the ears
C. Contraction of cervical vertebrae laterally
D. Formation of cataracts in the eyes

705. All of the following are local contraindications except
A. Sebaceous cyst
B. Carpal tunnel syndrome
C. Basal cell carcinoma
D. Umbilical hernia

706. Subacute Tennis Elbow is considered
A. A local contraindication
B. An absolute contraindication
C. An endangerment site
D. Not a contraindication

707. An injury to a tenoperiosteal junction could result in
A. Lymphoma
B. Tendonitis
C. Fracture
D. Synovitis

708. Infestation of mites that burrow beneath the skin
A. Warts
B. Scurvy
C. Shingles
D. Scabies

709. Tinea is a form of
A. Virus
B. Fungus
C. Bacteria
D. Parasite

710. Depletion of water content in the body results in
A. Hypothermia
B. Hydronephrosis
C. Dehydration
D. Frostbite

711. The definition of "ankyl/o" is
A. Ankle
B. Cheek
C. Knee
D. Crooked

712. Grave's disease, which forms a goiter in the neck, is considered
A. An endangerment site
B. An absolute contraindication
C. A local contraindication
D. Not a contraindication

713. A rheumatologist is a doctor that specializes in
A. Connective tissue
B. Lymph
C. Kidneys
D. Urinary bladder

714. Complete rupture of a ligament
A. Grade 3 strain
B. Grade 3 sprain
C. Grade 2 strain
D. Grade 2 sprain

715. The definition of the prefix "pro-" is
A. Near
B. Before
C. New
D. After

716. In a person with acquired immunodeficiency syndrome, diseases such as pneumonia or the flu are categorized as
A. Opportunistic infections
B. Retracted infections
C. Immunizations
D. Autoimmune disorders

717. Cellulitis is considered
A. An endangerment site
B. An absolute contraindication
C. A local contraindication
D. Not a contraindication

718. If diastolic pressure measures 90 or higher, a person may be diagnosed with
A. Myocardial infarction
B. Hypotension
C. Hyperemia
D. Hypertension

719. Inflammation of the bladder, usually due to a bacterial infection spreading upwards from the urethra
A. Nephritis
B. Cystitis
C. Urethritis
D. Cholecystitis

720. All of the following are local contraindications except
A. Herniated disc
B. Grade 2 sprain
C. Trigeminal neuralgia
D. Acute osteoarthritis

721. Tennis elbow is also known as
A. Olecranon bursitis
B. Medial epicondylitis
C. Tuberculitis
D. Lateral epicondylitis

722. Lice are mainly found
A. In the hair
B. Under the skin
C. On the chest
D. On the feet

723. A patient suffering from renal failure might need to have the following procedure in order to filter the blood properly
A. Pacemaker
B. Electrolysis
C. Angioplasty
D. Dialysis

724. Herpes zoster infection results in
A. Scurvy
B. Cold sores
C. Scabies
D. Shingles

725. Lack of oxygen to the brain may cause
A. Angina pectoris
B. Heart attack
C. Arrhythmia
D. Stroke

726. Wryneck is considered
A. A local contraindication
B. An absolute contraindication
C. An endangerment site
D. Not a contraindication

727. Involuntary spasms of muscles in the neck, turning the head to one side
A. Torticollis
B. Whiplash
C. Spondylitis
D. Laryngitis

728. Severe pain in the lower right quadrant is most likely the result of
A. Diverticulitis
B. Crohn's disease
C. Appendicitis
D. Celiac disease

729. Increased lipid accumulation along the walls of arteries, reducing blood flow to specific area of the body
A. Phlebitis
B. Arteriosclerosis
C. Atherosclerosis
D. Varicose veins

730. Part of the stomach protruding through the diaphragm
A. Esophageal hernia
B. Hiatal hernia
C. Umbilical hernia
D. Inguinal hernia

731. Tearing of a muscle is considered a
A. Sprain
B. Strain
C. Contracture
D. Subluxation

732. A cancer spreading from one location in the body to another makes it
A. Asymptomatic
B. Benign
C. Malignant
D. Asymmetrical

733. The definition of the prefix "anti-" is
A. Without
B. Against
C. Bad
D. One

734. Non-infectious pharyngitis is considered
A. A local contraindication
B. An absolute contraindication
C. An endangerment site
D. Not a contraindication

735. The study of disease
A. Pathology
B. Etiology
C. Radiology
D. Idiopathology

736. The definition of the prefix "tachy-" is
A. Rapid
B. Slow
C. Excessive
D. Below

737. Uremia
A. Blood in the feces
B. Urine in the blood
C. Blood in the urine
D. Feces in the abdomen

738. A blockage of a blood vessel may result in
A. Arrhythmia
B. Phlebitis
C. Ischemia
D. Hypertension

739. The definition of the prefix "quadri-" is
A. Three
B. Paralysis
C. Four
D. False

740. The definition of the prefix "intra-" is
A. Inside
B. Change
C. Excessive
D. Below

741. Hemorrhage is also referred to as
A. Bruising easily
B. Blood formation
C. Bleeding
D. Blood clot formation

742. Sprain
A. Tearing of cartilage
B. Tearing of a tendon
C. Overstretching of a muscle
D. Overstretching of a ligament

743. The definition of the prefix "pre-" is
A. Near
B. Before
C. New
D. After

744. Overabundance of water in fecal matter may result in
A. Constipation
B. Diarrhea
C. Diverticulitis
D. Ulcerative colitis

745. Etiology
A. Study of disease
B. Study of cause of disease
C. Study of tumors
D. Study of tissue

746. Paraplegia
A. Paralysis of only the legs
B. Paralysis of one side of the body
C. Paralysis of all four limbs
D. Paralysis of one side of the face

747. A bruise is considered
A. An endangerment site
B. An absolute contraindication
C. A local contraindication
D. Not a contraindication

748. Attack of the epithelial cells of the skin by the body's immune system results in
A. Rosacea
B. Acne
C. Psoriasis
D. Systemic lupus

749. The definition of the suffix "-derma" is
A. Skin
B. Break
C. Growth
D. Resembling

750. Gallbladder inflammation
A. Cholecystitis
B. Cystitis
C. Hepatitis
D. Jaundice

751. Upon dilation of blood vessels in the inflammatory response, the following type of cell moves into the location to destroy bacteria and debris
A. Leukocytes
B. Thrombocytes
C. Erythrocytes
D. Osteoclasts

752. Plantar fasciitis is considered
A. A local contraindication
B. An absolute contraindication
C. An endangerment site
D. Not a contraindication

753. Ulcerative colitis
A. Protrusion of the pylorus through the pyloric sphincter into the duodenum
B. Open sores along the large intestine, causing pain in the abdomen and diarrhea
C. Formation of pockets in the large intestine due to a lack of substances for the intestine to press against
D. Infection of diverticular pouches, resulting in abscesses and leakage of fecal matter into the abdominal cavity

754. Multiple sclerosis
A. Degeneration of the cerebrum resulting in loss of memory
B. Degeneration of myelin sheaths surrounding axons in the central nervous system
C. Reduction of dopamine, resulting in trembling movements
D. Paralysis of the facial nerve, resulting in loss of function of one side of the face

755. The definition of "encephal/o" is
A. Fat
B. Body
C. Brain
D. Kidney

756. Mister Greene suffers from ankylosing spondylitis, which affects his intervertebral discs. If he were to schedule a massage appointment, the massage therapist would
A. Perform the massage and do joint compression on the intervertebral discs
B. Reschedule the massage until the condition has subsided
C. Perform the massage while avoiding the affected area
D. Perform the massage if the massage does not result in pain

757. The most severe form of meningitis
A. Parasitic meningitis
B. Viral meningitis
C. Fungal meningitis
D. Bacterial meningitis

758. Common medication used in people who suffer from diabetes, hypertension, and heart disease
A. Anticoagulants
B. Antihistamines
C. Statins
D. Expectorants

759. All of the following are forms of parasites except
A. Ringworm
B. Tapeworm
C. Hookworm
D. Pinworm

760. Medications given to help control hypertension are known as
A. Statins
B. Antihistamines
C. Chemotherapy
D. Nitrates

761. The definition of "stomat/o" is
A. Stomach
B. Mouth
C. Intestines
D. Bladder

762. Stroke
A. Lack of oxygen and blood supply to parts of the myocardium, resulting in necrosis of heart tissue
B. Lack of oxygen and blood supply to parts of the brain, resulting in necrosis of brain tissue
C. Lack of oxygen and blood supply to parts of the skin, resulting in decubitus ulcerations
D. Lack of oxygen and blood supply to parts of the large intestine, resulting in diverticulitis

763. The definition of the prefix "endo-" is
A. Outside
B. Between
C. Inside
D. Against

764. Mononucleosis, warts, and cold sores are all caused by
A. Fungus
B. Bacteria
C. Virus
D. Parasite

765. The definition of the prefix "pseudo-" is
A. Change
B. Through
C. Inside
D. False

766. The definition of the prefix "inter-" is
A. Between
B. Through
C. Inside
D. False

767. HIV stands for
A. Hardening in-vitro
B. Human immunodeficiency virus
C. Acquired immunodeficiency syndrome
D. Hepatic inflammatory virus

768. Overstretching of veins resulting from excessive pressure
A. Arteriosclerosis
B. Phlebitis
C. Edema
D. Varicose veins

769. Compression of the median nerve under the flexor retinaculum, resulting in numbness in the hand
A. Thoracic outlet syndrome
B. Carpal tunnel syndrome
C. Bell's palsy
D. Writer's wrist

770. Acute mononucleosis is considered
A. A local contraindication
B. An absolute contraindication
C. An endangerment site
D. Not a contraindication

771. The definition of "hydr/o" is
A. Water
B. Cold
C. Kidney
D. Heat

772. Ankylosing spondylitis is considered
A. A local contraindication
B. An absolute contraindication
C. An endangerment site
D. Not a contraindication

773. Bleeding is also known as
A. Hemorrhage
B. Hemorrhoids
C. Hemiplegia
D. Hemopoiesis

774. Cyst found along a tendon, especially one on the hands, is known as
A. Hematoma
B. Sebaceous cyst
C. Lipoma
D. Ganglion cyst

775. Beta-blockers are medications that help
A. Reduce inflammation
B. Slow heart rate
C. Eliminate cholesterol
D. Increase heart rate

776. Bacterial infection resulting in severe headache, fever, and vomiting
A. Stroke
B. Osteomyelitis
C. Meningitis
D. Cellulitis

777. Psoriasis, multiple sclerosis, and lupus are all examples of
A. Autoimmune disorders
B. Bacterial infections
C. Degenerative joint disorders
D. Fungal infections

778. Multiple sclerosis is what type of disorder
A. Bacterial
B. Autoimmune
C. Viral
D. Ulcerative

779. A person trembling during fine motor movements is a sign of
A. Alzheimer's disease
B. Parkinson's disease
C. Anemia
D. Bell's palsy

780. Tinea unguium is a fungal infection found on the
A. Scalp
B. Feet
C. Groin
D. Fingernails

781. Cyst caused by a blockage in sebum, resulting in formation of connective tissue surrounding the blockage
A. Lentigo
B. Papilloma
C. Ganglion cyst
D. Sebaceous cyst

782. The definition of "phren/o" is
A. Movement
B. Hill
C. Canal
D. Diaphragm

783. Acute strains are considered
A. A local contraindication
B. An absolute contraindication
C. An endangerment site
D. Not a contraindication

784. Subacute shin splints are considered
A. A local contraindication
B. An absolute contraindication
C. An endangerment site
D. Not a contraindication

785. The definition of "scler/o" is
A. Crooked
B. Spine
C. Skin
D. Hard

786. Peripheral vascular disease
A. Degeneration of blood vessels in the arms and legs, restricting circulation
B. Constriction of blood vessels in the fingers and toes, increasing circulation
C. Dilation of blood vessels in head and neck, resulting in hypoxia
D. Constriction of extracranial blood vessels, producing migraine headaches

787. An increased amount of interstitial fluid in an area results in
A. Aneurysm
B. Inflammation
C. Edema
D. Thrombus

788. Displacement of the mandible from the temporal bone
A. Osteoarthritis
B. TMJ disorder
C. Synovitis
D. Bruxism

789. A verruca is considered
A. An endangerment site
B. An absolute contraindication
C. A local contraindication
D. Not a contraindication

790. Tinea cruris is a fungal infection found on the
A. Scalp
B. Feet
C. Groin
D. Fingernails

791. The definition of the suffix "-plegia" is
A. Pain
B. Eating
C. Paralysis
D. Removal

792. Dead white blood cells in a localized area will form
A. Pus
B. Wart
C. Mole
D. Cancer

793. Pain in the lower back present with fever, nausea and vomiting may be a sign of
A. Hepatitis
B. Pyelonephritis
C. Gastritis
D. Encephalitis

794. Hyperadrenalism is considered
A. A local contraindication
B. An absolute contraindication
C. An endangerment site
D. Not a contraindication

795. Shingles is the result of an infection of the following virus
A. Human papilloma virus
B. Herpes simplex
C. Herpes zoster
D. Staphylococcus

796. In a patient with renal failure, blood may need to be filtered through the following machine to eliminate harmful substances
A. Defibrillator
B. Centrifuge
C. Pacemaker
D. Dialyzer

797. Streptococci infection which enters the body through wounds, resulting in infection of the skin and surrounding tissues
A. Cold sore
B. Boil
C. Rosacea
D. Cellulitis

798. Stomach acid flowing backwards through the cardiac sphincter results in
A. Esophageal cancer
B. Heart burn
C. Diarrhea
D. Vomiting

799. Butterfly rash commonly seen due to irritation of hair follicles on the face
A. Rosacea
B. Lupus
C. Rhinophyma
D. Psoriasis

800. A malignant form of cancer does what
A. Doesn't spread
B. Spreads
C. Becomes filled with pus
D. Creates sun spots

801. Jaundice
A. Yellowing of the skin due to excessive levels of bilirubin in the bloodstream
B. Inflammation of the liver due to a viral infection
C. Hardening of the skin due to increased friction on an area, resulting in keratin production
D. Bluish tint of the skin, resulting from systemic hypoxia

802. A boil is considered
A. An absolute contraindication
B. A local contraindication
C. An endangerment site
D. Not a contraindication

803. Pain in the face around the mouth, nose, and eyes may be the result of
A. Trigeminal neuralgia
B. Bell's palsy
C. Cerebral palsy
D. Vascular headaches

804. Myocarditis is considered
A. A local contraindication
B. An absolute contraindication
C. An endangerment site
D. Not a contraindication

805. Systemic cyanosis may be the result of
A. Hypertension
B. Arteriosclerosis
C. Heart disease
D. Raynaud's disease

806. A client with arthritis would be referred to the following specialist
A. Rheumatologist
B. Cardiologist
C. Gastroenterologist
D. Nephrologist

807. Beta-blockers may be used to treat all of the following conditions except
A. Asthma
B. Angina
C. Arrhythmia
D. Hypertension

808. Inflammation of the skin resulting from contact of the skin by an irritant
A. Stasis dermatitis
B. Contact dermatitis
C. Seborrheic dermatitis
D. Eczema

809. Low-density lipoprotein is also known as
A. Neutral cholesterol
B. Good cholesterol
C. Bad cholesterol
D. Cystic cholesterol

810. The definition of the suffix "-phasia" is
A. Eating
B. Speech
C. Formation
D. Removal

811. Parasthesia
A. Complete paralysis
B. Tingling sensation
C. Pain
D. Pressure

812. The most common form of skin cancer
A. Kaposi's sarcoma
B. Squamous cell carcinoma
C. Malignant melanoma
D. Basal cell carcinoma

813. The definition of "cyst/o" is
A. Esophagus
B. Stomach
C. Small intestine
D. Bladder

814. A sebaceous cyst is considered
A. A local contraindication
B. An absolute contraindication
C. An endangerment site
D. Not a contraindication

815. The final stage of an HIV infection is known as
A. AIDS
B. PPALM
C. ARC
D. HBV

816. Inadequate oxygenation in the skin may result in
A. Cyanosis
B. Raynaud's syndrome
C. Diabetes mellitus
D. Atherosclerosis

817. The definition of "salping/o" is
A. Ovary
B. Uterus
C. Fallopian tube
D. Eye

818. Chronic cholecystitis is considered
A. A local contraindication
B. An absolute contraindication
C. An endangerment site
D. Not a contraindication

819. Of the following, which condition is contagious
A. Osteoporosis
B. Osteomyelitis
C. Ankylosing spondylitis
D. Basal cell carcinoma

820. Warts are considered
A. An endangerment site
B. An absolute contraindication
C. A local contraindication
D. Not a contraindication

821. The definition of the prefix "macro-" is
A. Small
B. Large
C. Around
D. Eating

822. Phlebitis
A. Inflammation of the liver caused by a viral infection or alcoholism
B. Hardening of an artery wall, caused by hypertension
C. Fatty plaque accumulation on the walls of an artery
D. Inflammation of a vein caused by trauma, pregnancy, or immobilization

823. All of the following are contagious conditions except
A. Mononucleosis
B. Herpes simplex
C. Arrhythmia
D. Osteomyelitis

824. A laceration is considered
A. An endangerment site
B. An absolute contraindication
C. A local contraindication
D. Not a contraindication

825. In the inflammatory response, histamines are released in order to
A. Dilate blood vessels
B. Constrict blood vessels
C. Decrease circulation
D. Increase lymphatic drainage

826. Atherosclerosis in the coronary arteries may lead to
A. Heart murmur
B. Myocardial infarction
C. Tachycardia
D. Bradycardia

827. Blockage of the ureters by a kidney stone results in
A. Pyelonephritis
B. Cystitis
C. Uremia
D. Hydronephritis

828. A person suffering from a myocardial infarction may be given the following type of medication during an attack
A. Expectorant
B. Antihistamine
C. Beta-blocker
D. Anticoagulant

829. Scoliosis is considered
A. A local contraindication
B. An absolute contraindication
C. An endangerment site
D. Not a contraindication

830. Hyperthyroidism could lead to a condition such as
A. Grave's disease
B. Hypothyroidism
C. Iodine deficiency
D. Hashimoto's disease

831. Multiple sclerosis, muscular dystrophy and ankylosing spondylitis are all examples of
A. Autoimmune disorders
B. Bacterial infections
C. Degenerative disorders
D. Fungal infections

832. Neurotransmitter involved in the trembling movements involved with Parkison's disease
A. Dopamine
B. Epinephrine
C. Norepinephrine
D. Melatonin

833. Antihistamines
A. Block actions of vasodilators, which increase the size of blood vessel lumen
B. Block actions of antibodies, which disable virus function
C. Block actions of statins, which reduce hypertension
D. Block actions of histamines, which produce allergic response

834. Emesis is also known as
A. Sneezing
B. Vomiting
C. Defecating
D. Urinating

835. The definition of "spondyl/o" is
A. Ribs
B. Cartilage
C. Large intestine
D. Vertebrae

836. The definition of "kinesi/o" is
A. Hill
B. Movement
C. Sugar
D. Muscle

837. An injury caused by detachment of part of the body from its normal point of insertion, such as the type of injury sustained in motorcycle accidents
A. Avulsion
B. Laceration
C. Burn
D. Amputation

838. Immobilization, pregnancy, and prolonged standing may all result in
A. Myocardial infarction
B. Hepatitis
C. Phlebitis
D. Anemia

839. Osteoarthritis is also known as
A. De Quervain's disease
B. Rheumatoid arthritis
C. Wear and tear arthritis
D. Carpal tunnel syndrome

840. A gastrologist is a doctor that specializes in
A. Skin
B. Heart
C. Stomach
D. Connective tissue

841. Of the following, which condition is contagious
A. Diverticulitis
B. Pneumonia
C. Emphysema
D. Alzheimer's disease

842. Tinea corporis is considered
A. A local contraindication
B. An absolute contraindication
C. An endangerment site
D. Not a contraindication

843. A herniated disc is considered
A. A local contraindication
B. An absolute contraindication
C. An endangerment site
D. Not a contraindication

844. Immediately after a fracture to a bone, the following type of bone cell exerts its action to speed the regeneration
A. Osteoblast
B. Osteoclast
C. Osteocyte
D. Periosteum

845. Inflammation of the pleural membrane, resulting in chest pain
A. Bronchitis
B. Pneumonia
C. Pleurisy
D. Asthma

846. Bursitis
A. Reduction of synovial fluid in a joint
B. Inflammation of a joint caused by uric acid buildup
C. Destruction of alveoli causing decreased oxygen intake
D. Inflammation of a bursa due to irritation

847. Rapid heart rhythm
A. Bradycardia
B. Tachycardia
C. Atrial fibrillation
D. Myocarditis

848. Lordosis is considered
A. A local contraindication
B. An absolute contraindication
C. An endangerment site
D. Not a contraindication

849. Pulmonary edema
A. Excessive fluid in the lungs
B. Blood clot in the lungs
C. Reduction of circulation to the lungs
D. Degeneration of alveoli in the lungs

850. The definition of "corp/o" is
A. Fat
B. Body
C. Brain
D. Kidney

851. A lack of erythrocytes in the body results in
A. Myocardial infarction
B. Raynaud's syndrome
C. Anemia
D. Decreased immune response

852. Contact dermatitis is considered
A. An absolute contraindication
B. A local contraindication
C. An endangerment site
D. Not a contraindication

853. The definition of "cyan/o" is
A. White
B. Blue
C. Red
D. Black

854. A doctor that specializes in the feet is known as a
A. Podiatrist
B. Oncologist
C. Radiologist
D. Rheumatologist

855. Tetany leads to
A. Lack of insulin in the blood stream
B. Spasms in muscles of the face, arms, and legs
C. Resistance to insulin in the blood stream
D. Hyperglycemia

856. Excessive movement in the neck resulting in trauma to ligaments, muscles and tendons
A. Spondylosis
B. Torticollis
C. Osteoarthritis
D. Whiplash

857. Heart murmur
A. Necrosis of myocardium due to blockages in coronary arteries
B. Irregular heart rhythm due to random electrical impulses stimulating myocardium of ventricles
C. Hole in the ventricular septum, resulting in blood passing freely between ventricles
D. Blood flow moving backwards in the heart due to valve incompetence

858. Medication helpful in the relief of a stuffy nose
A. Vasodilator
B. Expectorant
C. Antihistamine
D. Decongestant

859. High altitudes can cause altitude sickness, a common form of
A. Hypoxia
B. Hypothermia
C. Hyperplasia
D. Frostbite

860. Blockage of fluid in semicircular canals may result in
A. Torticollis
B. Tinnitus
C. Vertigo
D. Mastoiditis

861. Statins function by inhibition of certain enzymes in which structure
A. Small intestine
B. Stomach
C. Liver
D. Heart

862. Second phase of inflammation
A. Phagocytosis
B. Pinocytosis
C. Tissue repair
D. Histamine release

863. Low-density lipoprotein levels in the body can be reduced with the use of
A. Antihistamines
B. Beta-blockers
C. Statins
D. Expectorants

864. Shaking of a part of the body that is involuntary
A. Tourette's syndrome
B. Paralysis
C. Tremor
D. Trigeminal neuralgia

865. Acute shin splints are considered
A. A local contraindication
B. An absolute contraindication
C. An endangerment site
D. Not a contraindication

866. Tinea pedis is considered
A. Not a contraindication
B. An absolute contraindication
C. An endangerment site
D. A local contraindication

867. Bursting of an aneurysm may result in
A. Hyperemia
B. Death
C. Hypoxia
D. Hypothermia

868. Atopic dermatitis is also known as
A. Hyperemia
B. Topical dermatitis
C. Seborrheic dermatitis
D. Eczema

869. The presence of gallstones in the gallbladder may result in the development of
A. Cystitis
B. Cholecystitis
C. Hepatitis
D. Jaundice

870. Breaking down of cartilage between bones that articulate results in
A. Osteoarthritis
B. Rheumatoid arthritis
C. Osteoporosis
D. Osteomyelitis

871. Cystic fibrosis, hemophilia, and muscular dystrophy are all
A. Autoimmune disorders
B. Genetic disorders
C. Bacterial infections
D. Viral infections

872. Contact dermatitis
A. Inflammation of the skin caused by irritants coming in contact with the epidermis
B. Inflammation of the skin caused by blockages of the sebaceous glands
C. Inflammation of the skin caused by fluid buildup beneath the skin
D. Inflammation of the skin caused by exposure to cold

873. Impetigo
A. Bacterial infection resulting in inflammation around the hallux
B. Viral infection resulting in cold sores around the mucous membranes
C. Bacterial infection resulting in yellow scabs around the mucous membranes
D. Viral infection resulting in inflammation of the brain

874. A mole is an example of a
A. Lesion
B. Cancer
C. Cold sore
D. Abscess

875. Laryngitis may result in
A. Decreased tidal volume
B. Loss of voice
C. Difficulty swallowing
D. Increase thyroid production

876. The definition of "cutane/o" is
A. Cold
B. Life
C. Skin
D. Same

877. Subacute strains are considered
A. A local contraindication
B. An absolute contraindication
C. An endangerment site
D. Not a contraindication

878. Subacute asthma is considered
A. A local contraindication
B. An absolute contraindication
C. An endangerment site
D. Not a contraindication

879. Hydatid cysts are the cause of what type of infection
A. Parasitic
B. Viral
C. Bacterial
D. Fungal

880. Osteomalacia
A. Protrusion of the nucleus pulposus through the annulus fibrosis
B. Overabundance of vitamin D production resulting in thickening of bone tissue
C. Degeneration of intervertebral discs, resulting in loss of natural spine curvature
D. Insufficient vitamin D production resulting in softening of bone tissue

881. Cephalosporin is used to fight the following type of infection
A. Fungal
B. Viral
C. Bacterial
D. Parasitic

882. Trauma to a vein may result in
A. Varicose veins
B. Phlebitis
C. Arteriosclerosis
D. Anemia

883. Trigeminal neuralgia
A. Compression of the median nerve beneath the transverse carpal ligament, resulting in loss of sensation in the hand
B. Paralysis of one side of the face due to stimulation of the Herpes Simplex virus, which affects the facial nerve
C. Pain in the face around the eyes, nose, and mouth caused by compression of the trigeminal nerve
D. Damage to the spinal cord below T1, resulting in paralysis of the lower limbs

884. Of the following, which condition is contagious
A. Influenza
B. Osteoarthritis
C. Raynaud's disease
D. Sebaceous cyst

885. Decrease in dopamine levels in the body often results in
A. Sleep apnea
B. Alzheimer's disease
C. Anemia
D. Parkinson's disease

886. A blood clot is also known as
A. Plasma
B. Embolus
C. Aneurysm
D. Thrombus

887. The definition of the suffix "-poiesis" is
A. Breathing
B. Formation
C. Growth
D. Condition

888. An elderly client with a history of decubitus ulcers schedules a massage. An appropriate treatment modification would be
A. Perform the massage, applying medication and gauze to any ulcers found
B. Reschedule the massage and refer the client to a dermatologist
C. Perform the massage, avoiding any decubitus ulcers the massage therapist may come upon
D. Perform the massage, working directly atop any ulcers found to break up adhesions

889. Herniated disc
A. Protrusion of the gelatinous center of an intervertebral disc through the cartilaginous portion
B. Vertebrae moving out of place, resulting in pinching of spinal nerves
C. Degeneration of intervertebral discs, resulting in fusion of vertebrae and loss of natural curvature of the spine
D. Hyper-curvature of the vertebrae, forcing the vertebrae laterally

890. Dyspnea
A. Malformation of bone
B. Bacterial infection
C. Lung cancer
D. Shortness of breath

891. An injury at a musculotendinous junction may result in
A. Nephritis
B. Synovitis
C. Tendonitis
D. Fracture

892. Cholecystitis
A. Inflammation of the gallbladder
B. Inflammation of the urinary bladder
C. Inflammation of the liver
D. Inflammation of the kidneys

893. The definition of "mast/o" is
A. Milk
B. Breast
C. Tear
D. Uterus

894. Tearing of the fascia on the bottom of the foot
A. Flat feet
B. Plantar warts
C. Plantarfasciitis
D. Bunion

895. The definition of "enter/o" is
A. Esophagus
B. Stomach
C. Small intestine
D. Bladder

896. Pain in the chest and left arm resulting from myocardial ischemia
A. Angina pectoris
B. Atherosclerosis
C. Arteriosclerosis
D. Phlebitis

897. Device used to stimulate heart muscles to contract when they either beat too fast or too slow
A. Stent
B. Angioplasty
C. Pacemaker
D. Defibrillator

898. Rupture of a cerebral aneurysm results in
A. Thrombosis
B. Stroke
C. Embolism
D. Myocardial infarction

899. Migraine headaches
A. The result of severe muscle tightness in the suboccipital region, putting pressure on the base of the skull
B. Also called vascular headaches, result in dilated blood vessels in the cranium putting pressure upon the meninges
C. Also called glycemic headaches, the result of low blood sugar
D. Referred to as hypoxic headaches, caused by a lack of oxygen in the blood stream, resulting in anemia

900. Cancer of the lymph
A. Melanoma
B. Carcinoma
C. Sarcoma
D. Lymphoma

901. A fracture is considered
A. A local contraindication
B. An absolute contraindication
C. An endangerment site
D. Not a contraindication

902. Bacterial infection affecting the kidneys as a result of a urinary tract infection
A. Necrotising fasciitis
B. Cystitis
C. Pancreatitis
D. Pyelonephritis

903. In a client with lordosis, the following muscle might be tight, resulting in an exaggerated anterior tilt of the pelvis
A. Rectus abdominis
B. Latissimus dorsi
C. Quadratus lumborum
D. Psoas major

904. Acute edema is considered
A. A local contraindication
B. An absolute contraindication
C. An endangerment site
D. Not a contraindication

905. A client would be referred to a cardiologist for all of the following conditions except
A. Pleurisy
B. Endocarditis
C. Angina pectoris
D. Myocardial infarction

906. The definition of "gastr/o" is
A. Mouth
B. Stomach
C. Intestines
D. Bladder

907. The definition of the suffix "-gen" is
A. Breathing
B. Formation
C. Growth
D. Condition

908. Thrombosis
A. Creation of a blood clot within a blood vessel
B. Blood clot blocking a valve in the heart
C. Weakening of an arterial wall, resulting in necrosis
D. Blockage of coronary arteries in the heart, producing an infarct

909. The definition of the suffix "-clast" is
A. Discharge
B. Break
C. Growth
D. Resembling

910. Gangrene
A. Necrosis followed by a bacterial infection
B. Necrosis followed by localized ischemia
C. Necrosis followed by scar tissue formation
D. Necrosis followed by tissue regeneration

911. Thinning of mucous in the respiratory passages can be aided by which type of medication
A. Bronchodilator
B. Decongestant
C. Expectorant
D. Anticoagulant

912. The definition of the prefix "poly-" is
A. New
B. Near
C. Many
D. All

913. The definition of "lord/o" is
A. Disease
B. Curve
C. Side
D. Spine

914. The definition of "brachi/o" is
A. Extremity
B. Scapula
C. Abdomen
D. Arm

915. Peripheral vascular disease is usually the result of what other condition
A. Atherosclerosis
B. Myocardial infarction
C. Aneurysm
D. Muscular dystrophy

916. A neoplasm is another word for a
A. Abscess
B. Tumor
C. Mole
D. Skin tag

917. Cranial nerve V involves the following condition
A. Trigeminal neuralgia
B. Bell's palsy
C. Carpal tunnel syndrome
D. Fibromyalgia

918. The definition of the prefix "para-" is
A. Around
B. Near
C. Behind
D. Difficult

919. Osteoarthritis
A. Thinning of bone tissue as a result of decreasing calcium levels, post-menopause
B. Destruction of synovial membranes, which are replaced by fibrous tissue, reducing function of joints
C. Progressive erosion of hyaline cartilage between articulating bones, causing irritation
D. Fracture of a bone resulting in protrusion of the bone through the skin

920. Physical, uncontrolled reaction to a specific substance entering or coming in contact with the body
A. Allergy
B. Reflex
C. Shock
D. Phagocytosis

921. Ganglion cyst
A. Cyst located on a tendon which is idiopathic
B. Cyst formed by blockages in sebaceous glands
C. Cyst located on the back, formed by infection in the area
D. Cyst on the neck, formed by infected hair follicles

922. The definition of "pneum/o" is
A. Artery
B. Blood
C. Lung
D. Vein

923. Chronic bronchitis is considered
A. A local contraindication
B. An absolute contraindication
C. An endangerment site
D. Not a contraindication

924. A massage therapist comes across a fungal infection on the feet. The appropriate action would be
A. Apply a foot scrub to the affected area to treat the infection
B. Reschedule the massage until the fungal infection has resolved
C. Work atop the affected area, as fungal infections are not contagious
D. Avoid the affected area, but work on the rest of the body is indicated

925. Chronic bronchitis and emphysema are examples of
A. Chronic obstructive pulmonary disease
B. Asthma
C. Pleurisy
D. Congestive heart failure

926. Gastroenteritis is most often the result of
A. Dehydration
B. Ingestion of bacteria or virus
C. Lack of sufficient water in stool
D. Gastroesophageal reflux disease

927. Bronchodilators act on which structures of the respiratory system
A. Trachea
B. Alveoli
C. Smooth muscle
D. Larynx

928. A corn is considered
A. An absolute contraindication
B. A local contraindication
C. An endangerment site
D. Not a contraindication

929. A slipped disc is considered
A. An absolute contraindication
B. A local contraindication
C. An endangerment site
D. Not a contraindication

930. A client with Crohn's disease would be referred to which doctor
A. Gastroenterologist
B. Nephrologist
C. Neurologist
D. Dermatologist

931. The definition of the prefix "mono-" is
A. Two
B. Disease
C. Bad
D. One

932. Pain in the face around the mouth, nose, and eyes may be caused by compression of or injury to the following cranial nerve
A. Cranial nerve V
B. Cranial nerve VII
C. Cranial nerve X
D. Cranial nerve II

933. Inflammation of the meninges
A. Stroke
B. Encephalitis
C. Meningitis
D. Migraine

934. A pulmonary embolism is considered
A. A local contraindication
B. An absolute contraindication
C. An endangerment site
D. Not a contraindication

935. The definition of "arthr/o" is
A. Artery
B. Joints
C. Lung
D. Heart

936. Subacute whiplash is considered
A. A local contraindication
B. An absolute contraindication
C. An endangerment site
D. Not a contraindication

937. Necrosis with a subsequent bacterial infection is known as
A. Cellulitis
B. Ischemia
C. Gangrene
D. Frostbite

938. Excessive alcohol consumption may result in
A. Nephritis
B. Cirrhosis
C. Gastritis
D. Diverticulitis

939. A puncture wound is considered
A. A local contraindication
B. An absolute contraindication
C. An endangerment site
D. Not a contraindication

940. The definition of the prefix "af-" is
A. Against
B. Away
C. Center
D. Towards

941. Hardening of the skin is a condition known as
A. Rheumatoid arthritis
B. Microdermabrasion
C. Dermatitis
D. Scleroderma

942. The definition of "proxim/o" is
A. Back
B. Far
C. Side
D. Near

943. Thyrotoxicosis may be the result of
A. Grave's disease
B. Iodine deficiency
C. Hypothyroidism
D. Myxedema

944. Osteoarthritis located in the cervical vertebrae is also known as
A. Spondylitis
B. Whiplash
C. Torticollis
D. Pharyngitis

945. The definition of "dist/o" is
A. Back
B. Far
C. Side
D. Near

946. Viral infection most often spread by mosquitoes resulting in encephalitis
A. Meningitis
B. Herpes Simplex
C. West Nile virus
D. Tinea pedis

947. Diverticulosis is considered
A. A local contraindication
B. An absolute contraindication
C. An endangerment site
D. Not a contraindication

948. Ankylosing spondylitis is also known as
A. Bamboo spine
B. Kyphosis
C. Scoliosis
D. Swayback

949. Tachycardia, a form of arrhythmia, results in
A. Slow heart beat
B. Rapid heart beat
C. Heart murmur
D. Angina pectoris

950. The definition of the prefix "ef-" is
A. Towards
B. Away
C. Center
D. Against

951. Infection caused by bacteria or virus that causes inflammation of the meninges, resulting in vomiting, headache, and fever
A. Osteomyelitis
B. Meningitis
C. Impetigo
D. Encephalitis

952. Acute urticaria is considered
A. A local contraindication
B. An absolute contraindication
C. An endangerment site
D. Not a contraindication

953. Chronic fatigue syndrome is considered
A. A local contraindication
B. An absolute contraindication
C. An endangerment site
D. Not a contraindication

954. An increase of non-functioning leukocytes entering into medullary cavities may result in
A. Leukemia
B. Anemia
C. Melanoma
D. Non-Hodgkins Lymphoma

955. A bed sore is considered
A. A local contraindication
B. An absolute contraindication
C. An endangerment site
D. Not a contraindication

956. Infection of the skin by staphylococcus or streptococcus bacteria, forming yellowish scabs and sores around the mouth and nose
A. Psoriasis
B. Cold sore
C. Impetigo
D. Cellulitis

957. The definition of "chlor/o" is
A. Yellow
B. Green
C. Red
D. Black

958. Compression of the following nerve by the transverse carpal ligament results in carpal tunnel syndrome
A. Median
B. Ulnar
C. Radial
D. Musculocutaneous

959. A person who plays a sports such as basketball or volleyball might be more prone to developing
A. Golfer's elbow
B. Tennis elbow
C. Jumper's knee
D. Runner's ankle

960. Guillain-Barre syndrome is also known as
A. Acute lumbar epiduritis
B. Chronic myelin degeneration
C. Acute inflammatory polyneuropathy
D. Chronic neuropathic degeneration

961. Spreading of malignant cancer can be accomplished through
A. Lymph
B. Muscle
C. Nerves
D. Urine

962. Fever, fatigue, and nausea are all common symptoms of which form of lupus
A. Dermatomyositis
B. Discoid lupus erythematosus
C. Myasthenia gravis
D. Systemic lupus erythematosus

963. The definition of "pulm/o" is
A. Artery
B. Blood
C. Lung
D. Vein

964. Pain felt at the lateral epicondyle of the humerus is associated with
A. Tennis elbow
B. Golfer's elbow
C. Carpal tunnel syndrome
D. Synovitis

965. Benign skin lesion containing increased amounts of melanin
A. Lentigo
B. Melanoma
C. Wart
D. Mole

966. Sciatica is considered
A. A local contraindication
B. An absolute contraindication
C. An endangerment site
D. Not a contraindication

967. A cicatrix is also known as a
A. Scar
B. Nosebleed
C. Fracture
D. Ligament injury

968. The definition of the prefix "bi-" is
A. Life
B. Two
C. Head
D. One

969. Cholelithiasis is also known as
A. Gallstones
B. Kidney stones
C. Blood clot
D. Aneurysm

970. The definition of the suffix "-pathy" is
A. Formation
B. Disease
C. Specialist
D. Dissolve

971. An antipyretic is a type of medication responsible for
A. Eliminating increased glucose
B. Decreasing inflammation
C. Destroying bacteria
D. Lowering fever

972. Spasm of smooth muscle surrounding bronchial tubes, resulting in decreased air intake and excessive mucous production
A. Emphysema
B. Bronchitis
C. Asthma
D. Tuberculosis

973. The definition of the suffix "-cision" is
A. Blood condition
B. Cutting
C. To carry
D. Removal

974. The definition of "cost/o" is
A. Cartilage
B. Ribs
C. Large intestine
D. Vertebrae

975. Shortness of breath
A. Dyspnea
B. Apnea
C. Asthma
D. Bronchitis

976. Diabetes mellitus is considered
A. A local contraindication
B. An absolute contraindication
C. An endangerment site
D. Not a contraindication

977. The definition of "path/o" is
A. Curve
B. Disease
C. Side
D. Foot

978. A callus is considered
A. A local contraindication
B. An absolute contraindication
C. An endangerment site
D. Not a contraindication

979. Osteomyelitis and the most serious form of meningitis are the result of
A. Fungus
B. Bacteria
C. Virus
D. Parasite

980. An upper respiratory tract infection may result in
A. Acute bronchitis
B. Emphysema
C. Asthma
D. Pleurisy

981. Hyper-curvature in the thoracic region
A. Swayback
B. Dowager's hump
C. Scoliosis
D. Bamboo spine

982. The definition of "cholecyst/o" is
A. Liver
B. Gallbladder
C. Pancreas
D. Spleen

983. Osteomyelitis is considered
A. A local contraindication
B. An absolute contraindication
C. An endangerment site
D. Not a contraindication

984. Vascular headache caused by dilation of blood vessels in the cranium, which in turn put substantial pressure on the meninges
A. Glycemic headaches
B. Muscular tension headaches
C. Migraine headaches
D. Hypoxic headaches

985. Normal cells growing uncontrollably results in
A. Inflammation
B. Cyst
C. Cancer
D. Edema

986. Slow heart rhythm
A. Bradycardia
B. Tachycardia
C. Atrial fibrillation
D. Myocarditis

987. Lack of calcium entering into the bone can lead to
A. Scoliosis
B. Osteomyelitis
C. Dowager's hump
D. Osteoporosis

988. The third most common form of skin cancer
A. Squamous cell carcinoma
B. Malignant melanoma
C. Basal cell carcinoma
D. Kaposi's sarcoma

989. The definition of "gingiv/o" is
A. Gums
B. Teeth
C. Tongue
D. Hearing

990. Ibuprofen and acetaminophen are examples of
A. Antihistamines
B. Anti-inflammatory
C. Diuretics
D. Antipyretics

991. Impetigo is considered
A. A local contraindication
B. An absolute contraindication
C. An endangerment site
D. Not a contraindication

992. Addison's disease
A. Rapid formation of kidney tissue, resulting in increased filtration of blood
B. Overuse of corticosteroids, resulting in weight gain and muscle atrophy
C. Protrusion of part of the stomach through the diaphragm
D. Autoimmune disorder resulting in the destruction of the adrenal cortex

993. Atrial fibrillation is a form of
A. Heart murmur
B. Arrhythmia
C. Infarction
D. Aneurysm

994. The most common form of cancer is found in the
A. Breast
B. Lungs
C. Pancreas
D. Skin

995. Dizziness
A. Vertigo
B. Impetigo
C. Tinnitus
D. Labyrinthitis

996. Cancer of epithelial cells
A. Carcinoma
B. Sarcoma
C. Leukemia
D. Lymphoma

997. Inflammation of breast tissue
A. Angina pectoris
B. Mastectomy
C. Mastitis
D. Dermatitis

998. Acute Golfer's Elbow is considered
A. An absolute contraindication
B. A local contraindication
C. An endangerment site
D. Not a contraindication

999. Embolism
A. Bulge in an artery wall, usually caused by a weakened artery due to a condition such as hypertension
B. Inflammation of a vein due to trauma, resulting in blood clot formation
C. Blood clot in the blood stream becoming lodged in the heart, lungs, or brain, resulting in death of tissue
D. Ischemia in the myocardium due to a blockage in the coronary arteries, resulting in myocardial infarction

1000. A disease that has an unknown cause is known as
A. Pathological
B. Carcinogenic
C. Etiologic
D. Idiopathic

1001. Lateral epicondylitis is more commonly known as
A. Golfer's elbow
B. Tennis elbow
C. Football shoulder
D. Soccer knee

1002. Allergic reactions in the body may be controlled with use of
A. Vasodilators
B. Statins
C. Antihistamines
D. Beta-blockers

1003. The three stages of inflammation
A. Histamine release, phagocytosis, tissue repair
B. Constriction of blood vessels, phagocytosis, tissue repair
C. Tissue repair, phagocytosis, histamine release
D. Muscle contraction, pinocytosis, tissue repair

1004. Transient ischemic attack is a form of
A. Aneurysm
B. Heart attack
C. Stroke
D. Inflammation

1005. Type of drug that combats bacterial infection
A. Morphine
B. Antibiotics
C. Non-steroidal anti-inflammatory drugs
D. Immunizations

1006. A decubitus ulcer is considered
A. An endangerment site
B. An absolute contraindication
C. A local contraindication
D. Not a contraindication

1007. Dilation of a small portion of an artery, caused by a weakened arterial wall
A. Embolism
B. Aneurysm
C. Thrombus
D. Murmur

1008. Hypothyroidism is also known as
A. Myxedema
B. Grave's disease
C. Iodine deficiency
D. Hashimoto's disease

1009. During the course of a massage, a client notifies the massage therapist of a sunburn they recently suffered from that includes the presence of blisters. Which of the following is the best course of action for the massage therapist to take
A. Avoid the affected area as blisters are a local contraindication
B. Work on the affected area, as increased circulation helps speed recovery of blisters
C. Apply heat to the affected area to help open the blisters and drain fluid
D. Apply cold on the blisters to reduce additional blister formation during the course of the massage

1010. The definition of the suffix "-rrhage" is
A. Discharge
B. Bursting forth
C. Growth
D. Urine

1011. The definition of "cardi/o" is
A. Artery
B. Blood
C. Lung
D. Heart

1012. Bruising and inflammation resulting from partial tearing of a ligament
A. Grade 2 sprain
B. Grade 1 strain
C. Grade 3 sprain
D. Grade 2 strain

1013. An injury to the spinal cord between C5 and T1 may result in
A. Quadriplegia
B. Paraplegia
C. Hemiplegia
D. Triplegia

1014. Bell's palsy
A. Pain in the face around the eyes, nose, and mouth caused by compression of the trigeminal nerve
B. Paralysis of one side of the face due to stimulation of the Herpes Simplex virus, which affects the facial nerve
C. Compression of the median nerve beneath the transverse carpal ligament, resulting in loss of sensation in the hand
D. Damage to the spinal cord below T1, resulting in paralysis of the lower limbs

1015. Diarrhea may result in
A. Diverticulosis
B. Constipation
C. Ulcerative colitis
D. Dehydration

1016. Overuse of the leg causing pain along the medial side of the tibia
A. Osteomalacia
B. Osteoporosis
C. Paget's disease
D. Periostitis

1017. Bronchodilators, expectorants, and decongestants all affect the
A. Respiratory system
B. Endocrine system
C. Nervous system
D. Cardiovascular system

1018. The trigeminal nerve is involved in the following condition
A. Cerebral palsy
B. Bell's palsy
C. Trigeminal neuralgia
D. Carpal tunnel syndrome

1019. Carpal tunnel syndrome
A. Pain in the face around the eyes, nose, and mouth caused by compression of the trigeminal nerve
B. Paralysis of one side of the face due to stimulation of the Herpes Simplex virus, which affects the facial nerve
C. Compression of the median nerve beneath the transverse carpal ligament, resulting in loss of sensation in the hand
D. Damage to the spinal cord below T1, resulting in paralysis of the lower limbs

1020. Meningitis is considered
A. A local contraindication
B. An absolute contraindication
C. An endangerment site
D. Not a contraindication

1021. The antecubital region is considered
A. A local contraindication
B. An absolute contraindication
C. An endangerment site
D. Not a contraindication

1022. Inflammation of the kidneys
A. Hepatitis
B. Nephritis
C. Cystitis
D. Gastritis

1023. Endocarditis is considered
A. A local contraindication
B. An absolute contraindication
C. An endangerment site
D. Not a contraindication

1024. Beta-blockers should not be used on people with
A. Bradycardia
B. Angina pectoris
C. Hypertension
D. Hyperthyroidism

1025. Infectious pleurisy is considered
A. A local contraindication
B. An absolute contraindication
C. An endangerment site
D. Not a contraindication

1026. Osteomyelitis
A. Bacterial infection of skeletal muscle
B. Viral infection of the medullary cavity
C. Bacterial infection of the periosteum and bone canal
D. Viral infection of muscle and tendon

1027. A collection of pus, usually localized
A. Psoriasis
B. Lesion
C. Wart
D. Abscess

1028. Inflammation of the connective tissue surrounding the heart
A. Myocarditis
B. Pericarditis
C. Phlebitis
D. Endocarditis

1029. Weight gain, muscle weakness and atrophy, and hypertension may result from the excessive use of synthetic corticosteroids, a condition known as
A. Cushing's syndrome
B. Addison's disease
C. Grave's disease
D. Hodgkin's disease

1030. Inability to contract muscles
A. Neuralgia
B. Paralysis
C. Neuritis
D. Lupus

1031. Pericarditis
A. Inflammation of the muscle of the heart
B. Inflammation of the inner linings of the heart
C. Inflammation of the connective tissue surrounding the heart
D. Inflammation of the coronary arteries

1032. Hyper-curvature in the thoracic region
A. Kyphosis
B. Lordosis
C. Scoliosis
D. Spondylitis

1033. Kyphosis is considered
A. A local contraindication
B. An absolute contraindication
C. An endangerment site
D. Not a contraindication

1034. Addison's disease is considered
A. A local contraindication
B. An absolute contraindication
C. An endangerment site
D. Not a contraindication

1035. The definition of "melan/o" is
A. White
B. Green
C. Red
D. Black

1036. A third degree burn is considered
A. A local contraindication
B. An absolute contraindication
C. An endangerment site
D. Not a contraindication

1037. The definition of "cry/o" is
A. Tear
B. Cold
C. Skin
D. Same

1038. The definition of the suffix "-pnea" is
A. Breathing
B. Small
C. Growth
D. Condition

1039. Necrosis of myocardium due to blockages in the coronary arteries leads to
A. Aneurysm
B. Heart murmur
C. Myocardial infarction
D. Arrhythmia

1040. Blood clot in a blood vessel dislodging from its location and moving through the blood stream
A. Aneurysm
B. Lymphedema
C. Thromboembolism
D. Myocardial infarction

1041. Sleep apnea
A. Stoppage of breathing due to blockages in the airways while asleep
B. Inability to properly fall asleep, or sleeping for minimal amounts
C. Uncontrolled falling asleep at any time
D. Shortness of breath due to physical exertion or another more serious cause

1042. During the course of a massage, a massage therapist notices an open wound on the skin of a client. The massage therapist should
A. Avoid the wound and only work on the posterior of the body
B. Avoid the wound but work on the rest of the body
C. Work on the wound to increase circulation and speed healing
D. Stop the massage and reschedule until the wound is healed

1043. Pseudoepinephrine is a substance found in the following medications
A. Antihistamines
B. Expectorants
C. Bronchodilators
D. Decongestants

1044. Parkinson's disease is considered
A. A local contraindication
B. An absolute contraindication
C. An endangerment site
D. Not a contraindication

1045. A contusion is also known as
A. Bruise
B. Wart
C. Fracture
D. Hives

1046. Chris, who has recently suffered from a heart attack, has requested a massage. The proper course a massage therapist should take is
A. Reschedule the massage until medical clearance has been provided from the client's physician
B. Perform the massage to promote circulation
C. Perform the massage and use cold compress to lower blood pressure
D. Perform the massage while avoiding shaking or trembling actions

1047. Mole
A. Rapid formation of melanocytes resulting in a cancerous tumor
B. Benign skin lesion with increased production of melanin
C. Form of skin cancer that grows slowly and is easily detectable
D. Also known as sun spots, usually form during senescence

1048. Inflammation of a group of nerves
A. Polyneuritis
B. Trigeminal neuralgia
C. Bell's palsy
D. Neuritis

1049. Basal cell carcinoma
A. Most common, most serious, fastest growing form of skin cancer
B. Least common, most serious, fastest growing form of skin cancer
C. Most common, least serious, slowest growing form of skin cancer
D. Least common, least serious, slowest growing form of skin cancer

1050. Air bubble in the pleural membrane as a result of piercing of lung tissue
A. Pleurisy
B. Pneumonia
C. Pneumothorax
D. Acute bronchitis

1051. Inflammation of joints persistent with an increased accumulation of uric acid
A. Pyelonephritis
B. Osteoarthritis
C. Gout
D. Ankylosing spondylitis

1052. Tinea capitis is considered
A. A local contraindication
B. An absolute contraindication
C. An endangerment site
D. Not a contraindication

1053. Pyelonephritis
A. Inflammation of the liver due to a viral infection
B. Inflammation of the bladder due to a bacterial infection
C. Inflammation of the kidneys due to a bacterial infection
D. Inflammation of the colon due to a viral infection

1054. Pneumothorax
A. Spasm of smooth muscle surrounding bronchial tubes resulting in decreased oxygen intake
B. Bacterial infection of the lungs resulting in severe fluid buildup in alveoli
C. Inflammation of pleural membrane resulting in severe chest pain
D. Air bubble present in the pleural membrane as a result of a punctured lung

1055. Viral infection resulting in localized hyper-production of keratinocytes
A. Impetigo
B. Wart
C. Cold sore
D. Acne

1056. Myocarditis
A. Inflammation of the inner linings of the heart
B. Inflammation of the muscle of the heart
C. Inflammation of the connective tissue surrounding the heart
D. Inflammation of the coronary arteries

1057. Bell's palsy affects the following cranial nerve
A. Cranial nerve VII
B. Cranial nerve V
C. Cranial nerve IV
D. Cranial nerve XII

1058. A client with impetigo schedules a massage. An appropriate response would be
A. Perform the massage, applying heat on the affected patches to reduce infection
B. Perform the massage, avoiding the affected area
C. Perform the massage, working on the affected patches, as impetigo is not contagious
D. Reschedule the appointment until the impetigo has cleared, as impetigo is highly contagious

1059. The definition of the prefix "ana-" is
A. Outside
B. Self
C. Before
D. Against

1060. Endocarditis
A. Inflammation of the muscle of the heart
B. Inflammation of the inner linings of the heart
C. Inflammation of the connective tissue surrounding the heart
D. Inflammation of the coronary arteries

1061. Medication given to people who suffer from asthma to relax smooth muscle in the respiratory system
A. Bronchodilators
B. Expectorants
C. Decongestants
D. Statins

1062. The popliteal region is considered
A. A local contraindication
B. An absolute contraindication
C. An endangerment site
D. Not a contraindication

1063. The definition of the prefix "dys-" is
A. Before
B. Same
C. Behind
D. Difficult

1064. The definition of "oste/o" is
A. Vessel
B. Bone
C. Muscle
D. Heart

1065. The study of cause of disease
A. Pathology
B. Etiology
C. Cardiology
D. Oncology

1066. A myocardial infarction is considered
A. A local contraindication
B. An absolute contraindication
C. An endangerment site
D. Not a contraindication

1067. Carpal tunnel syndrome
A. Compression of the median nerve by the transverse carpal ligament
B. Paralysis of the ulnar nerve due to an injury at the thoracic outlet
C. Compression of the radial nerve by the transverse carpal ligament
D. Loss of sensation in the hand as a result of entrapment of the axillary nerve

1068. Multiple sclerosis during the course of a flare-up is considered
A. A local contraindication
B. An absolute contraindication
C. An endangerment site
D. Not a contraindication

1069. Inflammation begins with
A. Increase of interstitial fluid
B. Constriction of blood vessels
C. Dilation of blood vessels
D. Phagocytosis

1070. Decongestants are used to reduce the swelling in the
A. Throat
B. Lungs
C. Nose
D. Abdomen

1071. A high ankle sprain is which grade sprain
A. Grade 2
B. Grade 1
C. Grade 3
D. Grade 4

1072. Acute lupus erythematosus is considered
A. A local contraindication
B. An absolute contraindication
C. An endangerment site
D. Not a contraindication

1073. Well-defined borders of infection is typical of which condition
A. Contusion
B. Osteomyelitis
C. Thrush
D. Cellulitis

1074. Grade 1 sprain
A. Complete rupture of a tendon
B. Partial tearing of a ligament resulting in bruising and inflammation
C. Complete rupture of a ligament
D. Overstretching of a ligament without tearing

1075. Ankylosing spondylitis
A. Degeneration of intervertebral discs that results in fusion of vertebrae
B. Degeneration of articular cartilage between bones causing pain and bone spurs
C. Degeneration of synovial membranes surrounding diarthrotic joints
D. Formation of fibrous tissue around synovial joints reducing movement

1076. In carpal tunnel syndrome, the median nerve is compressed by the following structure
A. Transverse carpal ligament
B. Extensor retinaculum
C. Pectoralis minor
D. Scalenes

1077. A client with substantial scarring may best benefit from
A. Cold compress applied to the area
B. Friction over the area
C. Avoiding the affected area
D. Rescheduling the massage

1078. Kyphosis is also known as
A. Swayback
B. Dowager's hump
C. Scoliosis
D. Bamboo spine

1079. Bacterial infection of a hair follicle, most commonly seen on the face, neck, armpit, which may need to be surgically drained
A. Cyst
B. Acne
C. Boil
D. Impetigo

1080. Malignant cancer can spread via
A. Cartilage
B. Oxygen
C. Bone
D. Blood

1081. Kaposi's sarcoma is a form of cancer usually present in
A. Late stage AIDS patients
B. The elderly
C. People exposed to excessive ultraviolet light
D. Children with leukemia

1082. Vomiting is also known as
A. Defecation
B. Reflux
C. Emesis
D. GERD

1083. A bacterial infection that enters the blood stream results in
A. Septicemia
B. Anemia
C. Gout
D. Leukemia

1084. Blockage of air passages during sleep, caused by relaxation of muscles in the throat and tongue
A. Insomnia
B. Sleep apnea
C. Dyspnea
D. Narcolepsy

1085. Skin tags are considered
A. A local contraindication
B. An absolute contraindication
C. An endangerment site
D. Not a contraindication

1086. Metabolic imbalance leading to spasms of the muscles of the face, arms, and legs
A. Cerebral palsy
B. Bell's palsy
C. Tetany
D. Scurvy

1087. Swelling of the following gland results in a goiter
A. Pituitary
B. Thyroid
C. Thymus
D. Adrenal

1088. A generalized feeling of discomfort which can accompany a systemic infection
A. Malaise
B. Malignancy
C. Hypoxia
D. Hypothermia

1089. Malignant cancer of white blood cells
A. Leukemia
B. Anemia
C. Melanoma
D. Myeloma

1090. Inflammatory disorder affecting peripheral nerves, causing weakness in the muscles of the upper and lower limbs
A. Myasthenia gravis
B. Guillain-Barre syndrome
C. Systemic lupus erythematosus
D. Neuroma

1091. Melanoma is what type of tumor
A. Benign
B. Malignant
C. Idiopathic
D. Lymphatic

1092. Renal failure is considered
A. A local contraindication
B. An absolute contraindication
C. An endangerment site
D. Not a contraindication

1093. Gout is considered
A. A local contraindication
B. An absolute contraindication
C. An endangerment site
D. Not a contraindication

1094. The definition of the suffix "-phagia" is
A. Speech
B. Eating
C. Pain
D. Removal

1095. In a client with herpes simplex, exposure to sunlight, stress, or hormonal changes may result in the development of
A. Impetigo
B. Decubitus ulcers
C. Cold sores
D. Acne

1096. A cold sore is considered
A. An endangerment site
B. An absolute contraindication
C. A local contraindication
D. Not a contraindication

1097. The definition of the prefix "iso-" is
A. Many
B. Same
C. New
D. All

1098. Compression of the median nerve by the transverse carpal ligament, resulting in numbness and tingling distal to the affected area
A. Trigeminal neuralgia
B. Thoracic outlet syndrome
C. Bell's palsy
D. Carpal tunnel syndrome

1099. The second phase of inflammation is called phagocytosis, which is the responsibility of
A. Leukocytes
B. Erythrocytes
C. Thrombocytes
D. Histamines

1100. A tumor of the thymus may result in
A. Still's disease
B. Systemic lupus erythematosus
C. Polymyostitis
D. Myasthenia gravis

Pathology Answer Key

01. C
02. B
03. C
04. A
05. A
06. D
07. A
08. D
09. C
10. C
11. D
12. D
13. A
14. B
15. B
16. B
17. D
18. C
19. D
20. A
21. A
22. B
23. D
24. C
25. D
26. C
27. A
28. B
29. C
30. D
31. A
32. B
33. D
34. A
35. D
36. B
37. C
38. B
39. B
40. A

41. A
42. C
43. C
44. B
45. C
46. B
47. A
48. A
49. C
50. D
51. D
52. C
53. B
54. C
55. D
56. A
57. B
58. B
59. C
60. B
61. A
62. D
63. D
64. B
65. B
66. C
67. A
68. A
69. D
70. B
71. B
72. D
73. A
74. D
75. B
76. C
77. B
78. C
79. D
80. A

81. D
82. D
83. B
84. A
85. B
86. A
87. C
88. A
89. C
90. C
91. D
92. A
93. C
94. B
95. D
96. A
97. B
98. D
99. A
100. C
101. B
102. A
103. B
104. D
105. D
106. D
107. B
108. B
109. C
110. B
111. B
112. B
113. A
114. D
115. A
116. D
117. B
118. A
119. D
120. D

121. A
122. A
123. D
124. B
125. D
126. A
127. C
128. C
129. C
130. A
131. D
132. B
133. B
134. C
135. D
136. A
137. C
138. B
139. A
140. C
141. B
142. A
143. D
144. D
145. B
146. B
147. A
148. B
149. D
150. D
151. A
152. D
153. B
154. D
155. A
156. B
157. C
158. A
159. B
160. D

161. D
162. D
163. D
164. A
165. B
166. C
167. B
168. B
169. A
170. C
171. D
172. C
173. A
174. B
175. B
176. D
177. A
178. D
179. B
180. D
181. A
182. D
183. A
184. B
185. C
186. C
187. A
188. C
189. A
190. B
191. B
192. B
193. A
194. D
195. C
196. A
197. C
198. B
199. A
200. D

201. A	246. B	291. A	336. B	381. A
202. A	247. A	292. A	337. A	382. B
203. D	248. A	293. C	338. A	383. B
204. B	249. C	294. B	339. C	384. B
205. A	250. A	295. C	340. D	385. A
206. C	251. B	296. C	341. B	386. D
207. C	252. C	297. C	342. A	387. D
208. D	253. A	298. A	343. B	388. D
209. A	254. C	299. D	344. D	389. A
210. A	255. A	300. A	345. D	390. A
211. C	256. C	301. B	346. A	391. C
212. D	257. B	302. A	347. D	392. B
213. A	258. D	303. D	348. D	393. C
214. B	259. B	304. C	349. A	394. A
215. C	260. B	305. B	350. C	395. B
216. A	261. A	306. B	351. A	396. C
217. D	262. D	307. D	352. B	397. C
218. D	263. D	308. B	353. C	398. C
219. C	264. C	309. D	354. D	399. B
220. A	265. C	310. A	355. B	400. A
221. D	266. D	311. D	356. A	401. A
222. A	267. A	312. B	357. D	402. D
223. C	268. B	313. A	358. C	403. A
224. C	269. A	314. C	359. D	404. C
225. C	270. D	315. B	360. C	405. D
226. B	271. C	316. D	361. B	406. B
227. B	272. A	317. D	362. D	407. D
228. A	273. B	318. D	363. A	408. C
229. A	274. B	319. B	364. A	409. A
230. C	275. B	320. A	365. C	410. D
231. C	276. B	321. A	366. C	411. A
232. C	277. A	322. C	367. C	412. C
233. D	278. D	323. A	368. A	413. C
234. A	279. A	324. D	369. B	414. A
235. D	280. C	325. D	370. B	415. B
236. B	281. C	326. D	371. C	416. D
237. B	282. B	327. A	372. A	417. D
238. C	283. A	328. C	373. D	418. C
239. A	284. D	329. A	374. D	419. A
240. B	285. D	330. B	375. C	420. A
241. C	286. B	331. A	376. A	421. A
242. D	287. A	332. C	377. D	422. B
243. D	288. C	333. C	378. B	423. C
244. B	289. D	334. D	379. A	424. B
245. B	290. B	335. B	380. D	425. C

426. B	471. B	516. D	561. A	606. D
427. C	472. A	517. B	562. D	607. B
428. A	473. B	518. C	563. C	608. B
429. B	474. D	519. C	564. B	609. A
430. C	475. B	520. D	565. D	610. B
431. D	476. C	521. A	566. D	611. C
432. D	477. A	522. A	567. A	612. C
433. C	478. D	523. A	568. C	613. C
434. A	479. C	524. B	569. D	614. A
435. A	480. D	525. D	570. A	615. B
436. D	481. A	526. D	571. A	616. C
437. B	482. A	527. C	572. D	617. D
438. B	483. B	528. A	573. A	618. D
439. D	484. C	529. B	574. B	619. A
440. A	485. C	530. D	575. C	620. C
441. C	486. C	531. B	576. D	621. D
442. A	487. A	532. A	577. A	622. B
443. C	488. D	533. B	578. C	623. C
444. C	489. A	534. B	579. C	624. A
445. B	490. D	535. A	580. B	625. C
446. A	491. B	536. D	581. D	626. D
447. B	492. B	537. D	582. B	627. D
448. D	493. B	538. D	583. B	628. C
449. C	494. A	539. A	584. C	629. C
450. D	495. D	540. C	585. B	630. C
451. A	496. C	541. C	586. D	631. A
452. B	497. A	542. C	587. B	632. D
453. B	498. B	543. D	588. A	633. B
454. A	499. D	544. A	589. A	634. D
455. D	500. B	545. A	590. C	635. D
456. D	501. B	546. B	591. C	636. B
457. B	502. C	547. B	592. B	637. A
458. A	503. A	548. C	593. B	638. D
459. D	504. D	549. A	594. A	639. D
460. A	505. D	550. C	595. D	640. B
461. C	506. B	551. D	596. A	641. A
462. D	507. A	552. B	597. D	642. C
463. A	508. A	553. A	598. B	643. D
464. A	509. B	554. C	599. B	644. C
465. D	510. D	555. B	600. A	645. C
466. D	511. A	556. D	601. A	646. A
467. C	512. C	557. D	602. B	647. D
468. B	513. C	558. A	603. C	648. A
469. A	514. A	559. B	604. A	649. C
470. D	515. B	560. D	605. D	650. B

651. B	696. B	741. C	786. A	831. C
652. C	697. A	742. D	787. C	832. A
653. D	698. A	743. B	788. B	833. D
654. A	699. B	744. B	789. C	834. B
655. B	700. C	745. B	790. C	835. D
656. B	701. A	746. A	791. C	836. B
657. B	702. D	747. C	792. A	837. A
658. A	703. A	748. C	793. B	838. C
659. B	704. B	749. A	794. D	839. C
660. D	705. B	750. A	795. C	840. C
661. C	706. D	751. A	796. D	841. B
662. A	707. B	752. D	797. D	842. B
663. A	708. D	753. B	798. B	843. A
664. D	709. B	754. B	799. A	844. B
665. C	710. C	755. C	800. B	845. C
666. C	711. D	756. D	801. A	846. D
667. D	712. C	757. D	802. B	847. B
668. B	713. A	758. C	803. A	848. D
669. C	714. B	759. A	804. B	849. A
670. D	715. B	760. A	805. C	850. B
671. C	716. A	761. B	806. A	851. C
672. A	717. C	762. B	807. A	852. B
673. B	718. D	763. C	808. B	853. B
674. D	719. B	764. C	809. C	854. A
675. A	720. C	765. D	810. B	855. B
676. B	721. D	766. A	811. B	856. D
677. A	722. A	767. B	812. D	857. D
678. B	723. D	768. D	813. D	858. D
679. D	724. D	769. B	814. A	859. A
680. D	725. D	770. B	815. A	860. C
681. D	726. D	771. A	816. A	861. C
682. A	727. A	772. D	817. C	862. A
683. C	728. C	773. A	818. D	863. C
684. B	729. C	774. D	819. B	864. C
685. D	730. B	775. B	820. C	865. A
686. D	731. B	776. C	821. B	866. D
687. A	732. C	777. A	822. D	867. B
688. D	733. B	778. B	823. C	868. D
689. A	734. D	779. B	824. C	869. B
690. D	735. A	780. D	825. A	870. A
691. B	736. A	781. D	826. B	871. B
692. C	737. C	782. D	827. D	872. A
693. C	738. C	783. A	828. D	873. C
694. A	739. C	784. D	829. D	874. A
695. D	740. A	785. D	830. A	875. B

876. C	921. A	966. D	1011. D	1056. B
877. D	922. C	967. A	1012. A	1057. A
878. D	923. D	968. B	1013. A	1058. D
879. A	924. D	969. A	1014. B	1059. D
880. D	925. A	970. B	1015. D	1060. B
881. C	926. B	971. D	1016. D	1061. A
882. B	927. C	972. C	1017. A	1062. C
883. C	928. D	973. B	1018. C	1063. D
884. A	929. B	974. B	1019. C	1064. B
885. D	930. A	975. A	1020. B	1065. B
886. D	931. D	976. D	1021. C	1066. B
887. B	932. A	977. B	1022. B	1067. A
888. C	933. C	978. D	1023. B	1068. B
889. A	934. B	979. B	1024. A	1069. C
890. D	935. B	980. A	1025. B	1070. C
891. C	936. D	981. B	1026. C	1071. A
892. A	937. C	982. B	1027. D	1072. B
893. B	938. B	983. A	1028. B	1073. D
894. C	939. A	984. C	1029. A	1074. D
895. C	940. D	985. C	1030. B	1075. A
896. A	941. D	986. A	1031. C	1076. A
897. C	942. D	987. D	1032. A	1077. B
898. B	943. C	988. B	1033. D	1078. B
899. B	944. A	989. A	1034. D	1079. C
900. D	945. B	990. D	1035. D	1080. D
901. A	946. C	991. B	1036. A	1081. A
902. D	947. D	992. D	1037. B	1082. C
903. D	948. A	993. B	1038. A	1083. A
904. D	949. B	994. D	1039. C	1084. B
905. A	950. B	995. A	1040. C	1085. D
906. B	951. B	996. A	1041. A	1086. C
907. B	952. B	997. C	1042. B	1087. B
908. A	953. D	998. B	1043. D	1088. A
909. B	954. A	999. C	1044. D	1089. A
910. A	955. A	1000. D	1045. A	1090. B
911. C	956. C	1001. B	1046. A	1091. B
912. C	957. B	1002. C	1047. B	1092. B
913. B	958. A	1003. A	1048. A	1093. A
914. D	959. C	1004. C	1049. C	1094. B
915. A	960. C	1005. B	1050. C	1095. C
916. B	961. A	1006. C	1051. C	1096. C
917. A	962. D	1007. B	1052. A	1097. B
918. B	963. C	1008. A	1053. C	1098. D
919. C	964. A	1009. A	1054. D	1099. A
920. A	965. D	1010. B	1055. B	1100. D

Kinesiology Practice Test

Kinesiology questions will likely ask all aspects of a muscle, including origin, insertion, action, innervation, synergists, and antagonists. These questions could be posed similarly to those in Massage, where you are given a situation involving a muscle, and you will be expected to assess the situation and figure out which muscle is involved. If one of these questions states, "Client X experiences pain while performing Action Y", it's almost always asking in different words, "Which muscle performs Action Y?" Being able to break down a question and put it into a more easily understandable question can definitely help.

If presented with a question asking the action of a muscle, or which muscle performs a specific action, there's an easy way to figure out the answer: Move! If I get a question asking which muscle flexes the shoulder, I will flex my shoulder and palpate muscles around it, trying to identify the correct answer that way. If I get a question asking which action is performed by the biceps brachii, I will contract that muscle and use my powers of deduction to figure out which joints it is moving, and which way it is moving them. Your own body can be used to help answer questions!

If you study and learn everything there is about the 30 or so muscles listed in your study guide, you will have no problem with the kinesiology section. That isn't to say you won't have questions on muscles NOT in the study guide. You will definitely be asked about things not in the study guide. However, knowing those muscles in the guide will highly increase your chances of passing the exam!

1. Structure located on the proximal shaft of the humerus
A. Trochlea
B. Bicipital groove
C. Radial fossa
D. Capitulum

2. Insertion of the adductor longus
A. Lesser trochanter
B. Pectineal line
C. Linea aspera
D. Greater trochanter

3. Elbow extension and shoulder extension is performed by the following muscle
A. Triceps brachii
B. Biceps brachii
C. Coracobrachialis
D. Anconeus

4. Part of the scapula serratus anterior inserts onto
A. Medial border
B. Lateral border
C. Spine
D. Inferior angle

5. Bi-lateral contraction of the pectineus muscles would have what action on two abducted lower limbs
A. Bring them into an extended position
B. Take them further apart
C. Bring them closer together
D. Rotate them laterally

6. Large bony structures located at the proximal end of the humerus
A. Trochlea and capitulum
B. Medial and lateral epicondyles
C. Deltoid tuberosity and olecranon fossa
D. Greater and lesser tubercles

7. Muscle responsible for intentional blinking
A. Frontalis
B. Orbicularis oris
C. Temporalis
D. Orbicularis oculi

8. Adductor magnus has a common origination site with which muscle group
A. Wrist flexors
B. Quadriceps
C. Rotator cuff
D. Hamstrings

9. All of the following are located on the femur except
A. Medial condyle
B. Greater trochanter
C. Linea alba
D. Adductor tubercle

10. The second cervical vertebrae is also known as
A. Atlas
B. Axis
C. Occiput
D. Temporal

11. Muscle originating on the spinous processes of T7-L5, the iliac crest, and lumbar aponeurosis
A. Quadratus lumborum
B. Latissimus dorsi
C. Spinalis
D. Psoas major

12. The ethmoid bone is found in which part of the face
A. Eye socket
B. Nose
C. Cheek
D. Ear canal

13. Shoulder flexion, elbow flexion, and forearm supination are all performed by which muscle
A. Brachialis
B. Coracobrachialis
C. Brachioradialis
D. Biceps Brachii

14. Which of the following is a hinge joint
A. Knee
B. Hip
C. Shoulder
D. Wrist

15. Muscle inserting onto the medial lip of the linea aspera and adductor tubercle of the femur
A. Adductor longus
B. Adductor magnus
C. Adductor brevis
D. Gracilis

16. The pubic symphysis connects which part of the pubic bones together
A. Superior rami
B. Pubic crests
C. Inferior rami
D. Pubic bodies

17. The following muscle inserts onto the lateral lip of the intertubercular groove
A. Pectoralis minor
B. Pectoralis major
C. Latissimus dorsi
D. Teres major

18. The origin of teres minor
A. Lateral border of the scapula
B. Medial border of the scapula
C. Spine of the scapula
D. Greater tubercle

19. Origin of the rectus femoris
A. Anterior Superior Iliac Spine
B. Anterior Inferior Iliac Spine
C. Ischial tuberosity
D. Body of the pubis

20. Which two structures form the hip joint
A. Head of femur and obturator foramen
B. Head of femur and acetabulum
C. Head of humerus and glenoid fossa
D. Head of humerus and acromion process

21. Contraction of the middle fibers of the trapezius result in
A. Retraction
B. Protraction
C. Elevation
D. Depression

22. The coronal suture connects the following bones of the cranium
A. Occipital and parietal
B. Parietal and parietal
C. Parietal and frontal
D. Temporal and parietal

23. The interphalangeal joints can perform which actions
A. Adduction and abduction
B. Rotation
C. Flexion and extension
D. Protraction and retraction

24. Brachioradialis inserts onto which part of the radius
A. Styloid process
B. Radial tuberosity
C. Head
D. Interosseous border

25. The antecubital region is located on which side of the elbow
A. Posterior
B. Anterior
C. Medial
D. Lateral

26. Muscles originating on the spinous processes of C7-T5
A. Levator scapulae
B. Serratus anterior
C. Trapezius
D. Rhomboids

27. The socket of the hip is also called the
A. Ischial tuberosity
B. Obturator foramen
C. Acetabulum
D. Iliac crest

28. Primary muscle a massage therapist palpates on the lateral edge of the leg
A. Soleus
B. Tibialis anterior
C. Peroneus longus
D. Gastrocnemius

29. The ankle joint is comprised of which two bones
A. Tibia and talus
B. Tibia and fibula
C. Talus and calcaneus
D. Talus and fibula

30. Muscle controlling adduction of the hip
A. Adductor longus
B. Sartorius
C. Rectus femoris
D. Biceps femoris

31. Extension of the thumb can be accomplished by contraction of which muscle
A. Extensor pollicis longus
B. Flexor pollicis longus
C. Extensor hallucis longus
D. Flexor hallucis longus

32. The saddle joint is located where
A. Elbow
B. Thumb
C. Knee
D. Ankle

33. Structure located on the lateral distal end of the humerus
A. Medial epicondyle
B. Greater tubercle
C. Lateral epicondyle
D. Trochlea

34. Antagonist to the rhomboids, responsible for abduction of the scapula
A. Latissimus dorsi
B. Pectoralis major
C. Trapezius
D. Serratus anterior

35. Proximal attachment of coracobrachialis
A. Coracoid process
B. Coronoid process
C. Medial proximal shaft of humerus
D. Radial tuberosity

36. Joint located between the occiput and first cervical vertebrae, responsible for flexion and extension of the head
A. Atlantoaxial
B. Atlantooccipital
C. Occipitofrontalis
D. Occipitoaxial

37. An antagonist to the middle fibers of the trapezius
A. Pectoralis major
B. Serratus anterior
C. Triceps brachii
D. Teres major

38. Which of the following muscles crosses the glenohumeral joint
A. Pectoralis minor
B. Trapezius
C. Coracobrachialis
D. Brachialis

39. Distal attachment of the peroneus longus
A. Head of the fibula
B. Tuberosity of the fifth metatarsal
C. Base of first metatarsal
D. Lateral condyle of the tibia

40. Synergist to the hamstrings while flexing the knee
A. Gastrocnemius
B. Soleus
C. Tibialis anterior
D. Rectus femoris

41. A concentric contraction of this muscle causes the hip to extend and the knee to flex
A. Gastrocnemius
B. Rectus femoris
C. Biceps brachii
D. Semitendinosus

42. Structure located directly inferior to the coronoid process of the ulna
A. Ulnar tuberosity
B. Coronoid fossa
C. Olecranon fossa
D. Styloid process

43. If a client were to resist the actions of the pectineus, how would they move their body
A. Adduction and flexion of the hip
B. Abduction and extension of the hip
C. Abduction and flexion of the hip
D. Adduction and extension of the hip

44. Muscle originating on the sternum and clavicle, responsible for neck flexion and unilateral head rotation to the opposite side
A. Levator scapulae
B. Sternocleidomastoid
C. Scalenes
D. Pectoralis major

45. The capitulum articulates with
A. Head of the radius
B. Tibial plateau
C. Coracoid process
D. Greater trochanter

46. Which muscle originates on the sternum, ribs, and medial half of the clavicle
A. Teres minor
B. Pectoralis minor
C. Anterior deltoid
D. Pectoralis major

47. The rectus femoris is biaxial. What are the two actions performed by this muscle
A. Hip flexion, knee flexion
B. Hip extension, knee extension
C. Hip flexion, knee extension
D. Hip extension, knee flexion

48. Where does the biceps brachii insert?
A. Ulnar Tuberosity
B. Radial Process
C. Coronoid Process
D. Radial Tuberosity

49. Muscle originating on the medial lip of the linea aspera
A. Vastus medialis
B. Vastus lateralis
C. Semimembranosus
D. Semitendinosus

50. Triceps brachii is innervated by the following nerve
A. Ulnar
B. Radial
C. Musculocutaneous
D. Median

51. Muscle primarily responsible for supination of the forearm
A. Biceps brachii
B. Triceps brachii
C. Brachioradialis
D. Brachialis

52. Muscle laying deep to the rectus femoris
A. Sartorius
B. Vastus lateralis
C. Vastus medialis
D. Vastus intermedius

53. Most superior portion of the tibia
A. Soleal line
B. Tibial tuberosity
C. Medial malleolus
D. Tibial plateau

54. Pivot joint located in the forearm, responsible for pronation and supination
A. Radiocarpal
B. Proximal radioulnar
C. Distal radioulnar
D. Humeroulnar

55. Insertion of the stirrup muscles
A. Base of first metatarsal
B. Tuberosity of fifth metatarsal
C. Calcaneus
D. Distal phalange of the great toe

56. Which of the following is not a fossa located on the humerus
A. Coronoid fossa
B. Olecranon fossa
C. Ulnar fossa
D. Radial fossa

57. Muscle responsible for flexing the thumb
A. Flexor digitorum longus
B. Extensor pollicis longus
C. Flexor pollicis longus
D. Flexor hallucis longus

58. The median nerve innervates which muscle
A. Biceps brachii
B. Pronator teres
C. Brachialis
D. Brachioradialis

59. Muscle originating on the distal anterior shaft of the humerus
A. Brachialis
B. Brachioradialis
C. Biceps brachii
D. Coracobrachialis

60. Distal attachment of the gastrocnemius
A. Calcaneus
B. Posterior medial and lateral epicondyles of the femur
C. Tuberosity of the fifth metatarsal
D. Base of the first metatarsal

61. Muscle assisting in flexion and adduction of the hip, originating on the superior ramus of the pubis
A. Adductor brevis
B. Gracilis
C. Adductor longus
D. Pectineus

62. Upon contraction, gracilis performs what action
A. Adduction and extension of the hip and extension of the knee
B. Abduction and flexion of the hip and flexion of the knee
C. Adduction and flexion of the hip and flexion of the knee
D. Abduction and extension of the hip and extension of the knee

63. Synergist to the biceps brachii while performing supination of the forearm
A. Coracobrachialis
B. Brachialis
C. Supinator
D. Triceps brachii

64. Pain experienced at the iliofemoral joint upon flexion most likely involves the following muscle
A. Gastrocnemius
B. Biceps femoris
C. Rectus femoris
D. Gluteus maximus

65. Nerve that innervates the heart and digestive organs
A. Vagus
B. Trigeminal
C. Occulomotor
D. Cardiac

66. Proximal attachment site of gastrocnemius
A. Posterior medial and lateral epicondyles of the femur
B. Linea aspera
C. Calcaneus
D. Soleal line

67. The median and ulnar nerves innervate which muscle group
A. Extensors of the wrist
B. Flexors of the wrist
C. Flexors of the shoulder
D. Extensors of the shoulder

68. Insertion of the gracilis
A. Pubic symphysis
B. Tibial tuberosity
C. Inferior ramus of pubis
D. Pes anserinus

69. Contraction of sartorius has what action on the lower limb
A. Knee extension, hip flexion and medial rotation
B. Knee flexion, hip flexion and lateral rotation
C. Knee flexion, hip extension and lateral rotation
D. Knee extension, hip extension and lateral rotation

70. Antagonist to the soleus
A. Tibialis anterior
B. Gastrocnemius
C. Peroneus longus
D. Peroneus brevis

71. Which of the following is an action of the knee
A. Abduction
B. Adduction
C. Flexion
D. Protraction

72. The axillary nerve innervates which two muscles
A. Teres minor and deltoids
B. Deltoids and latissimus dorsi
C. Coracobrachialis and biceps brachii
D. Latissimus dorsi and teres major

73. External rotation of the hip is provided by contraction of which muscle
A. Rectus femoris
B. Sartorius
C. Pectineus
D. Adductor longus

74. Which of the following is a structure located on the humerus
A. Coracoid process
B. Radial fossa
C. Acromion process
D. Olecranon process

75. Flexor pollicis longus produces what action
A. Extends the thumb
B. Flexes the great toe
C. Flexes the thumb
D. Extends the great toe

76. Origin of piriformis
A. Greater trochanter
B. Posterior surface of sacrum
C. Lateral border of scapula
D. Anterior surface of sacrum

77. The anterior portion of the elbow is also known as which region
A. Brachial
B. Antecubital
C. Surral
D. Crural

78. The longest muscle in the body
A. Sartorius
B. Gracilis
C. Latissimus dorsi
D. Trapezius

79. Shallow depression located on the distal posterior surface of the humerus
A. Olecranon fossa
B. Trochlea
C. Bicipital groove
D. Capitulum

80. The distal row of carpals contains all of the following bones except
A. Hamate
B. Trapezium
C. Triquetrum
D. Capitate

81. Antagonist of the tibialis anterior
A. Peroneus longus
B. Extensor digitorum longus
C. Rectus femoris
D. Biceps femoris

82. Large hole in the pelvis that the obturator nerve passes through
A. Iliac crest
B. Iliac fossa
C. Sciatic notch
D. Obturator foramen

83. Pain experienced at the glenohumeral joint upon extension may be the result of hypertonicity of the following muscle
A. Biceps brachii
B. Triceps brachii
C. Coracobrachialis
D. Supraspinatus

84. Origin of teres major
A. Superior angle of scapula
B. Medial lip of intertubercular groove
C. Inferior angle of scapula
D. Lateral lip of intertubercular groove

85. What muscle originates on the supraglenoid tubercle
A. Long head of the biceps brachii
B. Short head of the biceps brachii
C. Long head of the triceps brachii
D. Lateral head of the triceps brachii

86. The pubic symphysis holds what parts of the pubic bones together
A. Superior ramus
B. Body
C. Inferior ramus
D. Pubic crest

87. Primary antagonist to the hamstrings
A. Adductors
B. Quadriceps
C. Glutes
D. Calf

88. Carpal bone that articulates with the ulna
A. Trapezium
B. Scaphoid
C. Lunate
D. Pisiform

89. Order of the hamstrings from medial to lateral
A. Semimembranosus, semitendinosus, biceps femoris
B. Biceps femoris, semitendinosus, semimembranosus
C. Semimembranosus, biceps femoris, semitendinosus
D. Semitendinosus, semimembranosus, biceps femoris

90. The lambdoid suture is located between which cranial bones
A. Temporal and parietal
B. Parietal and parietal
C. Occipital and parietal
D. Parietal and frontal

91. Extension is
A. Moving a structure toward the midline
B. Decreasing the angle of a joint
C. Increasing the angle of a joint
D. Taking a structure away from the midline

92. Flexion of the lumbar vertebrae can be accomplished by contraction of the following muscle
A. Rectus abdominis
B. Iliacus
C. Quadratus lumborum
D. Latissimus dorsi

93. All of the following muscles insert onto the scapula except
A. Rhomboids
B. Supraspinatus
C. Serratus anterior
D. Pectoralis minor

94. Antagonist to the quadriceps, responsible for hip extension and knee flexion
A. Calf
B. Adductors
C. Rotators
D. Hamstrings

95. Stretching of the quadriceps muscle group is achieved by moving the body in what ways
A. Knee extension, hip flexion
B. Knee extension, hip extension
C. Knee flexion, hip flexion
D. Knee flexion, hip extension

96. Action of psoas major on the hip
A. Medial rotation
B. Extension
C. Flexion
D. Lateral rotation

97. Actions of the tibialis anterior
A. Supination and plantarflexion
B. Pronation and plantarflexion
C. Supination and dorsiflexion
D. Pronation and dorsiflexion

98. Insertion of supraspinatus
A. Greater tubercle
B. Lesser tubercle
C. Supraspinous Fossa
D. Infraspinous Fossa

99. Circumduction is
A. Moving a structure around the circumference of a joint
B. Bringing a structure closer to the midline
C. Rotating a structure laterally
D. Flexing a joint

100. Structure on the posterior surface of the femoral shaft running from superior to inferior
A. Linea alba
B. Linea aspera
C. Greater trochanter
D. Lesser trochanter

101. Which of the following describes a fossa
A. Articulation
B. Small protrusion
C. Large protrusion
D. Shallow depression

102. Muscles inserting onto the medial border of the scapula, responsible for adduction of the scapula
A. Serratus anterior
B. Rhomboids
C. Upper fibers of the trapezius
D. Latissimus dorsi

103. The four rotator cuff muscles are
A. Supraspinatus, Subscapularis, Infraspinatus, Teres Minor
B. Subscapularis, Infraspinatus, Supraspinatus, Teres Major
C. Infraspinatus, Deltoids, Subscapularis, Teres Minor
D. Supraspinatus, Infraspinatus, Teres Minor, Pectoralis Minor

104. A fossa can be found on each of the following bones except
A. Humerus
B. Ulna
C. Scapula
D. Ilium

105. Muscle originating on the posterior medial and lateral epicondyles of the femur
A. Tibialis anterior
B. Soleus
C. Gastrocnemius
D. Biceps femoris

106. Insertion of the rhomboids
A. Medial border of the scapula
B. Superior angle of the scapula
C. Lateral border of the scapula
D. Spinous processes of C7-T5

107. Turning the foot out away from the midline is also known as
A. Dorsiflexion
B. Inversion
C. Eversion
D. Plantarflexion

108. The gracilis is innervated by which nerve
A. Radial
B. Femoral
C. Sciatic
D. Obturator

109. Actions of the adductor magnus include
A. Hip extension, adduction, and lateral rotation
B. Hip extension, abduction, and flexion
C. Hip flexion, lateral rotation, and abduction
D. Hip flexion, extension, and adduction

110. Nerve that can pass under, over, or sometimes through the piriformis muscle
A. Femoral
B. Obturator
C. Sciatic
D. Lumbosacral plexus

111. The hip joint is also known as
A. Coxal joint
B. Tibiofemoral joint
C. Talocrural joint
D. Glenohumeral joint

112. All of the following muscles extend the shoulder except
A. Teres major
B. Latissimus dorsi
C. Supraspinatus
D. Subscapularis

113. Antagonist to sartorius with regards to knee flexion
A. Biceps femoris
B. Rectus femoris
C. Semitendinosus
D. Semimembranosus

114. Proximal attachment of the short head of biceps brachii
A. Coracoid process
B. Supraglenoid tubercle
C. Infraglenoid tubercle
D. Coronoid process

115. The medial epicondyle of the humerus is the origination site of which muscle group
A. Adductors
B. Wrist extensors
C. Wrist flexors
D. Abductors

116. A concentric contraction of the subscapularis muscle causes which actions on the shoulder
A. Lateral rotation, flexion, and adduction
B. Lateral rotation, extension, and adduction
C. Medial rotation, flexion, and adduction
D. Medial rotation, extension, and adduction

117. Adduction moves a body part in which way
A. Across the body
B. Away from the midline of the body
C. Towards the midline of the body
D. In front of the body

118. Muscle originating in the iliac fossa, responsible for flexion of the hip
A. Iliacus
B. Psoas major
C. Rectus femoris
D. Piriformis

119. Muscle inserting onto the lesser tubercle of the humerus, responsible for medial rotation, adduction, and extension of the shoulder
A. Subscapularis
B. Pectoralis Major
C. Supraspinatus
D. Pectoralis Minor

120. Muscle originating on the posterior ilium, posterior sacrum and coccyx, responsible for abduction and extension of the hip
A. Gluteus medius
B. Gluteus maximus
C. Gluteus minimus
D. Piriformis

121. Muscle responsible for extension, flexion, medial rotation, and horizontal adduction of the shoulder
A. Biceps brachii
B. Pectoralis minor
C. Pectoralis major
D. Triceps brachii

122. The tarsals are classified as what kind of bone
A. Short
B. Long
C. Irregular
D. Sesamoid

123. Contraction of the biceps femoris causes
A. Hip extension and knee flexion
B. Hip flexion and knee extension
C. Hip extension and knee extension
D. Hip flexion and knee flexion

124. Muscle originating on the lateral two thirds of the proximal tibia
A. Soleus
B. Tibialis anterior
C. Peroneus longus
D. Gastrocnemius

125. This muscle is the most powerful flexor of the elbow
A. Biceps brachii
B. Brachialis
C. Brachioradialis
D. Triceps brachii

126. Shoulder extension, medial rotation, and adduction is performed by
A. Coracobrachialis
B. Teres minor
C. Biceps brachii
D. Latissimus dorsi

127. Insertion of the following muscle occurs at the styloid process of the radius
A. Brachioradialis
B. Biceps brachii
C. Brachialis
D. Flexor digitorum longus

128. The pes anserinus is an insertion site for three muscles. These three muscles are
A. Sartorius, semimembranosus, gracilis
B. Gracilis, semitendinosus, sartorius
C. Rectus femoris, tibialis anterior, peroneus longus
D. Sartorius, gracilis, biceps femoris

129. Proximal attachment of semimembranosus
A. Ischial tuberosity
B. Inferior ramus of pubis
C. Superior ramus of pubis
D. Medial condyle of tibia

130. Which rotator cuff muscle does not originate in a fossa
A. Infraspinatus
B. Teres Minor
C. Supraspinatus
D. Subscapularis

131. Tuberosity located between the greater and lesser trochanters
A. Adductor
B. Femoral
C. Gluteal
D. Deltoid

132. Distal attachment of psoas major
A. Linea alba
B. Greater trochanter
C. Linea aspera
D. Lesser trochanter

133. The lunate articulates with which bone of the forearm
A. Ulna
B. Radius
C. Hamate
D. Triquetrum

134. The following muscles are also known as the stirrup muscles
A. Tibialis anterior and peroneus brevis
B. Tibialis anterior and peroneus longus
C. Peroneus longus and extensor digitorum longus
D. Peroneus brevis and peroneus longus

135. Nerve responsible for stimulation of the soleus
A. Superficial peroneal
B. Deep peroneal
C. Tibial
D. Femoral

136. The common peroneal nerve passes through which body region
A. Popliteal
B. Antecubital
C. Thoracic
D. Abdominal

137. Which bone does pectoralis major not attach to
A. Sternum
B. Clavicle
C. Humerus
D. Scapula

138. With the hand in neutral position, flexion of the elbow is accomplished by contraction of the following muscle
A. Triceps brachii
B. Brachialis
C. Coracobrachialis
D. Brachioradialis

139. The trapezium joins with the metacarpal of the thumb to create which synovial joint
A. Condyloid
B. Hinge
C. Pivot
D. Saddle

140. Insertion of trapezius
A. Spine of scapula, acromion process, clavicle
B. External occipital protuberance
C. Spinous processes of T1-T12
D. Greater tubercle of humerus

141. The scaphoid articulates with which bone of the forearm
A. Ulna
B. Radius
C. Tibia
D. Fibula

142. The one muscle of the rotator cuff that does not originate inside of a fossa is
A. Supraspinatus
B. Infraspinatus
C. Teres Minor
D. Subscapularis

143. Structure located on the lateral proximal shaft of the humerus
A. Deltoid tuberosity
B. Lesser tubercle
C. Medial epicondyle
D. Lateral epicondyle

144. Antagonist to serratus anterior, responsible for adduction of the scapula
A. Pectoralis minor
B. Rhomboids
C. Upper fibers of trapezius
D. Infraspinatus

145. Which is the only quadriceps muscle that crosses two joints
A. Vastus medialis
B. Vastus intermedius
C. Vastus lateralis
D. Rectus femoris

146. Insertion of latissimus dorsi
A. Iliac crest
B. Lateral lip of intertubercular groove
C. Spine of scapula
D. Medial lip of intertubercular groove

147. Which of the following is a structure located on the scapula
A. Greater tubercle
B. Inferior angle
C. Coronoid process
D. Lesser tubercle

148. Disc of cartilage holding the pubic bodies together
A. Pubic symphysis
B. Meniscus
C. Labrum
D. Sacrotuberous ligament

149. Structure located on the top of the tibia
A. Medial malleolus
B. Tibial tuberosity
C. Tibial plateau
D. Soleal line

150. Latissimus dorsi originates on the spinous processes of T7-L5, the lumbar aponeurosis, and which other landmark
A. Anterior Superior Iliac Spine
B. Iliac Crest
C. Iliac Fossa
D. Anterior Inferior Iliac Spine

151. The tendon of which muscle passes through the intertubercular groove
A. Long head of the biceps brachii
B. Short head of the biceps brachii
C. Deltoid
D. Rectus femoris

152. The elbow joint is which type of synovial joint
A. Pivot
B. Hinge
C. Ball and socket
D. Gliding

153. Origination of brachialis
A. Ulnar tuberosity
B. Proximal medial shaft of humerus
C. Coronoid process
D. Distal anterior shaft of humerus

154. Structure emerging from the spine of the scapula, articulating with the lateral end of the clavicle
A. Spine of the scapula
B. Coracoid process
C. Glenoid fossa
D. Acromion process

155. All of the following are structures located on the scapula except
A. Subscapular fossa
B. Axillary border
C. Coronoid process
D. Acromion process

156. What two muscles join with the calcaneal tendon to insert onto the calcaneus
A. Peroneus longus and brevis
B. Tibialis anterior and tibialis posterior
C. Gastrocnemius and soleus
D. Flexor hallucis longus and extensor digitorum

157. Muscle inserting on the medial lip of the intertubercular groove of the humerus
A. Latissimus dorsi
B. Teres minor
C. Biceps brachii
D. Brachialis

158. Origin of subscapularis
A. Subscapular Fossa
B. Supraspinous Fossa
C. Infraspinous Fossa
D. Lesser tubercle

159. Contraction of latissimus dorsi causes which actions
A. Shoulder adduction, extension, medial rotation
B. Shoulder flexion, extension, abduction
C. Shoulder abduction, extension, medial rotation
D. Shoulder extension, abduction, medial rotation

160. Insertion of subscapularis
A. Greater tubercle
B. Lesser tubercle
C. Subscapular Fossa
D. Spine of scapula

161. Origin of vastus lateralis
A. Medial lip of linea aspera
B. Lateral lip of linea aspera
C. Anterior Superior Iliac Spine
D. Anterior Inferior Iliac Spine

162. The bone a person sits on is also called the
A. Head of the femur
B. Iliac crest
C. Ischial tuberosity
D. Sacrum

163. All of the following are located on the fibula except
A. Head
B. Styloid process
C. Pes anserinus
D. Lateral malleolus

164. The pelvis is formed by which three bones
A. Ilium, ischium, pubis
B. Ilium, ischium, sacrum
C. Pubis, ischium, coccyx
D. Sacrum, coccyx, L5

165. Actions of the pectoralis major include flexion of the shoulder, horizontal adduction of the shoulder, extension of the shoulder, and
A. Flexion of the elbow
B. Abduction of the shoulder
C. Lateral rotation of the shoulder
D. Medial rotation of the shoulder

166. Stretching the rhomboids can be accomplished by moving the body in which way
A. Depress scapula
B. Adduct scapula
C. Elevate scapula
D. Abduct scapula

167. Contraction of the lower fibers of the trapezius results in
A. Elevation
B. Depression
C. Retraction
D. Adduction

168. Origin of pectoralis major
A. Medial lip of intertubercular groove
B. Sternum, ribs, lateral half of clavicle
C. Lateral lip of intertubercular groove
D. Sternum, ribs, medial half of clavicle

169. Which of the following is not a carpal bone
A. Cuboid
B. Capitate
C. Triquetrum
D. Pisiform

170. Common attachment site of three muscles on the medial proximal shaft of the tibia
A. Tibial tuberosity
B. Pes anserinus
C. Medial condyle
D. Medial malleolus

171. Nerve innervating the quadriceps muscle group
A. Obturator
B. Femoral
C. Sciatic
D. Common peroneal

172. The origin of gracilis is found at what body region
A. Inguinal
B. Popliteal
C. Cubital
D. Antecubital

173. Biceps brachii is innervated by the following nerve
A. Sciatic
B. Radial
C. Musculocutaneous
D. Median

174. Origin of trapezius
A. External occipital protuberance, spinous processes of T1-T12
B. Spine of scapula
C. Spine of scapula and clavicle
D. Medial border of scapula

175. Proximal attachment of infraspinatus
A. Greater Tubercle
B. Supraspinous Fossa
C. Infraspinous Fossa
D. Lateral border of the scapula

176. The cranial suture found between the occipital bone and parietal bones is called
A. Squamous suture
B. Sagittal suture
C. Lambdoid suture
D. Coronal suture

177. Muscle responsible for extending the thumb
A. Extensor hallucis longus
B. Flexor pollicis longus
C. Extensor pollicis longus
D. Flexor hallucis longus

178. Origin of the flexors of the wrist
A. Medial epicondyle of the humerus
B. Lateral epicodyle of the humerus
C. Coronoid process
D. Radial tuberosity

179. Insertion of the temporalis
A. Maxilla
B. Temporal bone
C. Zygomatic arch
D. Coronoid process of the mandible

180. Adductor magnus is named for its
A. Location
B. Shape
C. Attachment sites
D. Size and action

181. Which region of the body is the capitulum located at
A. Antecubital
B. Popliteal
C. Axillary
D. Inguinal

182. Nerve that stimulates the gastrocnemius
A. Deep peroneal
B. Tibial
C. Superficial peroneal
D. Obturator

183. Which of the following bones contains a fossa
A. Fibula
B. Ilium
C. Tibia
D. Sternum

184. The bicipital groove is located between which two structures on the humerus
A. The greater and lesser tubercles
B. The greater tubercle and deltoid tuberosity
C. The radial and coronoid fossae
D. The olecranon fossa and trochlea

185. The proximal row of the carpals contains all of the following bones except
A. Lunate
B. Scaphoid
C. Trapezoid
D. Pisiform

186. Psoas major joins with what other muscle to assist in hip flexion
A. Biceps femoris
B. Rectus femoris
C. Piriformis
D. Iliacus

187. Synergist to pronator teres
A. Supinator
B. Coracobrachialis
C. Triceps brachii
D. Pronator quadratus

188. Stretching of the masseter requires the jaw to be
A. Elevated
B. Depressed
C. Retracted
D. Protracted

189. The condyles of the humerus are located at which end of the bone
A. Distal
B. Proximal
C. Medial
D. Lateral

190. Which of the following is not found on the scapula
A. Spine
B. Acromion process
C. Coronoid process
D. Superior angle

191. Cranial nerve V is also known as
A. Accessory nerve
B. Facial nerve
C. Trigeminal nerve
D. Hypoglossal nerve

192. Opponens pollicis moves the thumb in what way
A. Extension
B. Flexion
C. Adduction
D. Opposition

193. Adductor muscle originating on the inferior ramus of the pubis and inserting onto the pes anserinus
A. Gracilis
B. Adductor magnus
C. Adductor longus
D. Adductor brevis

194. Joint located at the medial end of the clavicle
A. Acromioclavicular
B. Sternoclavicular
C. Jugular notch
D. Sternal angle

195. Structure located directly inferior to the Anterior Superior Iliac Spine
A. Ischial tuberosity
B. Iliac crest
C. Anterior Inferior Iliac Spine
D. Superior ramus of the pubis

196. Coracobrachialis is innervated by which nerve
A. Median
B. Musculocutaneous
C. Radial
D. Ulnar

197. Which of the following muscles crosses the elbow joint
A. Teres minor
B. Coracobrachialis
C. Pronator teres
D. Deltoid

198. Origin of the splenius capitis
A. Mastoid process and occiput
B. Superior angle of scapula
C. Spine of scapula
D. Spinous processes of C3-T6

199. Flexion and extension of the head takes place at which joint
A. Atlantooccipital
B. Atlantoaxial
C. Lambdoid suture
D. Between C1-C2

200. The knee moves in how many planes
A. One
B. Two
C. Three
D. Four

201. The talus articulates with which bone in the leg to produce the ankle joint
A. Femur
B. Fibula
C. Tibia
D. Calcaneus

202. Order of the following muscles from superficial to deep
A. Serratus posterior, rhomboids, trapezius
B. Trapezius, rhomboids, serratus posterior
C. Trapezius, serratus posterior, rhomboids
D. Rhomboids, trapezius, serratus posterior

203. The bones of the face fall under which classification
A. Sesamoid
B. Short
C. Long
D. Irregular

204. Actions of the peroneus longus
A. Pronation and dorsiflexion
B. Supination and dorsiflexion
C. Pronation and plantarflexion
D. Supination and plantarflexion

205. Origin of the supinator
A. Lateral epicondyle of the humerus
B. Medial epicondyle of the humerus
C. Anterior and lateral surface of radius
D. Posterior and medial surface of radius

206. Which of the following is not an action performed by the hip joint
A. Abduction
B. Retraction
C. Extension
D. Rotation

207. Nerve innervating the muscles of the posterior leg
A. Common peroneal
B. Tibial
C. Obturator
D. Femoral

208. Action of pectoralis minor
A. Abduction of the scapula
B. Adduction of the scapula
C. Elevation of the scapula
D. Medial rotation of the humerus

209. Most medial muscle of the erector spinae muscle group
A. Longissimus
B. Semispinalis
C. Spinalis
D. Iliocostalis

210. Moving the hip into extension and abduction has what affect on the pectineus
A. Contracts
B. Shortens
C. Stretches
D. Spasms

211. Muscle inserting onto the base of the first metatarsal, responsible for eversion and plantarflexion of the foot
A. Tibialis anterior
B. Peroneus brevis
C. Peroneus longus
D. Tibialis posterior

212. Which of the following is a structure located on the radius
A. Olecranon process
B. Coronoid process
C. Capitulum
D. Styloid process

213. A massage therapist palpates the medial epicondyle of the humerus. If the therapist were to move their hand directly inferior, the structure they would then be palpating would be the
A. Capitulum
B. Trochlea
C. Coronoid fossa
D. Ulnar tuberosity

214. The squamous suture is located between which cranial bones
A. Parietal and parietal
B. Temporal and parietal
C. Frontal and Temporal
D. Occipital and parietal

215. Synergist to the gastrocnemius in performing plantarflexion, also performs eversion of the foot
A. Peroneus longus
B. Soleus
C. Tibialis anterior
D. Popliteus

216. Synergist to the hamstrings when extending the hip
A. Iliacus
B. Gluteus maximus
C. Psoas major
D. Sartorius

217. Muscle responsible for plantarflexion
A. Soleus
B. Tibialis anterior
C. Extensor digitorum
D. Biceps femoris

218. Nerve or nerves providing stimulation to the adductor magnus
A. Femoral
B. Obturator and sciatic
C. Lumbosacral plexus
D. Vagus

219. The most distal portion of the radius
A. Olecranon process
B. Head
C. Radial tuberosity
D. Styloid process

220. The metacarpal of the thumb articulates with which carpal bone to create the saddle joint
A. Capitate
B. Trapezoid
C. Hamate
D. Trapezium

221. Insertion of the tibialis anterior
A. Lateral two thirds of the proximal tibia
B. Tuberosity of the fifth metatarsal
C. Base of the first metatarsal
D. Tibial tuberosity

222. The deltoid is innervated by the following nerve
A. Axillary
B. Femoral
C. Radial
D. Median

223. Stretching of the pectoralis major can be accomplished by moving the shoulder in which way
A. Lateral rotation and horizontal abduction
B. Medial rotation and flexion
C. Horizontal adduction and extension
D. Flexion and extension

224. The bones of the carpals are considered which type of bone
A. Irregular
B. Long
C. Short
D. Flat

225. Psoas major inserts on the following structure of the femur
A. Lesser trochanter
B. Greater trochanter
C. Head
D. Linea aspera

226. Muscle responsible for external rotation and extension of the shoulder
A. Subscapularis
B. Supraspinatus
C. Infraspinatus
D. Latissimus Dorsi

227. The ulna is positioned where in relation to the radius
A. Proximal
B. Lateral
C. Medial
D. Distal

228. The suture connecting the parietal and temporal bones together is called
A. Coronal suture
B. Sagittal suture
C. Lambdoid suture
D. Squamous suture

229. The phrenic nerve innervates which muscle
A. Pectoralis major
B. Diaphragm
C. Pectoralis minor
D. Trapezius

230. Which of the following is a structure located on the distal shaft of the femur
A. Lesser trochanter
B. Greater trochanter
C. Gluteal tuberosity
D. Adductor tubercle

231. Hip extension and knee flexion is performed by which muscle group
A. Adductors
B. Quadriceps
C. Hamstrings
D. Glutes

232. How many muscles insert onto the scapula
A. Six
B. Eight
C. Sixteen
D. Twenty-two

233. Moving a structure toward the midline of the body
A. Adduction
B. Abduction
C. Flexion
D. Extension

234. Most distal point on the ulna
A. Ulnar tuberosity
B. Olecranon process
C. Coronoid process
D. Styloid process

235. Muscle, along with temporalis and pterygoid, that raises the mandible
A. Orbicularis oris
B. Frontalis
C. Masseter
D. Orbicularis oculi

236. Insertion of the platysma
A. Fascia of the upper chest
B. Jugular notch
C. Medial third of the clavicle
D. Body of the sternum

237. Which of the following is a structure located on the ilium
A. Inferior ramus
B. Ischial tuberosity
C. Superior ramus
D. Iliac fossa

238. Gastrocnemius takes what action on the knee when contracted
A. Extends
B. Flexes
C. Adducts
D. Abducts

239. Muscle inserting onto the posterior medial condyle of the tibia
A. Semitendinosus
B. Semimembranosus
C. Biceps femoris
D. Rectus femoris

240. Antagonist to the pronator teres
A. Biceps brachii
B. Brachialis
C. Brachioradialis
D. Coracobrachialis

241. Muscle inserting onto the medial border of the scapula, responsible for protraction of the scapula
A. Rhomboid minor
B. Rhomboid major
C. Serratus anterior
D. Pectoralis minor

242. When the diaphragm ascends into the chest cavity, what takes place
A. Collapsed lung
B. Inhalation
C. Exhalation
D. Force

243. The greater tubercle of the humerus lies in what position relative to the lesser tubercle of the humerus
A. Anterior
B. Medial
C. Lateral
D. Posterior

244. Most medial muscle of the hamstrings muscle group
A. Biceps femoris
B. Semitendinosus
C. Rectus femoris
D. Semimembranosus

245. An injury to the hamstrings might inhibit which actions
A. Hip extension and knee flexion
B. Hip flexion and knee extension
C. Hip extension and knee extension
D. Hip flexion and knee flexion

246. All of the following are located on the pubis except
A. Pubic crest
B. Superior ramus
C. Inferior ramus
D. Ischial tuberosity

247. The wrist extensors originate on which part of the humerus
A. Medial epicodyle
B. Lateral epicondyle
C. Trochlea
D. Capitulum

248. The scapula contains how many fossae
A. Four
B. Three
C. None
D. Two

249. The pubic symphysis is categorized as which type of synovial joint
A. Pivot
B. Hinge
C. Plane
D. Saddle

250. The greater tubercle of the humerus is the insertion site of which three muscles
A. Teres Minor, Supraspinatus, Infraspinatus
B. Teres Major, Infraspinatus, Supraspinatus
C. Subscapularis, Supraspinatus, Teres Minor
D. Infraspinatus, Teres Major, Latissimus Dorsi

251. In order to stretch the gracilis, the body must by positioned in what way
A. Hip adducted, knee extended
B. Hip adducted, knee flexed
C. Hip abducted, knee flexed
D. Hip abducted, knee extended

252. Which of the following is a structure found on the proximal end of the femur
A. Adductor tubercle
B. Greater tubercle
C. Medial condyle
D. Lesser trochanter

253. An elongated piece of bone is also known as a
A. Symphysis
B. Ramus
C. Fossa
D. Coronoid

254. Flexion and horizontal adduction of the shoulder is performed by which muscle
A. Coracobrachialis
B. Biceps brachii
C. Pectoralis minor
D. Triceps brachii

255. Muscle that performs abduction, flexion, and extension of the shoulder
A. Biceps brachii
B. Deltoids
C. Coracobrachialis
D. Supraspinatus

256. Action of the piriformis on the hip
A. Adduction and lateral rotation
B. Abduction and medial rotation
C. Abduction and lateral rotation
D. Adduction and medial rotation

257. Muscle originating in the subscapular fossa
A. Pectoralis Minor
B. Supraspinatus
C. Infraspinatus
D. Subscapularis

258. Primary synergist to latissimus dorsi, performing extension, adduction, and medial rotation of the shoulder
A. Teres minor
B. Teres major
C. Trapezius
D. Infraspinatus

259. The zygomatic bones form which part of the face
A. Lower jaw
B. Upper jaw
C. Cheeks
D. Nose

260. Rectus abdominis and the diaphragm share an attachment site. They both attach to
A. Xiphoid process
B. Body of pubis
C. Lumbar vertebrae
D. Superior seven ribs

261. Nerve innervating the pronator teres
A. Radial
B. Median
C. Musculocutaneous
D. Axillary

262. Name of the groove the tendon of the long head of the biceps brachii passes through on its way to its insertion site
A. Intertubercular groove
B. Long head groove
C. Humeral groove
D. Interbicipital groove

263. Of the following, which is not an action of the hip
A. Opposition
B. Circumduction
C. Rotation
D. Flexion

264. Action causing a decrease in the angle of a joint
A. Abduction
B. Extension
C. Medial Rotation
D. Flexion

265. Muscle responsible for extending the neck and rotating the head to the same side
A. Rhomboids
B. Sternocleidomastoid
C. Levator scapulae
D. Splenius capitis

266. The nerve that innervates the adductor muscle group is
A. Radial
B. Femoral
C. Tibial
D. Obturator

267. Suture located between the two parietal bones
A. Coronal suture
B. Lambdoid suture
C. Sagittal suture
D. Squamous suture

268. Pectineus is part of what muscle group
A. Adductors
B. Quadriceps
C. Hamstrings
D. Glutes

269. Distal attachment of triceps brachii
A. Radial tuberosity
B. Olecranon process
C. Coronoid process
D. Styloid process

270. If a client experiences pain upon flexion at the glenohumeral joint, the muscle most likely involved is
A. Triceps brachii
B. Biceps brachii
C. Pectoralis minor
D. Brachialis

271. Bone inside the patellar tendon
A. Tibia
B. Patella
C. Fibula
D. Femur

272. Distal attachment site of the deltoids
A. Deltoid tuberosity
B. Greater tubercle
C. Lesser tubercle
D. Acromion process

273. The acromioclavicular joint is considered which type of synovial joint
A. Hinge
B. Pivot
C. Gliding
D. Ball and socket

274. Distal attachment of the iliacus
A. Iliac crest
B. Greater trochanter
C. Iliac fossa
D. Lesser trochanter

275. Placing the body into knee extension and ankle dorsiflexion would stretch which muscle
A. Gastrocnemius
B. Tibialis anterior
C. Rectus femoris
D. Extensor digitorum longus

276. The sternoclavicular joint is considered which type of synovial joint
A. Hinge
B. Pivot
C. Saddle
D. Gliding

277. Which muscle inserts on the olecranon process
A. Brachioradialis
B. Biceps brachii
C. Triceps brachii
D. Biceps Femoris

278. Muscle originating on the body of the pubis
A. Adductor longus
B. Adductor magnus
C. Pectineus
D. Gracilis

279. The ischial tuberosity lies where in relation to the Iliac crest
A. Lateral
B. Superior
C. Medial
D. Inferior

280. Muscles that cross the glenohumeral joint include all of the following except
A. Trapezius
B. Deltoid
C. Pectoralis major
D. Triceps brachii

281. The scientific name of the hip joint
A. Acetabulum
B. Tibiofemoral
C. Iliofemoral
D. Iliosacral

282. An antagonist to the biceps brachii is
A. Coracobrachialis
B. Brachialis
C. Pronator Teres
D. Pectoralis Major

283. Proximal attachment of gluteus maximus
A. Posterior ilium, posterior sacrum, posterior coccyx
B. Iliac crest
C. Anterior ilium, posterior sacrum
D. Gluteal line

284. Pectineus lies where in relation to all other adductor muscles
A. Lateral
B. Inferior
C. Medial
D. Superior

285. Which muscle is not part of the adductor muscle group
A. Gracilis
B. Semimembranosus
C. Pectineus
D. Adductor magnus

286. Muscle inserting into the fascia of the upper chest
A. Sternocleidomastoid
B. Platysma
C. Pectoralis major
D. Subclavian

287. Actions of the hamstring muscle group
A. Hip extension, knee flexion
B. Knee extension, hip flexion
C. Knee flexion, hip flexion
D. Knee extension, hip extension

288. The region of the body found at the back of the knee is known as
A. Popliteal
B. Crural
C. Inguinal
D. Antecubital

289. The glenohumeral joint is made by combining the head of the humerus with which structure on the scapula
A. Supraglenoid tubercle
B. Acromion process
C. Coracoid process
D. Glenoid fossa

290. Sartorius attaches proximally to what structure of the pelvis
A. Anterior superior iliac spine
B. Anterior inferior iliac spine
C. Ischial tuberosity
D. Superior ramus of pubis

291. Which fiber of the deltoid originates on the acromion process of the scapula
A. Inferior deltoid
B. Anterior deltoid
C. Posterior deltoid
D. Middle deltoid

292. Muscle responsible for lateral rotation and abduction of the hip
A. Sartorius
B. Pectineus
C. Piriformis
D. Gluteus minimus

293. Facial bones which form the cheeks
A. Maxilla
B. Mandible
C. Zygomatic
D. Temporal

294. The intercondylar ridge is located between which structures on the femur
A. Greater and lesser trochanters
B. Lateral and medial epicondyles
C. Medial and lateral condyles
D. Adductor tubercle and medial epicondyle

295. The greater trochanter is located on which end of the femur
A. Proximal
B. Distal
C. Anterior
D. Posterior

296. The saddle joint is created by which two bones
A. Lunate and ulna
B. Scaphoid and radius
C. Medial cuneiform and metatarsal of the great toe
D. Trapezium and metacarpal of the thumb

297. The linea aspera is located on which side of the femur
A. Anterior
B. Posterior
C. Medial
D. Lateral

298. All three hamstring muscles originate on which bony marking
A. Ischial tuberosity
B. Head of the fibula
C. Pes anserinus
D. Femoral condyle

299. Innervation of the pectineus is primarily provided by the following nerve
A. Sciatic
B. Femoral
C. Tibial
D. Common peroneal

300. Structures located directly superior to the trochlea and capitulum of the humerus
A. Bicipital groove and deltoid tuberosity
B. Greater and lesser tubercles
C. Medial and lateral epicondyles
D. Olecranon process and coronoid process

301. Medial and lateral rotation can be performed at which of the following joints
A. Hip
B. Elbow
C. Ankle
D. Wrist

302. A massage therapist is working on the lateral side of the forearm. The bone they are working on top of is the
A. Radius
B. Ulna
C. Humerus
D. Fibula

303. The flexor retinaculum is also known as
A. Transverse carpal ligament
B. Flexor tendon
C. Extensor retinaculum
D. Horizontal flexor tendon

304. An injury to the adductor magnus muscle would make which movements more difficult to perform
A. Hip flexion, abduction, and extension
B. Hip flexion, adduction, and extension
C. Hip extension, abduction, and medial rotation
D. Hip flexion, abduction, and medial rotation

305. The acetabulum and head of the femur articulate to create which joint
A. Shoulder
B. Knee
C. Hip
D. Ankle

306. Nerve innervating muscles of the posterior arm, including triceps brachii and the wrist extensors
A. Ulnar
B. Median
C. Radial
D. Axillary

307. Distal attachment site of semimembranosus
A. Posterior medial condyle of tibia
B. Medial epicondyle of femur
C. Tibial tuberosity
D. Pes anserinus

308. Gracilis is a synergist to the following muscle
A. Tibialis anterior
B. Soleus
C. Gastrocnemius
D. Gluteus maximus

309. In order to stretch the gastrocnemius, the body must be positioned in what way
A. Knee flexed, ankle dorsiflexed
B. Knee flexed, ankle plantarflexed
C. Knee extended, ankle plantarflexed
D. Knee extended, ankle dorsiflexed

310. Muscle inserting onto the lesser trochanter of the femur, responsible for flexion of the hip
A. Piriformis
B. Rectus femoris
C. Iliacus
D. Sartorius

311. Which of the following is a structure located on the ischium
A. Ischial spine
B. Iliac crest
C. Anterior superior iliac spine
D. Inferior ramus

312. Most proximal structure of the fibula
A. Lateral malleolus
B. Head
C. Neck
D. Styloid process

313. Antagonist to sartorius in regards to hip flexion
A. Iliacus
B. Rectus femoris
C. Gracilis
D. Semitendinosus

314. Name of the tendon that connects the quadriceps to the tibial tuberosity
A. Rectus femoris tendon
B. Vastus tendon
C. Patellar tendon
D. Tibial tendon

315. Origin of pectoralis minor
A. Coracoid process
B. Ribs 3-5
C. Ribs 1-3
D. Sternum

316. Stimulation of the sartorius is provided by which nerve
A. Sciatic
B. Obturator
C. Femoral
D. Tibial

317. Muscle responsible for extension and support of the vertebrae
A. Spinalis
B. Rectus abdominis
C. Trapezius
D. Rhomboids

318. Eversion of the foot is also known as
A. Pronation
B. Supination
C. Plantarflexion
D. Dorsiflexion

319. The most distal structure on the tibia
A. Lateral condyle
B. Lateral malleolus
C. Medial condyle
D. Medial malleolus

320. Pain felt at the tibiofemoral joint upon flexion may involve the following muscle
A. Rectus femoris
B. Gastrocnemius
C. Soleus
D. Tibialis anterior

321. The phalanges are classified as which type of bone
A. Short
B. Long
C. Flat
D. Irregular

322. Which of the following is a bone that does not fuse together with other bones to form the pelvis
A. Ischium
B. Ilium
C. Sacrum
D. Pubis

323. The flexors of the wrist are innervated by the following two nerves
A. Ulnar and median
B. Median and radial
C. Axillary and musculocutaneous
D. Radial and ulnar

324. The intertubercular groove is located on the proximal end of which bone
A. Tibia
B. Radius
C. Femur
D. Humerus

325. Antagonist to supinator
A. Brachialis
B. Biceps brachii
C. Pronator teres
D. Coracobrachialis

326. Ligament holding teeth to the mandible or maxilla
A. Periodontal
B. Dental
C. Periodental
D. Molar ligament

327. Which of the following is a structure located on the ulna
A. Olecranon fossa
B. Coronoid process
C. Radial tuberosity
D. Capitulum

328. The most distal structures on the femur that articulate with the condyles of the tibia
A. Medial and lateral epicondyles
B. Medial and lateral condyles
C. Lesser and greater trochanters
D. Adductor tubercle and medial epicondyle

329. The humerus and scapula combine to form which joint
A. Humeroradial
B. Acromioclavicular
C. Sternoclavicular
D. Glenohumeral

330. Action resulting in the thumb moving toward the pinky
A. Opposition
B. Flexion
C. Abduction
D. Extension

331. Proximal attachment of semitendinosus
A. Linea aspera
B. Ischial tuberosity
C. Pes anserinus
D. Inferior ramus of pubis

332. Foramen located beneath the eye socket on the maxilla
A. Zygomatic foramen
B. Mental foramen
C. Infraorbital foramen
D. Temporal foramen

333. Largest muscle of the adductor muscle group
A. Gracilis
B. Adductor longus
C. Adductor brevis
D. Adductor magnus

334. The bone that comprises the upper jaw is also called
A. Mandible
B. Maxilla
C. Zygomatic
D. Vomer

335. The radius and ulna are positioned where in relation to the humerus
A. Distal
B. Proximal
C. Medial
D. Lateral

336. A client experiences pain while abducting the shoulder. The muscle most likely involved would be
A. Pectoralis Major
B. Rhomboid Major
C. Deltoids
D. Infraspinatus

337. Muscle inserting onto the anterior and lateral surface of the radius
A. Supinator
B. Biceps brachii
C. Triceps brachii
D. Brachioradialis

338. Muscle responsible for hip flexion, knee flexion, and lateral rotation of the hip
A. Sartorius
B. Gracilis
C. Pectineus
D. Rectus femoris

339. Muscle originating on the ischial tuberosity
A. Tensor fasciae latae
B. Semimembranosus
C. Rectus femoris
D. Pectineus

340. Temporalis assists in what specific action
A. Lowering the jaw
B. Raising the jaw
C. Shifting the jaw anteriorly
D. Shifting the jaw posteriorly

341. Rotation of the head takes place at the following joint
A. Acromioclavicular
B. Atlantooccipital
C. Atlantoaxial
D. Sternoclavicular

342. The proximal radioulnar joint, responsible for pronation and supination, is which type of synovial joint
A. Hinge
B. Pivot
C. Gliding
D. Ellipsoid

343. The bones of the cranium are classified as which type of bone
A. Flat
B. Irregular
C. Short
D. Long

344. Three of the four rotator cuff muscles insert onto the greater tubercle of the humerus. The only one that does not is
A. Teres Minor
B. Supraspinatus
C. Infraspinatus
D. Subscapularis

345. Nerve stimulating the hamstrings muscle group
A. Superficial Peroneal
B. Femoral
C. Obturator
D. Sciatic

346. The atlantooccipital joint connects which two bones
A. Occipital and parietal
B. Atlas and axis
C. Axis and occipital
D. Occipital and atlas

347. Muscle located on the lateral side of the leg, responsible for pronation and plantarflexion of the foot
A. Tibialis anterior
B. Peroneus longus
C. Gastrocnemius
D. Soleus

348. The adductor magnus performs all the following actions except
A. Adduction
B. Abduction
C. Flexion
D. Extension

349. All of the following are examples of short bones except
A. Cuboid
B. Scaphoid
C. Patella
D. Hamate

350. The deltoids originate on which bony landmarks
A. Acromion process, clavicle, spine of scapula
B. Acromion process, clavicle, lateral border of scapula
C. Deltoid tuberosity, clavicle, acromion process
D. Superior angle of scapula, acromion process, clavicle

351. An injury to the gracilis would partially inhibit which actions
A. Hip adduction, knee flexion
B. Hip flexion, knee extension
C. Hip abduction, knee flexion
D. Hip extension, knee extension

352. Muscles that cross the knee include all of the following except
A. Gastrocnemius
B. Gracilis
C. Adductor magnus
D. Biceps femoris

353. Muscle controlling adduction of the hip
A. Rectus Femoris
B. Tensor Fasciae Latae
C. Gracilis
D. Gluteus maximus

354. The facial nerve is also known as which number cranial nerve
A. V
B. VII
C. X
D. XII

355. Which muscle inserts onto the proximal medial shaft of the humerus
A. Brachialis
B. Biceps brachii
C. Coracobrachialis
D. Brachioradialis

356. The more anterior point of the mandible, which the muscles of mastication attach to
A. Ramus of the mandible
B. Mandibular tubercle
C. Coronoid process
D. Coracoid process

357. Joint located at the lateral end of the clavicle
A. Coracoclavicular
B. Glenohumeral
C. Sternoclavicular
D. Acromioclavicular

358. Nerve innervating the wrist extensor muscle group
A. Median
B. Obturator
C. Radial
D. Ulnar

359. Turning the foot in towards the midline of the body
A. Pronation
B. Inversion
C. Eversion
D. Dorsiflexion

360. Movement produced at the atlantoaxial joint
A. Extension
B. Flexion
C. Rotation
D. Adduction

361. Muscle originating on the medial epicondyle of the humerus
A. Brachioradialis
B. Biceps brachii
C. Brachialis
D. Pronator teres

362. Holes in the mandible, allowing a passageway for blood vessels into and out of the bone
A. Mental foramina
B. Ossobuco
C. Mandibular tunnels
D. Maxillary foramen

363. The ankle is considered which type of synovial joint
A. Pivot
B. Hinge
C. Ball and socket
D. Ellipsoid

364. Nerve innervating the diaphragm
A. Vagus
B. Phrenic
C. Trigeminal
D. Facial

365. Part of the ulna that wraps around the trochlea to make the elbow joint
A. Coronoid process
B. Ulnar tuberosity
C. Head of the radius
D. Radial tuberosity

366. Muscle surrounding the eye socket
A. Buccinator
B. Occipitofrontalis
C. Orbicularis oculi
D. Masseter

367. Insertion of brachialis
A. Coronoid process and ulnar tuberosity
B. Styloid process
C. Radial tuberosity
D. Olecranon process

368. Fossa located on the anterior surface of the scapula
A. Subscapular fossa
B. Glenoid fossa
C. Supraspinous fossa
D. Infraspinous fossa

369. The radial tuberosity is located on which side of the radius
A. Posterior
B. Lateral
C. Medial
D. Distal

370. Structure found between the pubic body and ischial tuberosity
A. Ischial spine
B. Superior ramus of the pubis
C. Pubic crest
D. Inferior ramus of the pubis

371. Muscle originating on the temporal bone, inserting onto the coronoid process of the mandible
A. Pterygoid
B. Buccinator
C. Masseter
D. Temporalis

372. The radiocarpal joint is comprised of the radius and which carpal bone
A. Hamate
B. Lunate
C. Trapezium
D. Scaphoid

373. Where do rhomboid major and rhomboid minor originate
A. Lateral border of the scapula
B. Medial border of the scapula
C. Superior angle of the scapula
D. Spinous processes of C7-T5

374. The first cervical vertebrae is also known as
A. Atlas
B. Axis
C. Occiput
D. Temporal

375. All of the following are bones of the skull except
A. Ethmoid
B. Zygomatic
C. Atlas
D. Sphenoid

376. The only hamstring muscle that attaches to the fibula
A. Biceps femoris
B. Rectus femoris
C. Semimembranosus
D. Semitendinosus

377. Which structure is located on the tibia
A. Styloid process
B. Pes anserinus
C. Lateral malleolus
D. Adductor tubercle

378. Bone that forms the lower jaw
A. Maxilla
B. Mandible
C. Parietal
D. Zygomatic

379. Distal attachment of the supinator
A. Lateral and lateral surface of the radius
B. Radial tuberosity
C. Posterior lateral epicondyle of the humerus
D. Styloid process of the ulna

380. Antagonist of levator scapulae
A. Lower fibers of trapezius
B. Pectoralis minor
C. Upper fibers of trapezius
D. Rhomboids

381. Cranial nerve VII is also known as
A. Trigeminal nerve
B. Facial nerve
C. Olfactory nerve
D. Optic nerve

382. The scientific name of the knee is
A. Tibiofibular joint
B. Talocrural joint
C. Tibiofemoral joint
D. Iliofemoral joint

383. The wrist extensor group is innervated by the following nerve
A. Median
B. Radial
C. Ulnar
D. Femoral

384. Cranial nerve with three branches, inserting into the eye socket, the nose and upper teeth, and mandible
A. Hypoglossal
B. Facial
C. Zygomatic
D. Trigeminal

385. The long head of the triceps brachii originates where
A. Supraglenoid tubercle
B. Infraglenoid tubercle
C. Olecranon process
D. Coracoid process

386. Muscle originating on the inferior angle of the scapula
A. Teres minor
B. Infraspinatus
C. Teres major
D. Levator scapulae

387. Proximal attachment of the psoas major muscle
A. Anterior surface of lumbar vertebrae
B. Posterior surface of lumbar vertebrae
C. Greater trochanter
D. Lesser trochanter

388. The knee joint is made of which two bones
A. Femur and fibula
B. Tibia and femur
C. Tibia and fibula
D. Humerus and ulna

389. Muscle inserting onto the pectineal line of the femur
A. Psoas major
B. Adductor magnus
C. Gracilis
D. Pectineus

390. The lateral supracondylar ridge of the humerus is the origination site of which muscle
A. Brachioradialis
B. Biceps brachii
C. Biceps femoris
D. Coracobrachialis

391. The adductor tubercle is located directly superior to which bony marking on the femur
A. Medial epicondyle
B. Lateral epicondyle
C. Greater trochanter
D. Lesser trochanter

392. Which of these muscles does not insert onto the medial border of the scapula
A. Rhomboid major
B. Serratus anterior
C. Pectoralis minor
D. Rhomboid minor

393. The widest muscle in the body is
A. Rectus abdominis
B. Trapezius
C. Latissimus dorsi
D. Pectoralis major

394. The head of the radius enters into the following fossa when the elbow is placed into flexion
A. Coronoid fossa
B. Radial fossa
C. Olecranon fossa
D. Glenoid fossa

395. The tibia sits on top of which bone to produce the ankle joint
A. Cuboid
B. Calcaneus
C. Navicular
D. Talus

396. Nerve passing through the popliteal region on its way to the plantar surface of the foot
A. Obturator
B. Common peroneal
C. Femoral
D. Tibial

397. Innervation of the brachioradialis is provided by which nerve
A. Radial
B. Median
C. Ulnar
D. Musculocutaneous

398. All of the following are structures on the humerus except
A. Greater tubercle
B. Greater trochanter
C. Intertubercular groove
D. Coronoid fossa

399. Which of the following movements is trapezius not responsible for
A. Elevation of the scapula
B. Medial rotation of the shoulder
C. Retraction of the scapula
D. Depression of the scapula

400. Large bony projection on the proximal end of the radius
A. Radial tuberosity
B. Styloid process
C. Radial fossa
D. Olecranon process

401. Shortening of the tibialis anterior can be achieved with the following actions
A. Dorsiflexion and eversion
B. Dorsiflexion and inversion
C. Plantarflexion and inversion
D. Plantarflexion and eversion

402. Muscle inserting into the iliotibial tract and gluteal tuberosity
A. Gluteus medius
B. Gluteus minimus
C. Gluteus maximus
D. Piriformis

403. Insertion of the two stirrup muscles
A. Calcaneus
B. Navicular
C. Base of the first metatarsal
D. Tuberosity of the fifth metatarsal

404. Origination of temporalis
A. Frontal bone
B. Coronoid process
C. Zygomatic arch
D. Temporal bone

405. The condyles of the femur articulate with which structures on the tibia
A. Tuberosities
B. Malleoli
C. Head
D. Condyles

406. Insertion of the gluteus maximus takes place where
A. Iliotibial band and gluteal tuberosity
B. Gluteal tuberosity
C. Linea aspera
D. Gluteal line

407. Innervation of the tibialis anterior
A. Femoral
B. Superficial peroneal nerve
C. Tibial
D. Deep peroneal nerve

408. Peroneus longus is stimulated by which nerve
A. Deep peroneal
B. Superficial peroneal
C. Tibial
D. Femoral

409. Muscle originating on the lateral lip of the linea aspera
A. Semimembranosus
B. Vastus medialis
C. Semitendinosus
D. Vastus lateralis

410. Lateral rotation of the humerus is performed by which two rotator cuff muscles
A. Supraspinatus, Infraspinatus
B. Infraspinatus, Teres Major
C. Teres Minor, Infraspinatus
D. Supraspinatus, Subscapularis

411. Proximal attachment of pectineus
A. Body of pubis
B. Inferior ramus of pubis
C. Superior ramus of pubis
D. Ischial tuberosity

412. The trigeminal nerve is which numbered cranial nerve
A. X
B. VII
C. V
D. III

413. Muscle group primarily responsible for extension of the hip and flexion of the knee
A. Glutes
B. Quadriceps
C. Adductors
D. Hamstrings

414. The lesser trochanter is positioned where in relation to the greater trochanter
A. Lateral
B. Medial
C. Anterior
D. Posterior

415. The radiocarpal joint is considered which type of synovial joint
A. Hinge
B. Ball and socket
C. Condyloid
D. Pivot

416. Abduction of the scapula can be accomplished by contraction of which muscle
A. Serratus anterior
B. Rhomboids
C. Latissimus Dorsi
D. Trapezius

417. The atlantooccipital joint is responsible for producing which two actions on the head
A. Lateral deviation
B. Rotation
C. Flexion and extension
D. Adduction and abduction

418. Plane joint connecting the scapula to the clavicle
A. Sternoclavicular
B. Acromioclavicular
C. Atlantooccipital
D. Atlantoaxial

419. Primary action of the pronator teres
A. Elbow extension
B. Supination
C. Elbow flexion
D. Pronation

420. Muscle inserting on the pes anserinus, responsible for flexing and externally rotating the hip, and flexing the knee
A. Gracilis
B. Sartorius
C. Semitendinosus
D. Biceps femoris

421. The suture connecting the frontal and parietal bones is called
A. Coronal suture
B. Lambdoid suture
C. Sagittal suture
D. Squamous suture

422. Muscle primarily responsible for elevation of the scapula
A. Middle fibers of trapezius
B. Supraspinatus
C. Levator scapulae
D. Sternocleidomastoid

423. Flexion is
A. Moving a structure towards the midline
B. Increasing the angle of a joint
C. Decreasing the angle of a joint
D. Taking a structure away from the midline

424. Which of the following is a hinge joint
A. Wrist
B. Shoulder
C. Hip
D. Elbow

425. Of the following, which is not a fossa located on the scapula
A. Supraspinous fossa
B. Glenoid fossa
C. Subscapular fossa
D. Coronoid fossa

426. Proximal attachment of the biceps femoris
A. Supraglenoid tubercle
B. Head of the fibula
C. Coracoid process
D. Ischial tuberosity

427. Proximal attachment of the tibialis anterior
A. Lateral two thirds of the proximal tibia
B. Base of the first metatarsal
C. Head of the fibula
D. Medial condyle of the tibia

428. Spinous processes extend which direction
A. Laterally
B. Dorsally
C. Medially
D. Ventrally

429. The hip joint is considered which type of synovial joint
A. Ball and socket
B. Pivot
C. Ellipsoid
D. Hinge

430. Insertion of pectoralis minor
A. Sternum
B. Ribs 3-5
C. Coracoid process
D. Intertubercular groove

431. Action of the brachioradialis
A. Elbow extension
B. Elbow flexion
C. Wrist flexion
D. Wrist extension

432. Insertion of infraspinatus
A. Greater Tubercle
B. Infraspinous Fossa
C. Lesser Tubercle
D. Intertubercular Groove

433. The groin is also known as which body region
A. Thorax
B. Popliteal
C. Antecubital
D. Inguinal

434. Eversion of the foot turns the foot which way
A. Toes pointed down
B. In towards the midline
C. Toes pointed up
D. Out away from the midline

435. The diaphragm descending produces
A. External pressure
B. Exhalation
C. Force
D. Inhalation

436. Nerve found running along the zygomatic bone, partially responsible for taste reception and facial movement
A. Hypoglossal
B. Trigeminal
C. Facial
D. Accessory

437. Nerve responsible for facial expression
A. Cranial nerve VII
B. Cranial nerve V
C. Cranial nerve I
D. Cranial nerve X

438. Muscle innervated by the superficial peroneal nerve
A. Soleus
B. Peroneus longus
C. Gastrocnemius
D. Tibialis anterior

439. Muscle inserting onto the calcaneus via the calcaneal tendon
A. Semitendinosus
B. Tibialis anterior
C. Gastrocnemius
D. Flexor hallucis longus

440. Part of the vertebrae that the intervertebral discs rest upon
A. Transverse process
B. Spinous process
C. Facets
D. Dens

441. Action of the masseter on the jaw
A. Depresses jaw
B. Elevates jaw
C. Protracts jaw
D. Retracts jaw

442. Name of the joint found between the atlas and axis
A. Spinous joint
B. Atlantooccipital
C. Occipitotemporal
D. Atlantoaxial

443. The long head of the biceps brachii originates where
A. Supraglenoid tubercle
B. Infraglenoid tubercle
C. Coracoid process
D. Radial tuberosity

444. Decreasing the angle of a joint
A. Extension
B. Flexion
C. Rotation
D. Abduction

445. Structure located immediately superior to the styloid process of the ulna
A. Ulnar tuberosity
B. Olecranon process
C. Head of the ulna
D. Coronoid process

446. The knee is considered which type of synovial joint
A. Ellipsoid
B. Pivot
C. Ball and socket
D. Hinge

447. The deltoid is an antagonist to itself. What does this mean?
A. It has actions that aren't connected
B. It has two of the same actions
C. It has actions that are similar
D. It has two opposing actions

448. Tendon attaching the gastrocnemius to the calcaneus
A. Tibial
B. Calcaneal
C. Gastroc
D. Patellar

449. Another term for inversion of the foot is
A. Supination
B. Pronation
C. Dorsiflexion
D. Plantarflexion

450. The quadriceps are located on which side of the body
A. Anterior
B. Posterior
C. Medial
D. Lateral

451. Muscle inserting onto the calcaneus via the calcaneal tendon
A. Tibialis anterior
B. Soleus
C. Extensor hallucis longus
D. Extensor digitorum

452. The antecubital region is located on the anterior portion of which joint
A. Elbow
B. Knee
C. Wrist
D. Ankle

453. Muscle group originating on the lateral epicondyle of the humerus
A. Flexors of the wrist
B. Extensors of the wrist
C. Abductors of the wrist
D. Adductors of the wrist

454. Distal attachment of the soleus
A. Head of the fibula
B. Talus
C. Calcaneus
D. Soleal line

455. The ridge of the ilium is also known as the
A. Anterior superior iliac spine
B. Iliac spine
C. Ischial spine
D. Iliac crest

456. The ankle joint produces which of the following movement
A. Abduction
B. Rotation
C. Adduction
D. Dorsiflexion

457. The joints found between the vertebrae are categorized as which type of synovial joint
A. Gliding
B. Hinge
C. Pivot
D. Ellipsoid

458. Which of the following is not a hinge joint
A. Knee
B. Shoulder
C. Elbow
D. Ankle

459. The radiocarpal joint can perform all of the following actions except
A. Circumduction
B. Rotation
C. Adduction
D. Flexion

460. The interphalangeal joints are which type of synovial joints
A. Hinge
B. Pivot
C. Ball and socket
D. Ellipsoid

461. Nerve responsible for stimulation of the smooth muscle in the digestive tract, allowing peristalsis to take place
A. Gastrointestinal
B. Trigeminal
C. Vagus
D. Hypoglossal

462. The two bones that comprise the elbow joint are
A. Ulna and lunate
B. Radius and scaphoid
C. Scapula and humerus
D. Ulna and humerus

463. Muscle group located on the posterior thigh
A. Hamstrings
B. Quadriceps
C. Adductors
D. Gluteals

464. Synergist to the gastrocnemius in performing plantarflexion of the ankle
A. Tibialis anterior
B. Peroneus longus
C. Biceps femoris
D. Rectus femoris

465. With the client moving their arm into abduction, pain might be felt in the following muscle
A. Pectoralis Minor
B. Infraspinatus
C. Supraspinatus
D. Coracobrachialis

466. Contraction of the supinator produces what action
A. Supination
B. Pronation
C. Wrist flexion
D. Wrist extension

467. The greater trochanter is the distal attachment site of the following muscle, responsible for abduction and lateral rotation of the hip
A. Piriformis
B. Pectineus
C. Sartorius
D. Gluteus maximus

468. The three muscles that attach to the coracoid process
A. Long head of biceps brachii, coracobrachialis, pectoralis major
B. Coracobrachialis, brachialis, pectoralis minor
C. Short head of biceps brachii, coracobrachialis, pectoralis minor
D. Short head of biceps femoris, coracobrachialis, pectoralis minor

469. Deltoid and supraspinatus share a common action. That action is
A. Extension of the shoulder
B. Abduction of the shoulder
C. Flexion of the shoulder
D. Adduction of the shoulder

470. Facial expressions are controlled by which cranial nerve
A. Vagus
B. Trigeminal
C. Olfactory
D. Facial

471. The linea alba separates the two sides of which muscle
A. Psoas major
B. Rectus abdominis
C. Rectus femoris
D. Biceps femoris

472. Muscle originating on the ischial tuberosity
A. Sartorius
B. Semitendinosus
C. Gracilis
D. Adductor longus

473. Muscle inserting on the mastoid process and occiput, responsible for extending the neck and rotation of the head to the same side
A. Trapezius
B. Sternocleidomastoid
C. Levator scapulae
D. Splenius capitis

474. Moving a structure away from the midline of the body
A. Rotation
B. Abduction
C. Extension
D. Adduction

475. All of the following are examples of long bones except
A. Sphenoid
B. Humerus
C. Clavicle
D. Fibula

476. The order of the hamstring muscle group from medial to lateral
A. Semitendinosus, Semimembranosus, Biceps Femoris
B. Semimembranosus, Semitendinosus, Rectus Femoris
C. Vastus Medialis, Vastus Intermedius, Vastus Lateralis
D. Semimembranosus, Semitendinosus, Biceps Femoris

477. Muscle responsible for stabilizing the glenohumeral joint and abduction of the shoulder
A. Supraspinatus
B. Subscapularis
C. Infraspinatus
D. Teres Minor

478. Which of the following is not a rotator cuff muscle
A. Infraspinatus
B. Teres major
C. Teres minor
D. Subscapularis

479. Antagonist to the extensors of the wrist
A. Biceps brachii
B. Brachioradialis
C. Wrist flexors
D. Triceps brachii

480. Origination of the pronator teres
A. Middle lateral shaft of ulna
B. Lateral epicondyle of the humerus
C. Middle lateral shaft of radius
D. Medial epicondyle of the humerus

481. Muscle originating on the ischial tuberosity
A. Biceps femoris
B. Biceps brachii
C. Gracilis
D. Triceps brachii

482. The head of the radius articulates with which structure on the humerus
A. Trochlea
B. Capitulum
C. Medial epicondyle
D. Lateral epicondyle

483. The most anterior muscle of the quadriceps muscle group
A. Vastus intermedius
B. Vastus lateralis
C. Vastus medialis
D. Rectus femoris

484. All of the following muscles attach to either the medial or lateral lip of the bicipital groove except
A. Pectoralis major
B. Infraspinatus
C. Latissimus dorsi
D. Teres major

485. Origin of supraspinatus
A. Subscapular Fossa
B. Infraspinous Fossa
C. Supraspinous Fossa
D. Lateral border of the scapula

486. Movement caused by moving a structure around the entire circumference of a joint
A. Adduction
B. Rotation
C. Circumduction
D. Abduction

487. Action of levator scapulae
A. Elevation of scapula
B. Retraction of scapula
C. Depression of scapula
D. Protraction of scapula

488. All of the following are located on the tibia except
A. Lateral malleolus
B. Tibial tuberosity
C. Pes anserinus
D. Soleal line

489. Sternocleidomastoid is named for its
A. Attachment sites
B. Size
C. Shape
D. Muscle fiber direction

490. Which of the following is a structure located on the pubis
A. Iliac crest
B. Superior ramus
C. Anterior inferior iliac spine
D. Ischial tuberosity

491. Abduction of the shoulder can be accomplished by a concentric contraction of which muscle
A. Coracobrachialis
B. Infraspinatus
C. Pectoralis Major
D. Deltoid

492. Which of the following is a structure of the fibula
A. Pes anserinus
B. Tibial tuberosity
C. Radial tuberosity
D. Styloid process

493. The atlantoaxial joint is considered what type of synovial joint
A. Ellipsoid
B. Ball and socket
C. Pivot
D. Hinge

494. Muscle originating on the zygomatic arch and inserting onto the angle and ramus of the mandible
A. Masseter
B. Temporalis
C. Frontalis
D. Pterygoid

495. Muscle originating on the ischial tuberosity and inferior ramus of the pubis
A. Biceps femoris
B. Adductor magnus
C. Semitendinosus
D. Semimembranosus

496. Distal attachment of teres minor
A. Lateral border of scapula
B. Greater tubercle
C. Lesser tubercle
D. Intertubercular groove

497. Muscle originating on the head of the fibula, superior third of the shaft of the fibula, and the soleal line
A. Biceps brachii
B. Gastrocnemius
C. Soleus
D. Brachioradialis

498. The glenohumeral joint is considered what kind of synovial joint
A. Hinge
B. Pivot
C. Gliding
D. Ball and socket

499. The glenohumeral joint combines which two bones together
A. Humerus and scapula
B. Scapula and clavicle
C. Clavicle and sternum
D. Humerus and ulna

500. Insertion of pectoralis major
A. Deltoid tuberosity
B. Medial lip of intertubercular groove
C. Lateral lip of intertubercular groove
D. Acromion process

501. The elbow joint performs the following actions
A. Flexion and extension
B. Adduction and abduction
C. Medial and lateral rotation
D. Protraction and retraction

502. Muscle responsible for flexion of the hip and extension of the knee
A. Tibialis anterior
B. Rectus femoris
C. Biceps femoris
D. Vastus intermedius

503. Plantarflexion and dorsiflexion takes place at which joint
A. Tibiofemoral
B. Talocalcaneal
C. Talotibial
D. Tibiofibular

504. The nerve that innervates the diaphragm, allowing breathing to take place
A. Trigeminal
B. Vagus
C. Phrenic
D. Facial

505. Distal attachment of what muscle is located at the tibial tuberosity
A. Biceps Femoris
B. Rectus Femoris
C. Sartorius
D. Tibialis Anterior

506. Insertion of levator scapulae
A. Superior angle of scapula
B. Transverse processes of C1-C4
C. Spinous processes of C5-T1
D. Inferior angle of scapula

507. Structure lying superior to the Anterior Inferior Iliac Spine
A. Greater trochanter
B. Posterior Superior Iliac Spine
C. Ischial tuberosity
D. Anterior Superior Iliac Spine

508. The radial nerve innervates which of the following muscles
A. Coracobrachialis
B. Brachialis
C. Brachioradialis
D. Biceps brachii

509. Insertion of the adductor magnus
A. Inferior ramus of the pubis
B. Ischial tuberosity
C. Lateral epicondyle of the femur
D. Medial lip of linea aspera and adductor tubercle

510. All of the following muscles cross the elbow joint except
A. Triceps brachii
B. Brachialis
C. Pronator teres
D. Coracobrachialis

511. Soleus originates on which part of the tibia
A. Tibial tuberosity
B. Soleal line
C. Lateral condyle
D. Medial condyle

512. The most inferior structure on the pelvis
A. Iliac crest
B. Pubic symphysis
C. Ischial tuberosity
D. Inferior ramus of pubis

513. Adductor muscle assisting in adducting the hip, flexing the hip, and flexing the knee
A. Adductor longus
B. Adductor magnus
C. Gracilis
D. Pectineus

514. Most lateral hamstring muscle
A. Biceps femoris
B. Semimembranosus
C. Semitendinosus
D. Rectus femoris

515. Most proximal structure on the anterior surface of the ulna
A. Coronoid process
B. Ulnar tuberosity
C. Olecranon process
D. Styloid process

516. Most medial of the humeral condyles
A. Capitulum
B. Trochlea
C. Greater tubercle
D. Lesser tubercle

517. Antagonist to the hamstrings, responsible for hip flexion and knee extension
A. Calf
B. Adductors
C. Quadriceps
D. Rotators

518. Pronation and supination takes place at the following joint
A. Elbow
B. Distal radioulnar
C. Proximal radioulnar
D. Radiocarpal

519. Muscle originating on the anterior surface of the sacrum
A. Psoas major
B. Pectineus
C. Sartorius
D. Piriformis

520. Plantarflexion of the ankle is primarily caused by contraction of which muscle
A. Gastrocnemius
B. Tibialis anterior
C. Rectus femoris
D. Flexor hallucis longus

521. The origin of vastus medialis can be palpated at
A. Medial lip of linea aspera
B. Lateral lip of linea aspera
C. Greater trochanter
D. Lesser trochanter

522. Which muscle, responsible for flexion of the elbow, inserts onto both the coronoid process and ulnar tuberosity
A. Brachioradialis
B. Brachialis
C. Coracobrachialis
D. Biceps brachii

523. Most distal insertion of the adductor longus
A. Adductor tubercle
B. Medial lip of linea aspera
C. Ischial tuberosity
D. Inferior ramus of the pubis

524. Sheath of tendon separating the two sides of the rectus abdominis muscle
A. Linea alba
B. Linea aspera
C. Interosseous ligament
D. Retinaculum

525. Bony projection protruding superiorly from the axis, which the atlas sits on top of
A. Vertebral body
B. Spinous process
C. Transverse process
D. Dens

526. Muscle inserting onto the mastoid process of the temporal bone
A. Masseter
B. Temporalis
C. Buccinator
D. Sternocleidomastoid

527. Inversion moves the foot in what way
A. In towards the midline
B. Out away from the midline
C. Points toes up
D. Points toes down

528. Insertion of the splenius capitis
A. Spinous processes of C3-T6
B. Mastoid process and occiput
C. Superior angle of the scapula
D. Superior nuchal line

529. Innervation of brachialis is accomplished by which nerve
A. Median
B. Radial
C. Musculocutaneous
D. Ulnar

530. Actions of infraspinatus
A. Medial rotation, extension
B. Lateral rotation, extension
C. Medial rotation, flexion
D. Lateral rotation, flexion

531. Teres Minor is innervated by which nerve
A. Median
B. Musculocutaneous
C. Radial
D. Axillary

532. The styloid process of the ulna lies where in relation to the olecranon process
A. Posterior
B. Proximal
C. Anterior
D. Distal

533. The greater trochanter lies in what position on the femur relative to the lesser trochanter
A. Medial
B. Lateral
C. Anterior
D. Posterior

534. Bony projection on a vertebral body that extends dorsally
A. Spinous process
B. Transverse process
C. Dens
D. Facet

535. Teres major has three actions. They are
A. Extension, adduction, medial rotation of the shoulder
B. Flexion, abduction, lateral rotation of the shoulder
C. Extension, abduction, medial rotation of the shoulder
D. Flexion, adduction, lateral rotation of the shoulder

536. Insertion of pectineus
A. Lateral lip of linea aspera
B. Greater trochanter
C. Pectineal line
D. Gluteal tuberosity

537. Which of the following is not an attachment site of biceps brachii
A. Supraglenoid tubercle
B. Radial tuberosity
C. Ulnar tuberosity
D. Coracoid process

538. An antagonist to the middle fibers of the deltoid
A. Brachialis
B. Supraspinatus
C. Biceps brachii
D. Latissimus dorsi

539. To stretch the triceps brachii, the arm must be placed in which position
A. Shoulder extended, elbow flexed
B. Shoulder flexed, elbow flexed
C. Shoulder flexed, elbow extended
D. Shoulder extended, elbow extended

540. The styloid process of the radius is located on which end of the bone
A. Anterior
B. Proximal
C. Distal
D. Posterior

541. Order of the hamstrings from lateral to medial
A. Semitendinosus, semimembranosus, biceps femoris
B. Semimembranosus, semitendinosus, biceps femoris
C. Biceps femoris, semitendinosus, semimembranosus
D. Biceps femoris, semimembranosus, semitendinosus

542. Synergist to brachialis, assisting in elbow flexion
A. Anterior deltoid
B. Coracobrachialis
C. Triceps brachii
D. Biceps brachii

543. Action of the flexors of the wrist
A. Abducting the wrist
B. Extending the wrist
C. Adducting the wrist
D. Flexing the wrist

544. Pectoralis major attaches to all of the following points except
A. Bicipital groove
B. Lesser tubercle
C. Sternum
D. Clavicle

545. Structure located on the distal end of the humerus
A. Capitulum
B. Head
C. Greater tubercle
D. Deltoid tuberosity

546. Muscle originating on the superior ramus of the pubis
A. Pectineus
B. Gracilis
C. Adductor brevis
D. Adductor magnus

547. The gluteal tuberosity is located between which two structures on the femur
A. Greater trochanter and lesser trochanter
B. Head and neck
C. Medial epicondyle and lateral epicondyle
D. Medial condyle and lateral condyle

548. Action of spinalis on the vertebrae
A. Flexion and extension
B. Rotation and flexion
C. Support and extension
D. Flexion and support

549. Contraction of the soleus causes what action
A. Dorsiflexion
B. Plantarflexion
C. Supination
D. Pronation

550. The inguinal region is located at which part of the body
A. Elbow
B. Knee
C. Shoulder
D. Hip

551. All of the following are located on the ilium except
A. Ischial spine
B. Anterior superior iliac spine
C. Anterior inferior iliac spine
D. Iliac fossa

552. Gastrocnemius takes what action on the ankle when contracted
A. Dorsiflexes
B. Plantarflexes
C. Inverts
D. Everts

553. The sphenoid bone is located in which region of the body
A. Eye socket
B. Carpals
C. Tarsals
D. Pelvis

554. Shrugging your shoulders is an example of what movement
A. Depression
B. Elevation
C. Protraction
D. Retraction

555. In order to stretch the tibialis anterior, the body must be positioned in what way
A. Dorsiflexion and inversion
B. Plantarflexion and inversion
C. Plantarflexion and eversion
D. Dorsiflexion and eversion

556. Structure located only on the posterior surface of the scapula
A. Inferior angle
B. Coracoid process
C. Subscapular fossa
D. Spine of the scapula

557. Proximal attachment of adductor magnus
A. Ischial tuberosity and anterior inferior iliac spine
B. Superior ramus of pubis and ischial tuberosity
C. Posterior inferior iliac spine and ischial tuberosity
D. Inferior ramus of pubis and ischial tuberosity

558. The proximal attachment of the rectus femoris is located at the
A. Ischial Tuberosity
B. Anterior Inferior Iliac Spine
C. Anterior Superior Iliac Spice
D. Tibial Tuberosity

559. Muscle originating in the supraspinous fossa
A. Teres Minor
B. Infraspinatus
C. Supraspinatus
D. Subscapularis

560. The hip joint can produce all of the following movements except
A. Protraction
B. Adduction
C. Flexion
D. Circumduction

561. Superficial muscle to the vastus intermedius
A. Rectus femoris
B. Vastus lateralis
C. Vastus medialis
D. Pectineus

562. Muscle originating on the spinous processes of C3-T6
A. Serratus posterior
B. Rhomboids
C. Trapezius
D. Splenius capitis

563. Structure located directly superior to the ulnar tuberosity
A. Styloid process
B. Olecranon process
C. Radial tuberosity
D. Coronoid process

564. The coronoid process wrapping around the trochlea produces what joint
A. Elbow
B. Knee
C. Hip
D. Shoulder

565. A synergist to the triceps brachii while performing extension of the elbow
A. Latissimus dorsi
B. Brachioradialis
C. Anconeus
D. Teres minor

566. Teres minor is innervated by the following nerve
A. Femoral
B. Musculocutaneous
C. Radial
D. Axillary

567. Muscle originating on the anterior surface of the lumbar vertebrae
A. Rectus femoris
B. Quadratus lumborum
C. Psoas major
D. Iliacus

568. Stretching of the hamstrings can be achieved by performing what actions
A. Hip flexion and knee flexion
B. Hip extension and knee flexion
C. Hip flexion and knee extension
D. Hip extension and knee extension

569. Muscle originating on the anterior superior iliac spine
A. Rectus femoris
B. Sartorius
C. Gracilis
D. Adductor magnus

570. To stretch the biceps brachii, the body must be placed in which position
A. Elbow flexed, shoulder extended
B. Elbow extended, shoulder extended
C. Elbow flexed, shoulder flexed
D. Elbow extended, shoulder flexed

571. Contraction of the splenius capitis has what action on the head and neck
A. Rotates head to the opposite side and flexes neck
B. Rotates head to the same side and extends neck
C. Rotates head to the same side and flexes neck
D. Rotates head to the opposite side and extends neck

572. Muscle inserting on the pes anserinus
A. Gracilis
B. Semimembranosus
C. Rectus femoris
D. Biceps femoris

573. The scientific name of the ankle joint is the
A. Talofibular joint
B. Talocrural joint
C. Tibiofemoral joint
D. Talocalcaneal joint

574. Structure located on the distal end of the fibula
A. Lateral malleolus
B. Medial malleolus
C. Styloid process
D. Head

575. The adductor tubercle is located on which portion of the femur
A. Medial
B. Lateral
C. Anterior
D. Posterior

576. The radius lies where in relation to the ulna
A. Superior
B. Medial
C. Lateral
D. Inferior

577. Pain experienced at the iliofemoral joint upon extension may be caused by hypertonicity of
A. Rectus femoris
B. Iliacus
C. Semimembranosus
D. Psoas major

578. Muscle that passes through the antecubital region
A. Supinator
B. Coracobrachialis
C. Brachialis
D. Rectus femoris

579. Insertion of the sartorius
A. Lateral epicondyle of the femur
B. Tibial tuberosity
C. Medial epicondyle of the femur
D. Pes anserinus

580. Bones that articulate with the maxilla include all of the following except
A. Frontal
B. Mandible
C. Zygomatic
D. Nasal

581. Ligament connecting the radius and ulna
A. Interosseous ligament
B. Parietal ligament
C. Intertubercular ligament
D. Radial ligament

582. Cartilage found surrounding the glenoid fossa which aids in structural support of the shoulder joint
A. Labrum
B. Coracoid process
C. Bicipital tendon
D. Acetabulum

583. Adductor longus attaches to the pelvis at what point
A. Body of pubis
B. Inferior ramus of pubis
C. Superior ramus of pubis
D. Pubic crest

584. Most proximal structure located on the humerus
A. Trochlea
B. Head of humerus
C. Greater tubercle
D. Deltoid tuberosity

585. Origin of the brachioradialis
A. Lateral supracondylar ridge of the humerus
B. Medial supracondylar ridge of the humerus
C. Lateral epicondyle of the humerus
D. Medial epicondyle of the humerus

586. Insertion of the piriformis
A. Lesser trochanter
B. Greater trochanter
C. Ischial tuberosity
D. Olecranon process

587. Bony projection on a vertebral body that extends laterally
A. Dens
B. Spinous process
C. Transverse process
D. Facet

588. Abduction moves a body part which way
A. Across the body
B. Towards the midline
C. Away from the midline
D. Behind the body

589. All of the following are located on the tibia except
A. Medial malleolus
B. Lateral condyle
C. Tibial tuberosity
D. Styloid process

590. Movement taking place at the proximal radioulnar joint
A. Supination
B. Flexion
C. Extension
D. Circumduction

591. Levator scapulae originates where
A. Inferior angle of the scapula
B. Spinous processes of C5-T1
C. Superior angle of the scapula
D. Transverse processes of C1-C4

592. Moving the body into plantarflexion and eversion would result in subsequent stretching of the following muscle
A. Tibialis anterior
B. Peroneus longus
C. Gastrocnemius
D. Soleus

593. Transverse processes extend which direction from a vertebral body
A. Dorsally
B. Laterally
C. Medially
D. Ventrally

594. Adductor muscle inserting on the pes anserinus
A. Adductor Magnus
B. Gracilis
C. Adductor Longus
D. Adductor Brevis

595. Increasing the angle of a joint
A. Adduction
B. Flexion
C. Extension
D. Circumduction

596. Large protrusion located on the proximal lateral shaft of the femur
A. Linea aspera
B. Lesser trochanter
C. Greater trochanter
D. Adductor tubercle

597. Muscle originating on anterior ribs 1-8
A. Rhomboids
B. Pectoralis minor
C. Pectoralis major
D. Serratus anterior

598. Which of the following is not an origin of the deltoids
A. Deltoid tuberosity
B. Clavicle
C. Acromion process
D. Spine of scapula

599. Muscle inserting onto the base of the first metatarsal, responsible for dorsiflexion and supination of the foot
A. Tibialis posterior
B. Tibialis anterior
C. Peroneus longus
D. Peroneus brevis

600. Antagonist to the gastrocnemius, responsible for dorsiflexion
A. Tibialis anterior
B. Peroneus longus
C. Soleus
D. Peroneus brevis

601. All of the following are parts of the ulna except
A. Trochlea
B. Olecranon process
C. Coronoid process
D. Styloid process

602. Proximal attachment of the iliacus
A. Lesser trochanter
B. Greater trochanter
C. Iliac fossa
D. Iliac crest

603. A client experiences acute pain during shoulder abduction. Which muscle is most likely involved
A. Teres minor
B. Infraspinatus
C. Deltoid
D. Coracobrachialis

604. Muscle responsible for flexion of the knee and plantarflexion of the ankle
A. Rectus femoris
B. Soleus
C. Tibialis anterior
D. Gastrocnemius

605. The sagittal suture is located between which two cranial bones
A. Occipital and parietal
B. Parietal bones
C. Parietal and frontal
D. Temporal and parietal

Kinesiology Answer Key

01. B	40. A	79. A	118. A	157. A
02. C	41. D	80. C	119. A	158. A
03. A	42. A	81. A	120. B	159. A
04. A	43. B	82. D	121. C	160. B
05. C	44. B	83. B	122. A	161. B
06. D	45. A	84. C	123. A	162. C
07. D	46. D	85. A	124. B	163. C
08. D	47. C	86. B	125. B	164. A
09. C	48. D	87. B	126. D	165. D
10. B	49. A	88. C	127. A	166. D
11. B	50. B	89. A	128. B	167. B
12. A	51. A	90. C	129. A	168. D
13. D	52. D	91. C	130. B	169. A
14. A	53. D	92. A	131. C	170. B
15. B	54. B	93. B	132. D	171. B
16. D	55. A	94. D	133. A	172. A
17. B	56. C	95. D	134. B	173. C
18. A	57. C	96. C	135. C	174. A
19. B	58. B	97. C	136. A	175. C
20. B	59. A	98. A	137. D	176. C
21. A	60. A	99. A	138. D	177. C
22. C	61. D	100. B	139. D	178. A
23. C	62. C	101. D	140. A	179. D
24. A	63. C	102. B	141. B	180. D
25. B	64. C	103. A	142. C	181. A
26. D	65. A	104. B	143. A	182. B
27. C	66. A	105. C	144. B	183. B
28. C	67. B	106. A	145. D	184. A
29. A	68. D	107. C	146. D	185. C
30. A	69. B	108. D	147. B	186. D
31. A	70. A	109. D	148. A	187. D
32. B	71. C	110. C	149. C	188. B
33. C	72. A	111. A	150. B	189. A
34. D	73. B	112. C	151. A	190. C
35. A	74. B	113. B	152. B	191. C
36. B	75. C	114. A	153. D	192. D
37. B	76. D	115. C	154. D	193. A
38. C	77. B	116. D	155. C	194. B
39. C	78. A	117. C	156. C	195. C

196. B	241. C	286. B	331. B	376. A
197. C	242. C	287. A	332. C	377. B
198. D	243. C	288. A	333. D	378. B
199. A	244. D	289. D	334. B	379. A
200. A	245. A	290. A	335. A	380. A
201. C	246. D	291. D	336. C	381. B
202. B	247. B	292. C	337. A	382. C
203. D	248. A	293. C	338. A	383. B
204. C	249. C	294. C	339. B	384. D
205. A	250. A	295. A	340. B	385. B
206. B	251. B	296. D	341. C	386. C
207. B	252. D	297. B	342. B	387. A
208. A	253. B	298. A	343. A	388. B
209. C	254. A	299. B	344. D	389. D
210. C	255. B	300. C	345. D	390. A
211. C	256. C	301. A	346. D	391. A
212. D	257. D	302. A	347. B	392. C
213. B	258. B	303. A	348. B	393. C
214. B	259. C	304. B	349. C	394. B
215. A	260. A	305. C	350. A	395. D
216. B	261. B	306. C	351. A	396. D
217. A	262. A	307. A	352. C	397. A
218. B	263. A	308. C	353. C	398. B
219. D	264. D	309. D	354. B	399. B
220. D	265. D	310. C	355. C	400. A
221. C	266. D	311. A	356. C	401. B
222. A	267. C	312. D	357. D	402. C
223. A	268. A	313. D	358. C	403. C
224. C	269. B	314. C	359. B	404. D
225. A	270. B	315. B	360. C	405. D
226. C	271. B	316. C	361. D	406. A
227. C	272. A	317. A	362. A	407. D
228. D	273. C	318. A	363. B	408. B
229. B	274. D	319. D	364. B	409. D
230. D	275. A	320. B	365. A	410. C
231. C	276. D	321. B	366. C	411. C
232. A	277. C	322. C	367. A	412. C
233. A	278. A	323. A	368. A	413. D
234. D	279. D	324. D	369. C	414. B
235. C	280. A	325. C	370. D	415. C
236. A	281. C	326. A	371. D	416. A
237. D	282. C	327. B	372. D	417. C
238. B	283. A	328. B	373. D	418. B
239. B	284. D	329. D	374. A	419. D
240. A	285. B	330. A	375. C	420. B

421. A	458. B	495. B	532. D	569. B
422. C	459. B	496. B	533. B	570. B
423. C	460. A	497. C	534. A	571. B
424. D	461. C	498. D	535. A	572. A
425. D	462. D	499. A	536. C	573. B
426. D	463. A	500. C	537. C	574. A
427. A	464. B	501. A	538. D	575. A
428. B	465. C	502. B	539. B	576. C
429. A	466. A	503. C	540. C	577. C
430. C	467. A	504. C	541. C	578. C
431. B	468. C	505. B	542. D	579. D
432. A	469. B	506. A	543. D	580. B
433. D	470. D	507. D	544. B	581. A
434. D	471. B	508. C	545. A	582. A
435. D	472. B	509. D	546. A	583. A
436. C	473. D	510. D	547. A	584. B
437. A	474. B	511. B	548. C	585. A
438. B	475. A	512. C	549. B	586. B
439. C	476. D	513. C	550. D	587. C
440. C	477. A	514. A	551. A	588. C
441. B	478. B	515. A	552. B	589. D
442. D	479. C	516. B	553. A	590. A
443. A	480. D	517. C	554. B	591. D
444. B	481. A	518. C	555. C	592. A
445. C	482. B	519. D	556. D	593. B
446. D	483. D	520. A	557. D	594. B
447. D	484. B	521. A	558. B	595. C
448. B	485. C	522. B	559. C	596. C
449. A	486. C	523. B	560. A	597. D
450. A	487. A	524. A	561. A	598. A
451. B	488. A	525. D	562. D	599. B
452. A	489. A	526. D	563. D	600. A
453. B	490. B	527. A	564. A	601. A
454. C	491. D	528. B	565. C	602. C
455. D	492. D	529. C	566. D	603. C
456. D	493. C	530. B	567. C	604. D
457. A	494. A	531. D	568. C	605. B

Flashcards

In the next pages, you will find pre-made flashcards. All you have to do is cut them out! These cover all the important information you need to know, and will save you a ton of time!

When studying using flashcards, make sure you use them backwards and forwards. Here's an example:

One side: Per Henrik Ling
Other side: Developed Swedish Gymnastics

The first time you go through the flashcards, you'd start with "Per Henrik Ling" and determine who he is or what he did, in which the answer is on the other side. The next time you do your flashcards, turn them around, so the side you start with is "Developed Swedish Gymnastics", which allows you to try to remember who the person was it's asking about. This prepares you for questions that are asked multiple ways while still looking for the same information!

About the Author

This study guide has been written by David Merlino, LMT, NCTM. David has been performing massage since 2005 in the State of Nevada, working for several world class resorts, therapeutic establishments, and local spas. David has been teaching students to pass the National Exam and MBLEx since 2011, achieving a pass rate and scores above local and national averages. David's information and methods have been proven to work.

References

All of the following resources were used in the creation of this study guide:

The Four Hour Chef – Timothy Ferriss, 2013
Anatomica: The Complete Home Medical Reference – Ken Ashwell, 2010
Pharmacology for Massage Therapy – Jean Wible, 2004
Trail Guide to the Body – AnatomyMapp
Basic Clinical Massage Therapy: Integrating Anatomy and Treatment – James Clay, 2003
Theory & Practice of Therapeutic Massage – Mark Beck, 1999
Mosby's Pathology for Massage Therapy – Susan Salvo, Sandra Anderson, 2004

For updates, new videos, and more, check out the official
Massage Test Prep blog, located at massagetestprep.wordpress.com!

Join the Massage Test Prep community, join our official forum, found at
MassageTestPrep.com!

This study guide is the copyrighted work of MassageTestPrep.com,
Massage Test Prep, and David Merlino, LMT, NCTM.
Unauthorized reproduction is prohibited.

Anytime Fitness

(14) $47.00
$39.75 year commitment $486.00

11:30 open until
7 days
$10 dep
24 hr access